Henry Chadwick has been Regiu[s Professor]
of Divinity in the University of Ox[ford]
(1959–69), Dean of Christ Church[, Oxford]
(1969–79), and Regius Professor [of Divinity]
in the University of Cambridge (19[79–83]).
He is now Master of Peterhouse, Cambridge.

G. R. Evans is Fellow of Fitzwilliam College,
Cambridge, Lecturer in History in the
University of Cambridge, and British
Academy Research Reader in Theology
(1986–8).

CHRISTIAN AUTHORITY

CHRISTIAN AUTHORITY

*Essays in Honour of
Henry Chadwick*

EDITED BY

G. R. EVANS

CLARENDON PRESS · OXFORD

1988

Oxford University Press, Walton Street, Oxford OX2 6DP
Oxford New York Toronto
Delhi Bombay Calcutta Madras Karachi
Petaling Jaya Singapore Hong Kong Tokyo
Nairobi Dar es Salaam Cape Town
Melbourne Auckland
and associated companies in
Beirut Berlin Ibadan Nicosia

Oxford is a trade mark of Oxford University Press

Published in the United States
by Oxford University Press, New York

British Library Cataloguing in Publication Data
Christian authority: essays in honour of
Henry Chadwick.
1. Church Authority
I. Chadwick, Henry   II. Evans, G.R.
(Gillian Rosemary)
262'.8   BT91
ISBN 0-19-826683-9

Library of Congress Cataloging-in-Publication Data
Christian authority.
Bibliography: p.
Includes index.
1. Authority (Religion)   2. Ecumenical movement.
3. Chadwick, Henry, 1920–   .   I. Chadwick, Henry,
1920–   .   II. Evans, G.R. (Gillian Rosemary)
BT88.C48   1988   262'.8   87–22113
ISBN 0-19-826683-9

Set by Promenade Graphics Ltd., Cheltenham
Printed in Great Britain
at the University Printing House, Oxford
by David Stanford
Printer to the University

Preface

THE theme of Christian authority carries a great deal on its shoulders. Theologically and historically it has raised divisive questions; today it lies at the heart of the ecumenical endeavour. Henry Chadwick's friends have gathered these papers together in recognition of the continuing importance and present topicality of a subject to which he has given much thought and scholarship. The resulting book has, we hope, much in it for historians and theologians, but we have also striven to exemplify here the theological method which is being developed by today's ecumenical conversations.

These essays approach the problems with which they are concerned as we believe he would wish: by looking at the sources of old controversies in context in their time, and asking what is to be learnt about the real issue in that way. It is a method which has proved indispensable in ecumenical conversations and which has made possible today's movement towards consensus in areas where there once seemed irreconcilable difference. This 'ecumenical method' of reading the sources together and looking for consensus, not difference, is establishing itself as a new theological process, and arguably the most important for the future of the Church in the world. It has always been the natural climate of Henry Chadwick's work.

Christian authority is Christ's authority. All talk of authority in the Church is concerned with the ways in which this authority operates in and through 'the common life in the body of Christ', so that the community as a whole and every individual member may be equipped 'so to live that the authority of Christ will be mediated through them' (ARCIC *Final Report*, Authority I. 1–3). Questions about the authority on which we believe are inseparable from questions about the authority by which we act. In his essay in this volume H. R. McAdoo writes on the 'inseparable linking of the two aspects of authority', 'authority as truth-maintaining' and 'authority as power to legislate and administer', within the framework of the *koinōnia*. Where these links have become broken and one or more aspects of authority in the Church have been emphasized at the expense of others, problems about Christian authority have become deeply divisive. We lose sight—to borrow a striking and lovely phrase—of the order which is 'love in regulative operation' (Report of the Anglican–Reformed International Commission, *God's Reign our Unity*, p. 82). The ecumenical task is both to restore a right balance and to resolve residual particular difficulties. The essays in this volume are attempts to untie some specific tangles, but we have tried to make them representative in their coverage of every aspect of Christian authority.

If we have concentrated disproportionately in any one area, it is in that of the process of 'reception'. This volume is going to press at a crucial period when the Churches are, by the various processes of their confessional traditions, 'receiving' the reports of a number of international ecumenical commissions. At the General Synod of the Church of England in November 1986, Henry Chadwick was present as a member of the House of Clergy when motions were carried in favour of welcoming the reports of *BEM* and ARCIC. In the sometimes impassioned debate on the Authority text of ARCIC in particular—for example, 'People still darkly purvey the myth that Rome never changes' or 'There is no sense in which we can claim a convergence on Papacy as it has existed in Rome for the past 1000 years'—the reception process could be seen actively at work. Old anxieties were voiced, sometimes interrogatively, as if to see how they sounded in fresh and clearer air. A number of individuals stood up to say that they were finding it agonizingly difficult to decide how to vote because attitudes and assumptions they had held all their lives had been brought into question for them by new insights; they felt the Holy Spirit moving them to let go of old prejudices and they found it painful to accept that what had once seemed right had perhaps been a misunderstanding. Gradual familiarization with new ideas and a new vocabulary was visibly changing minds, and with them the mind of the Church (in that place at least). Alongside such comments were others concerned with the nature of the decision-making process itself. There were expressions of an energetic wish on the part of the laity to play an active part in the reception process, which have their parallels in all other Christian communions today. There were signs of dawning realization of the complexities of the issues involved.

We are coming to a point in the ecumenical endeavour when the problems remaining are the really hard ones—'What do we mean by fundamental disagreement?' and 'Shall we ever be able to recognize one another's ministries so that we can become in practice the one Church of our baptism, living and working and worshipping together?' The method of reading the sources and looking for consensus is facing its severest tests. We are being stretched to reach a prize. As Henry Chadwick has more than once been heard to remark, it is when the going gets tough that it is most important not to give up. It is a sign that the goal is near.

Acknowledgements

I should like to thank members of the first and second Anglican Roman Catholic International Commissions and of the Faith and Order Advisory Group for contributing reminiscences and comments to the introduction on Henry Chadwick's work as ecumenist, as well as a large number of his friends for help of all kinds. Sir Richard and Lady Southern gave invaluable help with the summaries, proofs, and other matters. Sonia Argyle brought order to a mixed collection of typescripts; she, John Cordy, and Anne Ashby have given their services not only on behalf of the Press, of which Henry Chadwick was himself a Delegate for twenty years, but also as his friends of many years' standing.

G. R. E.

Contents

Abbreviations

ARCIC I	The *Final Report* of the First Anglican–Roman Catholic International Commission (London, 1982)
ARCIC II	The Second Anglican–Roman Catholic International Commission
BEM	*Baptism, Eucharist and Ministry: The Lima Report of the World Council of Churches*
CCSL	Corpus Christianorum, Series Latina
CR	Corpus Reformatorum
CSEL	Corpus Scriptorum Ecclesiasticorum Latinorum
CT	*Acta Concilii Tridentini*
DC	*Documentation catholique*
DS	*Dictionnaire de spiritualité*
DTC	*Dictionnaire de théologie catholique*
EETS	Early English Text Society
EP	Richard Hooker, *Ecclesiastical Polity*
FOAG	Faith and Order Advisory Group
HMC	Historical Manuscripts Commission
JEH	*Journal of Ecclesiastical History*
JTS	*Journal of Theological Studies*
PG	Patrologia Graeca
PL	Patrologia Latina
POC	*Proche-Orient chrétien* (Jerusalem)
SC	Sources Chrétiennes
WA	Luther, *Werke*, Weimar edition.

Henry Chadwick as Ecumenist

THE EDITOR

CHRISTIAN authority is a subject to which Henry Chadwick has given a lifetime's thought and scholarship. As a young scholar he was led from New Testament studies to patristics by a perception of the significance of the way in which the young Church produced the documents of the New Testament, the continuity of the second-century community with that of the first generations, and the emergence of the leadership of the church of St Peter and St Paul at Rome. In an article which appeared in the *Journal of Theological Studies* in 1957 and in a lecture given in Montreal in the same year, he was already exploring ideas on the implications of this last which he developed in his inaugural lecture as Regius Professor of Divinity in 1959, *The Circle and the Ellipse*. In a series of articles on Councils (1960, 1966, 1972, 1973), a study of Anglican Orders (1968), work on authority (1977), a delineation for Germans of the character of Anglicanism (1977), a piece on Anglican–Roman Catholic relations (1978), episcopacy (1980), full Communion (1981), assessments of progress and problems (1983), justification by faith (1984, in preparation for the work of ARCIC II), the Petrine Office (1984), he has written about many aspects of the nature and working of Christian authority.

His principal output as a scholar has been in the patristic field. But he has read equally widely in Reformation and Counter-Reformation materials, in the theology of the seventeenth century and beyond, and as anyone who has been present at a seminar or round a Commission table with him will attest, there are few matters on which he cannot produce the exact reference. A leading Evangelical theologian once remarked in amicable appreciation, 'Henry knows about *everything*.' A month before each ARCIC meeting he buries himself in sixteenth- and seventeenth-century polemical divinity in order to ensure that any questions raised then which still seem relevant now are not ignored. By keeping an eye impartially on the confessional formularies and historic debates of both traditions, he has sometimes saved a draft from falling accidentally into verbal contradictions of the positions it seeks to state.

The 'everything' is far from being shapeless. He is a bibliophile

who loves the contents rather than the covers of his overflowing
library in a thoroughly purposeful way. The consistent focus of his
reading is the history of theology, conceived in its fullness against
contemporary social and political events. He can produce an anec-
dote or a historical detail as readily as a theological idea and it is in
this largely conceived intellectual context that he seeks to trace the
ways in which Christian truth persists through the vicissitudes of
time. He always emphasizes that he is a historian, and it is perhaps
as a historian that he would wish to be judged by the scholarly
world. He has not been driven by uncertainties in his own faith to
write questioning works of theology; his own steady confidence in
the ancient truths of faith is underpinned by a historian's awareness
of continuities and he has sought to state them for today in terms
Christians of the past would happily recognize. He remarked at one
of the meetings of ARCIC I in England, 'This is no place to hold
such a meeting—the weight of history is too much upon us.' He has
been able to present the role of Rome through Anglican eyes in a
way which has made plain its catholicity as a gift it offers to other
Churches; his sympathetic presentation of primacy has been
especially important. He has been able to show Roman Catholics an
Anglican Church not made freshly in the sixteenth century, but
going back at one with the Church of Rome to Augustine of Canterbury, and to make plain the catholicity of classical Anglican six-
teenth- and seventeenth-century theology. It is here that we must
call him a theologian. He is one of the leading exponents, not to say
pioneers, of the new ecumenical method in theology.

Henry Chadwick's direct contribution to the ecumenical cause
has been massive. He served on the first Anglican–Roman Catholic
International Commission from its inception in 1970 until the completion of its Final Report in 1981. He is now a member of ARCIC
II. He served on the Anglican–Orthodox Commission until the
pressure of his duties as Dean of Christ Church made it impossible
for him to continue. He has always been willing to take on the hard
backroom work of subcommissions. He has served on the Faith and
Order Advisory Group of the General Synod of the Church of
England during the period in which it has been concerned with the
process of reception of the worldwide ecumenical reports in the
Anglican Church. His informal ecumenical work has been of
immense scale and variety. He has given talks to Diocesan and Deanery Synods, to parishes, to groups of clergy meeting for refresher

courses, to theology students and interested undergraduates, to Anglicans, Roman Catholics, and other Christians attending meetings of every sort. And individuals all over the world attest the word or phrase or casual conversation which has helped the progress of ecumenical understanding.

Those who have heard him speak have been struck by his power of making the realities of the ecumenical process plain. He takes his audience into the heart of the Commission's work, seats it round the table, and engages it in the discussion. He conveys both the pain and the joy of the process, the grinding slowness of progress at times, the surprises—above all the working of *koinōnia* in the life of the Commission itself as its members grow together in unity. His own contribution, as his fellow members describe it, bears the marks of the deep reflection of many years spent in coming to understand the ecumenical process.

Ecumenical understanding comes about through conversation. In the discussions of the Commissions Henry speaks fairly frequently but he is a good judge of when to keep silent—even to the point of occasionally holding back when the Commission joyously takes off in pursuit of a hare. But he has been known to stop the chase at such moments by pointing out forthrightly, but with the utmost good humour, that the last few minutes of discussion have been 'bosh'. His contributions have been balanced, rounded, judicious, never self-indulgent or partisan. He waits until he has formulated his view and can state it articulately. The directness of his response is mediated through reflection and a system of checks and balances; it is at once immensely complex and simple. Roman Catholic members have spoken with respect of a natural *magisterium*, a sense that his contributions are magisterial both because of the mastery of the material they reveal and because of his mastery of the issue. He has often been able to produce out of a hat the quotation which settles an argument. A story is told of an occasion when a Roman Catholic member, himself noted for his scholarship, cited a recondite passage from the *Acta* of the Council of Trent. There was an impressed silence. Then Henry ventured diffidently to point out that the Latin in fact ran thus . . . The correction was made for the sake of exactitude and not with any intention of outpointing a friend in erudition; that was so clear to everyone present that everyone, including the expert on Trent, was reduced to admiring friendly laughter. When he fights for a point he does so by sheer effort; he has an infinite capacity for taking pains. Not all the oral or written elements he has contributed have been accepted. He is always quick to withdraw a suggestion if it proves not to express the common mind, and he has never been known to resent it when a piece of wording which has taken many hours to arrive at has been rejected, or indeed when an idea or formulation which has been at first discarded by others has found its way back as their idea a year or two later.

Henry has a facility—the word is misleading if it obscures the intensive effort involved—for drafting a replacement passage while listening with one ear to the discussion. It is a skill which has been of great use to the Commissions. He has frequently produced new material by working late into the night after a session; the members of the Commission have come down next morning to find sheets distributed round the table with 'HC' at the bottom. They are offered in no spirit of putting one man's opinion, but as a straightforward contribution to the task in hand. He lets them go at once, like his comments, if they prove not to be helpful. He does so not only out of a respect for others' views on which several members have remarked, but also because he seeks to win their minds and not to force a position upon them. One contributor who has collaborated with him in other work has always found him that rarity among academics, the readiest of writers and the most willing to discard his own drafts for the sake of the progress of combined effort. He has made a massive and crucial contribution in the drafting of key phrases, passages, footnotes. The story is well known of how he framed the footnote on transubstantiation which appears in the ARCIC statement on the Eucharist (6 n. 2) which instantly won the acceptance of the Roman Catholic members who had not found it easy to state together what all of them could recognize. His style is unmistakable, with its implicit footnoting at every point and its spare, forceful imagery.

He has put the cause of unity first in a way which has been sacrificial of both time and energy. Time spent on meetings and talking to groups must be added to the vast amount of invisible time he has given to research and the writing of position papers, ground-clearing papers, drafts for discussion. The commitment of energy has been so complete that on one occasion during the period when ARCIC I was meeting in Venice he collapsed, because of the strain of what he afterwards described as 'a sticky patch'. One of the many friends who have offered reminiscences sums up the whole as a 'considerable personal contribution' to the ecumenical quest. He himself has been known to say that it is 'a good cause to die in'.

Yet this commitment is of a mind and spirit sane, balanced, and judicious. A peacemaker by temperament, inclination, and practice, Henry understands the working of the human propensity for war. He goes through battle scenes, not without nervous strain, but with equability, good humour, and what has been described as an 'awe-inspiring humility'. His 'gentle courtesy' has struck more than one participant as 'a most creative factor in the Commission's debates'. The victory of a faction would be of no interest to him. He sees the ecumenical task as one of turning old battle-grounds into rendez-vous for friends, friends who grow secure enough of one another to become more and more candid. In this way the tangle of ancient polemical abuse is cleared and it becomes possible to see what is being said. As the Commissions have again and again come to see, finding words with which everyone is happy, and, more impor-tantly, which express a common consent of view, is not a matter of compromise, but of discovering old enmities groundless and arriv-ing together at the truth.

Qualities of the man himself, both personal and intellectual, have been no small factor in his contribution to the ecumenical endeav-our. Many instances of his perceptiveness of others' needs have been recorded, and of his kindness and sympathy and understanding. The infinite capacity for taking pains is as evident in his dealings with people as in his scholarship and writing. Early on in the life of ARCIC I one helper recalls 'his offer of help on seeing two of us battling with an antediluvian duplicating machine late at night. We refused his help, but were touched to find a note from him saying how much he disliked to think of us being overworked and as he was "quite a competent typist" he would be ready to help us at any time.' Undergraduates in trouble, graduate students in despair over theses, secretaries working for the Commissions, all speak of his friendliness and approachability and his concern to make everyone feel a part of a common endeavour. He is much loved by the sisters of the convent where the Venetian meetings are held: 'Che gentil-lezza! Che cortesia! Com'è bravo!' These things are of a piece with the humility and simplicity of his approach to the Christian life. He is a very private man, and it is only occasionally that his deepest feelings are glimpsed. One Roman Catholic member of ARCIC mentions a moment when Henry confessed to feeling like weeping because the whole Commission could not join together in the celebration of the Eucharist.

Intellectually, he has a musician's capacity for entering wholly into what he is doing, and a musician's utter concentration, a quick perception of where the problem lies, reliable judgement, thoroughness, patience. He brings a sense of duty and a capacity for endurance to long meetings, as well as a liveliness and a sense of the ridiculous which has often lightened the mood. He commented after his collapse in Venice that when he came to and saw the members of the Commission standing anxiously round him, he 'knew he could not be in heaven'. His humour can be sophisticated, but simple things make him laugh and his impish irony is never sarcasm.

One co-worker in the ecumenical field, asked for reminiscences, smiled and said, 'Ah, you want the human—no the superhuman—touch.' Many of those who have contributed to this sketch of his ecumenical work have expressed a sense of having encountered greatness. 'Henry', one said, 'is a giant in his way.' That is not what Henry himself would want us to say. But he might allow us to speak of his loyalty, honesty, and seriousness in the ecumenical endeavour. That, and the delicacy and sweetness of nature which illuminate his work, set an example of ecumenical method and point a way forward for this new theological discipline. The contributors, friends among whom some are fellow workers in the ecumenical field or pupils—in some cases all three—offer these essays in his honour and for the furtherance of the cause to which he has given a remarkable life.

1

A Catholic Perspective on Ecclesial Communion

PIERRE DUPREY

THE expressions 'to be in communion', 'to be in full communion' are often used imprecisely. 'Full communion' in particular has a different sense in the Anglican Communion from that which it has in the Catholic Church. From this point of view it is hoped that the following reflections may be useful.

The final salutation of 2 Corinthians (13: 14) has been used in most liturgies.

This fact alone shows that we are here at the heart of the Christian mystery. The communion of the Holy Spirit, manifestation of the Father's love in the grace of the Lord Jesus, is the gift towards which the whole economy of salvation tends. The communion of the Holy Spirit is the gift of God, hence an eminently objective reality, freely received by us and independent of us in its fundamental existence. But as with all the gifts God makes to them, men have the awe-inspiring possibility of refusing it, as they have the obligation, having once received the gift, to live it, to make actual all its dimensions and potentialities, in submission and docility to Him who both gives and is given.

It is on this level first of all that ecclesial communion must be affirmed, because everything in the Church more or less immediately derives from this and is ordered towards it. For Irenaeus the history of salvation is a progressive introduction of man into communion with God.[1] Beyond all legislation, all past ruptures, and present divisions, one fact stands out which can be expressed by paraphrasing words of St Augustine: whether we like it or not, we are brothers. We are brothers not in the fashion of this passing world, not by blood, but according to the world to come, that last eternal world into which all will enter who have received the Word made flesh, who believe in His name and so are born of God, become children of God and thus brothers and sisters of one

[1] *Adv. haer.* iv. 14. 2, SC 100. 543–5.

another. It is with our brotherhood as with our sonship. Our brotherhood in its profound reality (cf. 1 John 3: 1–2) cannot be broken except by such culpable infidelity as will strike at our filial relationship and cut us off from the communion of the Holy Spirit.

What are the various aspects and different levels of realization of this communion of the Holy Spirit which is ecclesial communion? That is what we must outline together today. From the beginning I have wished to stress the unique character of this communion and of the community which results from it, to avoid at once whatever might tempt us to apply to the Church a profane model, which was and still often is the source of so many errors in this area.[2]

First, what does the word mean? *Koinōnia* comes from *koinos* 'common'[3] (the opposite of *idios* 'proper', 'particular', 'private').[4] *Koinoun* 'to put together,' 'to pool'. *Koinōnia* then will be 'the action of having in common', 'sharing in', 'participating in'.[5] The corresponding Latin term will be *communio* or *communicatio*.[6] The basic idea seems to be, in Plato, that of having in common, participating in. In Aristotle, two aspects are distinguished: community of interest and community of mind or spirit. For him the concept implies: a plurality of participants, a common purpose envisaged, an action in common and the difference between the participants.[7] Fr. Congar notes that the real sense of *koinōnia*, communion, is very close to *metochē*, participation.[8] For Fr. Tillard it is 'a solidarity

---

[2] J. Ratzinger, *Le Nouveau Peuple de Dieu* (Paris, 1977), 99.

[3] It is interesting to note here that Homer knows nothing of *koinos*, but uses its equivalent *xynos* and its derivatives *xynoun* 'to share'; *xynōnia* 'community', 'covenant'. We observe the links with words made up with the prefix *xyn = syn*, notably *synodos, synedrion* (cf. Ignatius, *Magn*. 6. 1; *Trall*. 3. 1: *Philad*. 8. 1), *synodia*. See Irenaeus, *Adv. haer*. iii. 4. 3 (SC 211. 50–1 and 210, 244–5: *aphistamenos tēs tōn adelphōn synodias*: 'separated from the communion of the brethren'; the SC translation has 'community'. The passage is about Cerdo convicted of heresy and excommunicated. There might be an interesting starting-point here for studying the links between communion, conciliarity, and collegiality.

[4] In the economy of the new covenant, because of its personal interiorization opposition between 'common' and 'particular' was to become outdated. This will be seen later.

[5] *Metechein* 'to have with'.

[6] Cf. L. M. Dewailly, 'Communio–communicatio: Brèves notes sur l'histoire d'un sémentème', in *Revue des sciences philosophiques et théologiques*, 54 (1970), 43–63.

[7] H. J. Sieben, in '*Koinōnia*, communauté–communion', in *DS* 1743–5. The elements of Aristotle's description of the concept might offer a useful framework for a theological development.

[8] *Le Concile de Vatican II: Son Église, peuple de Dieu et corps du Christ* (Théologie Historique, 71; Paris, 1984), 34; see also *Sainte Église: Études et approches ecclésiologiques* (Paris, 1963), 37–40.

founded on the participation of all in one good which is the Spirit of the Risen Lord binding them to the one Body of Christ. It is a matter of the relation of all to the same good which each possesses and which binds them together.'[9] But here we have already moved from the general meaning of the word, 'a relation existing between persons participating in the same good', to its properly Christian content.

I cannot here make a study of *koinōnia* in Scripture and the primitive Church.[10] I want merely to point to the preparation in the Old Testament for the theme of communion in the themes of inheritance and covenant.[11] Israel is the inheritance of Yahwe (e.g. Exod. 9), it is his particular possession. There is a relationship of unique intimacy between God and the people he has chosen and with whom he has made a covenant: they shall be my people and I will be their God (e.g. Jer. 24: 7). From the time of the first covenant (cf. Gen. 15) God promised to give as inheritance to this people a land where they could live. The idea of inheritance like that of covenant is progressively deepened and spiritualized. For the Levites, a tribe with no territory of their own, the inheritance is Yahwe (Deut. 10: 9) but this becomes thus a characteristic of the whole people: Yahwe is their portion (cf. Jer. 10: 16; Ps. 16: 5). To possess land becomes the conventional expression for perfect happiness (Ps. 37: 11). In the second beatitude (Matt. 10: 4) the land is the equivalent of the Kingdom. In the New Testament—the new covenant—it is the Kingdom (Matt. 25: 34),[12] the eternal life (Matt. 19: 29), the very fullness of God's gifts, which become the inheritance. The members of the new people of God are heirs of God and fellow heirs with Christ (Rom. 8: 17). The inheritance is participation in the life of the risen Christ (cf. 1 Cor. 15: 49–50). From now on we live by the promised Spirit which has been given to us and we hope for full possession (cf. Eph. 1: 14).

We come back here to 'the communion of the Holy Spirit' as the end of the whole economy of salvation. Although the Greeks only used *koinōnia* with the genitive of the thing shared in, in St Paul the

---

[9] In '*Koinônia*, communauté–communion, *DS* 1759.

[10] See J. M. McDermott, 'The Biblical Doctrine of *koinônia*', *Biblische Zeitschrift*, 19 (1975), 64–77 and 219–33; J. Coppens, 'La *koinônia* dans l'Église primitive' *Eph. théol. gov.* 46 (1970), 116–21; P. C. Bori, *Koinônia* (Brescia, 1972).

[11] Cf. 'Héritage et alliance', in *Vocabulaire de théologie biblique* (Paris, 1970).

[12] We cannot but recall here that for St Maximus the Confessor the kingdom of God *is* the Holy Spirit (*Exp. orat. Dom.*, PG 90. 884).

term is used with a genitive of the person; he thus demonstrates that the basis of the Christian community, namely salvation, is not a sharing in *something*, but an *intimate relationship with a divine person*.[13]

Koinōnia designates the relationship of the believer with the Father through the Son in the Holy Spirit and at the same time the new relation, established as a consequence, between believers. This relation between believers is just as real, mysterious, and spiritual as that established with God—when I say spiritual here I use the term in the strong sense: that which belongs to the Spirit, which appertains to a definitive, eschatological reality.[14] It is the communion of saints, that is, the communion existing between all those who are made saints by the gift of the Spirit uniting them to Christ on his way to the Father. This communion is on the increase throughout the course of history, of which it is the ultimate reason and the final goal.[15] At the end, as St Augustine says, there will be only one Christ, one only Son loving the Father for all eternity.[16]

During the time that separates the resurrection of Christ from the *parousia*, this communion, of its nature invisible, must yet manifest itself in and through a community. At the same time the community is the setting through which and in which that communion can be established and expanded.[17] In successive Christian generations this will also be the community of Christ's faithful which, by its unity resulting from its communion with the Father through the Son in the Spirit,[18] will witness before the world that the Father has really sent his Son;[19] that in the Son he has reconciled the world to himself and has entrusted to the Church the ministry of reconciliation.[20]

[13] J. M. McDermott, *DS* 1745. See Y. Congar, 'Pneumatologie dogmatique', in *Initiation à la pratique de la théologie* (Paris, 1982), ii. 497–500. It has recently been shown that the Covenant was a choice bringing about a living in common whose future was guaranteed by the Promise; the promise which was also a pledge of the indefectible fidelity of the divine partner. The term 'communion' makes clear what is at issue in the Covenant. The prophetic preaching calls Israel to 'a movement of withdrawal with regard to the granting of the goods' promised in order to direct it towards a searching for God, who ultimately promises himself. That means that the being together, the communion, is an end on its own and in itself.

[14] Cf. Epistle to the Hebrews.

[15] Cf. Rev. 6: 9–11; Eph. 1: 9–10; 1 Cor. 14: 24.

[16] Cf. *In epist. Joan. ad Parthos*, x. 3, PL 35. 2055–6.

[17] Cf. 1 John 1: 1–3.

[18] Cf. Cyprian, *De orat. Dom. 23*, PL 4. 553: 'The Church is the people that draws its unity from the unity of the Father, the Son and the Holy Spirit', cited in *Lumen Gentium*, 4.

[19] Cf. John 17: 21.

[20] Cf. 2 Cor. 5: 18–20.

What will be the elements of communion at this visible level where the unity of the community has its structure? They are found listed in some fashion in the summaries of Acts where St Luke traces the portrait of the ideal community: fidelity to the teaching of the Apostles; fraternal charity by which the believers are of one heart and one mind and hold everything in common; participation in the Eucharist and in the life of prayer.[21] Paul underlines the importance of baptism[22] and the Eucharist[23] for being integrated into, and living in, the community. He returns several times to the fact that community solidarity implies the service of the poorest brethren.[24]

Traditionally, and presupposing the gift of the Holy Spirit, these elements are: the bond of the one profession of faith, sacramental life, acceptance of the Church's hierarchy and its direction of the Church. These three components correspond to the power to preach, sanctify, and govern which Christ has entrusted to his Church.[25]

Thus the Christian community is gathered for a life of holiness by and about those who continue to exercise within it the pastoral charge which the Apostles first received from the Lord. This communion in, or sharing of, holy things which seems to have been the primitive meaning of the expression 'communio sanctorum' is ecclesial communion at the visible level; it is the criterion and the condition of the unity of the community[26] and of unity between communities.[27]

Ecclesial communion will be full and perfect between Churches if these constituent elements of the unity of the Church are lived in

[21] Cf. Acts 2: 42–6 and 4: 32.
[22] Cf. Gal. 3: 26–7, Rom. 6: 3–11; Col. 3: 3; etc.
[23] Cf. 1 Cor 10: 16–17.
[24] Cf. Rom. 15: 26–7: 2 Cor. 8: 2–4; 9: 12–14.
[25] Cf. *Lumen Gentium*, 14, and the commentary by Mgr. Philips in *L'Église et son ministère au deuxième Concile du Vatican*, (Report, text and commentary on the Constitution *Lumen Gentium*; Paris, 1967), i. 196. Henceforward the work will be cited as Philips. The perspectives and dimensions of this study do not allow us to show sufficiently how the reception of the word of God in faith is the basis of the unity of the community. 'Fidelity to the teaching of the Apostles' is the first characteristic mentioned by Luke. We know the importance for Paul of faith which responds to the preaching of the word of God (cf. e.g. Rom. 10: 14–17) and the necessity of fidelity to the authentic Gospel (cf. Gal. 1: 8–9). For John it is by receiving the apostolic witness that we enter into the apostolic community and into its communion with the Father and the Son. An ecclesiology of communion would have to give to this point its full weight.
[26] Cf. *Christus Dominus*, n. 11: *Sacrosanctum Concilium*, n. 41.
[27] *Tomos Agapis*, n. 176.

each Church.[28] It will be incomplete, imperfect in so far as they are lacking.[29] In this case it will be imperfect, but real—of the same reality as the gifts of God which are its basis. Moreover, in either case we are talking about realities used by the Spirit to give structure to a community and make it attain its end. By their profound natural dynamism as gifts of God to his Church they tend towards full realization. The unity which they manifest and maintain in such a Church and between it and others tends towards full unity. This is what *Lumen Gentium* calls 'catholic unity' without giving to the adjective a confessional meaning which has often been put upon it.[30] It was left to the Decree on Ecumenism to be more precise:

> . . . some, even very many of the elements or endowments which together go to build up and give life to the Church herself can exist outside the visible boundaries of the Catholic Church. . . . All of these, which come from Christ and lead back to Him, belong by right to the one Church of Christ.[31]

Of this one Church of Christ it is said in *Lumen Gentium* that it subsists in the Catholic Church. Hence it is not identified with the latter in an exclusive way. This also emerges clearly from the description which the Decree gives of the relations of the Catholic

---

[28] I refer here to the presence and putting into practice of all these elements in each Church. I do not wish to say that all these are fully and perfectly lived up to in all these Churches. In this sense communion within one Church and between the Churches still needs to grow and be perfected. It seems that the expression 'full and perfect' comes from Paul VI. To the references given by Philips we should add the great speech at Grottaferrata on 18 Aug. 1963, where Paul VI spoke of the Orthodox Churches (*DC*, 15 Sept. 1963). This expression assumes the possibility of incomplete and imperfect communion (cf. Philips, i. 196).

[29] This whole question is further developed in Cardinal Jean Willebrands, 'L'Avenir de l'œcuménisme', *POC* 25 (1975), 3–15. Prof. Oscar Cullmann said that it is possible to go beyond Christian fullness. From the Protestant point of view it is this something more, something too much, in Catholicism that is an obstacle to communion (cf. Thils, *Le Décret sur l'Œcuménisme* (Paris, 1966), 58–9).

[30] *Lumen Gentium*, nn. 8 and 15, and Philips's commentary, i. 119, 200–6; ii. 297–8. Note that in n. 15 in a general description the episcopate is pointed to as an element common to other Churches and ecclesial communities. 'Apostolic succession' was deliberately avoided, so as to include the Churches or ecclesial communities which preserve this structure of the Church, but with whom 'apostolic succession' is a 'subject of dispute' (Philips, i. 204).

[31] Cf. the whole of no. 3 and also 20 and 22. See Thils, op. cit. 45–59. He explains: these elements of the Church are living spiritual values, which tend of themselves towards their fulfilment and accomplishment (p. 53). See also Cardinal Jaeger, *Le Décret de Vatican II sur l'Œcuménisme* (Tournai, 1965), 68–77 and 151–7.

Church with the Oriental Churches, notably when it says of the latter that 'through the celebration of the Eucharist of the Lord in each of these Churches, the Church of God is built up and grows in stature.'[32]

We have here evidently an ontological, not a canonical or juridical, notion of communion.[33] The confusing of these two notions has created, and still often creates, difficulty. I shall return to this later on, but I should like to say at once about the passage just quoted that the 'visible boundaries of the Catholic Church' are determined by canonical or juridical communion, while beyond these boundaries there exist Churches with which it is in ontological communion which is more or less complete. Before going on, I should like to emphasize here the effort made by the Catholic Church in the Council to provide a secure theological basis for real ecumenical commitment. It was a question of respecting fully the faith in the oneness of the Church of Christ and the Catholic Church's awareness of being that Church. On the other hand it was necessary to recognize the fact of the existence and salvific efficacy of other ecclesial communities and to give a theological explanation of that fact. Here I am not speaking directly of Orthodox Churches because there was a long tradition, a tradition uninterrupted, even if obscured, for some hundred or so years, which regarded them as true Churches in the theological sense[34] and placed the separation of East and West within one Church: a separation of the east and west

---

[32] *Unitatis Redintegratio*, n. 15. This is opposed to a reductionist interpretation of 'subsistit in', an interpretation which was just what the Council fathers wished to avoid by refusing to put in 'est'. In the *expensio modorum* of Oct.–Nov. 1964 we read 'ut patet duae manifestantur tendentiae, una quae sententiam aliqua tenus extenderet, altera quae vellet eam restringere. De qua re commissio jam antea post largam discep-tationem, elegit vocem "subsistit in"; cui solutioni omnes praesentes adhaeserunt' (Alberigo, *Synopsis historica* (Bologna, 1975), 509). The *relatio* of the doctrinal com-mission July 1964 had already said 'quaedam verba mutantur: loco "est" 1. 21 dicitur "subsistit in", ut expressio melius concordet cum affirmatione de elementis ecclesiali-bus quae alibi adsunt' (ibid. 440). Philips had already foreseen that this formula would make 'streams of ink flow' (vi. 1, p. 199). Unfortunately they have not yet flowed and that part of *Lumen Gentium*, n. 8, crucial for ecumenism, still awaits the deeper studies it deserves. Such studies should explain the two tendencies of which the *expensio modorum* speaks, what they aimed at and what was their relative importance in the Council.

[33] Cf. Thils, op. cit. 46. From the canonical or juridical point of view, you are either in communion or not.

[34] Cf. Y. Congar, *Chrétiens désunis* (Paris, 1937), 381–2, and *Irenikon* (1950), 22–4.

parts of that Church.[35] I am speaking of the Churches which issued
from the Reformation, in order to take a new standpoint and to
ensure that that standpoint is consistent with the traditional Catholic faith. It is the working out of the dogmatic notion of communion
which has allowed the Catholic Church to take this step. If we do
not take this standpoint, we cannot understand the ecumenical commitment of the Catholic Church.[36] But if we do, we understand
why Cardinal Willebrands sees the future of ecumenism in the
development of an ecclesiology of communion in all its dimensions.[37]

It is possible to criticize what has been done, to judge it unsatis-
factory. It is not possible to deny that here was a central problem
which the Catholic Church has faced with courage and consistency
and thereby laid the foundation for further progress.[38] The problem
is also central in the World Council of Churches.[39] I know of no
other attempts made in this area which I would judge more satisfactory.

The communion which I call ontological and which others call
dogmatic, has been lived and experienced in eucharistic communion. The eucharistic synaxis is not only a gathering in unity of the
local assembly of the faithful communicating in the eternal life of
the triune God through the body and blood of Christ. It is also the
identifying in and through the Spirit of that celebrating community
with all the communities which throughout the world celebrate
these mysteries, and of these within the community contemplated
by the seer of the Apocalypse, the apostolic community, that of the
believers of all ages reunited with the Apostles about the throne of
'the Lamb standing as though it had been slain' for the eternal

---

[35] Council of Florence, 'Laetentur coeli: apheretai men gar to mesotoichon to tēn
dytikēn kai anatolikēn diairoun Ekklēsian' (Alberigo, *Conciliorum oecumenicorum
decreta* (Bologna, 1973), 524). This text is freely adapted in no. 18, *Unitatis redintegratio*.
[36] An example of this failure of understanding is D. Ols, 'Scorciatoie ecumeniche',
L'Osservatore romano 25–6 Feb. 1985. See on this subject A. Nichols, '*Einigung der
Kirchen*: An ecumenical controversy', *One in Christ*, 21 (1985), 139–66.
[37] Art. cit. in n. 29.
[38] Cf. *Unitatis redintegratio*, n. 24, where it is said that the Council does not wish
'to prejudice the future inspiration of the Holy Spirit'.
[39] The declaration of Toronto in 1950; cf. *Evanston to New Delhi* (Geneva, 1981),
245–50. The tendency of some in recent years to resume discussion of this declaration
has encountered firm opposition, notably from the Orthodox Churches.

heavenly liturgy, the end of history.[40] The Eucharist is the source at which communion in its vertical and horizontal dimensions is unceasingly renewed and unified. In the patristic epoch 'communion between churches keeps always an interior link with the eucharist. In turn, the use of the term in its sacramental sense looks back to interecclesial communion.'[41]

But this mystery of communion, these mysteries, must be celebrated in many places and in generation after generation. In proportion as the community grows and the years pass there will be the concern about harmony, about fidelity to apostolic truth, and a necessary juridical dimension will be given to the community, to the several communities.[42] But long before external forms had been found for organizing unity or union had been realized on the social level, the local Churches or communities felt themselves linked, at least when the Eucharist was being celebrated, with the other Churches, spread throughout the world, in the communion of unity.[43] The exchanging of confessions of faith,[44] letters of communion, 'a sort of ecclesiastical passport', hospitality, reciprocal visits, feast-day letters, eulogies, the gift of *fermentum*, then councils and synodal letters were the first spontaneous forms of expression, ensuring and consolidating communion. This gift of God had to be lived out, manifested in a community *homothymadon epi to auto*.[45] The ministry of unity, the episcopate plays a fundamental role here.

Beyond the ontological notion of communion to preserve it and keep it in fidelity, we have already encountered earlier, closely mingled with it, the canonical notion of communion. It is necessary and inseparable from the first, but totally at its service. I cannot examine here the various forms taken by the organization of hierarchical communion. I have done so elsewhere.[46] I would like merely to

[40] Cf. Rev. 5: 6 and 22: 1–5. On the role of the Eucharist in ecclesial communion see J. Zizioulas, *L'Unité de l'Église dans la divine eucharistie et l'évêque durant les trois premiers siècles* (Athens, 1965).

[41] H. J. Sieben, *DS* 1750.

[42] The pastoral epistles among others already show clearly this concern or, if you like, awareness of this necessity.

[43] H. J. Sieben, *DS* 1751.

[44] Orthodoxy of faith has always been in the forefront of criteria for granting or refusing communion.

[45] Acts 1: 14; 2: 46; 4: 24; 15: 26. This theme of the Acts is the heart of the book by S. Tyszkiewicz, *La Sainteté de l'Église christoconforme* (Rome, 1945).

[46] 'La Structure synodale de l'Église dans la théologie orientale', *POC* 20 (1970), 123–45.

touch here on the question of the delimitation of episcopal ministry. In the ancient Church this delimitation, or more precise indication, is found included in the actual rite of ordination for a given Church. But the question of delimitation of dioceses quickly arose.[47] On the other hand, even in the East, once the transfer of bishops from one see to another was allowed, it called for a decision by an ecclesiastical authority higher than that of the diocese. Is not this the equivalent of what in the West we call the 'missio canonica'? What is important is that for the West, as for the East, we believe that episcopal ordination gives, along with the grace, the charge to teach, to sanctify, and to rule. For Catholics this is clear in Chapter III of *Lumen Gentium* and in the *nota praevia*. But these texts also affirm that the Pope gives the final designation of powers which must permit their exercise. This is but 'the actual expression of the communion instituted by the Lord according to a hierarchical scheme.'[48] This is done in any case by election and nomination. Is it not the same in the Orthodox Churches, even though they do not speak of 'missio canonica'? How and by whom are future bishops actually designated in the different autocephalous Churches? As far as I know there is no longer any election of candidates by the people or by the bishops of neighbouring dioceses.

The *nota praevia* says:

Such an ulterior norm is demanded by the nature of the case, since there is question of functions which must be exercised by several subjects working together by Christ's will in a hierarchical manner. It is clear that this 'communion' has been in the life of the Church according to circumstances of the times, before it was, so to speak, codified in law.

Therefore it is significantly stated that hierarchical communion is required with the head of the Church and its members. Communion is an idea which was held in high honour by the ancient Church (as it is even today, especially in the East). It is understood, however, not of a certain vague feeling, but of an organic reality which demands a juridical form, and is simultaneously animated by charity.[49]

Whether we like it or not, whether we are allergic or not to terms like 'hierarchical communion' or 'hierarchical communities', here is

---

[47] Cf. H.-M. Legrand, 'Nature de l'Église particulière et rôle de l'évêque dans l'Église', in *La Charge pastorale des évêques* (Unam Sanctam, 74; Paris, 1969), 176–219.

[48] Cf. Philips, p. 274.

[49] Ibid. 270.

a reality received from the Lord and answering to the nature of all permanent human society, however small in extent. Anarchy is a utopia, a seductive eschatological dream, leading only to continuing anarchy. This is not to prejudge the various ways in which hierarchical authority can be organized and ensured. Now that discussions, at times passionate, have calmed down, it seems clear that Mgr. Philips is right when he says that this *nota praevia* in no way restricts the scope of Chapter III of the Dogmatic Constitution on the Church. It gives precision to the canonical requirements of hierarchical communion, the need for which is many times affirmed in Chapter III. How is this canonical communion organized? East and West have different traditions on this point, but they agree in asserting the need for hierarchical communion, even if they use different words. The *nota praevia* is not at all opposed to what I am saying together with Mgr. Philips: that ancient customary law and traditional oriental discipline retain for these Churches all their validity.[50] The fact remains, evidently, that the Catholic faith considers communion with the Bishop of Rome as necessary. There again, we cannot at all prejudge now what that canonical communion implies or does not imply. It will be for the dialogues in progress to work that out.

However that may be (and I have alluded to it above), whether canonical communion exists or not, and unhappily between the Bishop of Rome and the other Churches it does not, we know that ontological communion exists in the truth and in the realities of the mystery of salvation operating in and through the Church. *That* communion is 'almost total' with the Orthodox Churches.[51] It is real, but incomplete, with the other Churches and Ecclesial communities not in canonical communion with the Bishop of Rome.

Conclusion

Ecclesial communion is realized at three levels.

   1. At the spiritual, invisible, and definitive level, that of our life

[50] Ibid. 290.
[51] *Tomos Agapis*, 182, p. 614. Here we need to mention the very interesting study by André de Halleux, 'Fraterna communio', *Irenikon*, 58 (1985), 291–311, and his article 'Les principes catholiques de l'œcuménisme: Quelques réflexions', *Revue théologique de Louvain*, 16 (1985), 306–50, which I got to know about after this study had been written. In the first study de Halleux understands hierarchical communion more in the sense of a hierarchically structured communion than in that of

offered to the Father through the Son in the Holy Spirit and thus offered for our brethren. To serve this reality is the reason, more or less immediate, for the other levels. It was from this point of view that Paul VI could say at Bethlehem that the barriers of our divisions do not reach up to heaven. This communion results from the gift of the Spirit. That is why it is said to be at the *spiritual* level. It is He who is the source of ecclesial communion at this level and hence at the other two. Thus it can be said that ecclesial communion is truly the 'fellowship of the Holy Spirit'. Communion at this level is said to be *invisible* to distinguish it from the other levels. There is no question of undervaluing the influence of a life lived according to the Spirit by each believer and each community and the witness which such a life constitutes. 'The tree is known by its fruit.'[52] To say that this communion is *definitive* is to point to the eschatological reality already present.

2. At the visible level of the community within which and through which God's liberating and sanctifying action takes place. The unity of this community is a condition of its fulfilling its mission. Ecclesial unity is achieved through the acceptance and active reception of the elements making up the unity of the community: common profession of the apostolic faith, sacramental life, co-ordination of community life by those who have been given the ministry of word and sacrament and the charge to preside over the life of the community.

3. At the canonical or juridical level where an organizing of the unity of the community takes place to ensure that the different members (who have rights and duties at different levels) live in brotherly harmony and in fidelity to 'the faith which was once for all delivered to the saints'.[53] Here there can be many different juridical regimes giving practical expression to the same dogmatic truth (here lies the chief objection to the possibility of a 'fundamen-

communion between hierarchs, which is the sense we have given it in these pages. Consequently, he suggests that we aim rather at a 'fraternal communion' than at a 'hierarchical communion' with the Orthodox Churches. In this connection, see our reflections 'Primus inter pares', DC 70 (1973), 29–31. The word 'hierarchy' seems to have entered the Christian vocabulary with Pseudo-Dionysius, who seems to have created it. It then spread in the seventh century (Maximus, Sophronius). It entered ecclesiastical Latin only with the translation of Dionysius in the ninth century. It then had a fine innings.

[52] Matt. 12: 33.
[53] Jude 3.

tal law'). This third level is closely linked with the preceding one, to which it lends organization, but it has not the same necessity, given that it can be realized in various forms.

Hierarchical communion is often placed in this context. This is well enough if we are merely considering the canonical manner in which hierarchical relations are organized in the concrete. It will not do if we are estimating the *necessity* of these relations, if we are looking at how the communion between local Churches (the communion necessary to their very being) is articulated, and abstracting from the different ways in which hierarchical relations can be realized and organized in practice. Understood in this latter way, hierarchical communion is to be seen as an important element at our *second* level of communion, that which I have called ontological.

Hierarchical communion shows how juridical or canonical communion is closely linked to ontological communion. I would say that ontological communion always implies a minimum of juridical or canonical communion, but that the latter is not invariable and is always open to a certain diversity, whether with different communities or at different periods. The discernment needed here is always very delicate; it calls for great pastoral prudence. There is always the risk in changing certain forms of altering the essential which they are there to put into working order. We are always tempted to give absolute value to what we are used to, even to consider as apostolic those usages that may have only a few decades behind them. To be rooted in the essential is, here as elsewhere, the measure of freedom.

In using the term 'communion' we need to be aware of this complexity so as to avoid ambiguities.

Communion is founded on the gifts of God. It is an objective reality. It is realized in charity, but that does not at all diminish the importance of its foundation. It would be very reductionist to place communion first at the affective level. 'Koinonia puts the accent on the interior value which takes account of unity and on what is shared in common . . . ' The *societas* often designates the external tie, the web of relations which thereby unite Christians . . . Everything in the mystery of the Church is built around koinōnia in what God in Christ has given once for all.[54]

Once again, among Christians, whether we like it or not, we are brothers.

[54] J. Tillard, *DS* 1759, 1761.

2

La Réception de Vatican II par les non-Catholiques

J. M. R. TILLARD

Summary

The ecumenical movement has important ecclesiological implications. We must keep in view not only the unity we seek, but the profound changes of attitude already brought about in our progress towards unity. In the present climate of questioning whether the vision of the pioneers of the ecumenical movement was anything more than a dream, we need to reflect on these developments. The mutual reception of the ideas of other communions is something quite new. It is nowhere better exemplified than in the reception of Vatican II by non-Catholics.

To 'receive' is to make one's own. To recognize is to see a position as acceptable without necessarily adopting it oneself.

A special sort of reception is involved when it takes place between divided Churches and apart from the formal process of concluding an ecumenical agreement. The Roman Catholic Church sees itself as that within which the Church as Christ intended it subsists ('subsistit in'), and towards which we turn today ('hic' et 'nunc') in search of that Church. But it does not affirm that the Church of God cannot exist outside the limits of the Roman Catholic communities. It is important that this tension set out in *Lumen Gentium* is maintained. It is clear that the Holy Spirit has gone on working in the divided community wherever a true baptism is celebrated. In this way, since Vatican II, the Roman Catholic Church has 'received' some of the Reformers' ideas: the place of the Word in the Liturgy, for example, and communion in both kinds for the laity. It has 'received' from the East a theology of the 'local church'; the *epiklēsis*. If the process of conversion to the values of ecclesial *koinōnia* is seen as a work of the Holy Spirit guarding the indefectibility of the Church, then this is an authentic 'reception'. Vatican II was a Council in which many important elements of truth and practice were 're-received', thanks to the other Christian bodies.

At the Synod of Bishops held in Rome in November 1985, Henry Chadwick represented the Anglicans among the observers. He read their declaration to the Synod, saying that the observers from other communions had not thought of themselves as strangers, and had not felt themselves so; all met as brothers in Christ. The observers expressed a sense of sharing in the reception of Vatican II.

There remain, indeed, practical questions of the way in which each Church is to open itself to the rest. But non-Catholics have been struck by the fidelity to the Gospel shown by the work of Vatican II. They have opened themselves especially to the influence of Catholic liturgical reform in their own life of prayer. They have 'received' some of the main insights and decisions of the Council, and so 're-received' many key elements of the tradition.

It is in this context that we must set recent bilateral dialogues, which are not the cause but the consequence of this very process of mutual 'reception', the meetings of Pope Paul VI with Patriarch Athenagoras and Archbishop Ramsey, and John Paul II with the American Lutheran Bishop James R. Crumley.

It is becoming possible to perceive the common intention in expressions hitherto unfamiliar to some Churches and to see where the focal ideas lie. The emphasis placed by ARCIC I on *koinōnia* is a supremely important example. It is one of the most important fruits of this 'reception'.

L E mouvement œcuménique a d'importantes conséquences ecclésiologiques. Trop habitués à ne penser œcuménisme qu'en fonction du but final, qui est la soudure organique des Églises aujourd'hui encore séparées, nous avons jusqu'ici négligé l'évaluation des changements profonds d'attitude qu'il a provoqués. Ou si nous l'avons fait, nous nous sommes d'ordinaire bornés à scruter le registre de l'action en commun ou du témoignage commun. Or son influence s'est exercée aussi dans des registres fondamentaux de la pensée ecclésiale. C'est l'un de ces registres que nous nous proposons de présenter dans cette rapide étude.

Une Situation Ecclésiologique nouvelle

1. Une réflexion sur l'influence de l'œcuménisme est aujourd'hui d'autant plus nécessaire que plusieurs s'interrogent. Ils se demandent si l'intuition des grands pionniers n'était pas un rêve. En effet, sous nos yeux, après la grande espérance soulevée par les premiers résultats des dialogues bilatéraux[1], tout semble pour le moins piétiner. On s'attendait à des actes officiels qui, sans être déjà le sceau définitif mis aux projets d'union, auraient rendu irréversibles les importants résultats désormais acquis. La grande célébration de la levée réciproque des Anathèmes de 1054, simultanément à Constantinople et en plein cœur du concile du Vatican II, par Athénagoras

---

[1] Surtout par le *Final Report* de l'ARCIC.

et Paul VI[2] avait merveilleusement ouvert la voie dans ce sens. Peu de démarches du même type l'ont suivie. L'œcuménisme est devenu un œcuménisme de textes et non de décisions.

Bien plus, on a même souvent l'impression de reculs très nets sur des points cruciaux qui semblaient acquis. N'en donnons qu'un exemple. Alors que dans le dialogue anglican-catholique romain l'accord de l'ARCIC I sur l'Eucharistie et le ministère laissait entrevoir la possibilité d'un renversement du verdict d'*Apostolicae curae*[3], l'épineuse question de l'ordination des femmes au presbytérat et surtout à l'épiscopat vient créer un obstacle nouveau[4]. Et tout pousse à croire qu'il sera plus difficile à surmonter que ceux évoqués sous Léon XIII. On comprend que des œcuménistes brûlant leurs énergies pour la cause de l'Unité soient parfois effleurés par la tentation du découragement et du « à quoi bon? ».

2. Pourtant, quelque chose a changé. Tout particulièrement les relations profondes entre Églises sont devenues telles que souvent elles « reçoivent » l'une de l'autre des éléments importants pour leur propre fidélité, voire des décisions les impliquant. L'exemple le plus net — que nous allons analyser — est la façon dont Vatican II, qui est sans nul doute l'événement le plus central de la vie de l'Église catholique depuis un siècle, est « reçu » par les autres chrétiens.

Il importe de bien percevoir la nouveauté de cette situation. Par le

---

[2] On trouvera les textes officiels dans le *Tomos Agapis* (Rome–Istanbul, 1971), aux nᵒˢ 119–30. Voir en particulier le bref *Ambulate in dilectione* de Paul VI (lu durant une session solennelle du concile du Vatican II, le 7 décembre 1965) et le Tomos patriarcal d'Athenagoras, lu le même jour dans la cathédrale du Phanar. Voir aussi aux nᵒˢ 200–1, 236–7, 277–9 le rappel de cette levée des anathèmes, montrant son impact sur les relations des deux Églises.

[3] Voir la lettre du cardinal Willebrands aux deux co-présidents de l'ARCIC II : « If at the end of this process of evaluation the Anglican Communion as such is able to state formally that it professes the same faith concerning essential matters where doctrine admits no difference and which the Roman Catholic Church also affirms are to be believed and held concerning the Eucharist and the Ordained Ministry, the Roman Catholic Church would acknowledge the possibility that in the context of such a profession of faith the texts of the Ordinal might no longer retain that « nativa indoles » which was at the basis of Pope Leo's judgement. This is to say that, if both Communions were so clearly at one in their faith concerning the Eucharist and the Ministry, the context of this discussion would indeed be changed. » Parmi les nombreuses éditions de ce texte, daté du 13 juillet 1985, mais rendu public simplement le 5 mars 1986, renvoyons à *Origins*, 15 (1986), 662–3 (663).

[4] C'est ce que dans leur réponse à la lettre du cardinal Willebrands les deux co-présidents de l'ARCIC II reconnaissent, par la lettre du 14 janvier 1986, publiée le 5 mars 1986 (ibid. 664).

passé — nous ne parlons évidemment que des siècles ayant suivi les grandes ruptures entre Orient et Occident, Église de Rome et Églises de la Réforme — les « réceptions » des visions catholiques (romaines) par les autres groupes chrétiens se faisaient dans le déroulement même de ce que l'on appelait les « conciles d'Union » (Lyon, Florence). En d'autres termes, la « réception » par ces autres était partie intégrante de ce qui était censé être un acte d'union, conciliaire par sa nature propre. Et le groupe non-Catholique ne « recevait » les positions catholiques qu'après avoir participé à l'élaboration du document final dans lequel elles étaient assumées. Il suffit de parcourir les *Acta* du concile de Florence pour se rendre compte de la complexité de cette participation. Or dans le cas de Vatican II il en va autrement. La présence des Observateurs lors des sessions de ce Concile n'équivalait en rien — même s'ils étaient fréquemment consultés et écoutés — à une participation formelle de leur Église aux délibérations aboutissant aux décisions ou déclarations doctrinales qui constituent l'œuvre de Vatican II. Et si elle contribuait — trés fortement — à la création de l'esprit conciliaire et de sa toute nouvelle ouverture, elle demeurait pourtant tout autre chose qu'une « activité d'union ».

Dans cette situation, il est œcuméniquement crucial d'observer comment les autres Églises ont réagi face à Vatican II et surtout comment plusieurs des déclarations de ce concile, ne concernant directement et formellement que l'Église catholique romaine, ont été reçues en dehors des limites de celle-ci. Alors que, par exemple, les décisions du concile de Florence adoptées par l'Est et l'Ouest en un concile d'union ont ensuite été refusées par l'Orient, dans le cas de Vatican II des documents destinés uniquement à l'Église catholique romaine ont été « reçus » par d'autres Églises, auxquelles ils n'étaient pas destinés et qui y ont « reconnu » leur bien. Car « réception » et « reconnaissance » sont, selon nous, très proches. On « reçoit » quand on fait sien le point en cause; on « reconnait » quand on y voit une position acceptable sans pour autant l'assumer.

Il s'agit, certes, d'un type bien spécial de « réception ». Car celle-ci s'accomplit entre Églises divisées, souvent en dehors d'un processus immédiat et formel de conclusion d'accord œcuménique ou d'évaluation des valeurs doctrinales encore possédées en commun. Avant d'évoquer — dans les limites de cette étude — certains des points ainsi reçus, il nous parait nécessaire de réfléchir sur les implications écclésiologiques d'un tel phénomène. Car elles sont

importantes et constituent, à nos yeux, une page nouvelle de la théologie de l'Église de Dieu.

3. Du point de vue catholique romain, il est clair que cette « réception » est à comprendre dans la ligne de ce que la constitution dogmatique *Lumen Gentium* a affirmé au cœur même de sa prise de
conscience de l'identité de l'Église catholique. Il y a dans cette prise
de conscience deux pôles, en tension. Et l'important est de ne pas
détruire cette tension. D'une part, en effet, l'Église catholique
romaine se perçoit comme celle dans laquelle l'Église voulue par le
Christ Jésus *subsiste* avec tous ses éléments essentiels (le « subsistit
in »), en sorte que si l'on veut voir l'Église dans sa plénitude et sa
force, avec tout ce qu'elle requiert pour être dans l'histoire humaine
ce que Dieu veut qu'elle soit, c'est vers cette Église catholique telle
qu'elle demeure « hic et nunc » qu'il faut encore se tourner[5]. Mais
d'autre part ce « subsistit in » est utilisé — comme l'affirme en
plein concile la commission responsable du choix de cette
expression nouvelle — afin de « concorder mieux avec l'affirmation
des éléments écclésiaux qui existent ailleurs » et d'éviter l'expression
absolue « l'Église voulue par le Christ *est* l'Église catholique[6] ». En
d'autres termes — et telle est la tension, essentielle pour une juste
intelligence de la vision de Vatican II — on dit que l'Église de Dieu
n'est en toute sa plénitude et sa force que dans la communauté catholique, mais on ne dit pas que l'Église de Dieu n'est que dans l'Église catholique. Elle déborde les frontières de celle-ci, même si alors
elle n'a plus sa plénitude et sa force. L'Église de Dieu est comme la
rivière qui déborde de son lit dans des espaces où se répand l'eau
vive — c'est-à-dire l'Esprit-Saint et sa grâce — mais sans toute la
force du courant. Si donc elle se dit le fleuve en son lit, l'Église catholique ne peut pas se dire toute l'Église de Dieu, puisque l'eau vive
de l'Esprit porte ses fruits hors des berges et que cette eau, venant
du Seigneur ressuscité et de lui seul, est la même que celle qui coule
en elle avec tout son dynamisme. On se situe ici dans le registre de la
plénitude, non dans celui de l'existence pure et simple[7].

---

[5] Il s'agit du n° 8 de *Lumen Gentium*. Voir le commentaire du secrétaire même de
la commission responsable de ce texte Mgr G. Philips, *L'Église et son mystère au IIe
concile du Vatican*, i (Paris, 1967), 119.

[6] Voir *Acta synodalia sacrosancti concilii oecumenici Vaticani II*, iii. 1. 177.

[7] Le cas est clair en ce qui concerne les Églises d'Orient, dont on reconnaît du côté
catholique romain la nature d'Églises au sens strict, bien qu'elles soient séparées de la
communion avec l'Église de Rome. Ceci est net dans le décret conciliaire sur l'œcuménisme.

C'est d'ailleurs parce que l'Esprit de Dieu continue d'agir dans ces espaces écclésiaux même après la rupture, et sur la base du baptême, que dans sa démarche conciliaire l'Église catholique ellemême a pu « recevoir » des Églises ou communautés ecclésiales séparées d'elle des éléments importants de son *aggiornamento*. Que les chemins empruntés pour cette « réception » aient été souvent tortueux, peu importe. Compte avant tout le fait que des valeurs écclésiales insuffisamment mises en œuvre dans la tradition catholique romaine ont été gardées par d'autres traditions et que Vatican II les a — d'ordinaire par la médiation de la réflexion théologique des dernières décennies — « reçues » officiellement.

Ce fait se vérifie à plusieurs niveaux. Le processus est net en ce qui concerne la réforme liturgique[8]. Il nous paraît exact d'affirmer que l'Église latine a « reçu » des Églises d'Orient — au terme d'une histoire complexe[9] — l'épiclèse sacramentelle. Car c'est bien l'Orient qui gardait celle-ci, quoiqu'il en soit du caractère épiclétique implicite du canon romain et de la reprise de l'épiclèse par quelques liturgies de tradition anglicane[10]. L'Église catholique a également « reçu » la protestation de la Réforme en ce qui touche à l'usage de la langue vernaculaire dans la Liturgie, au calice aux laïcs, à la place de la Parole.

Mais cette « réception » a aussi joué à des registres fondamentaux de la pensée doctrinale. N'en donnons que trois cas majeurs. Il est difficile de nier que la théologie de l'Église locale, qui représente une des grandes acquisitions ecclésiologiques de Vatican II, a été « reçue » de l'Orient, ou tout au moins « re-reçue » après la longue parenthèse de l'écclésiologie universaliste. Il en va de même de l'écclésiologie eucharistique[11] où elle s'enchâsse. Et la belle constitution *Dei Verbum* est marquée par la « réception », à travers la recherche exégétique des Écoles catholiques, de plusieurs vérités défendues

---

[8] Voir J. M. R. Tillard, « La réforme liturgique et le rapprochement des Églises », dans *Liturgia, opera divina e umana; Studi sulla Riforma Liturgica offerti a S.E. Mons. Annibale Bugnini* (Rome, 1982), 215–40. Traduction partielle dans *One in Christ*, 19 (1983), 227–49.

[9] Voir les discussions internes au concile de Florence (mais la question n'était pas abordée au concile de Lyon).

[10] Voir J. M. R. Tillard, « La réforme liturgique et le rapprochement des Églises », pp. 236–7. On sait que Cranmer lui-même, dans le texte de 1549 du *Book of Common Prayer*, introduisait une épiclèse. Elle disparaît en 1552 et 1662. En dehors de la tradition anglicane mentionnons la Liturgie de l'Église d'Afrique du Sud, elle-même influencée par l'Orient.

[11] Au sens large du terme.

avec ténacité par les traditions nées de la Réforme. Sans cette
« réception », à tous ses niveaux, Vatican II n'aurait pas été le Concile de vérité et d'espérance qu'il a été.

Peut-être objectera-t-on que dans ce contexte le mot « réception » ne saurait être utilisé qu'avec prudence et qu'il faut éviter de
lui donner une connotation strictement théologique. Nous avons
souvent entendu cette objection. Elle ne nous paraît pas fondée. En
effet, il ne s'agit en rien d'un pur et simple retour de l'Église catholique soit au donné révélé comme tel, soit à l'antique Tradition,
comme certains l'insinuent. Ce retour ne s'opère — dans la plupart
des cas — que grâce à l'interpellation de l'autre tradition, dans
laquelle l'Église catholique trouve attestée, justifiée et vécue la
valeur en cause. Et c'est à travers *cette* présence dans *cette* autre
communauté que l'Esprit interpelle l'Église catholique, la poussant
à s'interroger sur les raisons justifiant face à la foi et à la pratique tra-
ditionnelles sa propre position.

En d'autres termes, c'est une vérité toujours actualisée dans la vie
ecclésiale, bien que hors de ses propres frontières, que l'Église catholique accepte. Elle la « reçoit » de la chair même de la vie ecclésiale,
par la médiation d'une autre Église — séparée d'elle mais néan-
moins encore habitée par l'Esprit — où elle a gardé ou retrouvé la
place qui lui revient dans l'équilibre de la doctrine ou de la *praxis*
chrétiennes. Le processus est proche, bien que les modalités et les
contextes soient différents, de celui par lequel la décision d'une
Église locale ou d'un concile local est « reçue » en un concile
universel[12]. Ici, au lieu de l'autorité pesée d'une décision nous trou-
vons l'autorité d'une conviction appuyée d'ordinaire sur un témoignage vécu ; et au lieu d'une Église locale en pleine communion avec
l'Église catholique nous avons une Église ou une communauté en
communion imparfaite avec elle. Mais l'imperfection de cette communion est celle que décrit le décret sur l'œcuménisme lorsqu'il
déclare : « bien que nous les croyions victimes de déficiences, les
Églises ou communautés séparées ne sont nullement dépourvues de
signification et de valeur dans le mystère du Salut » (*Unitatis Redintegratio*, 3). Les *elementa* authentiques d'ecclésialité qu'elles possè-
dent et vivent ont toute la puissance de témoignage et, par
conséquent, d'autorité évangélique, que leur vaut cette authenticité.
Ils sont donc matière à « réception ».

---

[12] Pensons au cas des décisions du concile d'Orange.

La même situation écclésiologique fondamentale explique que, sous l'action de l'Esprit qui les habite et les pousse elles aussi à la quête de la pleine communion par une constante conversion à la plénitude écclésiale, ces Églises ou communautés séparées de l'Église catholique « reçoivent » ce qui, venant d'elle, leur apparaît comme un bien *de* l'Église de Dieu ou un élément essentiel *pour* cette Église de Dieu. De toute évidence, cela relève du *kairos* œcuménique dans lequel depuis près d'un siècle l'Esprit-Saint enserre l'ensemble du monde chrétien. Quelque chose de l'état pré-œcuménique de ce monde est changé, et tout pousse à croire que le changement est irréversible.

Peu à peu, en effet, les Églises ont cessé — malgré leur persistante désunion — de se sentir étrangères, coupées les unes des autres. Et ceci est surtout significatif face à l'Église catholique. Le « nostra res agitur » du pasteur Visser 't Hooft au moment de Vatican II[13] traduisait la conscience d'une communion fondamentale — communion d'origine, communion de mission, communion de destinée finale, communion d'accueil du Christ Jésus, communion de repentance, communion d'Esprit-Saint — qui « subsiste » en dépit des ruptures. En sorte que si l'Église de Dieu subsiste dans, « subsistit in » l'Église catholique avec sa force et sa plénitude de moyens de grâce, la communion dans le « oui » global dit au kérygme apostolique comme tel continue de subsister dans (« subsistit in ») l'ensemble des communautés chrétiennes qui celèbrent un authentique baptême. Les divisions n'annulent pas la force unitive de ce « oui[14] ». Or c'est en lui que toute unité authentique doit s'enraciner. Sur la base de cette communion fondamentale, et face à une Église catholique en train de se réformer (en « recevant » plusieurs de leurs propres convictions), les autres Églises se sont vues, dans leur loyauté chrétienne, poussées à « recevoir » pour elles-mêmes plusieurs des points affirmés par les documents conciliaires. L'événement conciliaire a ainsi rejoint, par delà la communauté catholique, la strate de fond qui est précisément l'assise sur laquelle repose l'engagement œcuménique. Il faut voir dans ce phénomène un important progrès vers la *communion*. Il s'agit, en effet, de la qualité même de la souche commune de laquelle tout dépend et sans

---

[13] Texte dans *DC* 63, (1966), 511.
[14] Voir J. M. R. Tillard, « Pluralisme théologique et mystère de l'Église », dans *Concilium*, 191 (1984), 109–24 (119–23).

laquelle l'unité retrouvée risquerait fort de n'être qu'un aménagement poli et habile de concessions ou de compromis.

4. Il se pourrait même que certaines des affirmations de Vatican II ainsi « reçues » par d'autres communautés produisent chez celles-ci plus de fruits que dans les milieux catholiques. La déclaration sur la liberté religieuse, par exemple, a peut-être aujourd'hui plus d'impact chez certaines Églises protestantes classiques, confrontées à des groupes fondamentalistes, que dans l'ensemble des communautés catholiques. Chose étrange, plusieurs Églises, peu intéressées à la lettre même des documents, ont « reçu » l'esprit de ceux-ci d'une façon souvent plus convaincue que des cercles catholiques attentifs à une éxégèse minutieuse. C'est certainement le cas pour la « réception » de l'esprit du décret sur l'œcuménisme dans des milieux protestants. Il pourrait même arriver que des portions de l'œuvre de Vatican II s'effacent de la mémoire catholique, mais demeurent dans la conscience chrétienne grâce à leur « réception » par des non-catholiques. Une telle possibilité ne surprend pas lorsqu'on a compris que l'Esprit-Saint peut se servir d'un concile général de l'Église catholique pour un but plus large que le seul bien de la communauté catholique comme telle.

Réfléchissant, depuis de nombreuses années, sur ce que nous avons décrit comme un mouvement de « conversion mutuelle aux valeurs fondamentales de la *koinōnia* écclésiale », nous y voyons même un signe non équivoque de l'action de l'Esprit gardant l'Église indéfectible. Mais cette action — et cela est une dimension qu'on n'avait guère perçue jusqu'ici — passe par l'entrelacs des relations écclésiales renouées grâce au mouvement œcuménique. Selon la grande économie de la Révélation, l'Esprit agit *sur* l'Église de Dieu *par* l'Église de Dieu; il garde cette Église par le jeu de toutes les communautés censées déboucher dans la communion plénière. Ce sont celles-ci qui, attestant par leur propre vie l'authenticité et l'importance des valeurs écclésiales de leur tradition, les rappellent à la conscience des autres groupes. S'évangélisant mutuellement, elles se convertissent ensemble à ce que Dieu veut qu'elles soient ensemble. L'engagement œcuménique apparaît ainsi comme autre chose qu'une subtile diplomatie. Il s'inscrit en pleine chair de l'action de l'Esprit-Saint gardant l'Église indéfectible en dépit de tout — sur la base du « oui » global dit au kérygme — mais voulant que déjà dans cette indéfectibilité s'actualise la *communion*, qui est l'essence même

de l'Église de Dieu. Il les fait se donner ou se redonner mutuellement les grandes valeurs dont le tissu constitue l'Église que Dieu
veut. Et parmi elles, bien entendu, figure (l'Église catholique
romaine en est fermement convaincue) le ministère d'unité confié à
l'évêque de l'Église de Rome. Mais sur ce point on piétine...

Ce débordement de l'œuvre de Vatican II et cette efficacité hors
frontières, replongés comme nous venons de le faire dans l'ample
dynamisme d'influences réciproques dont ce concile lui-même a
été le bénéficiaire en des domaines importants, doivent dorénavant
être assumés par l'ecclésiologie. Un nouveau registre de la « communion qui persiste en dépit de nos brisures », insoupçonné en
plusieurs milieux écclésiaux même théologiques ou officiels, s'impose ainsi à notre réflexion. Il y a une « réception », elle aussi sus-
citée par l'Esprit-Saint, s'exerçant dans une sorte de capillarité que
permet la grâce baptismale, qui prépare lentement, mais à une
grande profondeur, la « réception » des grands accords qui scelle-
ront l'unité organique. Nos murs de division — peut-être bardés
d'anathèmes ou de jugements malveillants — ne sont plus
étanches. Ne serait-ce pas le grand acquis définitif du mouvement
œcuménique ?

*Quelques cas de « réception » hors frontières des décisions de
Vatican II*

1. Pour étayer la réflexion qui précède il suffira d'évoquer rapide-
ment certains faits, complétant ce que dans une autre étude nous
avons amplement développé[15], et qui permettent au moins de percevoir dans quel *sens* on peut parler d'une authentique « réception »
de Vatican II hors de l'Église catholique. Il nous semble d'ailleurs
que ce sens est remarquablement exprimé dans la déclaration des
observateurs au synode extraordinaire des évêques de novembre-
décembre 1985, lue par Henry Chadwick et portant la marque de sa
pensée :

Vous ne nous avez pas considérés comme des étrangers ou des rivaux, et
nous ne nous sommes pas sentis tels. Vous nous avez accueillis comme des
frères en Christ par la foi et le baptême, bien que nous ne soyons pas encore
en parfaite communion. Votre invitation est à considérer comme un signe
de la communion qui s'est développée entre nous et qui continue à croître.

[15] « La réforme liturgique et le rapprochement des Églises ».

Observateurs, nous ne sommes pas des spectateurs passifs : nous nous sentons profondément engagés dans vos discussions ...

Nous nous sommes réjouis de la ferme approbation des travaux du Concile Vatican II dans ses dimensions ecclésiologiques et œcuméniques. Nous ont réjouis aussi les rapports sur le renouveau de la vie liturgique, sur un nouveau recours à la Sainte Écriture, sur la croissante participation des laïcs dans la vie et le témoignage de l'Église. Avec satisfaction nous avons pris note de la réaffirmation du décret sur l'œcuménisme et des thèmes qui lui sont étroitement liés, comme la collégialité et le partage des responsabilités, a l'intérieur d'une unité ordonnée, par les Conférences épiscopales. Ces conférences et d'autres structures collégiales aux niveaux local et paroissial sont de grande importance pour l'œcuménisme, en augmentant les possibilités de coopération. L'accent mis à la fois par Vatican II et par ce Synode sur la communion (*koinonia*) comme clé pour comprendre la nature de l'Église est important pour l'œcuménisme. Cette communion est créée pour nous, non par nous; elle nous conduit au Père, en Christ, à travers l'Esprit-Saint[16].

Ceux qui font cette déclaration se disent impliqués de façon active dans l'œuvre de Vatican II ou du synode discutant de celle-ci. Elle ne leur est pas extérieure. Bien plus, son impact les réjouit en profondeur, tout comme la constatation que ses grands axes sont réaffirmés par l'ensemble de l'épiscopat catholique. En d'autres termes, ils font corps avec le dynamisme de « réception » qu'ils constatent dans la communauté catholique; ils s'y associent; ils *communient* à la « réception » catholique. Et leur langage ne détonnerait pas dans la bouche d'un évêque en communion avec Rome. Tel est bien le *sens* de la « réception » de Vatican II par les autres Églises : on *communie* à l'accueil que l'Église catholique fait à ce concile, on s'associe à la volonté de mettre en œuvre ses décisions. C'est pourquoi il faut y voir une démarche formellement œcuménique, et déjà un geste important d'unité ecclésiale.

2. Un fait global doit d'abord être souligné. Car il est crucial dans la situation qui nous préoccupe. Les déclarations de *Lumen Gentium* et du décret *Unitatis Redintegratio* sur l'ouverture œcuménique de l'Église catholique et son désir de s'intégrer dorénavant dans l'effort commun de tous les chrétiens pour la quête de l'unité ont été « reçues » par l'ensemble des Églises. Son entrée comme membre à part entière de la commission *Foi et Constitution*, où d'ailleurs certains de ses théologiens occupent des positions de direction, les dis-

---

[16] Texte dans *Origins*, 15 (1985), 454–5.

cussions sur son éventuelle appartenance au Conseil Œcuménique lui-même[17], la participation active de plusieurs de ses experts dans les consultations et même les Assemblées de celui-ci, la constitution du groupe mixte de travail entre elle et ce Conseil[18] en sont la preuve manifeste au plan universel. Quiconque connaît l'histoire de ses relations avec *Foi et Constitution* puis avec le Conseil œcuménique avant Vatican II devine ce que cette « réception » par ces organismes impliquait[19]. Il ne s'agissait ni de politesse, ni de tactique habile. On accueillait la nouvelle vision catholique; on l'intégrait avec joie et confiance à ce qui était né sans elle et même, à tout un plan, malgré elle. Citons à l'appui de cette affirmation deux des œcuménistes les plus lucides. D'abord Edmund Schlink :

Bien qu'une série de questions demeurent encore ouvertes, je ne tiendrais pas moins pour une erreur que de porter sur le décret sur l'œcuménisme un jugement négatif. Si nettes que soient les limites spécifiquement catholiques romaines, à l'intérieur desquelles le programme œcuménique a été discuté et arrêté par le concile, il n'en serait pas moins déplacé d'en faire un grief á ses auteurs. Chaque Église ne peut en effet s'ouvrir au reste de la chrétienté qu'en partant de ce préalable qu'en elle se trouve réalisée l'Église une, sainte, catholique, apostolique. La déclaration de Toronto, elle aussi, garantit à chaque Église membre la liberté de maintenir son ecclésiologie et de ne pas modifier le jugement qu'elle porte sur les autres Églises membres. C'est bien pourquoi existent au sein du Conseil œcuménique des manières différentes et convergentes d'œcuménisme. Certes, la plupart des Églises n'affirment pas leur identité avec l'Église une et sainte avec le même exclusivisme que l'Église romaine, encore ne faudrait-il pas commencer par rapprocher et comparer les prémisses des différentes Églises, mais au contraire, regarder à la volonté avec laquelle une Église dépasse ses prémisses pour s'ouvrir aux autres. Or, sous cet angle, comment ne pas constater ici un dynamisme œcuménique singulièrement impressionnant, — d'autant plus impressionnant qu'il s'est fait jour *malgré* les durcissements dogmatiques et juridiques bien connus de cette Église. Le Décret du second Concile du Vatican sur l'œcuménisme est en tous cas tellement important qu'aucune Église ne peut

---

[17] Voir *DC* 65 (1968), 1486, 1500. Lire W. A. Visser 't Hooft, « Ultimes réflexions », dans *DC* 83 (1986), 125–9 (127–8).

[18] Il est créé dès 1965 (cf. *DC* 62 (1965), 369, 643, 1109–10).

[19] Qu'on se souvienne de la réponse de Benoît XV à l'invitation de participer à la création de *Faith and Order* (voir O. Rousseau, « Le grand voyage œcuménique des fondateurs de Foi et Constitution », dans *Irenikon*, 43 (1970), 325–61). Et le ton de *Mortalium animos* du pape Pie XI est connu.

se permettre de l'ignorer. Il a créé une situation nouvelle dans les relations entre l'Église romaine et les autres[20].

Kristen Skydsgaard est peut-être plus net :

Tout cela ne laisse pas de nous impressionner, nous Luthériens, et nous nous voyons amenés à réviser notre conception de l'Église catholique romaine. Car qui de nous aurait attendu de cette Église, célèbre pour son « immobilité », qu'elle parvienne à un tel changement? Il est évident qu'elle est restée elle-même, cela se confirmera aussi dans l'avenir. Et cependant elle a changé. Comprendre ce paradoxe, c'est comprendre le concile ...

De graves questions sont posées au concile. Mais même mis en question, cet événement reste une invitation pressante faite autant à nous tous qu'à l'Église catholique romaine. « Toutes choses ont leur revers, le Christ seul n'en a point. » Ces termes « le Christ seul », voilà en définitive l'Évangile pour tous les hommes et pour toutes les Églises[21].

Il est significatif que, parmi les documents qu'elle considère comme essentiels pour sa réflexion sur la confession de foi, la commission *Foi et Constitution* inclue un large extrait de la constitution de Vatican II sur la Révélation, avec ce commentaire : « Ce document ouvre très large la porte pour un dialogue œcuménique sur la Révélation de Dieu tout autant que sur les relations entre écriture et tradition. Cette Constitution concorde, à un degré étonnant, avec le contenu de la déclaration de *Foi et Constitution* (Montréal 1963) sur Écriture, Tradition et tradition[22]. » Ici encore, il est clair que la « réception » s'appuie non sur un volonté vague de relations œcuméniques à nouer, mais sur le contenu objectif d'une doctrine de Vatican II dans laquelle on « reconnaît » un bien commun, exprimé d'une façon telle que toutes les Églises peuvent y trouver nourriture pour leur intelligence de la foi. D'ailleurs, déjà à Louvain (en 1971) la commission *Foi et Constitution* avait inclus dans sa réflexion des arguments doctrinaux empruntés aux documents conci-

---

[20] E. Schlink, « Le décret sur l'œcuménisme », dans *Le Concile vu par les observateurs luthériens*, i. *Le Dialogue est ouvert* (Neuchâtel–Paris, 1965), 185–221 (220).

[21] Kristen Skydsgaard, « Envers », ibid. iii. *Rome nous interpelle* (Neuchâtel–Paris, 1967), 161–8 (162, 167).

[22] *Apostolic Faith Today*, ed. Hans Georg Link, coll. *Faith and Order Paper* n° 124 (Genève, 1985), 156–64. Voici l'original anglais de la phrase citée, de l'introduction : « This document threw the doors wide open for ecumenical dialogue on God's revelation as well as on the relationship between scripture and tradition. To an astonishing degree this Constitution coincides in content with the Montreal Statement of the Faith and Order Commission in 1963 on « Scripture, Tradition and Traditions. »

liaires[23]. Ceux-ci entrent ainsi dans le processus œcuménique. Ils ne sont pas simplement des textes documentaires : ils appartiennent à la chair même de la recherche. Qui, sous Pie XI et Pie XII, aurait pensé pareil sort pour les *acta* d'un concile formellement catholique romain, convoqué par l'évêque de Rome ?

Quant à l'influence de la réforme liturgique catholique sur la vie de prière des autres Églises, qu'il nous suffise de dire[24] qu'elle manifeste une autre forme de « réception ». Sans que la perspective soit formellement œcuménique — c'est-à-dire orientée directement vers la *communion* organique — des Églises, de plus en plus nombreuses, voient dans ce que l'Église catholique a modifié chez elle *à cause de* Vatican II une incitation et souvent un modèle pour une réforme liturgique à instaurer de leur côté. Et par là plusieurs renouent avec la grande Tradition qu'elles avaient ignorée ou dont parfois elles s'étaient coupées. On ne se rallie pas à Rome, mais on retrouve le grand filon traditionnel dont l'Église de Rome se veut le témoin ou la gardienne et pour lequel elle-même a renouvelé sa vie liturgique[25]. C'est là, nul ne le niera, un pas en avant considérable vers ce qui doit être la norme d'une unité organique authentique : la possibilité de « reconnaître » chez l'autre les grandes valeurs écclésiales dont on vit soi-même.

3. Mais cette « réception » dans le réseau très large des relations avec les organismes plus universels n'est pas la seule « réception » œcuménique de Vatican II. Les dialogues bilatéraux qui se sont multipliés[26] ont été non la cause, mais la conséquence, de l'accueil que des Églises ont faites soit à l'esprit soit aux positions du concile.

Les rencontres de Paul VI avec Athénagoras et l'Archevêque Ramsey doivent être vues dans cette perspective. Jusqu'au pontificat de Jean XXIII, le fossé entre Orient et Occident semblait si grand que la possibilité de liens vrais était écartée de part et d'autre. Le Patriarche Athénagoras a « reçu » — avec tout son sens profond — la démarche de Paul VI, faite dans l'esprit de Vatican II, renouant

---

[23] Ainsi *Faith and Order, Louvain 1971*, coll. *Faith and Order Paper* n° 59 (Genève, 1971), 79, 97, 99, 147, 186, 229.

[24] En renvoyant à notre étude 'La réforme liturgique et le rapprochement des Églises', où nous avons présenté un assez large dossier de faits.

[25] Même à un registre purement pastoral, comme le manifeste la *Methodist Mass*, préparée par Donald Charles Lacy (Lima, Ohio, 1983).

[26] Sur leur impact et leurs limites voir le jugement de Visser 't Hooft, art. cit. 125-7.

avec l'ancienne coutume d'annoncer son élection aux Églises d'Orient et envoyant au Patriarche œcuménique une lettre autographe où il le « reconnaissait » comme un frère dans l'épiscopat[27]. A travers l'évêque de Rome, l'épiscopat catholique actualisait la nouvelle attitude déjà exprimée dans le concile[28] et, à travers le Patriarche œcuménique, l'Orient la « recevait ». Le baiser de Paul VI et d'Athénagoras au Mont des Oliviers (en janvier 1964) symbolisait cette « offre » et cette « réception ». Dans un tout autre contexte, l'Archevêque de Canterbury « recevait », avec l'invitation de Paul VI, qui « répondait » à son propre désir, la nouvelle possibilité ouverte par Vatican II[29]. C'est ainsi, en effet, que le cardinal Bea, dans son discours officiel, lui présentait la signification de l'événement[30].

Les relations, plus récentes, établies entre l'évêque luthérien américain James R. Crumley et le pape Jean-Paul II montrent que ce processus de « réception » se poursuit[31]. Et il est remarquable que cette correspondance soit entièrement centrée sur l'accueil, par les Églises luthériennes, des possibilités de *communion* offertes surtout par le décret sur l'œcuménisme. Pas assez connu, cet échange épistolaire nous paraît typique du nouvel esprit dont nous traîtons. Il faut en donner quelques extraits. L'évêque Crumley écrit à l'évêque de Rome, le 22 mai 1985, après avoir cité une importante déclaration œcuménique de son Église, « nous avons noté l'engagement exprimé dans le Décret sur l'œcuménisme de Vatican II; j'ai discuté avec le Secrétariat pour l'Unité chrétienne des voies possibles pour un travail visant les buts exprimés dans ces documents »[32]. Jean-Paul II lui répond en prenant acte de cette « réception » d'un des buts majeurs du concile : « dont l'un des soucis principaux a été la restauration de l'unité entre tous les chrétiens »[33].

Ces trois faits, qui ne sont pas les seuls, mais que nous choisissons

---

[27] Textes dans *Tomos Agapis*, nos 29, 33; *POC* 13, (1963) 336–7; *Irenikon*, 36 (1963), 541–2.

[28] Et qui s'exprimera officiellement en novembre 1964, par la promulgation de *Lumen Gentium* et du décret sur l'œcuménisme.

[29] Voir Alan Clark et Colin Davey, *Anglican/Roman Catholic Dialogue: The Work of the Preparatory Commission* (Londres, 1974), 5–7.

[30] Texte du cardinal Bea dans *DC* 63 (1966), 677–8, qui renvoie explicitement à l'ouverture rendue possible par Vatican II.

[31] *A Correspondence Between Pope John Paul II and Bishop James R. Crumley Jr.*, produced by Department for Ecumenical Relations, Lutheran Church of America, 231 Madison Avenue, New York, NY 10016 (1985).

[32] Ibid. 7.

[33] Ibid. 11.

parce qu'ils ont pour acteurs les responsables de trois Églises largement impliquées dans le drame de la rupture entre Rome et le reste
de la chrétienté, sont lourds d'implications. Le Patriarche œcuménique, l'Archevêque de Canterbury, l'évêque luthérien des États Unis
acceptent la proposition d'une Église dont, durant des siècles, leurs
communautés s'étaient méfiées et qu'elles avaient même combattue.
Il est évident que la raison de ce changement d'attitude est non seu-
lement la bonne volonté exprimée par l'Église catholique depuis
Vatican II, mais la garantie apportée par la doctrine de celui-ci. On
« reconnaît » en cette doctrine, au moins pour l'essentiel, celle de la
grande Église des temps apostoliques et celle de « l'Église rendue à
sa pureté ».

4. Dans ces conditions, on ne s'étonne guère de trouver dans les
documents préparés par les Commissions bilatérales de dialogue
avec l'Église catholique une « réception » ample, quoique souvent
nuancée et circonspecte, de plusieurs pans de l'œuvre conciliaire.
Les exemples que nous pourrions verser au dossier sont nombreux.
Nous nous contenterons de trois.

Le Rapport de la Commission mixte entre l'Église catholique et la
fédération luthérienne, publié sous le titre *Facing Unity*[34], commence par souligner comment depuis le concile, grâce à la doctrine
de celui-ci, à l'action de Paul VI et de Jean-Paul II en accord avec
elle, à la collaboration qu'elle a permise, « l'Église catholique
romaine n'est plus regardée (par les luthériens) comme une Église
fausse (*a false Church*). » Ainsi la fonction de l'évêque de Rome est
mieux comprise, ce qui « rend intenables les anciennes condamna-
tions et les images hostiles d'antan »; « la condamnation amère de la
Messe catholique est perçue comme chose du passé. » La « réception » produit donc déjà un fruit concret: un changement du regard
porté sur la communauté catholique. A un autre plan, peut-être plus
profond, on admet l'importance cruciale du n°. 8 de *Lumen Gentium* (le « subsistit in »), l'enjeu de l'accent mis sur la hiérarchie des
vérités et le perpétuel retour à la pureté des origines[35]. On les
« reçoit » comme les marques de la vérité du jugement que l'Église
catholique porte sur elle-même. Bref, on « reçoit » avec joie et

---

[34] Roman Catholic/Lutheran Joint Commission, *Facing Unity: Models, Forms
and Phases of Catholic–Lutheran Church Fellowship* (Genève, 1985).
[35] Ibid. 24–7, avec la note 53.

action de grâces la nouvelle façon dont l'Église catholique se situe face aux autres groupes chrétiens.

Par la suite, traîtant de l'unité de la foi et de la diversité de ses expressions, le même texte assume largement la position de Paul VI, elle-même enracinée dans les déclarations de *Lumen Gentium* (n° 23) et du décret sur l'œcuménisme (n° 4)[36]. Or une étude attentive de ces paragraphes montre qu'on ne se borne pas à « reconnaître » dans ce que dit Paul VI une option valable, mais destinée à demeurer le bien propre de la tradition catholique. On la « reçoit » comme une optique appelée à devenir le bien commun des deux traditions. On comprendra le sens de cette « réception » si on la compare à la remarque des luthériens, insérée après la discussion de la vie sacramentelle :

La raison pour laquelle du côté catholique on parle aujourd'hui de l'Église comme sacrement devient claire. La tradition luthérienne n'est pas encore familière avec cette pensée et est souvent portée à la critiquer. Mais son intention doit être acceptable pour les Luthériens : en tant que Corps du Christ et *koinōnia* du Saint Esprit, l'Église est le signe et l'instrument de la grâce de Dieu, un instrument qui de lui-même ne peut rien faire[37].

Dans ce dernier cas, la « réception » de l'esprit de Vatican II permet de « reconnaître » la légitimité de façons de parler autrefois irritantes pour les luthériens.

Si l'on ajoute à ces points l'accueil des visions de *Lumen Gentium* sur le Peuple de Dieu et le Corps du Christ[38], on est forcé de constater que cet accord, important et prometteur, a comme assise principale, du côté luthérien, la « réception » de plusieurs des re-formulations de la doctrine catholique faites à Vatican II. Celles-ci sont passées dans le dynamisme de la croissance ensemble vers l'Unité.

Alors que dans l'accord luthérien-catholique l'accueil de Vatican II était explicite, il l'est moins dans le *Final Report* de l'ARCIC I. Le style concis choisi par les auteurs de celui-ci, leur désir de ne rien ajouter qui alourdirait la lecture du document, interdisaient toute citation. Pourtant ce silence ne doit pas laisser croire que les positions de Vatican II n'auraient joué qu'un rôle secondaire dans les discussions, puis les déclarations, de la Commission.

[36] Ibid. 31–2.
[37] Ibid. 42.
[38] Ibid. 43–5.

L'insistance sur la *koinōnia*, qui marque tout le document et que l'Introduction générale du *Report* explicite, vient pour l'essentiel d'une lecture de *Lumen Gentium* et du décret sur l'œcuménisme, dans laquelle les rédacteurs ont cherché à dégager ce qui leur semblait être l'intuition majeure de ces textes et à la resituer dans la grande Tradition écclésiale. Il est certain qu'elle traduit une « réception » — longuement analysée et pesée — de l'axe sur lequel Vatican II a situé sa présentation de l'Église de Dieu. C'est cette vision, exprimée dans un langage commun aux deux traditions et explicitée en fonction du but poursuivi par la commission, qui a guidé la recherche de l'ARCIC I et continue de guider celle de la nouvelle commission (ARCIC II). Il s'agit, on le voit, de la « réception » non de tel ou tel texte conciliaire, mais de la vision inspiratrice qui a comme porté l'écclésiologie du concile, en dépit de la ré-émergence çà et là de la théologie que Vatican I avait cristallisée[39]. Grâce à cette « réception », l'écclésiologie de *communion* est maintenant inscrite par les deux partenaires dans leur quête de l'unité visible. Bien plus — l'impact des interventions du cardinal Hume et du document de la Bishops' Conference of England and Wales au dernier Synode romain en fait foi[40] tout comme la déclaration des Primats de la communion anglicane réunis à Toronto en mars 1986 — elle s'impose avec plus de force dans la vie interne de chacune des deux Églises. Elle devient l'écclésiologie de base.

Sur cette toile de fond se situe la « réception » de tel ou tel point particulier de Vatican II. Certains cas sont évidents, comme le paragraphe sur la multiforme présence du Christ, inspiré de la Constitution sur la Sainte Liturgie (n° 7) et surtout de l'Instruction sur le culte eucharistique du 25 mai 1967 (n° 9) qui explicite celle-ci. D'autres sont plus voilés. Il est clair, par exemple, que la commission n'est parvenue à son consensus sur l'autorité — beaucoup plus riche qu'on le dit parfois — et en particulier sur la fonction de l'évêque de Rome que grâce à la « réception » (à la fois lucide, critique et sereine) par les anglicans des chapitres centraux de *Lumen Gentium*. Certes ces chapitres leur étaient présentés par des membres catholiques soucieux d'en montrer l'harmonie avec la grande Tradition patristique, et ils n'adhéraient à la vision de Vatican II que parce qu'ils y retrouvaient celle des Pères. Mais — pour

[39] Comme l'a bien analysé A. Acerbi, *Due ecclesiologie: Ecclesiologia giuridica ed ecclesiologia di communione nella Lumen Gentium* (Bologne, 1975).
[40] L'intervention du cardinal Hume est dans *Le Tablet* (7 Dec. 1985), 1297.

avoir vécu cette merveilleuse expérience — nous pouvons certifier qu'il s'agissait bien d'une « réception », pesée et toujours appuyée sur des raisons intellectuellement honnêtes, de ce que l'Église catholique s'était dit d'elle-même à Vatican II. Sans cette « réception », jamais l'ARCIC I n'aurait pu produire son *Final Report*[41].

C'est dans un tout autre climat que nous plonge le Dialogue entre l'Alliance Réformée mondiale et le Secrétariat pour l'Unité des chrétiens. Car s'il choisit pour thème « la présence du Christ dans l'Église et le monde », c'est précisément afin de dégager et d'éclairer les différences entre les deux groupes sur ce point et d'autres qui lui sont reliés. On vise plus une harmonie du témoignage que l'unité comme telle[42].

Il est alors remarquable qu'abordant le problème épineux de l'autorité de l'Écriture on invoque la constitution *Dei Verbum* sur la Révélation pour faire percevoir que certaines différences sont dorénavant effacées[43]. Ici, comme ailleurs dans cette suite mal unifiée de rapports regroupés en un seul *Final Report*[44], les Réformés ne cherchent pas à « recevoir » de l'Église catholique quelque apport doctrinal susceptible soit d'enrichir leur propre tradition, soit de construire une base commune. En d'autres termes, ils ne s'ouvrent pas à un progrès par accueil mutuel des richesses de l'autre. De leur côté les catholiques sont dans la même attitude. On se borne à faire le point, en indiquant les convergences, « le degré d'accord et de désaccord, les questions en suspens »[45]. Pourtant, on prend pour critère de cette évaluation les positions de Vatican II. Celles-ci sont donc « acceptées », « reconnues » comme l'expression authentique de ce que l'Église catholique affirme d'elle-même et de sa foi. C'est là, on le voit, une « réception » minimale, bien différente de celle que nous rencontrions dans les deux autres documents bilatéraux. On « reçoit » ce que l'autre dit de lui-même, sans y « reconnaître » nécessairement un bien pour soi, sans même y lire nécessairement une authentique interprétation du donné chrétien. Mais cette « réception » — froide et formelle — est cependant importante au

---

[41] Il est intéressant de comparer le rapport de l'ARCIC I avec les discussions de Lambeth 1968!

[42] Le *Final Report* est publié dans Harding Meyer et Lukas Vischer, *Growth in Agreement*, coll. *Ecumenical Documents*, ii (Genève–New York, 1984), 434–63. Voir p. 435.

[43] Voir ibid. 440–1.

[44] Sur cette présentation finale de travail de la commission, voir ibid. 436.

[45] Ibid. 437.

plan œcuménique, et c'est pourquoi nous avons voulu présenter ce *Report*. En effet, elle permet d'avancer dans la connaissance et la confiance mutuelles, en sachant à quoi s'en tenir avec l'autre groupe. On sait qui il est, on l'accepte pour qui il est, bref on le « reçoit » comme un partenaire loyal et fiable. Toute tentation d'un dialogue fondé sur des compromis bancals ou même sur un double langage se voit ainsi radicalement écartée.

Au terme de cette réflexion, il nous faut simplement faire une constatation. Certes la ressoudure des Églises dans l'Unité que Dieu veut prendra plus de temps que nous le pensions. Et peu parmi les artisans du dialogue œcuménique en verront durant leur vie les premières réalisations. Pourtant dans les profondeurs de l'âme écclésiale l'Esprit est à l'œuvre. Le cas de la « réception » de Vatican II n'est qu'un exemple, parmi plusieurs, qui montre que mystérieusement les plaies de la désunion se cicatrisent, qu'un tissu conjonctif se récrée. Dans la grande vallée, la chair du Corps du Christ commence à se tendre par-dessus les membres déchirés. Dieu est un Dieu patient.

3

Two Aspects of Reception

ROGER GREENACRE

FOR the Church of England the year 1845 was difficult, and for the Oxford Movement it was critical. In October, after a long agony, John Henry Newman renounced Anglicanism and entered the Roman Catholic Church. As early as July this denouement was feared and anticipated by his closer friends and collaborators, and in particular by Dr Pusey, who was to become—with reluctance—his successor at the head of the Movement. During that month of July Dr Pusey tried to define his own position in relation to Newman's theory of the development of doctrine and at the same time to explain the evolution of his own attitude towards the Church of Rome in a correspondence with the redoubtable Archdeacon of Chichester, who, though a supporter of the Oxford Movement, was still very sharply anti-Roman. Pusey wrote in one of his letters to Manning—who was in turn to renounce Anglicanism and finally to become Cardinal Archbishop of Westminster and champion of the Ultramontanes—in these terms:

> . . . I can not but hope that it may prove that the Council of Trent may become the basis of union, that those assembled there, were kept providentially free from error . . . again, the Council of Trent might, by subsequent reception, become a General Council, and it might be so now virtually, although unrecognized as such by the whole Church, but in a state of suspense . . . [1]

In addition to the historical interest of this letter, which affords a notable example of the use of a word that has become today a standard part of our ecumenical jargon, I believe that we can already discern in Pusey's thought two aspects of a theology of reception which should interest all the Churches, but which are of particular significance for Anglicans. The first is that of reception as a means of digesting, accepting, absorbing, and assimilating new theological ideas or formulations which are foreign to our own denominational

---

[1] Cf. R. H. Greenfield, 'Such a Friend to the Pope', in P. Butler (ed.), *Pusey Rediscovered* (London, 1983), 174.

tradition or our own confessional vocabulary, and which previously would have been greeted with suspicion, or even hostility. The second is that of reception by the *consensus fidelium* as a constitutive—if not the determinative—factor in the totality of different elements which confer upon a doctrinal definition its authority and its ecumenicity. These are precisely the two aspects of 'reception' with which I propose to deal in this chapter; two aspects which must be clearly distinguished, but never separated.

Before speaking in more detail of the reception of the texts of bilateral and multilateral dialogue within Anglicanism, I should perhaps point out that a distinction of the greatest importance, which is certainly not specifically Anglican, applies with a quite particular pertinence to Anglicans. It is the distinction, made very clearly, for example, in the Official Report of the Assembly of the World Council of Churches in 1983 at Vancouver,[2] between the 'critical evaluation' by the Churches of the Lima text (*Baptism, Eucharist and Ministry*) leading up to their 'official responses' on the one hand and the 'spiritual process of reception' on the other. This Report explains that the distinction is a double one. In the first place, the process of evaluation and response will vary considerably from one confession to another according to each one's structures of authority: the process of reception, by contrast, will engage the whole body of the faithful and cannot be summarized or pinned down in a series of propositions, a text, or a vote. In the second place, official responses have been requested from the Churches within a fixed time-limit and with precise questions to be settled. The responses therefore will of necessity have a provisional quality; one should perhaps add that even the texts themselves have this provisional quality. When, for example, in the case of ARCIC we speak of a 'Final Report', that is not the same as calling it 'definitive'. In the case of ARCIC as in the case of Lima, the Commissions completed the tasks assigned to them, and published their conclusions; in neither case, however, was it a matter of a plenary agreement already finished and complete, but rather of a stage in the dialogue at which the need was felt to submit the results so far achieved to the Churches concerned before carrying on further. It was in some sense a recourse to the principle: *reculer pour mieux sauter*. Moreover, reception is a process which cannot really be submitted to a time-limit; it is essentially a long-term operation.

[2] *Gathered for Life* (World Council of Churches; Geneva, 1983), 46–7.

Anglicans are called upon to reflect on the nature of reception by the fact that it constitutes a major theme in the *Final Report* of ARCIC, and also because the Churches of the Anglican Communion have tried to reduce to a minimum the gulf which separates the process of official response from that of reception. With regard to this ambition it is not, I believe, appropriate for an Anglican to assess to what extent we have been successful: he can however set himself the task of giving an account of our efforts.

First, it is perhaps useful to remind ourselves that the Anglican Communion is composed of thirty or so autonomous Churches, each with its own ecclesiastical structures and its own Synods. It is not therefore a question in the first place of a single response, but rather of the responses of all the Anglican Churches which will require, at a further stage, a process of harmonization and co-ordination on the part of the institutions of the Anglican Communion. In explaining what is taking place in the Church of England, one can none the less give a general picture of what is happening in the other Churches of the Anglican Communion, for every one of them tries to incorporate into its own structures the episcopal and the synodical elements and includes in the latter the full participation of lay representatives.

In February 1985 the General Synod of the Church of England set aside a considerable space of time over two days to the formulation of a response to the BEM and ARCIC texts. The basic document before the Synod was a report *Towards a Church of England Response to BEM and ARCIC*, prepared by its Faith and Order Advisory Group (FOAG) under the chairmanship of Dr Eric Kemp, Bishop of Chichester.[3]

This Report insists on the fact that the Church of England through its Synod and its synodical institutions has already exercised a certain influence on the form and content of the texts in question. For example, FOAG had to respond in detail to the Accra text of 1974, the original draft which preceded the carefully revised Lima text of 1982.[4] As far as ARCIC is concerned, the General Synod had to consider the documents on the Eucharist and the Ministry in 1974 and the first document on Authority in 1977, and on both occasions it passed encouraging resolutions. Later, in 1977, the

---

[3] *Towards a Church of England Response to BEM and ARCIC* (London, 1985).
[4] *One Baptism, One Eucharist and a Mutually Recognized Ministry* (World Council of Churches, Faith and Order Paper no. 73; Geneva, 1975).

Anglican Consultative Council (ACC), an organ of the Anglican Communion, requested replies to certain precise questions related to these first three texts from all the member Churches of the Anglican Communion; after receiving a report from FOAG the General Synod of the Church of England approved three resolutions on ARCIC in 1979. It is worthy of note that one of them asked for a study of the doctrine of the Church capable of providing an 'over-all context' for the Agreed Statements. It can therefore be claimed that the *Final Report* of ARCIC, to the extent that it includes 'Elucidations' of the first three texts, which respond to certain specific questions and criticisms, and also an 'Introduction', which outlines an ecclesiology of *koinōnia* as an 'over-all context' for the statements that follow, is already the result of a certain measure of response and reception on the part of the Churches—including the Church of England. More recently still, in 1983, Henry Chadwick in a masterly introduction presented these two documents, *Baptism, Eucharist and Ministry* (Lima) and the *Final Report* of ARCIC, to the General Synod: this was the occasion for a first and very general debate with no resolutions and no voting. In February 1985 the FOAG report was warmly approved by the Synod on the first of the two days consecrated to BEM and ARCIC. Two days later the Synod had to consider some rather more specific resolutions, to which we must now turn our attention.

As far as BEM was concerned, there was very little disagreement. The three resolutions, which asked the Synod to recognize in the text 'the faith of the Church through the ages', to pursue certain recommendations of FOAG, and to commend another section of FOAG's report to the attention of the Faith and Order Commission of the World Council of Churches, were accepted and approved without difficulty. When it came to the *Final Report* of ARCIC, things were not so easy. Of course it has to be remembered that, where BEM only claims to record a convergence, ARCIC claims to record (at least on the Eucharist and the Ministry) a substantial agreement. A stronger claim inevitably provokes a sharper debate. The first resolution was of absolutely crucial importance and had been drawn up with great care so that it could be submitted in the same form to all the Churches of the Anglican Communion. It consisted of three paragraphs and, in the end, each one was voted on separately.

The first two paragraphs asked the Synod to recognize that the

ARCIC agreements on the Eucharist and on Ministry are 'consonant in substance with the faith of the Church of England'. Two
amendments as proposed by a priest in the Evangelical tradition
would have substituted the phrase 'convergent with' for 'consonant
in substance with'; if these amendments had been accepted, it
would have been a very serious blow to ARCIC. They were, however, rejected by decisive majorities, and many Evangelicals voted
against them. One of the most prominent Evangelical leaders, Colin
Buchanan (now Bishop of Aston), had already proclaimed that
Cranmer could have signed the Windsor Statement on Eucharistic
Doctrine, but that those who burned him could not. Whatever the
historical accuracy of such a claim, it is encouraging that it can be
made.

The third paragraph asked the Synod to accept that the ARCIC
texts on Authority in the Church 'record sufficient convergence on
the nature of authority in the Church for our communions together
to explore the structures of authority and the exercise of collegiality
and primacy in the Church.' The wording of this resolution was
clearly more modest in its claims, speaking no longer of 'consonance', but of 'convergence'. The debate, however, revealed a fairly
general malaise and provoked the then Chairman of the House of
Laity—a well-known Anglo-Catholic—to utter some sharp criticisms, in particular about the absence of any real participation of the
laity in the structures of authority of the Roman Catholic Church.
It was difficult at this point of the debate not to be seized by strong
apprehensions, but finally the motion was accepted with 238 voting
in favour, 38 against, and 25 abstaining.

I do not have room here to speak of all the other General Synod
resolutions on the subject of ARCIC, but only of the last, which
referred to the Diocesan Synods five of the motions on BEM and
ARCIC which the General Synod had just approved. The voting in
the General Synod on that 14 February 1985 represented only its
provisional response to the texts of BEM and ARCIC. The General
Synod had then to await the responses of the Diocesan Synods,
which had to be given before the end of September 1986 and in their
light give its own final response in November 1986. This, in turn,
must be handed on to the Anglican Consultative Committee, which
will meet in 1987 and prepare for the plenary meeting of all the
bishops of the Anglican Communion at the Lambeth Conference of
1988.

It should be pointed out that there is a difference between the procedure adopted for the two texts. Because the Churches of the Anglican Communion are members of the World Council of Churches as national or provincial Churches, each one has to send its response to BEM directly to Geneva; but because it is the Anglican Communion as such that is in dialogue with the Roman Catholic Church, it is the response to ARCIC of the Communion that must be sent to Rome. It is a very complex process, and even the Lambeth Conference cannot give a definitive answer to all the questions—since, for example, on the subject of authority in Anglican–Roman Catholic dialogue, ARCIC II (the second International Commission) has still a lot of work to do. Two other factors complicate the situation even further.

In the first place, the General Synod expressed the hope that all the Diocesan Synods would agree to consult in their turn the Deanery Synods. I believe that all the dioceses accepted this recommendation, and in the diocese of Chichester, for example, the Diocesan Secretary requested the rural deans to let him know of the voting results in their synods before the end of February 1986. If a consultation at this level promotes the reception of dialogue texts by the whole body of the clergy and people, it also poses real problems of organization, formation, and communication in the dioceses and renders urgent the need to make available publications of a more popular kind, relatively simple and adapted to the needs of non-specialists.

In the second place, there is the fact that there are now other reports; those concerning Anglican–Lutheran, Anglican–Reformed, and Anglican–Orthodox dialogues. These do not report on dialogues which have reached the same point of maturity as BEM and ARCIC, and so in July 1985 the General Synod passed them on to FOAG for further study, while it invited the dioceses not to give them formal evaluation, but to recommend them for study in particular situations in which Anglicans might already be in close collaboration with Christians of those traditions. Here again the process of reception can be seen to be anticipating and preparing the process of evaluation and official response.

But there are already some indications that at diocesan level the quantity of reports referred to local synods for their judgement is a matter of resentment and serious questioning. If this is not yet a red light, it is perhaps already an amber one. The Church of England does have to tackle the very serious question as to whether it is imposing upon its synodical structures a weight they can no longer bear.

This question leads me directly to the problem posed very pertinently by the FOAG report in the course of its analysis of the distinction between 'response' and 'reception':

The process of handling texts will differ according to the structures of authority that exist in different churches. Indeed, the need to respond officially to ecumenical texts has already raised questions about the self-understanding of churches and where their authority lies. For example, for Anglicans the way of dialogue throughout the communion is important in 'forming the mind of the church'. However, it is precisely this strength of Anglicanism that is also a weakness for how do we know when the Anglican Communion has formed its mind and what organ or what person/s is to announce that common mind to our partners in dialogue? As in the case of discovering a common mind over the question of the ordination of women to the priesthood, we see that the Anglican Communion is striving to understand the relationship of provinces to one another and the process by which common decisions, which are binding on all, are to be made.

If the need to respond officially to ecumenical statements raises questions for Anglican self-understanding it does so also for others. Those in the 'congregational tradition' have even less magisterial apparatus for officially determining what is the 'faith of the church through the ages' and no forms of *episkope* with authority to make an official declaration with binding authority on their members. On the other hand, the Roman Catholic Church which has the structures for this appears to be showing interesting changes in the workings of its structures. Not only has the *Final Report of ARCIC*, but also the *Lima Text* been sent to all the Episcopal Conferences for response. In an unprecedented way doctrinal materials co-authored by theologians from communions which are still officially anathematised are being dealt with by the highest level of authority. What is more, the Observations of the Sacred Congregation for the Doctrine of the Faith have not been taken as the final Roman Catholic response to ARCIC but, together with the *Final Report* have been sent for discussion to the Episcopal Conferences. Clearly the enterprise on which we are jointly engaged, the process of convergence, is forcing all the churches to re-examine their understanding of the essentials of the Christian faith and also their structures of decision making and their ways of pronouncing authoritatively on behalf of their communion.[5]

---

[5] Op. cit. 8–9, paras. 17–18.

In other words, the means by which a Church articulates and formulates its response to the dialogues imply, express, and reveal an ecclesiology—an ecclesiology which perhaps has never before been made fully explicit. More than that, the process does not allow that ecclesiology to remain static and immutable, but obliges it to advance, to launch out into the deep.

It is on this note of spiritual challenge that I would wish to conclude this examination of the reception of the conclusions of the dialogue texts. Reception can never be assimilated to a process of verifying the absolute conformity of the dialogue texts with the official confessional documents of our Churches. That approach leads only to an impasse, and it is one that has been adopted by some unlikely allies: certain conservative Evangelicals among the Anglicans, who feel themselves strictly bound by the 39 Articles, and certain hardline Roman Catholics, who take a similar view of Trent and Vatican I, have launched 'parallel' attacks on the *Final Report* of ARCIC.

The language of the fundamental question about ARCIC has been very carefully chosen: is the teaching of the ARCIC texts 'consonant in substance with the faith of the Church of England'? It is not in fact the General Synod that has chosen this formula. The same question has been sent to all the Churches of the Anglican Communion, and, moreover, the letter sent by Cardinal Willebrands to all the episcopal conferences of the Roman Catholic Church puts the same question, requesting them to assess whether the *Final Report* is 'consonant in substance with the faith of the Catholic Church'. But 'consonance', unlike 'conformity', is a word that designates a certain openness. In a little book which we wrote as a study guide to the *Final Report*, the late Dennis Corbishley and I posed the following question: 'Will both Anglicans and Roman Catholics be able to say in the end that nothing in the Report seems to them to betray the faith as they have learned it but, on the contrary, that their vision of the faith has been enlarged and confirmed?' We added: 'We say "in the end", because the immediate reaction of many people to a new way of expressing things may be unfavourable.'[6] Certainly our Anglican vision of the faith has been 'enlarged' by ecumenical dialogue and sometimes we have even been

---

[6] English Anglican/Roman Catholic Committee, *Study Guide to the Final Report of ARCIC* (London, 1982), 28.

able to pass from vision to action. A small example of this is the insertion of an *epiklēsis*—with explicit mention of the power of the Holy Spirit—in the new eucharistic prayers of the Church of England, a direct consequence of ARCIC's Windsor Agreement on the Eucharist in 1971.

It is not, however, enough to 'enlarge and confirm' our vision of the faith: we have to go further than that. In the end it is a question of a process of *metanoia* (repentance) and *epiklēsis* (docility to the Holy Spirit), as Lukas Vischer explains:

What happens when divided churches struggle together with a controversial subject and seek to reach agreement on it? Does consensus mean that each party gives up its own view, so that all join finally in some 'average' position? Is ecumenical dialogue like a political negotiation, so that the agreement which is reached is comparable to a 'joint communiqué'? That would be a most unfortunate misunderstanding. Ecumenical dialogue is not only the encounter of two parties with different interests. Rather it brings both parties together in the presence of God. It is nothing less than the readiness of the partners to stand together in their responsibility to the Gospel itself, as it has been delivered to us. Its source lies in Jesus Christ and the cloud of witnesses who have confessed him throughout the centuries. We do not create the results ourselves; they are not due to clever inspirations which enable us to make fancy proclamations. What is won in the dialogue is more that the partners turn together to Jesus Christ, that they correct each other in their hearing and understanding, that they are ready to learn from the other something which they have overlooked up to this point.[7]

A perspective of a spiritual pilgrimage towards the common understanding and expression of the apostolic faith has been opened up before us. And on this point too BEM and ARCIC are again unanimous.

In the Preface to the Lima text we read these words:

Certainly we have not yet fully reached 'consensus' (*consentire*), understood here as that experience of life and articulation of faith necessary to realise and maintain the Church's visible unity. Such consensus is rooted in the communion built on Jesus Christ and the witness of the apostles. As a gift of the Spirit it is realised as a communal experience before it can be articulated by common efforts into words. Full consensus can only be pro-

---

[7] 'The Process of "Reception" in the Ecumenical Movement', *Mid-Stream*, 23/3 (1984), 222.

claimed after the churches reach the point of living and acting together in unity.[8]

In similar vein the *Final Report* of ARCIC affirms:

Contemporary discussions of conciliarity and primacy in both communions indicate that we are not dealing with positions destined to remain static. We suggest that some difficulties will not be wholly resolved until a practical initiative has been taken and our two Churches have lived together more visibly in the one *koinōnia*.

[And further on]

The convergence reflected in our *Final Report* would appear to call for the establishing of a new relationship between our Churches as a next stage in the journey towards Christian unity.[9]

We move now to the second part of our task, an examination of the contribution of reception by the *consensus fidelium* to the authoritative character of a doctrinal definition. Among the bilateral dialogues in which the Anglican Communion is engaged, only the Anglican–Roman Catholic dialogue has so far considered this subject formally.

But before beginning to attempt a résumé of what is said about it in the *Final Report*, I think it not inappropriate to insert at this point a quotation from a speech made in the General Synod by Henry Chadwick in February 1985 during the debate on BEM and ARCIC, in which—to use his own words—he tried to 'tease out' the 'rather complex notion of reception'.

We take it, I think, that it is a technical term for that process by which in the Church of God we digest and assimilate a definition of doctrine in the making of which we ourselves may not have participated except indirectly. And yet if the definition presented to us, perhaps received from those who have faithfully transmitted to us the faith, if that definition which is presented to us truly belongs to the authentic deposit of faith or to what the Church sees that it needs for the safeguarding or the clarifying of that, then our receiving has a positive, vital effect. It is in that sense, I take it, that reception is distinct from the submission of obedience to duly constituted authority. It is totally unlike my normal response to the tax inspector's demands or even to my respect for the highway code. It implies not a passive acquiescence but

---

[8] *Baptism, Eucharist and Ministry*, (World Council of Churches, Faith and Order Paper no. 111; Geneva, 1983), p. ix.
[9] ARCIC I, pp. 98–9.

an active exercise of the trained, critical judgment; it is a consent of the believing mind and heart which, perhaps slowly but surely, comes to see that through that definition, whether it was of a synod or a primate, the authentic, living voice of faith has been spoken in the Church, to the Church, by God.[10]

The first ARCIC Statement on *Authority in the Church* (Venice, 1976) starts by giving a broad account of Christian authority in the context of the Church's mission. It is 'the Spirit of the risen Lord' who 'continues to maintain the people of God in obedience to the Father's will' and who 'safeguards their faithfulness to the revelation of Jesus Christ . . .' Further on, the role of the laity is touched upon: 'The perception of God's will for his Church does not belong only to the ordained ministry but is shared by all its members . . .' The Statement speaks of the ministry of discernment and teaching committed to those who have been ordained, but it continues:

The community, for its part, must respond to and assess the insights and teaching of the ordained ministers. Through this continuing process of discernment and response, in which the faith is expressed and the Gospel is pastorally applied, the Holy Spirit declares the authority of the Lord Jesus Christ . . .

At this point it is not without interest to refer to the Co-Chairmen's Preface to this Statement, in which we read: 'The Roman Catholic Church has much to learn from the Anglican synodical tradition of involving the laity in the life and mission of the Church.' Later, in the Statement itself, the word 'reception' appears for the first time:

When decisions . . . affect the entire Church and deal with controverted matters which have been widely and seriously debated, it is important to establish criteria for the recognition and reception of conciliar definitions and disciplinary decisions. A substantial part in the process of reception is played by the subject matter of the definitions and by the response of the faithful. This process is often gradual, as the decisions come to be seen in perspective through the Spirit's continuing guidance of the whole Church.

This description of reception evidently did not pass unquestioned, for in the 'Elucidation' of its Statement, published in the *Final Report* and dated 1981, the Commission explains its thinking in these terms:

---

[10] General Synod, *Report of Proceedings*, 16/1 (Feb. 1985), 75.

The Commission has also been asked to say whether reception by the whole people of God is part of the process which gives authority to the decisions of ecumenical councils.

By 'reception' we mean the fact that the people of God acknowledge such a decision or statement because they recognise in it the apostolic faith. They accept it because they discern a harmony between what is proposed to them and the *sensus fidelium* of the whole Church. As an example, the creed which we call Nicene has been received by the Church because in it the Church has recognised the apostolic faith. Reception does not create truth nor legitimize the decision: it is the final indication that such a decision has fulfilled the necessary conditions for it to be a true expression of the faith. In this acceptance the whole Church is involved in a continuous process of discernment and response (cf. para. 6).

The Commission therefore avoids two extreme positions. On the one hand it rejects the view that a definition has no authority until it is accepted by the whole Church or even derives its authority solely from that acceptance. Equally, the Commission denies that a council is so evidently self-sufficient that its definitions owe nothing to reception.

In its second statement on *Authority in the Church* (Windsor, 1981) the Commission pursues its reflection on this theme. After speaking of the great conciliar definitions, it continues:

The Church in all its members is involved in such a definition which clarifies and enriches their grasp of the truth. Their active reflection upon the definition in its turn clarifies its significance. Moreover, although it is not through reception by the people of God that a definition first acquires authority, the assent of the faithful is the ultimate indication that the Church's authoritative decision in a matter of faith has been truly preserved from error by the Holy Spirit. The Holy Spirit who maintains the Church in the truth will bring its members to receive the definition as true and to assimilate it if what has been declared genuinely expounds the revelation.

The Commission then proceeds to tackle the doctrinal authority of the Bishop of Rome as universal primate. A footnote makes it clear that the celebrated phrase from Vatican I—'ex sese, non autem ex consensu ecclesiae'—'does not deny the importance of reception of doctrinal statements in the Roman Catholic Church', but only the opinion that such declarations become 'irreformable' only subsequently, after approval by other bishops. But a little farther on, for the first and only time in the *Final Report*, a measure of disagreement has to be recorded:

When it is plain that all these conditions have been fulfilled, Roman

Catholics conclude that the judgment is preserved from error and the proposition true. If the definition proposed for assent were not manifestly a legitimate interpretation of biblical faith and in line with orthodox tradition, Anglicans would think it a duty to reserve the reception of the definition for study and discussion.

In order to illustrate this difference the Commission examines the two Marian definitions of 1854 and 1950 and draws the following conclusion:

In spite of our agreement over the need of a universal primacy in a united Church, Anglicans do not accept the guaranteed possession of such a gift of divine assistance in judgement necessarily attached to the office of the bishop of Rome by virtue of which his formal decisions can be known to be wholly assured before their reception by the faithful. Nevertheless the problem about reception is inherently difficult. It would be incorrect to suggest that in controversies of faith no conciliar or papal definition possesses a right to attentive sympathy and acceptance until it has been examined by every individual Christian and subjected to the scrutiny of his private judgement. We agree that, without a special charism guarding the judgement of the universal primate, the Church would still possess means of receiving and ascertaining the truth of revelation. This is evident in the acknowledged gifts of grace and truth in churches not in full communion with the Roman see.

However, only a little further on, the *Report* is able to affirm:

We have already been able to agree that conciliarity and primacy are complementary (Authority I, paras. 22–23). We can now together affirm that the Church needs both a multiple, dispersed authority, with which all God's people are actively involved, and also a universal primate as servant and focus of visible unity in truth and love.

The situation in which we are left by the second statement on Authority is dramatic; it could even be described as cruelly tantalizing. The great abyss which for four centuries has separated Rome and Canterbury has almost been bridged; the ladder which has been thrown across it by the *Final Report* of ARCIC only lacks (at least in the conviction of the members of the Commission) a single rung—a complete agreement on the exact relationship between a papal definition and its reception by the whole body of the People of God. It is now our duty to see to what extent there has been a response—from both sides—to this challenge.

First of all, there were the *Observations* of the Sacred Congregation for the Doctrine of the Faith, published at the same time as the *Final Report* itself. This document states that ARCIC's affirmations on the doctrine of reception 'are inexact and not acceptable as Catholic doctrine.' In particular, 'the formula of agreement' in the *Final Report* which 'makes reception by the faithful a factor which must contribute, under the heading of an "ultimate" or "final indication", to the recognition of the authority and value' of doctrinal definitions is judged to be incompatible with the Constitution *Pastor Aeternus* of Vatican I and the Constitution *Lumen Gentium* of Vatican II.[11]

Later on, the Episcopal Conferences of the Roman Catholic Church began to formulate their own official Responses at the request of the Roman Secretariat for Christian Unity. To my knowledge, three of these Responses have already been published in English,[12] those of the Bishops' Conferences of the United States, of France, and of England and Wales.

The American Response[13] is curious; it devotes just over five pages to the Eucharist, one and a quarter to the Ministry, and just over one to Authority. This being so, it is hardly surprising that nothing is said about reception.

The French Response[14] devotes a lengthy section to reception. It begins by approving and underlining what was said by the Commission: 'Reception is a fact of the Church. It is regrettable that Catholic theology in modern times forgot it. It has only been rediscovered since the Second Vatican Council.' As it proceeds, the analysis becomes more critical.

The ecumenical difficulty [say the French bishops] is to make the proper connection between the recognition and confirmation of a council by the Roman primate and its reception by the whole body of the Church. These two facts do not operate at the same level and care must be taken not to treat them as if what is allowed to one is taken away from the other.

A third section of this part of the Response explores reception as 'a fact which becomes clear after the event'.

---

[11] *Observations on the Final Report of ARCIC* (London, 1982), D 1 d and B III 5.

[12] This was originally written in the summer of 1985, but is still true in January 1987.

[13] Dated 22 Jan. 1984 and published in this country in *One in Christ*, 21/4 (1985), 320–9.

[14] The French text was published in *La Documentation Catholique*, 1902 (1–15 Sept. 1985) and an English translation in *One in Christ*, 21/4 (1985), 329–48.

It usually extends beyond a single generation because it enters the life and thinking of the Church gradually. It expresses the concrete meaning which the People of God recognize in and bestow upon the definition as they absorb it in their own way into the flesh and blood of Church life . . . As we see it, the Anglican members of ARCIC are wrong to speak of 'a duty to reserve the reception of the definition for study and discussion' . . . For if the decision is recognised to be an expression of the evangelical truth borne by the living tradition, reception will come about in its own kind of rhythm . . . Can one imagine an official decision not being received? This has, beyond argument, happened in the case of decisions which did not involve the Church's inerrancy: and it can be envisaged as a limit situation for decisions of that kind.[15] It would not mean that the decision taken was formally in error, but that for reasons needing analysis . . . it has not spoken to the living faith of the Church.

Before going on to tackle the treatment of reception in the English Response,[16] it is right for an Anglican to express joy and thankfulness at the entirely generous, open, and eirenic tone of that Response—the sign of a radical change in the relations between our two Communions in England and Wales. On the subject of reception the English Response begins by saying:

The Final Report presents the exercise of authority in the Church with due and balanced emphasis on the reception of teaching. The basis for this emphasis is a clear understanding that doctrinal definitions draw their authority both from the inner truth which they proclaim ('id quod docetur') and from the authority of the person or persons who proclaim them ('a quo docetur'). The response to these two aspects of authority is by faith and obedience, and such reception of teaching is the work of the Holy Spirit in the Church. In the Final Report the Commission has sought to express the essential complementarity of both elements in reception.

(37) The Final Report also develops the role of reception in the definitive proclamation of teaching. It successfully avoids the extremes of either making reception the criterion of doctrinal truth, or excluding it totally from the conditions needed to be sure that teaching is in accordance with the truth. When the Commission declares 'although it is not through reception by the people of God that a definition first acquires authority, the assent of the faithful is the ultimate indication that the Church's authoritative

---

[15] The original French reads: 'et on peut l'envisager comme une situation limite dans des décisions de ce dernier type'—i.e. for decisions which *do* involve the Church's inerrancy.

[16] *Response to the Final Report of ARCIC I*, approved by the Bishops' Conference of England and Wales during its meeting on 18 Apr. 1985 (London, 1985). Cf. also *One in Christ*, 21/2 (1985), 167–80.

decision in a matter of faith has been truly preserved from error by the Holy Spirit' (Authority II, paragraph 25), we believe that its thinking is compatible with Catholic teaching.

(38) Reception may indeed be the only grounds for complete assurance that all the conditions for the exercise of infallible magisterium have been present. We would wish to add, however, that in the lived faith of the Church such reception may take some considerable time to emerge.

It concludes with the following point for further consideration:

(41) While accepting as sound all that the Commission says about the nature and role of the reception of teaching, we also wish to comment that, in our view, both Communions would benefit from a continuing dialogue on this point. The importance of the reception of teaching is not well understood in the Catholic community and ongoing study would help to clarify the differences evident in the treatment of this theme.

Before turning to what is said about ARCIC's understanding of reception in the FOAG Report *Towards a Church of England Response to BEM and ARCIC*, three preliminary remarks perhaps need to be made. First, it should be emphasized that Anglicans have been intensely relieved to note that the *Observations* of the Congregation for the Doctrine of the Faith have had no negative influence—up till now at any rate—upon the responses of Roman Catholic Episcopal Conferences. Secondly, it needs to be held in mind that the FOAG Report does not constitute the official Response of the Church of England—given over a year later in November 1986—but is rather the most substantial element in the dossier destined to enable the Church of England to make that Response. Thirdly, it needs to be remembered that the Response of the Church of England is itself only one contribution towards the Response of the Anglican Communion.

The FOAG Report has this to say:

We believe that the Commission's statements on reception are soundly based, and fully in line with characteristically Anglican ways of thinking about authority and the active part played by the body of the faithful. At the same time it is also characteristically Anglican to understand a special responsibility for the safeguarding of unity and truth as resting on the episcopate . . . It would not . . . be consistent with Anglican forms for the ordination of bishops to doubt that the commission entrusted to bishops (and therefore also the gift of God proportionate to the task) includes the care for true doctrine and the proclamation of that to the faithful . . . Hence it would be misleading, as ARCIC observes, to suggest that in controversies of faith no definition, whether by council or primate, possesses a right to attentive sympathy and acceptance until it has been examined by every individual Christian and subjected to his or her private judgment. Such a suggestion would make nonsense of the proposition that the Church has authority in matters of faith. . . . Reception by the faithful is a continuing process of assimilation which is also a critical appropriation and interpretation.

It is important that Anglicans should maintain their position on this point for three reasons in particular. First, there is the matter of historical precedent. If it took three centuries for the Canon of the New Testament to be finally received, and half a century for the Council of Nicaea, should we expect any papal utterances to be accepted overnight? ARCIC mentions the reception of the so-called Tome of Leo by the Council of Chalcedon but does not make it sufficiently clear that this Council accepted it as an authoritative statement of faith only after careful examination. Secondly, Anglicans are not alone in believing that there is no office or institution in the Church which can claim the power to make statements whose preservation from fundamental error the Church may be sure of before their reception by the whole Church. The Orthodox Churches are as committed to the doctrine of the Church's infallibility as is the Roman Catholic Church, but they equally affirm that the power of such utterance is a gift of the Holy Spirit which when given, demands recognition and cannot be presumed upon beforehand in virtue of office. And thirdly, it is surely of theological significance that the dogmas which are particularly in question, those of 1854, 1870 and 1950, are precisely those which have been proclaimed within a deeply broken Church.[17]

I wish now to conclude with three questions for our further reflection and consideration, since it is clear that the doctrine of reception must find an important place in the continuing dialogue between our two communions—and indeed with other Churches also.

    1. The first question is suggested by that last phrase quoted from the FOAG Report about 'a deeply broken Church'. Does not the deadlock in which ARCIC found itself on the subject of the relationship between a definition and its reception have its roots in two very different conceptions of the frontiers of the Catholic Church? A definition which expresses only the faith of the Roman Catholic Church, even when profound attention has been paid to the living faith of all the members of that Church, cannot hope to find the same reception on the part of the faithful of the other Churches that

[17] Op. cit. 87–9, paras. 227–30 (*passim*).

it can expect from its own members. In his book *The Bishop of Rome*, Jean Tillard draws attention to a way forward opened up by Paul VI when he spoke of the Second Council of Lyons as 'the sixth of the general synods held in the West'.[18] Can one then make some distinction between an 'ecumenical council' and a 'general synod'? If Fr Tillard has correctly interpreted the mind of Paul VI—and he is not alone in making this interpretation[19]—then there is to be found in the quotation from Dr Pusey which I placed at the beginning of my article a striking and happy proximity to this thinking. Can an act of reception made by another Church give to a definition made since the separation a certain ecumenical plenitude which it lacked before?

2. The Anglican and Roman Catholic members of ARCIC I found themselves close to full agreement on the question of reception. Unfortunately it is undoubtedly true that for many others in both Churches the distance remains enormous. In order to bridge that gap is a strictly theological dialogue sufficient? Clearly the answer is no, as the *Final Report* itself recognizes. What then are the practical initiatives required for the spiritual and psychological transformation of the members of our Churches and of their ecumenical attitudes?

3. When we speak of reception we generally envisage either the 'yes' of acceptance or the 'no' of rejection. But does there not exist a third possibility, worse even than rejection—the deafening silence of the total indifference of the majority of the faithful?

Postscript

This paper was delivered in French at a Colloquium on the theme of Reception held at the Monastery of Chevetogne in Belgium in September 1985 and subsequently published (with the title 'La réception des textes des dialogues et la réception de la doctrine: deux problèmes pour les Anglicans') in the review *Irénikon*, 58/4 (1985). It is with the kind permission of the editor, Dom Emmanuel Lanne, that I reproduce this article in English, having made only some minor alterations in the course of translation. I am however aware

[18] Op. cit. (Paris, 1982), in English trans. (London 1983), 17.
[19] Cf. (e.g.) B. de Margerie, as quoted in Aidan Nichols, '*Einigung der Kirchen*: An Ecumenical Controversy', in *One in Christ*, 21/2 (1985), 161–6.

that it needs to be up-dated, at least very briefly, in the form of a postscript.

The reference to the Diocesan Synods of motions relative to *BEM* and ARCIC by the General Synod, as part of its provisional approval in February, 1985, elicited an overwhelmingly positive response. At the General Synod of November, 1986, all the motions relating to BEM and ARCIC were approved. Two following motions approved by the Synod drew particular attention to the role of the laity in the decision-making processes of the Church and to the need for further exploration of the relation between laity, clergy, and bishops in the exercise of authority.

It has to be admitted both that the margin of approval given by the General Synod of the Church of England was much narrower than that achieved in February 1985 and that the *Final Report* has provoked some reservations in other parts of the Anglican Communion. In particular it is now apparent that the Lambeth Conference of 1988 will have to conclude that much more work is needed on Authority in the Church before the majority of Anglicans can accept that the gap between the teaching of our two Communions in this field is as narrow as the *Final Report* suggested.

As Professor John Zizioulas (now Metropolitan of Pergamum) has pointed out,[20] in the final analysis reception is not a matter of texts alone; it is the Churches which are being challenged to receive each other. If this is the case (as surely it is), then the process of reception requires much more than study and discussion; it requires mutual trust, mutual commitment and a much closer sharing in life, worship and mission. Present hesitations and reservations in our Churches with regard to the reception of agreed statements and the doctrine of reception only underline the need to intensify such trust, such commitment and such sharing.

[20] Cf. 'The Theological Problem of "Reception" ', in *One in Christ*, 21/3 (1985) 193.

4

The Authority of Scripture
The Book of Genesis and the Origin of Evil in Jewish and Christian Tradition[1]

JAMES BARR

WHERE does religious authority ultimately reside? It may be said to reside, most obviously, in God himself and in the deeds of salvation that he has wrought. But our knowledge of these deeds comes to us through authoritative persons, whose interpretation of them is recognized as weighty and luminous in the Church. On the other hand our access to these persons is mediated through the texts that they have left to us. And these texts themselves contain interpretations of still older texts, which were understood to be authoritative from before the beginnings of Christianity itself.

In what way then are these different grades or manifestations of authority related? How far, for instance, does an ancient text continue to have authority, if understood in a way different from that in which authoritative persons later understood it? And how far is the interpretation which these authoritative persons give itself mediated through, and dependent on, an intervening history of interpretation, rather than arising directly from the ancient text taken in itself? Is the history of interpretation then itself authoritative? Nowhere can these questions be more suitably illuminated than in our ideas of the origin of evil.

How did evil begin? What was the origin of sin? These are questions of perennial interest. Although they look, at first sight, like prehistorical or palaeontological questions, they are actually very much questions about the present day, and indeed about the future. Our ideas about the origin of evil have an effect on our ideas about humanity and its potentialities and limitations in the present-day

---

[1] This essay was originally the Rabbi Julian B. Feibelman Memorial Lecture, delivered under the Chair of Judeo-Christian Studies at Tulane University, New Orleans, Louisiana, on Thursday, 7 November 1985. Permission to publish here is gratefully acknowledged. It is worthy of note that Henry Chadwick had himself delivered at an earlier time a lecture under the same Chair on 'St Augustine and the Origin of Evil'.

world. One picture of the origin of evil may suggest that irremediable disaster is inevitable unless some cataclysmic change occurs; another may suggest that humanity has potentialities that may yet find development in future history. Thus an old story has power to mould our estimation of ourselves, and differently according to the way in which we interpret it.

And this relationship between ideas of the origin of evil on the one hand, and values of the present day on the other, is no new thing: on the contrary, it existed already in biblical times. The men of the Bible had no direct knowledge of how evil began, just as they had no direct knowledge of how the world had come into being. Their picture of origins was composed from two basic sources. First, there were inherited depictions and legends, whether (earlier) drawn from the surrounding world of culture and religion, or (later) derived from earlier strata within the Bible or within Jewish or Christian tradition. Secondly, there was their experience of themselves, their beliefs, their God, their history, and their world. Thus ideas of the origin of evil correlate, though not directly or simply, with our attitude to problems of the present day, and this was already so for the men of the Bible.

Now I propose to begin with the position in Christianity, then to go back to the Old Testament seen in itself, then to turn to Jewish traditions and interpretations, and finally to return to Christianity. For the traditional Christian conception of the origins of evil, the dominant passages are in St Paul, and the central thought is that of the analogy between Adam and Christ. By one man sin entered into the world, and death through sin; and so death passed to all men (Rom. 5: 12); one man's disobedience meant condemnation for all men, and so also one man's act of righteousness means justification and life for all men (Rom. 5: 18); as through a man comes death, so through a man comes also the resurrection of the dead; as in Adam all die, so in Christ shall all be brought to life; the first man is of the earth, the second man is from heaven; as we have borne the image of the earthly, so we shall also bear the image of the heavenly one (1 Cor. 15: 21–2, 47, 49). These are familiar thoughts. For our purpose, the most noticeable thing about them is the stress they throw upon the disobedience of Adam. Right from the beginning sin came in; and its effect was instant and completely catastrophic. There is no matter of degree or development. The slightest sin was total and universal in its effect: sin, it seems, completely, and not partially, altered man's relation to God. And, in particular—and indeed this is the only particular that is mentioned—sin brought death into the world. Because he sinned, man had to die; and this is passed on, after Adam, to all humanity. The sin of Adam, and their own consequent sin, meant that all must die; only a redemption that overcame death, that brought life out of death, could overcome the sin inherited from Adam.

Later theologians worked out, on this basis, the doctrine of original sin. Sin was the lot of all human beings, through inheritance; and through the idea of concupiscence it might be connected with sexuality and with birth, even with femininity. 'In sin did my mother conceive me' (Ps. 51: 5, Hebrew 51: 7) was often so understood: it is, in fact, one of the very few Old Testament texts to point in this direction.

In traditional Protestantism original sin continued to be emphasized, but the stress was different, lying less on the mode of transmission and more on the complete heinousness of original sin or of any sin at all, so that in extreme cases 'total depravity' became, and has remained, a favoured term. The effect of sin was so great, some thought, that the image of God in man had been distorted, or even totally obliterated, an idea for which, however, there is no biblical evidence at all (none of the passages which use the term 'image of God' speaks of the loss of it, still less of its obliteration).

All this has been the familiar and traditional Christian position. It is so familiar, so deeply implanted in our traditions, that it comes as something of a surprise to realize that it is after all a rather rare emphasis within the New Testament itself; and, in particular, it is an emphasis that seems to be lacking from the teaching of Jesus himself. He, it seems, does not talk about Adam and the origin of sin at all. Sin and evil, yes: he is come 'to save his people from their sins' (Matt. 1: 21), and he is familiar with the ways of evil, how it enters the souls of people, deceives them, how evil spirits come back after they have been cast out. But all this belongs more to the present operations of sin and evil, their modes of working within people: the interest to *explain* this sin and evil by reaching back to the beginnings of humanity seems not to press in Jesus' mind. Sin, it seems, is not to be accounted for. It is there all right, but there is no doctrine of original sin to be found in Jesus' teaching, no appeal back to Adam and Eve and the Garden of Eden. And, if it is not in Jesus' teaching, it is equally absent from many other parts of the

New Testament; as has been said, it is intrinsically Pauline. 1 John
3: 8 says that sin belongs to the devil, and the devil sinned from the
beginning; but he does not mention Adam and Eve, though just a
few lines further down he mentions Cain, who murdered his
brother (3: 12). Jesus was well aware of the stories of the beginning
of the world, and he could appeal back to the time of creation: 'from
the beginning it was not so' that divorce was allowed, and Jesus
cited the marriage arrangements of Genesis 1–2 as the principle that
should guide in the matter (Matt. 19: 3–9; Mark 10: 2–11), but there
is no similar appeal back to the disobedience of Adam as the basis
for all sin and evil. It seems likely that the emphasis on the typology
of Adam and Christ is a Pauline creation, absent from Jesus' own
teaching and absent from many other currents of New Testament
thought. To say this is not to say that there is anything wrong with
the Pauline emphasis on the Adam–Christ relationship: on the contrary, it is an extremely powerful and important theological position. But the fact remains that it is by no means widely distributed
within the New Testament.

Nevertheless, as it turned out, the main Christian tradition in this
respect followed Paul. It emphasized the disobedience of Adam.
This one first sin was a totally cataclysmic event which very
seriously disrupted relationships between God and humanity; it
brought death into human existence; and its effects are immediate
and universal.

Now let us turn to the Old Testament story of Adam and Eve in
itself. Here we have a remarkable contrast. It is clear that the disobedience of Adam and Eve is a serious matter, and yet it is doubtful whether it is conceived as a cataclysmic 'fall' of man which
immediately and totally alters the status of humanity in relation to
God. There are several aspects in this:

First, it is not without significance that the term 'sin' is not used
anywhere in the story. The first use of this Hebrew word, as of the
corresponding Greek word (taken by the Greek as a verb, and so
hamartanō), in the Bible comes later, in the story of Cain:

> If you do well, you are accepted;
> if not, sin is a demon crouching at the door.
>
> (Gen. 4: 7 NEB)

—if this is the right sense, since text, grammar, and meanings remain
obscure. And not only 'sin', but other words, such as those com-

monly rendered as 'evil', 'transgression', 'rebellion', and the like, though not uncommon in Hebrew narrative style, are also absent from Gen. 2–3. The story proceeds on the level of practical actions: 'don't eat this', 'if you eat it, in that day you will die', 'how did you know that you were naked?', 'God made them coats of skins', and so on. The actual identification of sin or evil, their designation by name, is lacking. Moreover, nowhere does God say such things as 'this has totally ruptured the relationship between you and me', or 'you have now fallen from the sort of status that you used to enjoy', or 'you have lost the image of God in which you were created.' God punishes the man and the woman, as he does the snake; he tells them of the deprivations they will have to undergo; he drives them out of the Garden of Eden. But it is just not the case that all communion between God and Adam and Eve is broken: on the contrary, they keep on talking, the human pair with God, and God continues to care for them. They used fig leaves to cover their nakedness, and God improves upon this and makes them tunics of skin—just as later, after he expels Cain from his presence, he gives him a protective sign to prevent others from murdering him. It just is not the case that communion between God and humanity is broken down by the disobedience of Adam and Eve. They know God's displeasure, they hide from him among the trees, they feel guilty, they are afraid of God, they blame one another (the man blames the woman, the woman blames the snake), but they remain on speaking terms with God all along.

This in itself might not be so decisive, but we are pressed much farther in the same direction when we consider the all-important matter of death. This topic is emphasized from the beginning. The snake says to Eve: 'You will certainly not die. For God knows that when you eat of the fruit your eyes will be opened, and you will be like God, knowing good and evil.' They ate of the fruit; their eyes were opened; they found that they knew good and evil; and they did *not* die. The serpent was the one who was right in these matters. They did not die. Indeed, the punishment brought upon man does include the mention of death: because of man the ground is cursed (Gen. 3: 17 ff.) and man will suffer toil and frustration all his life: in the sweat of his face he will eat, until he returns to the ground, for from the ground he was taken: 'dust you are, and to dust you will return.' Yes indeed, but this is not death 'in the day that' they disobeyed, it is not death that is in itself the punishment: rather, the punishment upon man is toil and frustration in toil, and the final frustration is death, the final proof, far off in the future, that all his work will get him nowhere.

Sometimes it is said that, though the humans do not die, and in fact live a long time afterwards (Adam lived 930 years, Gen. 5: 5), they had 'died spiritually.' This is a fiction, completely contrary to the Hebrew conceptions within which the passage is written; moreover, it is proved wrong by the emphasis of the passage itself. For the problem created—and created *for God*!—by the disobedience of Adam and Eve is that they are now likely to gain *immortality*! Far from dying in the day of their offence, they will live for ever! All they have to do is to eat of the fruit of the tree of life: having eaten of the tree of knowledge, it is only a matter of time before they find the tree of life and eat of it, and that is the whole and the only reason why they are expelled from the Garden of Eden. 'The Lord God said, "Behold, the man has become like one of us, knowing good and evil; and now, lest he put forth his hand and take also of the tree of life, and eat, and live for ever"—therefore the Lord God sent him forth from the Garden of Eden' (Gen. 3: 22 f.), and put there the cherubim with flaming sword, to ensure that he would never get back in. Man is, as a result of his disobedience, on the point of gaining eternal life! Eternal life!—that this is the point is well confirmed by other stories from the ancient East which also emphasize this aspect. This enormously alters the focus of the story, when seen in itself as contrasted with the Pauline idea of Adam. In the story, it is not so much death that enters the world through disobedience: on the contrary, it is the glimmering distant vision of immortality. Indeed, the relations between life and death, within the story taken in itself, are probably very largely reversed as against our usual Christian ideas. Within the story, most probably, it was assumed that man was going to die in any case. Man was mortal, only gods were immortal, as in all the ancient orient. He would have had a good life, and died in old age among his family, as was esteemed in Israel to be natural, good, and right. The problem that is opened up by the 'Fall' is the possibility of eternal life for man.[2]

There is another familiar aspect that alters when we study the

---

[2] What has been said about the Genesis passage would require, were it to be fully documented, a detailed discussion of many questions of text and meaning concerning (*a*) the question whether man was originally mortal or immortal, and (*b*) the question of the location and function of the tree of life. The view I have taken seems to me to

story in itself. According to traditions familiar in Western Christianity at least, the primal sin of man consisted in *pride*, in the longing to be greater than one is, the longing to be as God. St Paul himself, however, nowhere says this, nor is the identification of the primal sin with pride in this sense to be found anywhere in the New Testament. But neither is it to be found in the Genesis story taken in itself. It is true that the snake, speaking to the woman, says (Gen. 3: 5) that if they eat of the forbidden fruit they will be like God, knowing good and evil; and this has commonly been understood to mean that this formed the motivation for their disobedience, the desire to be like God, to know good and evil. But the Genesis passage gives no hint that this is the *motivation* for their act. The snake said this as *explanation* of why *God* had forbidden the fruit of this tree. But there is no suggestion in the passage that the desire to be like God, to depart from human limitations and finitude and move into the class of the divine, formed the motivation of the woman's choice. It was the quality *of the tree* that attracted her: it was good for food, delightful to the eyes to look upon, and it had a third quality which *might be* 'to be desired to make one wise' (so RSV), but might be 'tempting to contemplate' (so NEB, and earlier Brown, Driver, and Briggs). At the most the woman was attracted by the food value, the pleasant appearance, and the educative prospects of the fruit. There is no indication that the will to become more than human, to put oneself in the place of God, formed her motivation: if it did, the narrative is at fault in not making this important point clear.

These then are perhaps the most important changes of perspective that emerge when we look at the material of Genesis in its own categories. But another must be added: there is significant evidence in the Hebrew Bible for another and quite different conception, namely that of a sort of gradual evolution and building up of evil. Seen in this way, the story of Adam and Eve may be only the first step towards a much more serious outbreak of evil. The next step comes with Cain, who murders his brother Abel—out of jealousy, as it seems, because God favours his brother more than himself. Cain is not put to death—yet another argument against the idea that

---

be the greatly most likely one. Only one point needs special mention: the whole tenor of the story seems to me to forbid any interpretation according to which the fruit of the tree of life had already been accessible to, and eaten by, Adam and Eve before their disobedience.

Adam was punished with death by God—but exiled and made to wander on the earth. It is here, as has been mentioned, that the word 'sin' first appears. Murder is a serious matter, yet Cain is still protected by God, so that his life will not be taken. Cain, it seems, was no irreligious man: Cain loved God, he was shattered when he discovered that he had to live away from God's presence; it was his jealous love for God, his need for God's favour, that had caused the original murder of Abel. The story of Cain's family ends with continuing aggravation of violence, with Lamech boasting about the multiple vengeance he has taken or is ready to take (Gen. 4: 23 f.).

Even more emphatic in Genesis is the place of the angel marriages and the story of the flood. The sons of God saw that the daughters of men were fair, and they took to wife such of them as they chose. Dark and obscure of import, this passage, doubtless of ancient mythological origin, seems to betoken, within Genesis as it now stands, a very serious breakdown in the order of the world. The lines that separate divinity and humanity are being overrun, and this is happening physically, with the production of giants and supernatural beings. Is this good or bad? The text is at first a little ambivalent. The children thus born were great people, mighty men, men of renown: these were great times, it seems to be about to say; 'there were giants in the earth in those days', as we still say proverbially. But the Genesis text then checks this positive impulse and the mood turns dark: it is here, and here for the first time in the Hebrew Bible, that we hear of total evil, of radical corruption. 'God saw that the wickedness of man was great in the earth', and it is here (Gen. 6: 5) that we first get the proof-text, the only real proof-text, for the idea of total depravity: 'every formation of the thoughts of man's heart was *only evil all the time*.' And at once we proceed to the flood: the Lord repented that he had made man on the earth, and he resolved to blot out all life. Is not this, within Genesis read for itself, the real recognition of something like 'original sin', something like 'total depravity'—here, and not in the story of Adam and Eve? It is here that real revolt against God is recognized, and here that God very properly responds with the decision to destroy the corrupt world.

But did Genesis mean that all men, everywhere and always, were purely and desperately wicked? Did they not mean that this was the case with the generation of the flood, but not with normal humanity? After the flood is over and life on earth begins again, we have the slightly puzzling and certainly remarkable words of God, as he smells the pleasing odour of Noah's first sacrifice: 'I will never again curse the ground because of man, for the formation of man's heart is evil from his youth' (Gen. 8: 21). This is enigmatic. It takes up again the theme announced before the flood: man is hopelessly evil. But it is now expressed in another way. Before the flood the sense was: man is hopelessly evil, and so I will destroy the world. Now the sense is: man is hopelessly evil, and so I will never again destroy the world. Or does he mean it otherwise? Perhaps we have to see a different syntax here: 'Never again will I curse the ground because of man, however evil his inclinations may be from his youth upwards' (NEB). A final determination of this problem must be left aside for the present.

But, to sum up to this point, it is possible to see in Genesis a culminating growth of evil with its highest point at the beginning of the flood, with the angel marriages. Seen in this way, the story of Adam and Eve is not the central or the most catastrophic point of origin of sin, and in particular it is not the major point of entry for death. The disobedience of Adam is part of a cumulative series, and is not in itself a primary display of human wickedness or pride.

One strong reason in favour of this construction is another fact: nowhere in the entire Hebrew Bible is the disobedience of Adam and Eve cited as explanation for sin or evil in the world. This reference, which to us seems so natural, simply does not occur. Isa. 43: 27 'Your first father sinned' is a good example, for the reference is not to Adam, but to Jacob or to other pioneers of the people of Israel. Nowhere is the existence or profundity of evil accounted for on the ground that Adam's disobedience made this inevitable. To this must be added another important argument: the Old Testament, far from taking the universal sinfulness of man as an obvious and ineluctable fact, seems rather, taken as a whole, to insist upon the possibility of avoiding sin. People often talk about the Psalms as poems deeply imbued with the sense of sin and the need for atonement, but this is because people read them through the eyes of a later perspective. The striking thing about the Psalms, taken generally, is the insistence of the poet that he (or the worshipper for whom he speaks) is free from blame and guilt: 'The Lord rewarded me according to my righteousness . . . for I have kept the ways of the Lord and have not wickedly departed from my God . . . I was blameless before him, and I kept myself from guilt' (Ps. 18: 20–3). To this may be added the clear testimony of the book of Job. In general, the whole atmosphere of the Hebrew Bible works against the assumption that sin and evil were taken, as a matter of theological principle, as something that belonged of necessity to all human life. The few areas, such as the matter of the angel marriages and the coming of the flood, which seem to betoken total and unbroken human evil, were clearly not taken to be universally applicable.

It is thus not at all surprising that the main Jewish tradition, as we know it since the Middle Ages, has refused to accept any sort of doctrine of original sin. It is simply not the view of the main stream of Jewish tradition, as we today know it, that man has inherited a basically faulted and corrupt constitution through the disobedience of Adam. Moral problems are serious choices for the Jew, and they are serious choices because one has freedom to sin or not to sin. There is indeed the idea of the two *yeṣers*, formations or inclinations (the same word as in Gen. 6: 5), the good and the bad, both of which are implanted in man and between which he has to choose: but this, if it is a recognition of a certain degree of implanted or innate tendency that may be bad, is also an insistence that no one such tendency is necessarily universal or dominant. There are indeed here and there traditions that suggest that in Judaism also faults could bring retribution, almost by implanted necessity, upon succeeding generations.[3] But on the whole, for Judaism as we know it, the disobedience of Adam is by no means so shocking a break as it is in traditional Christianity, by no means so catastrophic a 'fall', by no means the fateful incident through which alone all came to be condemned to be victims of sin and death. After all, Adam, like the other men of the first beginnings, was often regarded with admiration: he was a very great man. As Ben Sira put it, looking back over the worthies of the Bible who should be remembered:

> Shem and Seth were honoured among men
> but Adam is above every living being in the creation.
>
> (Ecclus. 49: 16).[4]

[3] I am grateful to Professor James L. Crenshaw of Vanderbilt University for calling some cases to my attention. A good example is the matter of the guilt incurred through the making of the golden calf: any retribution that comes upon the world contains a small fraction of that guilt (B. Sanh. 102a). I have not thought it necessary, however, to discuss such cases in detail.

[4] Since there are some questions as between the Hebrew and the Greek text, I do not insist on this rendering as being the true thought of Ben Sira himself; but, even if it is not, it is what his grandson thought when he put it into Greek.

All this then raises the serious question: was St Paul really at all right in his understanding the story of Adam and Eve as the cataclysmic entrance of sin and death? Did he perhaps, in fastening upon the great architectonic typology of Adam and Christ, the first man and the last man, fail to take into account all sorts of indications in the Genesis story which, if taken seriously, would have led in another direction? Before attempting to answer this, we have to look at another body of traditions which are very important. We turn to those early Jewish traditions which are known to us through the apocryphal books and other intertestamental literature.

First of all we may look at a passage in the Wisdom of Solomon:

> God created man for incorruption,
> and made him the image of his own eternity;
> but through the devil's envy death entered the world,
> and those who belong to his party experience it.
>
> (Wisdom, 2: 23 f.)

Here we see at once an emphasis that lies close to Paul's. The world was created to be incorrupt; the Devil's envy caused death to enter into it. The world would have been without death, man without corruption, but for the intervention of the snake, now already identified as the Devil. This is very important: Paul's reading of Genesis is not direct, but is mediated through the late tradition, well represented in Wisdom, a work of characteristic Hellenistic Judaism.

Similarly, unless we consider Fourth Ezra to have been already influenced by Christian ideas, which is hardly likely, we have thoughts like Paul's in:

> O Adam, what have you done?
> For though it was you who sinned, the fall was not yours alone,
> but ours also who are your descendants.
>
> (4 Ezra, 7: 118)

or again:

> The first Adam, burdened with an evil heart, transgressed,
> and was overcome, as were also all who were descended from him.
>
> (4 Ezra, 3: 21)

In this same period the matter of the angel marriages received considerable attention. Books like Jubilees and Enoch concerned themselves with it. The angel marriages were seen as the major and prototypic manifestation of evil. The rebel angels, known as the Watchers, a term found in Daniel itself, had come to earth and spread abroad the knowledge of certain technologies—a work that in the Hebrew Bible is related especially to the descendants of Cain, who had been the first shepherds, the first musicians, and the first metal-workers (Gen. 4: 20 ff.); this fact itself connects the Cain material with the traditions about the rebellious Watchers. The Watchers of Enoch brought down into the world the maleficent arts: notably the three worst of all, namely astrology, the making of armaments for the shedding of blood, and the production of cosmetics for the decoration of women. The whole matter of the rebel angels meant something profound: it showed a strong interest in the manifestation of sin in the beginnings of the world and its connections with modes of life that still continue. All this was worked out in detail: the names of the rebel angels, the sciences that they taught, the necessity that they should be bound and confined in a place beneath the earth (whence comes, perhaps, the idea of Christ's going and preaching to the 'spirits in prison', 1 Pet. 3: 19). Unlike the trends that we know from more modern Judaism, it all manifested a strong interest, perhaps an unhealthy interest, in the manifestations of sin and its connections with life, death, technology, and sex.

Women: that is the subject we have just touched upon. Genesis told how the woman first spoke with the snake and first tasted of the forbidden fruit; later she was punished with pain in childbirth and subjection to her husband. But the Hebrew Bible, in its canonical books, avoids too much moral judgement and too much morbidity about such things. In general, as we have seen, it appeals back very little, or not at all, to the story of Adam and Eve, and it spends little time on speculation about whether more or less of the blame rested on one or the other. Nowhere does it say that woman is more to blame for the origin of sin than is man. The existence of woman, in the Hebrew Bible, is taken very straightforwardly: a good wife is a treasure, a bad woman is a snare, and that's about all there is to it. But in the Hellenistic period consciousness of women, and sensitivity about them, seems to have become much greater. For instance, Ben Sira, a good example of Jewish piety and prudence, worried endlessly about the trouble and anxiety that a man could suffer because of the women of his household. Take daughters, for example: a father could never sleep at nights for worrying about his daughter. When she was young, he worried lest she should never marry; when she was married, he worried lest she should be disliked; if she was a virgin, he worried because she might be defiled, or become pregnant in her father's house; if she had a husband, he worried lest she should be unfaithful, and even if happily married he worried lest she should be barren and have no children (Ecclus. 42: 9–10). All this, moreover, was concern for the father's loss of sleep; the girl's unhappiness was left unmentioned. And all this was not incidental, for by this time it was thought that women were a sort of natural source of evil, and so we have the immortal words:

> For from garments comes the moth,
> and from a woman comes woman's wickedness;
> better is the wickedness of a man
> than a woman who does good . . .
>
> (Ecclus. 42: 13)

This attitude existing, it was natural that the story of Adam and Eve should be read in a similar way, and so also that of the rebel angels: 'Women are wicked, my children: because they have no power or strength as against men, they use wiles and tricks in order to draw them to themselves . . . It was thus that they allured the Watchers before the flood . . .' (Testament of Reuben, 5: 1, 6.)

Now St Paul himself in his analogy between Adam and Christ, as we have seen, confined himself to a broad comparison of the two persons and did not go into all the details of the story of the Garden of Eden. But whether this was always his policy depends on our view of the authorship of the Pastoral letters, for there we find: 'I permit no woman to teach or to have authority over men; she is to keep silent. For Adam was formed first, then Eve; and Adam was not deceived, but the woman was deceived and became a transgressor. Yet woman will be saved through bearing children . . .' (1 Tim. 2: 12–15.)

Probably, one would guess, not directly from St Paul: but of course, if not, then from people influenced by him, who thought they were saying what he would have said. In any case it is all interesting. Paul's whole concept of sin and death entering through Adam and passing upon all creatures is apparently dependent on mediation of the Genesis story through Hellenistic Judaism as seen in the books quoted. Yet these 'intertestamental' books also built up an emphasis on other loci for the origin of sin, and especially the angel marriages, which Paul neglected to mention. His view of Adam depended on the reading of the story with one single, very broad, theological perspective, that of the total comparison of Adam and Christ, death and life, living person and life-giving spirit, earthly and heavenly. Many details of the story as it was in Genesis would have conflicted with this reading of it, or could be fitted in only through forcible distortion. But once the story was read, as a whole, in Paul's manner, then the details, or some of them, could be re-read also, and that is what we see in Timothy: ideas of the place of woman are slotted into the conception that this is the central and total cataclysm in the drama of all humanity.

The case is of central importance for any idea of an authority that is attached to scriptural texts. St Paul's use of the typology of Adam, we have suggested, really depends on a broad theological conception, that of the analogical but differentiated roles of Adam and of Christ. To take this conception as authoritative does, of course, imply reference to the text of Genesis, which is agreed as authoritative in every detail. And yet one cannot say that the Genesis pericope, and it in itself, was St Paul's authority. Rather, from the field of images that Genesis afforded, he selected those that were specially relevant to his case. There remained a host of points and aspects in the Genesis text that Paul's interpretation, to say the least, does not account for without violence; or, putting it more strongly, they could easily contradict his use of the image of Adam altogether. And thus, if one is to take the text in itself as the basis for interpretation, it would be hard to say that the traditional Christian understanding, *on the basis strictly of the text taken in itself*, has more to be said for it than the traditional Jewish understanding.

But of course Paul did not take the text, strictly for itself, as his authority. Christ himself was, on one side, his authority; no doubt he might have created an imagery for his needs, like that of the Adam–Christ typology, even if scripture had not provided him with one. But on the other side he read Genesis through the lens of Hellenistic Jewish interpretation, much of which we know best through books of the 'Apocrypha'. This affects authority again, and in a different way. For if Paul's use of Adamic imagery is to be canonical, as it is to most traditional Christians and communities, surely it makes better sense if Wisdom is canonical too? Or, putting it conversely, surely the gap between Genesis and Paul is the greater if Wisdom is left out of the reckoning, as in almost all Protestant history it has been. But, if there is something in that argument, it is really an appeal to the authority of *history*: for Wisdom, and other books from the same period and tendency, are important, whether or not they are canonical, just because they witness to the history of interpretation that links Genesis with St Paul, and thus make it more natural that he read the text as he did.

These considerations may have much ecumenical importance. Authority, tradition, and the history of interpretation are very closely interrelated and interdependent. For St Paul's use of the story of Adam and Eve, the ultimate authority base seems to have lain in the finality, the completeness, the life-giving character of the redemption secured through Jesus Christ; for the statement of these, the Genesis story provided central, dramatic, and effective imagery. If on the other hand we should take the Genesis text as the authority base in itself, then the general tenor of the text, coupled with many of its details, seems to point in a very different direction. This being so, the history of the later Jewish understanding becomes all-important, for it provides a basis of intelligibility, within contemporary thought, for the way in which Paul used the figure of Adam, and it also provides an important guide for our understanding of what Paul must have meant. This same later Jewish understanding, on the other hand, should make the Christian treatment of the stories of the origin of evil less strange to Jewish readers than it would otherwise seem: for, clearly, in the older post-biblical Judaism there were more lines that led towards an understanding of the type now known as Christian than might seem natural on the basis of Judaism as it has been in more modern times. But conversely, if we take the Genesis text as our datum and starting point, then even traditional Christians who understand it in terms of 'original sin' and 'the Fall of Man' must admit that the passage falls far short of pointing unambiguously in that direction, and they must therefore be understanding of the traditional Jewish view of the matter, and also of those Christian interpretations which diverge radically from the traditional.

Genesis 3, then, is at best ambiguous as a description of 'the' Fall of Man, as a pointer to 'original sin'. To say this is not at all to dispute the validity of these doctrines: it is only to say that these hallowed doctrines are accepted less purely because Scripture requires them, and to a much larger extent because of other factors—in particular because of experience, because of viability as a guiding principle of faith, and above all because of theological explanatory power. It is these factors, in greater or in lesser degree, that bear upon the exegetical process and cause the interpreter to 'see' in the text the points and the evidences which can be built into a doctrinal structure. It is exactly the same factors, and not any will to 'deny' the teaching of Scripture, that cause other interpreters to go in directions very different from the traditional. Within traditional Christianity, after all, from St Paul onwards and down to the present day, the centrality of Adam and his disobedience has 'worked', and worked so magnificently—even if the text of Genesis suggests something very different. By contrast, no major current of Christianity found much use for the angel marriages, over which men of biblical times seem to have laboured rather seriously, and they were allowed to gather dust in the lumber-room of outdated and meaningless legend. As an explanatory device within theology, they never had worked very well: they did not give an account of anything within experience, and even to talk about them strained belief even more than most of the things that were believed.

Before we leave the subject, however, we should give another moment's thought to the interpretation of Genesis 3 'in itself' which we have adumbrated: a story, not primarily of how death came into the world, but primarily of how man came quite near to gaining immortality. Most of us would be perplexed by such an understanding, not because it contradicts the text—it does not—but because it seems strange to our tradition; we cannot at first see how or where it could fit in. In this way we find how much our tradition is our authority. But in fact, when we begin to explore it, we find that typological connections running through Scripture can be found for this interpretation as well as for others. Immortality, after all, is one of the things that religion is about. St Paul too can have connections here: 'this mortal must put on immortality' (1 Cor. 15: 53 AV). Christ has brought 'life and immortality' to light (2 Tim. 1: 10). And in the new heaven and the new earth the apocalyptist saw no less than the tree of life, whose leaves were for the healing of the nations (Rev. 22: 2). And perhaps we would not be left so far from Christian tradition after all: for here and there among the Fathers, especially among the Greek, there may be signs that pointed in a similar way, though it would be an impertinence for this writer, when writing in honour of Henry Chadwick, to suggest where these signs are to be found. And perhaps the healing of the nations might include some bridging of the gaps of comprehension, as far as concerns our notions of the origin of evil and of sin, between Jewish and Christian understandings, and also between traditional, conservative, Christianity and those who call for a fresh and open exploration of the inheritance of faith.

5

Revelation in Early Christianity

WOLFHART PANNENBERG

In his discussion with Maurice Wiles on the concept of revelation in
1980, Basil Mitchell started from a reflection on the drastic change
in theological attitudes toward that issue.[1] While not long ago the
basic function of revelation in Christian theology could be considered self-evident, this has been no longer the case after the criticism of F. G. Downing and James Barr.[2] Both argued that in the
biblical writings revelational language is neither fundamental nor
uniform, but occurs in considerable diversity while its importance
seems marginal in comparison to the central issues of the biblical
tradition.

Judgements like this became possible because in most modern
literature on the subject assertions about divine revelation on the
basis of the biblical witness were often made without a detailed
examination of the revelational terminology in the biblical writings
themselves. The same has been true with respect to theological literature of the patristic period.[3] Too readily modern or medieval concepts of revelation and of its basic importance in theology are
imputed to biblical or patristic authors, wherever revelational
language occurs. Sometimes the question is only whether the revelation is considered to have taken place in Jesus Christ or also in creation. But structure and function of such conceptuality deserve and
need closer examination. Such examination can also help to bring
out the modern (and medieval) concepts of revelation in sharper

---

[1] B. Mitchell and M. Wiles, 'Does Christianity Need a Revelation?', *Theology*, 83
(1980), 103–14.
[2] F. G. Downing, *Has Christianity a Revelation?* (Philadelphia, 1964); J. Barr,
Old and New in Interpretation (London, 1966), 65–102 (The Concepts of History
and of Revelation), esp. pp. 83 ff., and his earlier essay 'Revelation through History
in the Old Testament and in Modern Theology', *Interpretation*, 17 (1963), 193–205.
[3] See e.g. R. Latourelle, 'L'Idée de révélation chez les pères de l'église', *Science
ecclésiastique*, 11 (1959), 297–344; and P. Stockmeier, ' "Offenbarung" in der
frühchristlichen Kirche', in *Handbuch der Dogmengeschichte*, i. 1a, ed. M. Seybold
(Fribourg–Basle–Vienna, 1971), 26–87. Stockmeier, to be sure, indicates his awareness of the problem (pp. 29 f.).

relief. The following remarks are an attempt to contribute some pre-liminary observations to a study of this kind, which needs to be done on a much larger scale.

The early patristic usage of revelational terminology must, of course, be evaluated in the light of terminology and conceptions as they occur in the New Testament writings, but also in connection with Jewish apocalyptic literature which exerted considerable influence on the revelational terminology of the New Testament and still in the period of the apostolic fathers. Although the extent of that influence is still a matter of dispute, the fact as such seems beyond reasonable doubt.

In the apocalyptic writings revelational terminology was used in at least two different, but related, forms: On the one hand it referred to mantic experiences of 'disclosure' granted to apocalyptic seers.[4] On the other the terminology referred to events of the escha-tological future, when 'all the hidden things of heaven that shall happen on earth' (Enoch 51: 2) will come true (ibid. 91: 14). These two forms of revelation belong together, because precisely what will be 'revealed' in the endtime is also the content of the proleptic 'reve-lation' to the seer. Thus it corresponds to the way everything happens on earth—its beginning being in words, but its consum-mation manifest to all.[5]

In the New Testament, revelational language refers in many places to what will happen in the eschatological future. At the day of judgement 'each man's work will become manifest', for 'it will be revealed with fire' (1 Cor. 3: 13; cf. 4: 5; 2 Cor. 5: 2, 10). According to Mark 4: 22 'there is nothing hid, except to be made manifest; nor is anything secret, except to come to light.' The same idea occurs in different terminology (*apokalyptein* instead of *phaneroun*) in Matt. 10: 26 (Luke 12: 2), and in both cases it is extremely close to Enoch 51: 5. But it is not only the deeds of men that will be 'revealed' in the *eschaton*. The same is said of Jesus Christ with respect to his return in order to judge the world: This is called 'the revealing of our Lord Jesus Christ' (1 Cor. 1: 7; cf. 2 Thess. 1: 7). Again, it is only a terminological difference, when the same event is termed *epiphania* (2 Thess. 2: 8; cf. 1 Tim.

---

[4] See e.g. Enoch 1: 2; 80: 1; also 106: 13, 19; IV Ezra 3: 31; 6: 33.
[5] IV Ezra 9: 5: 'consummatio in manifestatione'; cf. 6: 28; II Bar. 29: 3; 39: 7; 70: 7.

6: 14; 2 Tim. 4: 8). In this event the glory of Christ will be revealed (1 Pet. 4: 13, cf. Titus 2: 13), and the believers will participate in it. His glory will be revealed upon them too (1 Pet. 5: 1; cf. Rom. 8: 18 f.).

While these phrases sound quite traditional in the line of apocalyptic literature, the situation is different when the present disclosure of what shall be revealed in the end is described. Even here, however, a number of words correspond closely to the proleptic revelation the apocalyptic seers received of things that will become manifest in the eschatological future. Here belongs Paul's affirmation that God 'revealed' his Son to him (Gal. 1: 16): It was the future Messiah and judge of the world who appeared to Paul. Jesus' answer to Peter's confession at Caesarea Philippi (Matt. 16: 17) may belong to the same category. In that case, the meaning is that 'such things', i.e. Jesus' Messiahship, which is to become publicly manifest only in the eschatological future, were 'revealed' to Peter now by the heavenly Father. In both cases it is characteristic, however, that the multitude of revelations the apocalyptic seers claimed to have received is reduced to one single content, the Messiahship of Jesus. This christological focus also characterizes the introductory sentence of Rev. 1: 1: Everything that follows is here described as 'revelation' of God to *Jesus Christ*, which only secondarily was communicated to his 'servant' John through the service of an angel. This again is a reminder in a peculiar way of Matt. 11: 27 (Luke 10: 22): The Father transferred everything to the Son, so that nobody knows the Father but the Son and to whom he will 'reveal' it. Here the Son himself functions in the place of the apocalyptic *angelus interpres*.

A more radical modification of the apocalyptic understanding of proleptic revelation of what will become manifest in the endtime can be found in Paul, where the earthly history of Jesus is termed 'revelation' in that sense. According to Rom. 3: 21 the atoning death of Christ (3: 24 f.) 'revealed' the righteousness of God which had been 'witnessed' to before by law and prophets—'witnessed', that is, in order to become manifest in the future (cf. Rom. 1: 2). Therefore, in Rom. 1: 17 Paul could claim that through his Gospel the righteousness of God becomes manifest already. This does not mean that the Gospel was revealed to the apostle by way of an apocalyptic vision. Rather, the content of the Gospel, the story of Christ it proclaims, is the place where the righteousness of God has been revealed.[6] Thus the two aspects of the apocalyptic conception of revelation, the eschatological one and its present anticipation, are in a peculiar way combined. The 'witness' of the prophets and of the law, which in Jewish tradition was understood to refer to the eschatological fulfilment and manifestation of God's righteousness, was now related to an event which preceded the *eschaton* and had become a past to be memorized soon after it happened. But if the eschatological witness of the Scriptures, the content of which was considered mysterious in Jewish tradition, had become manifest already in the story of Jesus, then the divine 'mystery', as Paul said (Rom. 11: 25), the divine plan of history's course toward the salvation of all humanity,[7] was already 'revealed' in him. This was explicitly stated in the final sentence of Romans, a sentence which is probably a secondary addition,[8] but nevertheless summarizes the argument of the apostle himself. The content of the Gospel is 'the revelation of the "mystery" which was kept secret for long ages, but is now disclosed and through the prophetic writings is made known to all nations' (Rom. 16: 25 ff.). Essential elements of this summary of the content of the Gospel recur in slightly modified versions in a number of other writings, in the letter to the Colossians (1: 26 f.), in Ephesians (3: 5 and 9 ff.), in the pastoral letters (2 Tim. 1: 9 f., Titus 1: 2 f.), as well as in 1 Peter (1: 20). According to all these words, the content of the divine 'plan' (mystery) of salvation consists in extending that salvation by means of the death of Christ, to all nations. Paul himself made that point in Rom. 11: 25 and there he also used the term 'mystery' in this special connection.

In view of all the evidence from Paul and other letters in the New Testament it is hard to see how James Barr in his critique of the concept of revelation could miss in the New Testament explicit reference to a revelation as a 'source of knowledge Christians now have.'[9] I am afraid that here we have explicitly stated even a kind of

---

[6] For the crucial importance of Rom. 3: 21 in relation to the whole theme of the Epistle to the Romans and especially for its relation to Rom. 1: 17 see U. Wilckens, *Der Brief an die Römer*, i (EKK VI 1; Neukirchen, 1978), 199 ff. (cf. pp. 101 ff.).

[7] That the word 'mystery' was an apocalyptic term referring to the divine plan for history was shown by G. Bornkamm in his article on that term in Kittel's *Theological Dictionary to the New Testament*, iv (1942), 820–3.

[8] See U. Wilckens, *Der Brief an die Römer*, iii (1982), 147 ff.

[9] J. Barr, op. cit. 88. Barr makes this point in relation to the 'eschatological type' of revelational language in the New Testament, which he distinguishes from 'special revelation' (his only other type), without however paying attention to the interrelation of these two types of revelational language in the Jewish apocalyptic tradition.

'revelation through history' which Barr so vehemently attacked. His criticism may have to be explained as an overreaction to a then recent awareness of the diversity of biblical conceptions of revelation and of their difference from theological notions then current of revelation, together with a lack of a detailed analysis of the relevant materials, at least in New Testament exegesis.[10] Nevertheless, Barr was correct in rejecting any assumption of a revelation that would grant knowledge of a hitherto completely unknown God. Such a notion is absent not only from the Old Testament traditions,[11] but also from the New Testament.[12] In addition, the function of the conception of revelation in Rom. 16: 25–7 and in similar places is that of a summary of the content of the Gospel, not that of a principle of theological argument as in medieval and modern theology. It remains to be seen whether this had already changed in the patristic period.

In the writings of the apostolic fathers revelational language is in many places still reminiscent of the apocalyptic usage, especially of course in the Shepherd of Hermas. This also includes the apocalyptic idea (Dan. 9) that the mysterious meaning of the Scriptures can be grasped only with the help of some special revelation.[13] More

[10] In relation to the Pauline writings, however, such an analysis has been produced by D. Lührmann, *Das Offenbarungsverständnis bei Paulus und in den paulinischen Gemeinden* (1965). See also the unpublished dissertation of E. Kamlah, 'Traditionsgeschichtliche Untersuchungen zur Schlußdoxologie des Römerbriefes' (Diss. Tübingen, 1955). Concerning the Old Testament cf. the article of R. Rendtorff in W. Pannenberg (ed.), *Revelation as History* (London 1969), 38–46 (the German edition was published in 1961). Although Barr mentioned that volume, he did not enter into a detailed critique of the evidence presented by Rendtorff, esp. in relation to the prophetic 'word of demonstration' (*Erweiswort*) which occurs in Ezekiel and Deutero–Isaiah (e.g. Isa. 41: 20; 45: 3, 6; 49: 23) with reference to future events which will induce Israel (or even all the nations) to 'recognize that I am Yahweh'. The same formula was used in Deuteronomy with reference to the events of the Exodus story (Deut. 4: 39, cf. 7: 9). Here it is explicitly said that this specific history, which became constitutive of the existence of Israel as a nation, was intended by God to make himself known. Therefore it is unfortunate that Barr, in his criticism of the concept of 'revelation through history' did not discuss this evidence in detail, although its special importance for the issue had been emphasized by Rendtorff. Barr's short remark that this 'striking phrase' may not be taken as indicating revelation but rather some 'realization of something already known' (p. 92) simply rules out this evidence by recourse to a preconceived idea of revelation.

[11] Barr, pp. 86 ff., 89 ff.

[12] The only exception is the knowledge of God from creation, which Paul in Rom. 1: 19 attributes to a revelational activity of God himself.

[13] Hermas, *Vis.* ii. 2. This idea was particularly important in the Qumran writings. Cf. O. Betz, *Offenbarung und Schriftforschung in der Qumransekte* (Tübingen, 1960).

important are a number of statements asserting the 'appearance' or epiphany of the Lord in the flesh (Barn. 5.6; 6 7), in correspondence with prophetic predictions. The most interesting and original conception, however, occurs in the famous dictum of Ignatius (*Magn.* 8. 2) that 'God revealed himself through his Son Jesus Christ who is his word, which proceeds from silence.' Here, for the first time, occurs an explicit statement of divine self-revelation in Jesus Christ. The peculiar reference to 'the word which proceeds from silence' indicates perhaps that Ignatius' phrase was coined in the tradition of the 'revelational scheme' documented in Rom. 16: 25–7 and in the other related words in the New Testament, because there the idea of the divine silence which was broken in Jesus Christ seems to have its roots. But while this idea in the New Testament writings was related to the conception of the divine plan of history (mystery), in Ignatius it is related to God himself by means of another idea, that of the divine word. Thereby, the Johannine concept of the word also gains a new connotation: it is now not primarily the cosmic Logos, but the word of divine self-communication. No doubt, the connotations of the cosmological function of the Logos and of the divine 'mystery' of history, now replaced by the term *logos*, are still present in Ignatius' phrase. But for the first time all these elements become subordinate to the idea of divine self-revelation.

In a more complicated way, the same idea was expressed later by Irenaeus. When he wrote that the Son revealed the Father by becoming manifest himself in the flesh (*Adv. haer.* iv. 6. 3), the word of Jesus (Matt. 11: 27), that only the Son can reveal the Father, is combined with the appearance of the Son in the flesh. But a little further on, Irenaeus presents the matter from the point of view of the Father, when he asserts that the Father wanted the Son to become manifest in order to become known himself through the Son (iv, 6. 5). According to Irenaeus, the Father is not revealed for the first time by the incarnate Son, but was already revealed through the pre-existent Son, in the creation of the world as well as through the witness of law and prophets (iv. 6. 6). In a similar way Justin had already spoken of the pre-existent word as revealing the Father. According to Justin, it was the Son or Word that appeared to the Old Testament patriarchs in their encounters with God, because the Father himself remains invisible. Here again Matt. 11: 27 may be in the background. In order to let the Father be known, the Son has to become visible to human beings in some way (*Dial.* 127. 3–128. 2), which of course happened definitively in the incarnation. As soon as the eternal Logos was conceived as mediator of all human know-ledge of the Father, according to Matt. 11: 27, the question could not fail to arise which form the Logos should assume to become 'visible' to human beings. Thus the ideas of revelation and incar-nation became convergent. God's self-revelation became the moti-vation for the incarnation of the eternal word. Yet in the thought of Justin this idea could not yet function as a theological argument for the fact of incarnation. For that purpose, rather, he had recourse to the Old Testament prophecies (*Apol.* 30–53). Our faith in Jesus Christ, he said, would have no basis 'unless we have testimony of announcements that were proclaimed before his appearance in the flesh and which we find fully confirmed' (*Apol.* 53). The basis of argument, then, for the incarnation of the Son, is not its motivation by God's intention to be revealed. The basis of argument is scrip-ture, and notably the prophetic witness of the Old Testament. The importance of this argument was by no means restricted to apolo-getic discourse with Jews. On the contrary, the authority of the Old Testament itself was established for non-Jewish Christians by the 'historical' evidence of the fulfilment of its prophecies in Jesus Christ.

This can be seen in a particularly interesting passage from Ori-gen's *Principles*. Like many other patristic theologians, Origen was deeply influenced by the claim of Matt. 11: 27 that only the Son can reveal the Father. But he added that such revelation is always mediated through the Spirit.[14] This idea, however, led to Origen's doctrine of the inspiration of the biblical Scriptures. At the end of the chapter devoted to this issue in his *Principles* (iv. 1. 7), Origen quoted Rom. 16: 25–7, but he understood the grammar of that sentence in a different way from that of modern exegesis, so that he could derive from it his idea that the prophetic Scriptures *mediate* the revelation that occurred in the Son. In his reading the sentence says that the revelation of the divine mystery occurred 'through the prophetic writings and the epiphany of our Lord and Saviour Jesus Christ', while the authentic form of the final sentence of Romans distinguishes between the revelation in Jesus Christ and

---

[14] Origen, *Princ.* i. 3. 4: 'Omnis scientia de patre revelante filio in spiritu sancto cognoscitur.'

its announcement to all the nations through the prophetic writings.[15] According to Origen, however, the 'prophetic writings' are themselves instruments of divine revelation. He was able to derive that idea from 2 Tim. 3: 16, but he did so with an interesting comment (iv. 1. 6): the manifestation of the Son in the incarnation alone demonstrated the divine inspiration of the Old Testament Scriptures, because their divine truth now became evident, with the old prophecies fulfilled.[16] To Origen, this was an indication of the interrelatedness of Son and Spirit in the event of revelation. And therefore he could further conclude that also 'the writings that proclaim his arrival and his teaching have been composed with all [sc. divine] power and authority', to the effect that the apostolic writings have to be considered as inspired literature as well. If the revelation of the Son is mediated through the Spirit and if the working of the Spirit produced scriptures as its deposit, then the writings of the Apostles who received the full share of the Spirit can hardly be considered less inspired than the prophetic writings of the Old Testament.

With Origen's doctrine of scriptural inspiration, patristic theology comes close to the position that became basic in the medieval doctrine of revelation. But even Origen was still far from equating revelation with the inspiration of Scripture. Nor was the idea of revelation considered to provide the basis of theological argument. It was rather its result, because—as Origen's argument shows as well as that of Justin—the basic argument was the correspondence of the prophetic predictions with their fulfilment in the story of Jesus Christ. Even the authority of Scripture, the divine inspiration of the Old Testament, was established on that basis. That God had revealed himself in Jesus Christ was the conclusion reached from those premises. As in the New Testament, the concept of revela-

---

[15] Cf. C. E. B. Cranfield, *The Epistle to the Romans* (6th edn., 1975), 811 ff., followed by U. Wilckens, op. cit. iii. 150, n. 708.

[16] There is no reason why the same idea could not have been already intended in Rom. 16: 25–7, so that it would be unnecessary to read the phrase 'prophetic scriptures' in 16: 26 as referring to early Christian writings rather than to the Old Testament prophets. Such a reading, which would be unparalleled in early Christian usage and is also contrary to Rom. 3: 21, is nevertheless postulated by some modern exegetes because of the function attributed to 'the prophetic scriptures' by Rom. 16: 26, that they lead 'all the nations' to the obedience of faith (cf. Wilckens, op. cit. iii. 150 n. 709), but this has been precisely the function of the fulfilment of prophetic predictions in early Christian theology as it was also assumed in Origen's interpretation of the passage.

tion functioned as a summary of the Christian faith, not as a basis for theological argument.

In medieval and in modern theology very different conditions for theological argumentation developed. In the Latin Christianity of the Middle Ages the authority of the Church had become so overwhelming that the inspired authority of the biblical writings, proposed by the witness of the Church, was able to become the basis of the theological exposition of the content of faith in dialogue with philosophical reason. In modern Protestantism the authority of the Church was reduced to that of Scripture, but the authority of Scripture itself was eroded as a result of historical-critical scrutiny of the biblical writings. Nor was it possible to have recourse to the patristic argument of the fulfilment of the prophetic predictions in Jesus Christ. The historical reading of the prophetic words demonstrated that the original intentions of the various prophecies in the Old Testament were different from what New Testament writings claimed as their fulfilment. Only if one allows for modifications of the reading of traditional texts in the process of changing experiences, can the Christian claim of a fulfilment of Old Testament prophecies in Jesus Christ be defended. In any event, such an argument already presupposes some other basis of theological reasoning.

It was in connection with the rise of the notion of positive religion and as a result of deriving claims about religious truth from experiences of divine reality that the modern concept of divine self-revelation as the source of religious truth developed. Its function in modern theology has not been identical with its first explicit emergence in patristic theology, nor with the basis of that emergence in the revelational language of the New Testament and, behind that, in the prophetic 'word of demonstration'.[17] Nevertheless, contemporary theology, in arguing for the idea of divine self-revelation as a principle of religious knowledge, can call upon the emergence of that idea in the biblical traditions. To do so expresses a consciousness of continuity with Christian origins and, indeed, with the prophetic traditions of the Old Testament, a consciousness of continuity which is not at all unfounded.

The slow process of the emergence of an explicit idea of divine self-revelation in the biblical traditions has an additional advantage, at least a potential advantage for the argumentation of modern theo-

---

[17] See n. 10 above.

logy. It allows us to trace the process of transition from the type of revelational experiences and conceptions of intuitive mantics, which are found everywhere in the history of religions, to a concept of God's making himself 'known' to his people through his action in history (Deut. 4: 39; 9. 7), thus replacing the function of mythology in constituting the order of society by that primordial history, the function of which was extended later on, in Ezekiel and Deutero-Isaiah, to the further course of history toward an eschatological future, the function of which, later still in Jewish apocalypticism, was explicitly described as 'revelation', before the New Testament could talk of the 'revelation' of God's 'mystery', his plan for the course and goal of history, in Jesus Christ, which in turn was called by Ignatius the self-revelation of God through his eternal word. This slow emergence of the idea of divine self-revelation in Jesus Christ provides the advantage for modern theology, that in claiming divine self-revelation it need not start with a *petitio principii*, because the mediation of that concept which summarizes the content of the Christian faith, or of Christianity as a positive religion, is to be found in history itself. This might be a little different from traditional ideas on 'revelation through history', but nevertheless it may be important.

6

Der Terminus 'sola fides' bei Augustinus

ADOLAR ZUMKELLER

Summary

The expression 'sola fides', which plays a fundamental part in Luther's teaching on justification, is found about thirty times in Augustine's writings. Apart from a few places where the combination of the two words may reasonably be taken as coincidental, the phrase occurs in two senses: first in comparison with the faith which seeks understanding, and secondly in contrast to the faith which works through love (Gal. 5: 6).

1. In spite of his principle 'Crede, ut intellegas', which also set the pattern for his pastoral endeavours, Augustine stood up for the 'sola fides' of a large number of contemporary Christians. He defended them against the presumptuousness of the Manichees, who boasted of imposing no 'iugum credendi' on their followers, but rather of leading them to knowledge. He defended them, too, against the Neo-Platonists, who prided themselves on having succeeded in arriving at a vision of God through their own efforts, and mocked the many Christians who lived without this vision, 'ex fide sola'. In spite of all this, Augustine was convinced that the well-informed Christian ascended gradually to holiness of life 'non iam sola fide, sed certa ratione'. He conceded, however, that certain beliefs about historical events, such as Christ's death and resurrection, had to be accessible only to faith and not to insight. In commenting on 1 Cor. 3: 1 ff., Augustine sometimes describes believers as 'carnales' and contrasts these 'intellegendo cernentes' with 'spiritales'.

2. Augustine often uses the term 'sola fides' in connection with justification. He saw the difficulty of reconciling Rom. 3: 28 with Jas. 2: 17, 20 and Gal. 5: 6), justification by faith with 'fides mortua' and 'fides quae per caritatem operatur'. The 'misericordes' in the contemporary Church made the subject topical with their reassurance of eventual salvation for all the baptized, even unrepentant sinners. Augustine saw here not only a pastoral, but also a doctrinal, error. He wrote on the matter in the *De Fide et Operibus* (c. 413), and in a series of sermons and writings during the last twenty years of his life.

He argues that the gift of justification by faith cannot be earned. Paul asserts in Gal. 5: 6 that 'fides viva' works through love, because faith and grace bear fruit in the individual when they are present. He identifies the 'fides mortua' of James (2: 17, 20) with that faith even the devils have (cf. Mark 1: 24), and which is not rewarded with everlasting bliss. Living faith keeps God's commandments out of love and that is made possible by the gift of grace. So the Christian has nothing to boast of in his good works, and the reward he receives in everlasting life is a gift of God's mercy.

DER AUSDRUCK „sola fides", der in der Rechtfertigungslehre Martin Luthers eine grundlegende Rolle spielen sollte[1], war auch dem christlichen Altertum nicht völlig fremd. So dürfte eine Untersuchung über Verwendung und Sinn dieses Ausdrucks bei Augustinus von einigem Interesse sein.

Man begegnet dem Terminus „sola fides" in Augustins Schriften, Briefen und Predigten etwa dreißigmal[2]. In einigen Fällen handelt es sich zweifellos nur um eine ziemlich zufällige Verbindung beider Wörter. So bemerkt er in einer Predigt zu dem Psalmvers (88, 45): „Dissoluisti eum ab emundatione": Weil nur der Glaube an Christus (*sola fides* Christi) rein mache, würden die Juden, die nicht an Christus glauben, von dieser Reinigung nicht erfaßt[3]. In ähnlicher Weise gebraucht er den Ausdruck in Sermo 215: „Nur dieser Glaube (*sola haec fides*) [an Christi Auferstehung] ist es, der die Christen von allen anderen Menschen unterscheidet und trennt.[4]" Noch einer Äußerung dieser Art begegnet man in einer Predigt über Psalm 101; dort spricht Augustinus von der „partus uirginis..., ubi nullus hominum operatus est, nulla transfusa concupiscentia, sed *sola fides* accensa, et Verbi caro concepta"[5].

Doch gibt es in Augustins Schrifttum auch nicht wenige Stellen, an denen die Wortverbindung „sola fides" schon zum festen Terminus geworden ist. Und zwar begegnet man ihr in doppeltem Sinnzusammenhang: als „sola fides" in Gegenüberstellung zur „fides", die nach Einsicht verlangt, und als „sola fides" im Gegensatz zur „fides quae per dilectionem operatur" (Gal. 5, 6).

I

Augustins Imperativ: „Crede, ut intellegas!"[6], hat man als sein „programme théologico-philosophique" bezeichnet[7]. Er beruft sich

---

[1] Cf. etwa K. Haendler, „Sola-fide-Prinzip (in der evangelischen Theologie)", Lex. für Theol. und Kirche[2], IX (Freiburg 1964), 860 f. und die dort verzeichnete Literatur.

[2] Dank schulde ich den Herausgebern des Augustinus-Lexikons (erscheint seit 1986 im Verlag Schwabe und Co., Basel–Stuttgart), die mir, mit Hilfe der von ihnen erarbeiteten EDV-Augustinus-Wortkonkordanz, unentgeltlich eine Liste aller Sätze zur Verfügung stellten, in denen Augustinus den Ausdruck „sola fides" gebraucht.

[3] En. in ps. 88, 2, 7, 57 f.: CCSL 39, 1240.

[4] Serm. 215, 6: PL 38, 1075.

[5] En. in ps. 101, 1, 1, 44—46: CCSL 40, 1426.

[6] Serm. 43, 7, 145 f.: CCSL 41, 511.

[7] R. Holte, Béatitude et sagesse (Paris 1962), 381 f.; cf. ibid. 367 ff.

dafür gerne auf Is. 7, 9: „Nisi credideritis, non intellegetis[8]", und auf das Herrenwort (Mt. 7, 7): „Quaerite et inuenietis[9]". In seinem Brief an Consentius vom Jahre 410 hat er dieses Programm näher erläutert: „... fides praecedat rationem, qua cor mundetur, ut magnae rationis capiat et perferat lucem[10]". Als erhabenes Ziel erscheint ihm die „plenitudo cognitionis" und die „summitas contemplationis[11]". Dabei gibt Augustinus zu bedenken: „... homo fidelis debet credere, quod nondum uidet, ut uisionem et speret et amet[12]". Ähnlich schreibt er in De agone christiano, einer Schrift aus der Zeit um 396: „... priusquam mens nostra purgetur, debemus credere quod intellegere nondum ualemus[13]".

Augustinus wendet sich damit gegen die Anmaßung der Manichäer, die sich rühmten, nur solche Lehren vorzutragen, die sie mit der Vernunft beweisen könnten, während die Christen auf den Glauben verwiesen seien: „... se autem non iugum credendi imponere, sed docendi fontem aperire gloriantur[14]". Schon in seiner Schrift De utilitate credendi vom Jahre 391 weist Augustinus diese Haltung der Manichäer entschieden zurück. Er hält dem manichäischen Gegner vor: Wenn dieser ihm befehle, nicht zu glauben, dann würde er selbst auch nicht glauben dürfen, daß es unter Menschen eine Religion geben könne, und würde sich deshalb nicht an den Manichäer wenden, um durch ihn zu ihr zu gelangen. Augustinus schließt mit der rhetorischen Frage: „Estne ulla maior dementia quam ut ei (sc. Manichaeo) *sola*, quae nulla scientia subnixa est, *fide* displiceam, quae ad eum ipsum me sola perduxit?[15]"

Die „sola fides" der meisten Christen seiner Zeit hat Augustinus zwei Jahrzehnte später in seinem Werk De Trinitate nochmals gegen ähnliche Angriffe verteidigen müssen: Er spricht von gewis-

---

[8] Serm. 43, 7, 146: CCSL 41, 511; De lib. arb. I, 2, 4 und II, 2, 6: CSEL 74, 6, 7 und 41, 15 f.; De ag. christ. 13, 14: CSEL 41, 118, 12 f.; De Trin. xv, 2, 2, 28: CCSL 50A, 461 und öfter. Augustins altlateinische Übersetzung von Is. 7, 9 entspricht dem Text der Septuaginta, während die Vulgata nach dem hebräischen Urtext liest: „Si non credideritis, non permanebitis."
[9] Contra Acc. II, 3, 9: CSEL 63, 29, 26; De Lib. arb. II, 2, 6: CSEL 74, 22 f.; Conf. I, 1, 1, 13 f. und XII, 1, 1, 7: CCSL 27, 1 und 217; De Trin. I, 5, 8, 38: CCSL 50, 37 und öfter.
[10] Epist. 120, 1, 3: CSEL 34/2, 706, 24 f.
[11] Ibid. 120, 1, 4: CSEL 34/2, 707, 16 und 24.
[12] Ibid. 120, 2, 8: CSEL 34/2, 711, 24 f.
[13] De ag. christ. 13, 14: CSEL 41, 118, 10 f.
[14] De util. cred. 9, 21: CSEL 25/1, 26, 6 f.
[15] Ibid. 14, 30: CSEL 25/1, 38, 2—4.

sen Leuten (quidam), mit denen er offensichtlich die Neuplatoniker meint, die sich stolz rühmten, „ad contemplandum Deum et inhaerendum Deo uirtute propria posse purgari[16]". Sie verwiesen darauf, daß einige von ihnen, wobei sie wohl an Plotin dachten, mit ihrer „acies mentis" die „lux incommutabilis ueritatis" ein wenig berühren konnten. Dabei spotteten sie, wie Augustinus berichtet: „christianos multos *ex fide* interim *sola* uiuentes [hoc] nondum potuisse". Augustinus antwortet mit dem anschaulichen Vergleich: Es bringe dem Hochmütigen keinen Nutzen, die Heimat jenseits des Meeres von weitem schon zu erblicken, wenn er sich schämt, das Boot (nämlich des Glaubens) zu besteigen, das ihn hinüberbringt. Dagegen schade es dem Demütigen in keiner Weise, wenn er die Heimat in der weiten Ferne zwar noch nicht erblickt, aber in jenem Boot zu ihr gelangt[17].

Wenn Augustinus in dieser Weise auch die „sola fides" der großen Menge der damaligen Christen verteidigt hat, so war doch Richtschnur für ihn selbst und für sein seelsorgliches Bemühen das schon erwähnte Programm: „Crede, ut intellegas!" Dies kommt schon in seiner philosophischen Frühschrift De ordine klar zum Ausdruck, in der er mehrfach auf die Bedeutung der „auctoritas" und auf ihr Verhältnis zur „ratio" zu sprechen kommt[18]. Dabei bekennt er sich zu dem Satz: Die „anima bene erudita" steige stufenweise zu einem sittengemäßen Leben empor und zwar „non iam *sola fide*, sed certa ratione[19]".

Freilich weiß Augustinus, daß es auch Wahrheiten gibt, die nicht der Einsicht zugänglich sind, die vielmehr nur geglaubt werden können, etwa der Glaubenssatz, daß Christus für unsere Sünden gestorben und von den Toten erstanden ist. In seinem Brief an Consentius von 410 hat er deshalb die Regel aufgestellt: „Et uisibilium quidem rerum praeteritarum, quae temporaliter transierunt, *sola fides* est, quoniam non adhuc uidenda sperantur, sed facta et transacta creduntur[20]."

---

[16] De Trin. IV, 15, 20, 1—3: CCSL 50, 187.
[17] Ibid. 11—19. Übrigens findet sich auch in einem wörtlichen Zitat des Julian von Aeclanum ein anerkennender Hinweis auf die „sola fides" der „simplices", die mit anderen Dingen beschäftigt sind und keinerlei Bildung besitzen (C. Jul. V, 1, 4: PL 44, 783).
[18] Vor allem De ord. II, 5, 16 und 9, 26 f.: CSEL 63, 157 f. und 165 f.; cf. auch K.-H. Lütcke, „Auctoritas" bei Augustin (Stuttgart, 1968), 70 ff., 119 ff., 166 ff.
[19] De ord. II, 19, 50: CSEL 63, 182, 16—19.
[20] Epist. 120, 2, 9, 1—3: CSEL 34/2, 711.

Im selben Sinn wie hier erscheint der Terminus „sola fides" nochmals viele Jahre später in Augustins Enchiridion von ca. 421. Wie Augustinus berichtet, hatte der Adressat der Schrift, der Diakon Laurentius von Karthago, ihm den Wunsch vorgetragen, er möge doch ein Buch schreiben, in welchem unter anderem auch enthalten sei, „in quantum ratio pro religione contendat, uel quid in ratione, cum *fides* sit *sola*, non ueniat²¹".

Jene Christen, denen nicht nur das „credere", sondern auch das „intellegere" der göttlichen Wahrheit von Gott geschenkt ist, bezeichnet Augustinus in seiner Erklärung zum Psalm 135 aus der Zeit um 415 als die „spiritales sancti" und findet sie versinnbildet durch die „caeli in intellectu", von denen der Psalmvers (135, 5) spricht: „Fecit Deus caelos in intellectu." Ihnen stellt er als die „infra caelos terra" jene Christen gegenüber, „qui [hoc] nondum possunt, et *solam fidem* firmissimam tenent²²".

Die gleiche Gegenüberstellung und den Terminus „sola fides" im selben Sinn gebraucht Augustinus auch in einer seiner Homilien zum Johannesevangelium aus der gleichen Zeit. Dabei bezeichnet er im Anschluß an 1 Cor. 3, 1 f. die Nur-Glaubenden als die „carnales". Sie sind für ihn die „tantum credendo tenentes", die „spiritales" aber die „intellegendo cernentes". Den ersten ist die Glaubenswahrheit „lacteus potus", den anderen „solidus cibus". Augustinus schließt: „Solidam profecto [apostolus] uoluit esse scientiam spiritalium, ubi non *sola fides* accomodaretur, sed certa cognitio teneretur; ac per hoc illi [carnales] ea ipsa credebant, quae spiritales insuper agnoscebant²³."

II

Schon in einer frühen Predigt Augustins, die noch in seine Priesterzeit datiert wird²⁴, erscheint der Terminus „sola fides" in einem ganz anderen Sinnzusammenhang, nämlich bei der Frage nach der Bedeutung des Glaubens für die Rechtfertigung des Sünders. Das Thema des Sermo ist die „temptatio Abrahae a Deo". Ausgehend

---

²¹ Ench. 1, 4, 32—34: CCSL 46, 49 f.
²² En. in ps. 135, 8, 2—6: CCSL 40, 1962. Zur Datierung siehe CCSL 38, S. xviii. Nach A.-M. La Bonnardière, Recherches de chronologie augustinienne (Paris, 1965), 139 dürfte diese Enarratio jedoch nicht vor 419/420 anzusetzen sein.
²³ In Joa. euang. 98, 2, 4—14, 29—32: CCSL 36, 576 f.
²⁴ Cf. A. Kunzelmann, „Die Chronologie der Sermones des hl. Augustinus", Miscellanea Agostiniana, II (Rom, 1931), 417-520, ss. 432 f.

von dem Wort des Jac. 2, 23: „Credidit Abraham Deo, et reputatum est illi ad iustitiam, et amicus Dei appellatus est", stellt der Prediger fest: „Quod credidit Deo, intus in corde, in *sola fide* est. Quod
autem immolandum duxit filium... magna fides est utique, et mag-
num opus."

In diesem Zusammenhang wirft Augustinus nun die Frage auf:
„Quare ergo apostolus Paulus ait (Rom. 3, 28): ‚Arbitramur iustificari hominem per fidem sine operibus legis' et alio loco dicit (Gal. 5,
6): ‚Et fides quae per dilectionem operatur'? Quomodo fides per
dilectionem operatur, et quomodo iustificatur homo per fidem sine
operibus legis[25]?" Augustinus antwortet: „... potest iustificari
homo ex fide sine operibus legis,... cum fides per dilectionem operetur in corde, etiam si foras non exit in opere[26]." Als Beispiel
erwähnt er den „latro, qui cum domino crucifixus est: corde credidit ad iustitiam, ore confessus est ad salutem (cf. Rom. 10, 10). Nam
‚fides quae per dilectionem operatur', et si non sit in quo exterius
operetur, in corde tamen feruens seruatur[27]."

Diese Gedanken hat Augustinus in der Quaestio 76 der ziemlich
gleichzeitigen Schrift De diuersis quaestionibus 83 aus seiner Priesterzeit noch weiter ausgeführt. Deutlicher als in der erwähnten
Predigt unterscheidet er hier zwischen den Werken, die der Rechtfertigung vorausgehen, und denen, die ihr folgen. Er schreibt:

... apostolum Paulum non ita per Abraham docere iustificari hominem per
fidem sine operibus, ut si quis crediderit, non ad eum pertineat bene operari, sed ad hoc potius, ut nemo arbitretur meritis priorum operum se per-
uenisse ad donum iustificationis, quae est in fide... Nam iustificatus per
fidem quomodo potest nisi iuste deinceps operari, quamuis antea nihil iuste
operatus ad fidei iustificationem peruenerit non merito bonorum operum
sed gratia Dei, quae uacare in illo non potest, cum iam per dilectionem bene
operatur[28]?

Augustinus ist deshalb überzeugt: „Quapropter non sunt sibi con-
trariae duorum apostolorum sententiae Pauli et Iacobi..., quia ille
dicit de operibus quae fidem praecedunt, iste de his quae fidem
sequuntur[29]."

Die ganze Frage, die hier also ein vorwiegend exegetisches Pro-

[25] Serm. 2, 9, 223—233: CCSL 41, 15 f.
[26] Ibid. 250—253.
[27] Ibid. 240—243.
[28] De diu. quaest. 83, qu. 76, 1, 15—30: CCSL 44A, 219.
[29] Ibid. qu. 76, 2, 79—84: CCSL 44A, 221.

lem erscheint und bei deren Lösung der Terminus „sola fides" nur ein einziges Mal an unbedeutender Stelle erwähnt wird, sollte rund zwanzig Jahre später für Augustinus sehr aktuell werden. Infolge des Zustroms der Volksmassen zur Kirche seit den Zeiten des Kaisers Konstantin war auch die Zahl jener Christen gewachsen, die kein wirklich christliches Leben führten. Deshalb fanden sich in der damaligen Kirche Leute — Augustinus nennt sie „misericordes nostri[30]" — die unter Berufung auf Gottes Barmherzigkeit die Heilsbedingungen erleichtern wollten. Wie Augustinus in seinen Retractationes berichtet, empfing er um das Jahr 413 „a quibusdam fratribus laicis quidem, sed diuinorum eloquiorum studiosis scripta nonnulla, quae ita distinguerent a bonis operibus christianam fidem, ut sine hac non posse, sine illis autem posse perueniri suaderetur ad aeternam uitam[31]". Dementsprechend wünschten diese Leute „indiscrete omnes admittendos esse ad lauacrum regenerationis, quae est in Christo Iesu domino nostro, etiamsi malam turpemque uitam facinoribus et flagitiis euidentissimis notam mutare noluerint[32]". Sie hielten es nämlich, wie Augustinus mitteilt, für völlig verfehlt (peruersum... atque praeposterum), die Taufbewerber schon vor der Taufe über die Verpflichtungen eines christlichen Lebens zu unterrichten. Das sollte nach ihrer Ansicht erst danach geschehen. Würde dann einer trotzdem ein schlechtes Leben führen, so könne er doch „tamquam per ignem" das Heil erlangen, wenn er nur den christlichen Glauben bewahrte[33]. Augustinus vermutete, der konkrete Anlaß zu dieser Lehre sei ein falsches Mitleid mit den Bigamisten gewesen, die nach der Gewohnheit der damaligen Kirche zur Taufe nicht zugelassen wurden[34].

Wohl noch im Jahre 413, kurz nach seiner Schrift De spiritu et littera[35], verfaßte der Kirchenvater eine ausführliche Schrift De fide et operibus, in der er sich mit diesen Vertretern einer „sola fides" auseinandersetzte. Entschieden wendet er sich gegen die These, den Täuflingen sei vor der Taufe nur die „sola fides" darzulegen, erst nach der Taufe sei die Ermahnung zu einem guten Lebenswandel

---

[30] De ciu. Dei XXI, 17, 1: CCSL 48, 783; cf. ibid. XXI, 21: CCSL 48, 786.

[31] Retr. II, 64 (38): CSEL 36, 177.

[32] De fid. et op. 1, 1: CSEL 41, 35, 3—6.

[33] Ibid. 35 f.

[34] Ibid. 1, 2: CSEL 41, 36, 8—12.

[35] Augustinus selbst bezeugt in De fid. et op. 14, 21 (CSEL 41, 62, 5—7): „ . . . ex hac quaestione prolixum librum edidi, qui inscribitur De littera et spiritu". In Retr. (ibid.) erscheint das Werk unmittelbar nach „De spiritu et littera".

angebracht[36]. Denn die Ansicht, daß die Täuflinge „de sola fide" zu unterweisen seien, könne sich nicht auf die Briefe der Apostel berufen[37]. Auch werde zu Unrecht behauptet, Petrus habe am ersten Pfingstfest den Dreitausend, die nach seiner Predigt getauft wurden, die „sola fides" verkündet[38].

Doch handelte es sich bei der neuen Theorie für Augustinus nicht nur um eine Frage der pastoralen Praxis, sondern um Anschauungen, die unmittelbar die christliche Lehre berührten: „... promittitur scelestissime turpissimeque uiuentibus, etiamsi eo modo uiuere perseuerent et tantummodo crederent in Christum eiusque sacramenta percipiant, eos ad salutem uitamque aeternam esse uenturos[39]". Diese These stützte sich anscheinend auch auf Rom. 3, 28: „Arbitramur enim iustificari hominem per fidem sine operibus legis." Jedenfalls bezieht Augustinus in seine Widerlegung eine kurze Interpretation dieser Paulusstelle ein: Der Apostel wolle nicht sagen, „ut percepta ac professa fide opera iustitiae contemnantur, sed ut sciat se quisque per fidem posse iustificari, etiamsi legis opera non praecesserint; sequuntur enim iustificatum, non praecedunt iustificandum[40]". Auch habe Paulus nicht irgendeine „fides... in Deum" im Auge gehabt, „sed eam salubrem planeque euangelicam definiuit, cuius opera ex dilectione procedunt[41]". Augustinus verweist hier auf seine Schrift De spiritu et littera, wo er darüber schon ausführlich gehandelt habe[42].

Dafür, daß man „per solam fidem" nicht zum ewigen Leben gelangen kann, beruft sich Augustinus auf das Herrenwort (Mt. 19, 17): „Si uis uenire ad uitam, serua mandata", auf Jac. 2, 20, wonach der Glaube ohne Werke tot ist[43], und auf zahlreiche andere Stellen[44].

---

[36] Ibid. 13, 19: CSEL 41, 59, 5—8. Ähnlich ibid. 27, 49: CSEL 41, 96, 3—5.
[37] Ibid. 7, 11: CSEL 41, 48, 5—10.
[38] Ibid. 8, 12: CSEL 41, 48, 20—23.
[39] Ibid. 27, 49: CSEL 41, 96, 14—17.
[40] Ibid. 14, 21: CSEL 41, 62, 1—4.
[41] Ibid.: CSEL 41, 62, 10—12.
[42] Cf. De spir. et litt. 8 f., 14 f., und 26, 44 f.: CSEL 60, 166 ff. und 197 ff. — Auch in einem späteren Kapitel (ibid. 21, 39: CSEL 41, 84, 7—10) bringt Augustinus Gedanken, die an die Schrift De spir. et litt. (14 ff., 26—32: CSEL 60, 180 ff.) anklingen: „... uiolentia fidei Sanctus Spiritus impetratur, per quem diffusa caritate in cordibus nostris lex non timore poenae, sed iustitiae amore completur."
[43] De fid. et op. 15, 25: CSEL 41, 67, 3—7.
[44] Er zitiert 1 Cor. 13, 2; Jac. 2, 14; 1 Cor. 6, 9 f.; Gal. 5, 19—21 und Mt. 25, 41—44: ibid. 15, 25: CSEL 41, 65, 24—66, 14 und 67, 7—16.

Auch die Behauptung, Getaufte, die die „sola fides" besäßen,
aber die „bona opera" vernachlässigten, würden gemäß 1 Cor.
3, 13 „per ignem" Rettung finden[45], ist nach Augustinus eine Fehldeu-
tung des zitierten Apostelwortes und steht außerdem in Widerspruch zu vielen anderen Schriftstellen[46]. Ebensowenig lasse sich
eine solche Kraft der „sola fides" mit Berufung auf 1 Cor. 7, 12—15
nachweisen, wo der Apostel nach Augustinus sagen wollte: „...
propter fidem Christi uxor legitima societate coniuncta sine ulla
culpa relinquatur, si cum uiro christiano propter hoc, quia christianus est, permanere noluerit." Denn die Rechtmäßigkeit der Entlas-
sung der Gattin gründe darin, daß der getaufte Christ „ueraciter egit
paenitentiam ab operibus mortuis, quando accessit ad baptismum
habetque in fundamento fidem, quae per dilectionem operatur[47]".

Wie hier stellt Augustinus auch sonst in seiner Schrift der „fides
mortua" im Sinn von Jac. 2, 17—20 oftmals die „fides quae per
dilectionem operatur" (Gal. 5, 6) gegenüber[48]. Die „fides mortua"
identifiziert er mit der „fides... daemonum, cum et ipsi credant et
contremiscant et filium Dei confiteantur Iesum[49]"; von diesem
Glauben gelte: „non est fides, quae operatur per dilectionem, sed
quae exprimitur per timorem[50]". Dagegen sei die „fides quae per
dilectionem operatur" jener Glaube, durch den nach Eph. 3, 17
Christus in den Herzen wohnt[51]. Augustinus nennt ihn deshalb
auch „fides Christi, fides gratiae christianae[52]". Schlußfolgernd
stellt er fest: Das ewige Leben sei den Gläubigen nur in der Weise
verheißen, „ut non etiam per fidem mortuam, quae sine operibus
saluare non potest, ad eam se quisque peruenire posse arbitretur, sed
per illam fidem gratiae, quae per dilectionem operatur[53]".

Übrigens setzt Augustinus die „fides sola" nicht grundsätzlich
mit der „fides sine operibus mortua" des Jakobusbriefes (Jac. 2, 20)
gleich. Denn, wie er einmal bemerkt, könne man mit Recht sagen:
„ad *solam fidem* pertinere Dei mandata, si non mortua, sed uiua illa

---

[45] Ibid. 15, 26: CSEL 41, 68, 15—17.
[46] Cf. ibid. 15 f. 24—27: CSEL 41, 64—72.
[47] Ibid. 16, 28: CSEL 41, 72, 4—10, 17—20.
[48] Siehe etwa ibid. 16, 30; 21, 38; 27, 49: CSEL 41, 74, 7, 19—21; 83, 19—22; 97, 4—7.
[49] Ibid. 16, 27: CSEL 41, 70, 1—2. Cf. ibid. 16, 30: CSEL 41, 74, 19—21; und ibid. 21, 38: CSEL 41, 83, 19—22.
[50] Ibid. 16, 27: CSEL 41, 70, 3—5.
[51] Ibid. CSEL 41, 69, 22 f.
[52] Ibid. 70, 5. Cf. ibid. 21, 38: CSEL 41, 83, 19—22.
[53] Ibid. 27, 49: CSEL 41, 97, 3—7.

intellegatur fides, quae per dilectionem operatur[54]". Freilich wird man auch von dieser positiven Würdigung der „sola fides" nicht behaupten können, daß sie in etwa dem entspricht, was mehr als tausend Jahre später Martin Luther mit seinem Sola-fide-Prinzip ausdrücken wollte. Dafür dürfte das Verständnis der „fides" und der „iustificatio" bei Augustinus und Luther zu verschieden sein. Immerhin könnte ein solcher Text beim heutigen oekumenischen Gespräch den Brückenschlag erleichtern.

Eine wertvolle Ergänzung zu diesen Ausführungen in De fide et operibus gibt Augustinus in seiner Enarratio secunda zu Psalm 31, die er um die gleiche Zeit — im Januar 413 — in einer Predigt vorgetragen hat[55]. Ausgehend von Rom. 4, 3: „Credidit autem Abraham Deo; et reputatum est illi ad iustitiam", bringt der Prediger die Sorge zum Ausdruck: „Vides ergo, quia ex fide, non ex operibus iustificatus est Abraham; faciam ergo quidquid uolo, quia etsi bona opera non habuero, et tantum credidero in Deum, deputatur mihi ad iustitiam[56]." Um seinen Zuhörern zu zeigen, daß dies ein grobes Mißverständnis des Apostelwortes darstelle, verweist Augustinus auf den Jakobusbrief: „Iacobus enim in epistula sua, contra eos qui nolebant bene operari de *sola fide* praesumentes, ipsius Abrahae opera commendauit, cuius Paulus fidem;... fides sine operibus mortua esset, et tamquam radix sine fructu sterilis atque arida remaneret[57]."

Ganz anders beurteilt Augustinus „die Werke vor dem Glauben", d.h. die Werke des Ungläubigen:

Ea enim ipsa opera quae dicuntur ante fidem, quamuis uideantur hominibus laudabilia, inania sunt. Ita mihi uidentur esse ut magnae uires et cursus celerrimus praeter uiam. Nemo ergo computet bona opera sua ante fidem; ubi fides non erat, bonum opus non erat. Bonum enim opus intentio facit, intentionem fides dirigit[58].

So gilt nach Augustinus für jeden Menschen, daß er — wie Abraham — nur aufgrund des Glaubens gerechtfertigt wird. Aber dem Glauben müssen Werke folgen: „Sed si fidem opera non praecesserunt, tamen secuta sunt. Numquid enim fides tua sterilis erit?...

---

[54] Ibid. 22, 40: CSEL 41, 84, 25—85, 2.
[55] Zur Datierung cf. CCSL 38, S. xvii.
[56] En. in ps. 31, 2, 3, 2—5: CCSL 38, 226.
[57] Ibid. 3, 12—14, 24—26: CCSL 38, 226 f.
[58] Ibid. 4, 2—8: CCSL 38, 227.

Tene ergo fidem operaturus[59]." Auf den Einwand, daß der Apostel
Paulus in Rom. 4, 3 nichts von Werken sage, erwidert Augustinus:

> Immo hoc ait Paulus apostolus (Gal. 5, 6): ,Fides', inquit, ,quae per dilec-
> tionem operatur'; et alio loco (Rom. 13, 10): ,Plenitudo ergo legis, caritas'...
> Itaque si fides sine dilectione sit, sine opere erit. Ne autem multa cogites de
> opere fidei, adde illi spem et dilectionem, et noli cogitare quid opereris. Ipsa
> dilectio uacare non potest[60].

Nun beschäftigt sich Augustinus ausführlich mit der Frage, wie
das Wort des Römerbriefes von der Rechtfertigung aus dem Glauben ohne Gesetzeswerke (Rom. 3, 28) mit der Aussage Gal. 5, 6,
daß der Glaube durch die Liebe wirkt, zu vereinbaren ist: „... dilec-
tio uacare non potest, nisi et mali nihil operetur, et quidquid potest
boni operetur... Quomodo ergo iustificabitur homo per fidem sine
operibus?[61]" Augustinus läßt den Apostel antworten — und es ist
eine starke Betonung der völlig ungeschuldeten und unverdienten
Gnade der Rechtfertigung:

> Propterea hoc tibi dixi, o homo, ne quasi de operibus tuis praesumere
> uidereris, et merito operum tuorum te accepisse fidei gratiam. Noli ergo
> praesumere de operibus ante fidem. Noueris quia peccatorem te fides inue-
> nit, etsi te fides data fecit iustum, impium inuenit quem faceret iustum.
> ,Credenti', inquit, ,in eum qui iustificat impium, deputatur fides eius ad ius-
> titiam[62].'

> Gratis constat. Nihil boni fecisti, et datur tibi remissio peccatorum.
> Adtenduntur opera tua, et inueniuntur omnia mala... Non tibi Deus reddit
> debitam poenam, sed donat indebitam gratiam. Debebat uindictam, dat
> indulgentiam. Incipis ergo esse in fide per indulgentiam; iam fides illa
> assumpta spe et dilectione incipit bene operari; sed nec tunc glorieris, et
> extollas te[63].

Mit dem Apostel zieht Augustinus die Schlußfolgerung (Rom. 4, 5):

> ,Credenti autem in eum qui iustificat impium, deputatur fides eius ad iusti-
> tiam.'... Iustitiam autem quam? Fidei, quam bona opera non praecesserunt,
> sed quam bona opera consequuntur... Nemo iactet bona opera sua ante
> fidem, nemo sit piger in bonis operibus accepta fide. Dat Deus ergo indul-
> gentiam omnibus impiis, et eos iustificat ex fide[64].

---

[59] Ibid. 5, 1—5.
[60] Ibid. 5, 6—8, 20—22: CCSL 38, 227 f.
[61] Ibid. 6, 12—13, 19: CCSL 38, 229.
[62] Ibid. 6, 20—26.
[63] Ibid. 7, 10—12, 17—21: CCSL 38, 230.
[64] Ibid. 7, 32—37 und 8, 10—13: CCSL 38, 231.

Ähnliche Gedanken, wie sie sich in De fide et operibus vom Jahre
413 breit ausgeführt finden, bietet Augustinus — oft nur kurz skiz-
ziert — auch in Predigten aus dieser Zeit und den Schriften aus den
folgenden Jahrzehnten. In einem Sermo, den er zwischen 412 und
416 in der „Basilica Restituta" zu Karthago[65] über das königliche
Gastmahl (Mt. 22, 1–14) gehalten hat, bezeichnet er als das „uestis
nuptialis" des Gleichnisses die „caritas" und bemerkt: Auch die
„fides" verdiene Lob, aber nicht jede „fides". Dem Glauben, mit
dem Petrus bekannte (Mt. 16, 16): „Tu es Christus, filius Dei uiui",
stellt der Prediger den Glauben der Dämonen gegenüber, die auch
bekannten (Mc. 1, 24): „Tu es filius Dei", und folgert: „Petrus dixit
in amore, daemones a timore. Denique ille dicit (Lc. 22, 33):
‚Tecum sum usque ad mortem.' Illi dicunt (Mt. 8, 29): ‚Quid nobis
et tibi?'[66]" Augustins Anwendung für die Zuhörer lautet: „Ergo,
qui uenisti ad conuiuium, noli de *sola fide* gloriari. Distingue et
ipsam fidem, et tunc in te agnoscitur uestis nuptialis... Quae ergo
fides? Qualis fides? ‚quae per dilectionem operatur' (Gal. 5, 6)[67]."
    In einer Predigt, die Augustinus wahrscheinlich am Sonntag, dem
18. Juni 411, ebenfalls in Karthago gehalten hat[68], bemerkt er zu
dem Psalmwort (Ps. 38, 5): „Notum fac mihi, domine, finem
meum", daß der Christ durch den Glauben Christus als das Ziel
seines Lebensweges erkannt hat. Dann fährt er fort:

Sed non in fide tantum res est, sed in fide et opere: utrumque necessarium
est; nam et daemones credunt — audistis apostolum — et contremiscunt,
non est autem prode illis quia credunt. Parum est *fides sola*, nisi et opera
coniungantur: ‚Fides quae per dilectionem operatur', ait apostolus (Gal. 5,
6)[69].

Etwas ausführlicher kommt Augustinus in seinem Enchiridion von
ca. 421 auf das Ungenügen der „sola fides" zu sprechen. Unter aus-
drücklicher Berufung auf die Schrift De fide et operibus wendet er
sich gegen gewisse „catholici", welche — „humana quadam
beneuolentia" getäuscht — die Ansicht verträten: „... etiam hi, qui
nomen Christi non relinquunt, et eius lauacro in ecclesia baptizan-
tur,... in quantislibet sceleribus uiuant... salui futuri per ignem[70]".

[65] Cf. Kunzelmann, op. cit. 480 f.
[66] Serm. 90, 8: PL 38, 564.
[67] Ibid.
[68] Cf. Kunzelmann, op. cit. 502.
[69] Serm. Denis 20, 11: Miscellanea Agostiniana, I (Rom, 1930), 122, 11—15.
[70] Ench. 18, 67, 1—6: CCSL 46, 85.

Auch hier stellt er einem solchen Heilsversprechen „propter solam fidem" als Lehre der Heiligen Schrift entgegen, daß nur der Glaube zum Heile führt, „quae per dilectionem operatur" (Gal. 5, 6), nicht aber jener, der „mortua est in semetipsa" (cf. Jac. 2, 17)[71].

Einige Zeit später, wahrscheinlich im Jahre 424, sah sich Augustinus nochmals veranlaßt, zu der erwähnten Frage Stellung zu nehmen. Der kaiserliche „tribunus et notarius" Dulcitius legte ihm unter anderem auch die Frage vor: „Utrum aliquando qui sunt post baptismum peccatores exeant de gehenna?" In seiner Schrift De octo Dulcitii quaestionibus erteilte Augustinus ihm seine Antwort, indem er für ihn die entsprechenden Kapitel aus De fide et operibus (14 ff., 23—30) und aus dem Enchiridion (18, 67—68) kopieren ließ[72]. Abschließend gibt er zu: Die vorgeschlagene mildere Lösung der Frage „familiarius meum tangit affectum, quem habemus erga eos qui nobiscum corporis et sanguinis Christi sacramenta communicant, quamuis eorum mores perditos oderimus". Doch könne diese mildere Lösung nicht der Wahrheit entsprechen, da sie im offenen Widerspruch zu dem Apostelwort (Eph. 4, 5) stehe: „Hoc autem scitote intellegentes, quoniam omnis fornicator aut immundus aut auarus, quod est idolorum seruitus, non habet hereditatem in regno Christi et Dei[73]."

Eine ähnliche Stellungnahme findet sich auch in Augustins Schrift De continentia, die aus beachtlichen Gründen heute in die letzten 15 Jahre seines Lebens (416—418 oder gar 426—429) datiert wird[74]. Im Anschluß an das Wort des Apostels (Col. 3, 6): „Propter quae [uitia] uenit ira Dei in filios infidelitatis", schreibt Augustinus:

Utique salubriter terruit, ne putarent fideles propter *solam fidem* suam, etiamsi in his malis uiuerent, se posse saluari apostolo Iacobo contra istum sensum uoce manifestissima reclamante ac dicente (Jac. 2, 14): „Si fidem quis dicat se habere, opera autem non habeat, numquid poterit fides saluare eum?[75]"

Daß aber nicht nur die „filii infidelitatis", die solche Laster verüb-

---

[71] Ibid. 15—28: CCSL 46, 85 f.

[72] De octo Dulc. quaest. 1, 1—13: CCSL 44A, 255—269. Zur Datierung siehe A. Mutzenbecher, in CCSL 44A, SS. cx f.

[73] Ibid. 1, 14, 361—377: CCSL 44A, 269 f.

[74] A.-M. La Bonnardière, „La date du ‚De continentia‘ de Saint Augustin", Rev. des études aug. 5 (1959), 121—127, und D. O'B. Faul, „The date of the ‚De continentia‘ of Saint Augustine", Studia Patristica, VI (Berlin, 1962), 374—382.

[75] De cont. 14, 30: CSEL 41, 181, 1—7.

ten, Gottes Zorn treffen werde, sieht Augustinus durch die nachfolgenden Worte des Apostels bezeugt (Col. 3, 8): „Nunc autem deponite et uos uniuersa [uitia]." Durch die Beifügung „et uos" habe Paulus die Getauften vor der Selbsttäuschung bewahren wollen, „ne propterea se putarent haec mala facere atque in eis uiuere impune, quia fides eorum liberaret eos ab ira, quae uenit in filios infidelitatis ista facientes[76]."

Auch in seiner Spätschrift De gratia et libero arbitrio, verfaßt 426/427 für ein Mönchskloster in Hadrumetum, erwähnt Augustinus nochmals die Gefahr einer Mißdeutung von Worten des Apostels Paulus im Sinn der „sola fides". Zu dem Wort Eph. 2, 8: „Gratia salui facti estis per fidem, et hoc non ex uobis, sed Dei donum est; non ex operibus, ne forte quis extollatur" führt er aus: „Vidit [apostolus] utique putare posse homines hoc ita dictum, quasi necessaria non sint opera bona credentibus, sed eis *fides sola* sufficiat[77]."

Bei der Widerlegung dieses Mißverständnisses knüpft Augustinus an den nachfolgenden Vers (Eph. 2, 10) an: „Ipsius enim sumus figmentum, creati in Christo Iesu in operibus bonis, quae praeparauit Deus, ut in illis ambulemus." Hier spreche der Apostel durchaus von guten Werken, aber nicht „tamquam tuis ex te ipso tibi existentibus, sed tamquam his in quibus te Deus finxit, id est formauit et creauit[78]."

Augustinus schließt mit Worten, die in nuce seine ganze Rechtfertigungs- und Gnadenlehre enthalten:

Itaque, carissimi, si uita bona nostra nihil aliud est quam Dei gratia, sine dubio et uita aeterna, quae bonae uitae redditur, Dei gratia est; et ipsa enim gratis datur, quia gratis data est illa cui datur[79].

Sed quia ipsa bona opera ille (sc. Deus) in bonis operatur, de quo dictum est (Phil. 2, 13): „Deus est enim qui operatur in uobis et uelle et operari pro bona uoluntate", ideo dixit psalmus (Ps. 102, 4): „Coronat te in miseratione et misericordia"... Non extollimini tamquam de uestris operibus bonis, quia Deus est qui operatur in uobis[80].

Augustinus ist also der Überzeugung, daß die Gnade dem gefallenen Menschen aus reiner Erbarmung und Huld verliehen und

---

[76] Ibid. 14, 31: CSEL 41, 181, 21—182, 3.
[77] De grat. et lib. arb. 8, 20: PL 44, 892.
[78] Ibid.: PL 44, 893.
[79] Ibid.
[80] Ibid. 8, 21: PL 44, 893 f.

dadurch der menschliche Wille aus einem bösen in einen guten ver-
wandelt wird — nunmehr fähig, gute verdienstliche Werke zu
vollbringen. Doch braucht er dazu die ständige Hilfe der göttlichen
Gnade, so daß auch das ewige Leben, das er für diese Werke der
Gerechtigkeit empfängt, im Grunde Gnadencharakter besitzt.

Zusammenfassend läßt sich sagen, das Thema der „sola fides"
wurde für Augustinus sehr aktuell durch jene „misericordes" in der
damaligen Kirche, die im Hinblick auf Gottes Barmherzigkeit allen
Getauften, auch unbußfertigen Sündern, die Erlangung des ewigen
Heiles „aufgrund des bloßen Glaubens" versprachen. Augustinus
hat deshalb in den letzten zwei Jahrzehnten seines Lebens diese
Auffassung oftmals in Schriften und Predigten bekämpft. Seine Stel-
lungnahmen enthalten folgende Grundgedanken:

1. Das Apostelwort Rom. 3, 28, wonach die Rechtfertigung „per
fidem sine operibus legis" erfolgt, ist nicht im Sinn der erwähnten
„sola fides" zu verstehen, sondern schließt nur jene Werke aus, die
dem Glauben vorausgehen. Sie sind nach Augustinus, weil ihnen die
rechte Ausrichtung auf das Ziel mangelt, keine wirklich guten
Werke. Das „donum" der Rechtfertigung durch den Glauben kann
sich niemand durch Werke verdienen; es ist ungeschuldete Gnade.

2. In Gal. 5, 6 behauptet der Apostel vom rechtfertigenden Glauben, der „fides uiua": „per dilectionem operatur"; denn der Glaube
und Gottes Gnade können im Menschen nicht ohne Frucht bleiben.

3. Die „sola fides" des unbußfertigen Sünders läßt ihn nicht zum
ewigen Leben gelangen. Das beweist Augustinus mit Schriftstellen
wie Mt. 19, 17 und 25, 41—44, 1 Cor. 6, 9. und 13, 1 ff, Gal. 5,
19—21, Eph. 4, 5 usw. Die „sola fides" in diesem Verständnis identifiziert er mit der „fides mortua" des Jakobusbriefes (2, 17—20)
und mit der „fides" der Dämonen (cf. Mc. 1, 24).

4. Versteht man aber darunter die „fides uiua", die durch die
Liebe wirkt, so besitzt die „sola fides" einen Bezug zu den Geboten
Gottes.

5. Die „uita bona" der Gerechtfertigten ist eine Gnadengabe
Gottes, der nach Phil. 2, 13 auch die „opera bona" in uns wirkt.
Der Christ hat deshalb nie Grund, sich seiner guten Werke zu rüh-
men. Auch die „uita aeterna", der Lohn für diese Werke, ist Gottes
Gnadengeschenk.

7

Die Autorität des Lehrers nach Thomas von Aquin

CHRISTOPH SCHÖNBORN

Summary

1. Thomas Aquinas is regarded by the Roman Catholic Church as the 'Doctor communis'. How did Thomas himself look upon his authority as a teacher? What did he understand to be the authority of a teacher? Thomas examines this question thoroughly in his *Quaestio disputata* 'De magistro' (De ver. q. 11). In the context of epistemological debate, this question takes a position between the representatives of the Augustinian tradition of Illumination and the supporters of the newly received Aristotelianism. Most of the objections which Thomas investigates originate in Augustine's dialogue *De magistro*. It is common to all of them that they have little confidence in the human teacher and his instrument, language: only God can be the true teacher, in leading us to the light of truth, for the teacher's language is tied to the sense perceptions, and cannot transmit the certainty of truth.

2. In Thomas's answer to these objections it is noticeable that he is not criticizing Augustine, although he develops his view 'secundum doctrinam Aristotelis'. The reason for this reticence should not be seen as a 'political' tactic. Rather, as É. Gilson has shown, Thomas is reacting not against Augustine himself, but against the 'augustinisme avicennisant' which was common in his time, and which equates Avicenna's *intellectus agens separatus* with Augustine's *magister interior*. Thomas's position comes closer to Augustine's *intentio profundior* than that of many of his Augustinian contemporaries.

3. Thomas sets a middle course between two extremes, which Gilson calls 'extrinsécisme intégral' and 'intrinsécisme intégral'. The first position ascribes the operation of all created beings to the direct influence of God: the second views all actualization as being already latently present in the potentialities. In the first case, knowledge is direct inspiration from God, and in the second it is recollection. In both positions Thomas sees the denial of the real effectiveness of secondary causes. Both positions magnify God at the expense of created beings. Thomas sees God's greatness precisely in this, that he gives creatures not only their being, but their *own* activity as well. Primary and secondary causes are both directly operative, but at different levels: they are not in competition.

4. Thomas's own solution could be called a 'modified intrincisism'. The

forms of being do not come 'from outside', as Avicenna would have it; they are pre-existent in matter, not actually, but potentially. The case of the forms of understanding is similar: they do not come from above, from the *dator formarum* (Avicenna); they pre-exist in the human soul, though admittedly only as 'seeds of knowledge' (*scientiarum semina*). This seminal knowledge, which is innate in everyone, is the knowledge of the *prima principia*, the clear and most common principles of knowledge. These exist in the soul as *potentia activa*, like the power of health in the body. Just as the physician can only stimulate the operation of the power of being healthy, so the teacher can only encourage the growth of this seed of knowledge; as the physician cannot make health, so the teacher cannot create knowledge— both are 'servants of nature'.

5. Knowledge comes from the senses, but at the same time we know only in the light of the *prima principia*. How do these two aspects of knowledge operate together? What do we know through the *prima principia*? What sort of thing is this inborn seminal knowledge? It is nothing other than that the images received from sense data are truly knowable, and become thereby part of our intellectual stock. That we come to true knowledge out of the multiplicity of sense perceptions is only possible thanks to that inner, innate standard which Thomas calls the 'light of understanding'. By this light we recognize and accept what is offered to our understanding in its transcendental properties, such as *ens, unum, verum, bonum*. Inasmuch as God is the originator of the 'light of understanding', only God teaches men the truth. Thomas thinks that there is no significant difference between his view of the 'magister interior' and that of St Augustine.

6. But, unlike Augustine, Thomas attributes very positive powers to language. Certainly, language belongs to the world of sense symbols, yet our intellect is capable of understanding the intellectual intentions (*intentiones intelligibiles*) of the teacher's words, just as it is also capable of drawing intellectual contents (*species intelligibiles*) out of the sense impressions. If we can understand the language of reality we can also understand the teacher's language. Learning follows the same path as understanding, but learning from a teacher has one great advantage over personal study and search for knowledge: the master's teaching does not offer the random material of knowledge, but knowledge in an ordered form. The master's language should transmit the *intentiones intelligibiles* of his knowledge. Thomas sees language above all as the transparent medium of intellectual information.

7. Can angels teach men? This astonishing question, to which Thomas answers Yes, gives him the opportunity to expound his concept of a teacher once more. In the perspective of Dionysius's doctrine of Illumination, Thomas sees the role of angels as one in which they 'strengthen' (*confortare*) the *lumen intellectus* in man. It is not ready-made understanding, which

flows from higher intelligences to lower, but the power to know *for oneself.* God himself teaches man, in that he gives him the light of understanding. A good teacher follows this original pattern; he helps man to know *for himself.* There is a strong ethical factor in this view: only when we know *for ourselves* are we truly responsible for our own actions. Thomas sees teaching as leading to freedom, therefore the teacher must be freed from himself, and totally dedicated to truth. Thomas himself demonstrates what he teaches, that truth means freedom.

THOMAS VON AQUIN wird in der katholischen Kirche als der „doctor communis" bezeichnet. Er gilt (oder galt langezeit) als d i e theologische und philosophische Lehrautorität[1]. Was war und ist es an Thomas von Aquin, das ihm einen so hervorragenden Platz unter den christlichen Lehrern einbrachte? Warum mißt man ihm eine so große Autorität zu?

Einen Weg, auf diese Frage zu antworten, wollen wir hier zu gehen versuchen: Wie verstand Thomas von Aquin selber die Autorität des Lehrers? Aus seiner Sicht der Rolle des Lehrers können wir erschließen, wie Thomas selber seine Autorität verstanden wissen will. Thomas spricht häufig vom Lehren, vom Lehrer, vom Lernen, meist um dadurch das Verhältnis des Menschen zu Gott zu erhellen. Gelegentlich wird die Frage nach dem Lehren und Lernen auch eigens und ausdrücklich thematisiert, am Ausführlichsten in seiner *quaestio disputata* De magistro, der 11. Frage der *quaestiones disputatae* De veritate.

Dieser Text soll uns als Leitfaden dienen, von ihm wollen wir uns die Fragen und den Blickpunkt vorgeben lassen, nicht ohne gelegentliche Ausblicke in andere Texte des hl. Thomas, die unser Thema berühren. Unser Vorhaben beansprucht nicht, neue oder besonders originelle wissenschaftliche Resultate zu diesem Traktat vorzubringen. Große Meister der Thomasinterpretation haben das Wichtigste bereits gesagt, besonders was das Verhältnis der thomasischen zur augustinischen Sicht des Lehrers betrifft[2]. Kommen-

---

[1] Vgl. S. Szabo, Die Auktorität des hl. Thomas von Aquin in der Theologie (Regensburg–Rom. 1919); J. Ude, Die Autorität des hl. Thomas von Aquin als Kirchenlehrer und seine Summa Theologica (Salzburg, 1932); I. M. Ramirez, De auctoritate doctrinali S. Thomae Aquinatis (Salamanca, 1952); vgl. auch Art. 16 des Dekrets Optatam totius des II. Vatikanischen Konzils.

[2] É. Gilson, „Pourquoi saint Thomas a critiqué saint Augustin", Archives d'histoire doctrinale et littéraire du moyen âge, 1 (1926—1927), 5—127; P. Wilpert, Das Problem der Wahrheitssicherung bei Thomas von Aquin: Ein Beitrag zur Geschichte des Evidenzproblems (Münster i.W., 1931); M. Grabmann, Der göttliche Grund

tierte Übersetzungen erschließen die *quaestio* De magistro hinläng-
lich[3]. So bleibt uns eine sehr bescheidene und doch schwierige Aufgabe, der wir uns im Folgenden stellen wollen: d i e S a c h e s e l b s t ,
um die es Thomas geht, möglichst unverstellt in den Blick zu nehmen. Wenn das Resultat nichts wesentlich Neues bringt, so genügt
uns doch die Freude, Thomas „nach-zudenken", den Weg seiner
Gedanken nachzugehen und uns sozusagen von ihm selber auf diesem Weg bei der Hand nehmen zu lassen[4].

1. Ist nicht Gott allein Lehrer?

Die *quaestio disputata* De magistro wird allgemein in das zweite
Jahr der ersten Pariser Lehrtätigkeit des hl. Thomas datiert (1257—
1258)[5]. Ihr Platz in der Reihenfolge der unter dem Titel De veritate
zusammengefaßten Disputationen ist leicht einzusehen. Sie steht
mitten in einer Serie von Disputationen über Fragen, die verschie-
denste Probleme der Erkenntnislehre behandeln, angefangen von
der Erkenntnis der Engel (qq. VIII und IX) über Fragen der menschlichen Erkenntnis (z.B. de mente, q. X; de prophetia, q. XII; de con-
scientia, q. XVII) bis hin zur Frage der scientia animae Christi
(q. XX). Der epistemologische Kontext unserer *quaestio* De magistro
erklärt zum Teil die Eingrenzung auf die Frage der Erkenntnisvermittlung. Die pädagogischen Anschauungen des hl. Thomas lassen
sich nur indirekt aus unserem Text ermitteln. Sie sind freilich durch

menschlicher Wahrheitserkenntnis nach Augustinus und Thomas von Aquin (Münster i.W., 1924); A. Hufnagel, Intuition und Erkenntnis nach Thomas von Aquin
(Münster i.W., 1932).

[3] T. Gregory, Tommaso d'Aquino, „De magistro (Rom 1965), mit ausführlichem
Kommentar"; I. V. McGlynn, St. Thomas Aquinas, Truth, q. X—XX, Bd. II (Chi-
cago, 1953); Saint Thomas d'Aquin, Questions disputées sur la Vérité: Question XI,
Le Maître (De Magistro), texte latin, introduction, traduction et notes par Bernadette
Iollès (Paris, 1983); Des hl. Thomas von Aquino Untersuchungen über die Wahrheit,
in deutscher Übertragung von Edith Stein, Bd. I (Breslau, 1931), 309—325; unsere
Übersetzungen lehnen sich gelegentlich an diese Übersetzung an; vgl. ferner I. M.
Collera, The Treatises De Magistro of Saint Augustine and Saint Thomas (New
York, 1945). Nicht einsehen konnte ich die Arbeit von A. Caturelli, La doctrina
augustiniana sobre el maestro y su desarollo en S. Tomas d'A. (Cordoba, Argenti-
nien, 1954).

[4] Mein besonderer Dank gilt Frau Dr. Dorothée Welp für die kostbaren Ges-
präche über dieses Thema, die mir zu einer wirklichen *manuductio* hin zu der von
Thomas gemeinten Sache wurden.

[5] I. A. Weisheipl, Friar Thomas d'Aquino: His Life, Thought, and Works
(Oxford, 1975), 123.

aus klar und bis heute bedenkenswert. Gerade die Art und Weise, wie Thomas die Frage des Lehrers angeht, sagt schon viel über seine Auffassung von der Rolle des Pädagogen. Er beginnt nicht bei der Frage der pädagogischen Methoden, als ginge es nur darum, die erfolgreichste Methode herauszufinden. Die Ausgangsfrage in De magistro ist viel grundsätzlicher: Kann überhaupt ein Mensch einen anderen Menschen lehren? In einer Zeit, da metaphysische Fragen zu den Tätigkeiten unseres Alltags gar nicht gestellt werden, mag uns die metaphysische Frage nach den letzten Gründen des Lernens überraschen. Und doch liegt gerade in diesen überraschenden Fragen die Stärke der mittelalterlichen Universität. Die *quaestiones disputatae* führen uns in eine Welt, die über alles staunen kann, für die nichts einfach selbstverständlich ist, nicht um alles in Zweifel zu ziehen, sondern weil alles, selbst das Alltägliche, Anlaß zur Verwunderung, zur Bewunderung werden kann. Ist es nicht etwas Staunenswertes, dass in der Seele eines jungen Menschen Erkenntnisse aufleuchten, Einsichten wachsen? Woher kommt es, daß einem Hörer oder Leser etwas einleuchtet? Solches staunendes Nachdenken frägt nicht zuerst nach funktionalen Zusammenhängen, wie es im neuzeitlich-naturwissenschaftlichen Denken üblich geworden ist. Nicht wie das Lernen als psychologisches Phänomen zu erklären sei, ist die erste Frage, sondern was es darum ist, daß ein Mensch lernen kann.

Gemäß der Methode der *quaestio disputata* wird zuerst eine beachtliche Liste von Einwänden formuliert, die in unserem Falle alle das eine gemeinsam haben: sie scheinen auszuschließen, daß überhaupt ein Mensch einen anderen Menschen lehren kann. Den achtzehn Einwänden des ersten Artikels ist, bei aller Verschiedenheit, dies gemeinsam: daß sie den menschlichen Lehrer für überflüssig und unnütz erklären. Man kann sich lebhaft vorstellen, daß diese Einwände von den Kollegen und Studenten der Pariser Universität nicht ohne Ironie und Spott vorgebracht wurden, stellen sie doch das Amt und den Titel des „magister" selbst in Frage. P. Mandonnet hat die mittelalterliche Disputation „das Turnier der Kleriker" genannt[6]. Sehen wir uns den Verlauf des Turniers nun an!

Mit einem Paukenschlag beginnen die Einwände. Der Herr selber

---

[6] „Chronologie des questions disputées de saint Thomas d'Aquin", Revue Thomiste, 23 (1918), 267 f.; vgl. auch L.-J. Bataillon, „Les conditions de travail des maîtres de l'Université de Paris au XIIIᵉ siècle", Revue des sciences philosophiques et théologiques, 67 (1983) 417—433.

sagt im Evangelium unmißverständlich: „Einer ist euer Lehrer (magister)" und „Laßt euch nicht Lehrer nennen" (Mt. 23, 8). Ein Zitat aus der Glossa verschärft den Einwand: „... damit ihr nicht Menschen göttliche Ehre zuweist oder euch anmaßt, was Gott alleine zusteht". Das Evangelium selber verwehrt es, Menschen die Ehre des Magister-Titels zu geben. Hinter diesem biblischen Argument steckt ein brisanter Konflikt. Es ist eben erst ein Jahr her, daß der sogenannte „Mendikantenstreit" (vorerst) beendet wurde. Im Herbst 1256 hatte Thomas seine Streitschrift Contra impugnantes Dei cultum et religionem gegen die heftigen Angriffe des Wilhelm von Saint-Amour auf die Bettelorden verfaßt. Im zweiten Kapitel dieser Schrift („An religioso liceat docere") behandelt Thomas die Einwände gegen die Lehrtätigkeit der Mendikanten. Der erste Einwand, dem er hier begegnet, ist wieder das Herrenwort aus Mt. 23, 8. Ist es nicht ein Skandal, daß die Bettelorden, die sich so viel auf ihre evangelische Lebensweise zugute halten, sich gegen den Rat des Herrn „magistri" nennen lassen[7]? Auch wenn in unserer *quaestio* De magistro vom Mendikantenstreit nichts direkt durchscheint, so steht doch die ganze Brisanz dieses noch lange nicht beendeten Konfliktes zwischen gewissen Kreisen des Weltklerus und den neuen, vom Papsttum stark geförderten evangelischen Ordensbewegungen im Hintergrund. Die Antwort des hl. Thomas auf den Einwand, die Ehre des Magistertitels sei mit der evangelischen Schlichtheit unvereinbar, wird ein neues, ganz vom Geist der evangelischen Erneuerung erfülltes Bild des Lehrers und des Lehrens zeichnen. Thomas wird das Magisterium als demütigen Dienst und nicht als standesbewußten „honor" darstellen: „hoc enim falsum est, quod magisterium sit honor: est enim officium, cui debetur honor"[8]. Doch davon später noch!

Vorerst gilt es, auf ein anderes Konfliktfeld hinzuweisen, das sich hinter unserer *disputatio* abzeichnet: die Spannungen zwischen dem traditionellen Augustinismus und dem neu eindringenden Aristotelismus. Gerade im Bereich der Erkenntnislehre traten die Unterschiede der beiden Richtungen besonders deutlich hervor. Es ist nicht verwunderlich, daß sie in der Frage der Erkenntnisvermittlung durch den Lehrer geradezu in den Mittelpunkt rückt. Augustins

---

[7] Contra impugnantes, cap. 11: zum Mendikantenstreit vgl. I. A. Weisheipl, op. cit. 80—92.

[8] Contra impugnantes, cap. 11; Opera omnia, ed. Leonina, Bd. xli (Rom, 1970), s. A 61, Zeilen 518 f.

Lehre vom „magister interior" liefert denn auch die meisten Einwände im ersten Artikel unserer *quaestio*, während die Antwort des Thomas ausdrücklich „secundum doctrinam Aristotilis" formuliert wird[9].

Augustins zentralen Gedanken finden wir im neunten Einwand formuliert: Lehren heißt die Wahrheit lehren. Wer aber die Wahrheit lehrt, erleuchtet den Geist, ist doch die Wahrheit das Licht des Geistes. Gott alleine aber „erleuchtet jeden Menschen, der in diese Welt kommt" (Joh. 1, 9). Wahrhaft Lehrer sein kann daher nur Gott. Echtes Wissen kann nur innerlich im Menschen verursacht werden, nicht äußerlich, durch die Sinne (7. Einwand), Gott alleine aber kann den Menschen innerlich lehren. Damit Wissen und nicht nur Meinen zustande kommt, bedarf es der Gewißheit der Erkenntnis. Erst dann sprechen wir von W i s s e n („scientia est certitudinalis cognitio"). Solche Gewißheit kann aber nicht alleine vom Hören kommen. Das Gehörte muß vielmehr am inneren Maßstab der Wahrheit gemessen werden. Diese Wahrheit, die innerlich spricht, ist aber Gott selber (17. Einwand). Aus all diesen Einwänden folgt, daß Gott alleine Lehrer des Menschen sein kann und ist.

Auch von einem anderen Gesichtspunkt her kann die Möglichkeit menschlichen Lehrens in Frage gestellt werden. Eine Reihe von Argumenten kommt aus sprachtheoretischen Überlegungen zu diesem Schluß. Augustins früher Dialog De magistro hat die schlichte Feststellung, daß Lehren ein Sprachvorgang ist, dadurch „mehr und mehr ins Feuer der Kritik gebracht"[10], daß er die Komplexheit solcher Sprachvorgänge bewußt machte. Die meisten Einwände, die unter dem Aspekt der Sprache erhoben werden, berufen sich daher auch ausdrücklich auf Augustins De magistro.

„Wenn ein Mensch lehrt, so tut er es durch Zeichen", seien sie hörbar oder sichtbar, „... Doch kann man durch Zeichen (*signa*) nicht zur Kenntnis der Dinge (*rerum*) gelangen" (2. Einwand). Die Lehrtätigkeit scheint in der Welt der Zeichen verhaftet zu bleiben. Die Zeichen gehören zur Sinnenwelt, Wissen aber ist Sache des Geistes, es kann also durch sinnliche Zeichen nicht vermittelt werden (4. Einwand). Noch radikaler ist der 3. Einwand: Entweder kennt der Schüler die Dinge (*res*), von denen der Lehrer durch

---

[9] Opera omnia, ed. Leonina, Bd. XXII, ii (Rom, 1972), s. 350, Zeile 251. In dieser Ausgabe sind die Zeilen der einzelnen Artikel durchnummeriert. Die Zahlen in unserem Text verweisen auf die entsprechenden Zeilen im jeweiligen Artikel.
[10] H. Chadwick, Augustine (Oxford, 1986), 47.

Zeichen spricht, dann bedarf er freilich dieser Zeichen nicht mehr. Kennt er die Dinge nicht, dann versteht er auch die Zeichen nicht, die sie bezeichnen. Wenn aber ein menschlicher Lehrer nichts anderes tun kann als Zeichen mitzuteilen, dann kann kein Mensch einen anderen lehren. Der letzte (18.) Einwand verschärft nocheinmal dieses Argument: Thomas übernimmt es fast wörtlich der Rede Augustins an seinen Sohn Adeodatus: Ein Schüler ist von seinem Lehrer nur dann wirklich belehrt worden, wenn er selber zustimmend erklären kann, er habe erkannt, daß das vom Lehrer Gesagte wahr sei. Wenn er diese Zustimmung geben kann, dann heißt das aber, daß er sie auch hätte geben können ehe der Lehrer zu ihm sprach, daß er, anders gesagt, die Erkenntnis nicht aus den Worten des Lehrers sondern aus der eigenen inneren Einsicht schöpft[11].

„Certainly Augustine was the last person to deny that words are useful. So great a master of their employment was unlikely to think they played no part[12]." Gerade als Meister des Wortes wußte Augustinus aber auch, wie mißverständlich Worte sein können. Je höher die Wirklichkeit steht, von der zu sprechen ist, desto schmerzlicher wird die Unadäquatheit des Wortes empfunden. Augustinus betont nicht deshalb so stark die Ohnmacht des menschlichen Lehrers, weil er ein Skeptiker wäre, sondern weil er von der Aufgabe des Lehrens eine so hohe Auffassung hat. Aus den augustinischen Einwänden, die Thomas referiert, läßt sich ein beeindruckendes Bild von der Gestalt des Lehrers zeichnen. Aufgabe des Lehrers ist es, die Wahrheit zu lehren (9. Einwand). Dazu genügen die Zeichen nicht. Lehren heißt nicht, die Regeln eines Sprachspieles zu vermitteln, auch nicht, ein Begriffssystem einzupauken. Lehren, wie Augustinus es sieht, zielt auf Wissen ab, Wissen (*scientia*) aber heisst nicht nur Meinen (*opinio*) oder Dafürhalten (*credulitas*), sondern Gewißheit (*certitudo*)[13]. Gewißheit über die Wahrheit der Dinge, und nicht bloß Meinungen über das, was andere reden: das soll der Lehrer vermitteln. Augustinus bezweifelt nicht, daß solches Lehren möglich ist, er wagt es nur nicht, diese Aufgabe einem Menschen zuzuweisen: Gott alleine kann den Menschen wahrhaft lehren.

---

[11] Augustins Argumente, auf die Thomas sich bezieht, finden sich in *De magistro*, x. 29 (PL 32, 1212), für den 2. Einwand; XI. 36 (PL 32, 1215), für den 4. Einwand; XII, 40 (PL 32, 1217), für den 18. Einwand.

[12] H. Chadwick, op. cit. 48.

[13] *De magistro*, XII 40 (PL 32, 1217); vgl. 13. Einwand.

2. *Warum der hl. Thomas den hl. Augustinus nicht kritisiert hat*

Liest man nach all den Einwänden die „magistrale" *responsio* des ersten Artikels unserer *quaestio* De magistro, so ist man überrascht, festzustellen, daß der hl. Augustinus mit keinem Wort erwähnt wird, obwohl doch die meisten Einwände sich ausdrücklich auf seine Lehren beziehen. Statt dessen wird Avicenna genannt und ausführlich widerlegt. Augustinus scheint, den Einwänden zufolge, Gott allein als Lehrer gelten zu lassen, da Gott alleine den Menschen innerlich mit dem Licht der Wahrheit erleuchten kann, ohne das keine gewisse Erkenntnis möglich ist. Ohne Augustinus nochmals zu erwähnen bringt Thomas nun in seiner eigenen Antwort die Argumente gegen die Möglichkeit eines menschlichen Lehrers auf einen einzigen Nenner: eine Metaphysik, die für Zweitursachen keinen Raum läßt und die vor allem mit dem Namen Avicenna in Verbindung gebracht wird. Erst in den Antworten auf die Einwände wird Augustinus wieder genannt, ohne ein Wort der Kritik.

Diese rein äußerliche Beobachtung bietet noch mehr Anlaß zur Verwunderung, wenn wir uns daran erinnern, daß die Frage über den Lehrer vor allem eine Debatte über die Illuminationslehre des hl. Augustinus darstellt. Man kann sich gut vorstellen, in welch gespanntem Klima die Einwände aus Augustinus in der Debatte mit „magister" Thomas vorgebracht wurden, der als der führende Vertreter der nicht unumstrittenen Aristotelesrezeption galt. Nun wurde der Streit zwischen augustinischer Tradition und neuer Aristotelesrezeption gerade und besonders im Bereich der Erkenntnislehre ausgetragen. Kommt die Gewißheit unserer Erkenntnis immer unmittelbar von Gott? Welche Rolle kann die Sinnestätigkeit im Erkenntnisprozeß spielen? Trügen uns die Sinne und spricht nur Gott im Inneren uns die Wahrheit zu? Oder geben uns die Sinne zuverlässige Kunde von der Wirklichkeit? Welche Rolle kommt dem menschlichen Geist zu? Ist er der Erleuchtung Gottes gegenüber rein empfangend? Ist er es den Sinnen gegenüber? Oder ist er auch selber tätiger, hervorbringender Geist, „intellectus agens"?

Augustinus oder Aristoteles, so scheint bei vielen die Alternative gelautet zu haben, und da Thomas den Ruf eines Aristotelikers hatte, war, nach den damals (und heute noch?) gängigen Vorurteilen, zu erwarten, daß er gegen Augustins Illuminationslehre und für

Aristoteles' Abstraktionslehre Stellung nehmen werde. Warum hat
er es nicht getan? Eine naheliegende Antwort, die oft zu hören ist,
besagt, er habe dies aus taktischen Gründen getan. Es sei zu gefähr-
lich gewesen, offen Augustinus, die größte christliche Lehrautorität, zu kritisieren. So habe Thomas seine Kritik hinter einer Kritik
an dem Mohamedaner Avicenna versteckt, von Augustinus aber
eine „pie interpretatio" gegeben. Diese These ist unseres Erachtens
völlig unglaubwürdig. Thomas ist so wenig Taktiker, für ihn ist die
schlichte, unverstellte Wahrheitsfrage so unbedingt und ausschließlich im Vordergrund, daß solche Überlegungen nicht der Grund
dafür sein können, daß Thomas Augustinus nicht kritisiert hat.

Sehr viel glaubwürdiger ist die These von E. Gilson[14], Thomas
habe den „augustinisme avicennisant" seiner Zeit kritisiert, das
heißt jene weitverbreitete Schulrichtung, die Augustins Illuminationslehre mit Avicennas Aristotelesinterpretation verband und den
„intellectus agens separatus" des Avicenna mit dem „magister interior" Augustins gleichsetzte, mit der Folge, daß nun Augustins Illumination des menschlichen Geistes durch die göttliche Wahrheit
identifiziert wurde mit Avicennas „dator formarum", sodaß nun —
was Augustinus nie behauptet hatte — die „formae intelligibiles",
die unser Erkennen ausmachen, direkt von Gott unserem Geist
eingegossen werden. Nach Gilson wollte Thomas Augustinus
gegenüber diesem hybriden Augustinismus verteidigen, der sich für
authentisch augustinisch hielt: „Ayant désolidarisé saint Augustin
d'avec Avicenne, saint Thomas devait éprouver l'impression d'être
moins éloigné de l'augustinisme véritable que de celui de ses propres
contemporains[15]." Worum es geht, wird wohl deutlicher werden,
wenn wir uns nun der inhaltlichen Seite der thomasischen Antwort
zuwenden.

---

[14] Vgl. É. Gilson, op. cit. Der Titel ist irreführend, da Gilsons Studie eigentlich zu
dem Resultat kommt, daß Thomas Augustinus nicht kritisiert hat. Die bekannten
Texte, in denen Thomas vom Platonismus des hl. Augustinus spricht, sind offensichtlich nicht als Kritik formuliert: De spiritualibus creaturis, a. 10, ad 8 („Augustinus autem Platonem secutus quantum fides catholica patiebatur...": Thomas geht es
hier ausdrücklich darum, „ut profundius intentionem Augustini scrutemur");
Summa theologica, I^a, q. 84, a. 5 („Augustinus, qui doctrinis Platonicorum imbutus
fuerat, si qua invenit fidei accommoda in eorum dictis, assumpsit: quae vero invenit
fidei nostrae aversa, in melius commutavit"). Gilson scheint uns, *salva reverentia*,
dann doch eine zu große Kluft zwischen Augustinus und Thomas zu behaupten, und
dies wohl deshalb, weil er beide zu sehr als Philosophen und zu wenig als Theologen
sieht. Beide betreiben Philosophie a l s Theologen!
[15] É. Gilson, op. cit. 118.

3. *Alles kommt von Gott, auch das Wirken der Geschöpfe*

Die Lektüre der Antwort des hl. Thomas überrascht. Die Diskussion geht über den Lehrer und das Lernen. Thomas aber spricht von den höchsten metaphysischen Gründen. Wer Thomas liest, stellt immer wieder fest, daß er ein Problem löst, indem er es ins Licht der höchsten Seinsprinzipien stellt. So auch hier! Die Frage lautet ja: Kann ein Mensch einen anderen lehren oder kann das nur Gott? Thomas stellt also diese konkrete Frage in den denkbar weitesten Rahmen: wie verhalten sich göttliches und geschöpfliches Wirken?

Es klingt sehr „fromm", wenn Gott alles, dem Geschöpf kein Wirken zugesprochen wird. Thomas hat unentwegt diese scheinbare Frömmigkeit entlarvt[16] und ihr die wahre Größe Gottes und seiner Schöpfung entgegengehalten. Zwei Formen kann diese Sicht der Alleinwirksamkeit Gottes annehmen. Gilson nennt sie den „extrinsécisme intégral" und den „intrinsécisme intégral[17]", der erste, den Thomas in unserem Text mit dem Namen Avicenna verbindet, läßt alle Formen von außen, von oben kommen, nicht nur in der Erkenntnisordnung, sondern auch in der Seins- und Handlungsordnung: der zweite, den Thomas hier anonym referiert, sieht alle Seinsformen als in der Materie latent enthalten, alle Tugendhabitus als der Seele angeboren, alle Ideen als dem Denken eingeboren. Im ersten Falle verleiht Gott unmittelbar in jedem Augenblick neu alle Wesensformen, alle Tugendhabitus und alle Erkenntnisse: im zweiten Falle hat er sie ein für allemal in die Materie beziehungsweise in die Seele gelegt. Im ersten Fall ist Erkennen ein Zufluß des Wissens aus Gott, im zweiten Fall ist Erkennen Wiedererinnern[17]. Beiden Systemen ist gemeinsam, daß sie den Zweitursachen kein eigenes Wirken zusprechen. Im ersten Fall kommt ihnen nur die Rolle zu, das Wirken der Erstursache vorzubereiten, im zweiten Fall können sie höchstens Hindernisse beseitigen, die das Hervortreten der latenten Formen hemmen.

Die Leugnung der Eigentätigkeit der Zweitursachen hat schwerwiegende Konsequenzen. In der Summa contra gentiles (III, 69) hat Thomas diese Konsequenzen nachgezeichnet. Drei seien

---

[16] Ein berühmtes Beispiel ist seine Ablehnung der Lehre des Petrus Lombardus, daß die Liebe in den Geschöpfen der Hl. Geist selber sei: „Si quis recte consideret, hoc magis redundat in caritatis detrimentum", da die Liebe hier nicht mehr ein Akt des Menschen wäre (Summa theologica, II^a II^{ae}, q. 23, a. 2).

[17] É. Gilson, op. cit. 44.

hier kurz erwähnt. 1. Die Evidenz der Erfahrung spricht dafür, daß es ein je eigenes Wirken der verschiedenen Kreaturen gibt. Feuer bewirkt Feuer; ein Mensch zeugt einen anderen Menschen. Jedem Geschöpf kommt ein unverwechselbar eigenes Wirken zu. Wenn wir Gott in allem die Erstursache zuzusprechen haben, so doch nicht in der Weise, daß die Eigenwirksamkeit der Geschöpfe aufgehoben würde. 2. Gäbe es nicht das je eigene Tätigsein der Geschöpfe, so könnte es keine Wissenschaft geben, denn wir können die Ursachen nur durch ihre Wirkungen erkennen. Hätten die Geschöpfe keine e i g e n e, sie selber bezeichnende und bekundende Wirksamkeit, so gäbe es auch keine Kenntnis von ihnen. 3. Die schwerwiegendste Konsequenz bezieht sich aber auf das Gottesbild, das hinter der Leugnung der Zweitursachen steht: „Detrahere perfectioni creaturarum est detrahere perfectioni divinae virtutis." Wer Gott groß zu machen glaubt, indem er alles ihm und nichts den Kreaturen zuweist, der verkennt die wahre Größe und Weisheit Gottes. Wenn Gott, der reiner Akt ist, etwas schafft, so gibt er an seiner Wirklichkeit Anteil. „Wenn er anderen seine Ähnlichkeit (*similitudinem*) hinsichtlich des Seins mitteilt, indem er die Dinge ins Sein hervorbringt, so ist es nur folgerichtig, daß er ihnen auch seine Ähnlichkeit hinsichtlich des Wirkens (*quantum ad agere*) mitteilt, sodaß auch die geschaffenen Dinge ihre eigene Wirksamkeit (*proprias actiones*) haben." Soweit der Text aus der Summa contra gentiles.

Das zentrale Argument in der *responsio* unseres 1. Artikels in De magistro greift diesen letztgenannten Gedanken auf und führt ihn noch ein Stück weiter. Werden alle Wirkungen im geschöpflichen Bereich alleine der Erstursache zugesprochen, so wird damit die Schöpfungsordnung zerstört, die „aus der Ordnung und dem Zusammenhang der Ursachen gewoben wird (*ordine et connexione causarum contexitur*)" (239). Diese Schöpfungsordnung hat aber ihren Ursprung in der unfaßlichen Güte der ersten Ursache: „prima causa ex eminentia bonitatis suae rebus aliis confert non solum quod sint sed et quod causae sint" (240—242). Gott gibt den Dingen nicht nur ihr Sein, sondern auch das diesem Sein gemäße Wirken. Gerade d a r i n zeigt sich die Überfülle des Wirkens der Erstursache, daß sie Zweitursachen das Wirken gibt. Beide scheinbar so theozentrischen Richtungen, der Extrinsezismus und der Intrinsezismus, sind nicht theozentrisch genug. Sie wollen Gott a l l e s zuschreiben, wagen es aber nicht, ihm auch das zuzuschreiben, daß er seinen Geschöpfen das eigene Wirken gibt.

Hier stößt unser Denken freilich an eine Grenze, genauer unsere Vorstellungskraft. Wie sollen wir uns vorstellen, daß — um zu unserem Thema zurückzukommen — Gott alleine unser Lehrer ist, und doch wirklicher Raum für das Lehren menschlicher Lehrer vorhanden ist? Ehe wir uns dieser Frage zuwenden, sei noch einmal ein Text aus der Summa contra gentiles herangezogen. Er schließt unmittelbar an den zuvor zitierten an (III, 70): „Manchen scheint es schwer verständlich (*difficile ad intelligendum*) zu sein, daß die natürlichen Wirkungen Gott und dem Geschöpf (*naturali agenti*) zugesprochen werden", so beginnt Thomas. Wenn Gott, die Erstursache, all es wirkt, wozu noch Zweitursachen? Was bliebe diesen noch zu tun übrig? Der Einwand trifft nur scheinbar! Wir stellen uns die geschöpflichen Wirkenden meist isoliert vor. In Wirklichkeit gibt es, wie wir sahen, Einzelwirkendes immer nur in einer Gesamtordnung, die aus der Zuordnung und der Verbindung der Ursachen (*ordine et connexione causarum*) gewoben wird. Keine Ursache wirkt alleine. Vielmehr wirkt jede Ursache aus eigener Kraft, aber auch kraft all der anderen, höheren Ursachen, deren Wirken mit hereinspielt, wobei beide Wirkungen, die eigene und die der höheren Ursachen, unmittelbar sind, auf je eigene Weise: „So ist es auch nicht ungeziemend (*inconveniens*), daß dieselbe Wirkung von einem Geschöpf (*ab inferiori agente*) und von Gott hervorgebracht wird, und zwar von beiden unmittelbar (*ab utroque immediate*), wenn auch auf je eigene Weise." Thomas präzisiert: wir dürfen uns dies nicht so vorstellen, daß ein T e i l von Gott, ein T e i l vom Geschöpf gewirkt werden, sondern „die ganze Wirkung wird von beiden hervorgebracht, auf je verschiedene Weise, wie dieselbe Wirkung g a n z dem Werkzeug und auch g a n z dem Gebraucher des Werkzeugs zugesprochen wird"[18].

Dieser lange Weg über die Frage des Verhältnisses von Erstursache

---

[18] Summa contra gentiles, III, 70, ad fin.: „Non sic idem effectus causae naturali et divinae virtuti attribuitur, quasi partim a Deo, partim a naturali agente fiat, sed totus ab utroque secundum alium modum, sicut idem effectus totus attribuitur instrumento, et principali agenti etiam totus." Man darf hier nicht übersehen, daß das „sicut" nicht univok, sondern analog zu verstehen ist. Der Vergleich bezieht sich nur darauf, daß b e i d e, das Instrument und sein Gebraucher, g a n z wirken: er besagt dagegen nicht, daß etwa Gott die menschliche Freiheit gebrauche wie ein Handwerker sein Werkzeug. Um diesem möglichen Mißverständnis des Vergleichs entgegenzuwirken hat Thomas den Begriff des „instrumentum" gelegentlich

sache und Zweitursache hat uns nur scheinbar vom Thema weggeführt. Augustinus betrachtet in seinem Dialog De magistro staunend das Wirken des „magister interior", der das Licht ist, „das jeden Menschen erleuchtet, der in die Welt kommt" (Joh. 1, 9). Die Illuminationslehre, die in diesem Dialog zum ersten Mal klar thematisiert wurde, tritt zur Zeit des hl. Thomas nicht mehr in ihrer ursprünglichen Gestalt auf. Nach Gilsons Darlegungen erscheint sie im 13. Jahrhundert amalgamiert mit einem mohamedanisch geprägten Aristotelismus, der Gottes Alleinwirksamkeit unter mehr oder weniger vollständigem Ausschluß aller geschöpflichen Zweitursachen lehrt. Wo immer Thomas dieser verkürzenden Sicht begegnet, scheut er keine Mühe, sie zu widerlegen. Thomas ist überzeugt davon, daß Augustinus einen solchen Ausschluß der Eigenwirksamkeit der Geschöpfe nie gelehrt hat. In der Antwort auf den 8. Einwand des 1. Artikels sagt er es ausdrücklich: „Augustinus in libro De magistro per hoc quod probat solum Deum docere non intendit excludere quin homo exterius doceat, sed quod ipse solus Deus docet interius" (429—433).

Ist das ein „reverenter exponere", eine „pia interpretatio"? Thomas wird selber in aller Klarheit sagen: „Gott alleine ist es, der innerlich und hauptsächlich (*interius et principaliter*) lehrt...; dennoch wird vom Menschen im eigentlichen Sinne (*proprie*) gesagt, daß er lehre" (359—362). Wie kommt Thomas zu dieser Schlußfolgerung am Ende seiner „responsio" im ersten Artikel?

4. Vom Lernenden zum Lehrer

Beide Wege, der „extrinsécisme intégral" und der „intrinsécisme intégral", haben gemeinsam, daß sie den Zweitursachen nicht den ihnen gebührenden Raum geben. Wie sieht nun die „via media" aus, die Thomas bei Aristoteles zu finden meint, und der man in allen drei genannten Bereichen, in der Seinslehre, in der Ethik und in der Erkenntnislehre, folgen soll? Man könnte bei Thomas von einem „gemäßigten Intrinsezismus sprechen". „Die Naturformen existieren sehr wohl im voraus in der Materie, aber nicht aktuell (*in actu*), sondern nur potentiell", und es ist nicht alleine das Werk der

differenziert (vgl. Summa theologica, III^a, q. 7, a. 1, ad 3: „instrumentum animatum...quod ita agit quod etiam agitur"; De veritate, q. 24, a. 1, ad 5: „ab instrumento non oportet quod omnino excludatur ratio libertatis; quia aliquid potest esse ab alio motum, quod tamen seipsum movet: et ita est de mente humana").

Erstursache, daß sie vom potenziellen ins aktuelle Sein geführt werden, sondern auch das Werk der entsprechenden Zweitursachen. Nicht anders ist es im Bereich der Ethik. Noch ehe sie ihre vollverwirklichte Gestalt erreichen präexistieren die Tugenden in uns, und zwar in der Weise von gewissen natürlichen Neigungen (*in quibusdam naturalibus inclinationibus*), die eine Art „Tugend im Ansatz" (*quaedam virtutum inchoationes*) darstellen. Um aber zur Vollgestalt wirklicher Tugenden zu werden, müssen sie tatsächlich ins Werk gesetzt werden (251—264).

Was nun das Lernen betrifft, das heißt das Erwerben von Wissen, so gibt es auch hier im Menschen angelegte Vorgaben, die Thomas als „Wissenssamen" (*scientiarum semina*) bezeichnet. Thomas hat für diese „Wissenssamen" die verschiedensten Namen. Alleine in der *responsio* unseres 1. Artikels finden wir nicht weniger als sechs: „primae conceptiones intellectus" (267); „principia universalia" (273); „universales cognitiones" (275 f.); „principia communia per se nota" (326 f.); „principia innata" (347); oder einfach „principia" (354). Häufig spricht Thomas auch von den „prima principia". In ihnen ist alles Wissen einbeschlossen wie „in quibusdam rationibus seminalibus" (274 f.). Lernen heißt nichts anderes als das, was in diesen „rationes seminales" potentiell enthalten ist, in ein aktuelles Wissen überzuführen (275—279).

Aufs erste gesehen nimmt der hl. Thomas hier eine Position ein, die dem „intrinsécisme intégral" kaum nachzustehen scheint. Lernen scheint hier eher im platonischen Sinne als Erinnern verstanden zu sein. Die entscheidende, aber auch besonders schwierige, Frage ist daher, welcher Art die „scientiarum semina" sind, die „principia universalia", in denen alles Folgende samenartig enthalten ist. Handelt es sich um wirkliche Wissensinhalte oder um bloße Funktionsgesetze unseres Geistes? Von der Antwort auf diese Frage hängt es ab, ob der Lehrer wirklich lehren kann oder ob er nur den Anlaß bietet, daß das latente Wissen des Schülers ans Licht kommt.

Um einer Antwort näher zu kommen, klärt Thomas den Begriff des „in potentia praeexistere" (281). Etwas kann ja in einem doppelten Sinne potentiell existieren: als aktive oder als passive Möglichkeit. Eine aktive Möglichkeit („potentia activa completa") trägt in sich selber die ausreichende Kraft, Wirklichkeit zu werden. Als Beispiel nennt Thomas das Gesundwerden (*sanatio*). Im Kranken muß die aktive Möglichkeit zur Genesung vorhanden sein, damit er wirklich wieder gesund werden kann. Eine rein passive Möglichkeit genügt dazu nicht, weil sie nicht in sich selber das Prinzip der Verwirklichung trägt. Holz kann brennen, aber nicht aus sich selber. Ohne äußere Einwirkung entflammt sich das brennbare Holz nicht. Anders im Genesungsprozeß: äußere Wirkfaktoren (der Arzt, die Medikamente) können die aktive Gesundheitspotenz fördern, unterstützen, mehr nicht. Die aktive Potenz ist hier die eigentliche Wirkkraft, denn nicht Arzt und Medizin heilen den Kranken, sondern seine eigene Natur, mit oder ohne Unterstützung von außen (280—303).

Ähnlich liegen nun für den Aquinaten die Verhältnisse beim Lehrer. Das Wissen, das im Menschen „keimhaft", als „scientiarum semina" (266 f.) vorausexistiert, ist nicht eine rein passive Möglichkeit, sondern eine „potentia activa"! Die Begründung dafür, daß wir in den in uns vorhandenen Wissenskeimen die innere, hinreichende Kraft besitzen, zum wirklichen Wissen zu kommen, sieht Thomas darin, daß wir s e l b e r Wissen erwerben können (305 f.) wenn unser Verstand s e l b e r zu Erkenntnissen gelangt, so nennen wir das „Entdeckung" (*inventio*), wenn er dazu vermittels äußere Hilfen kommt, so nennen wir das „Unterweisung" (*disciplina*). Di „Lernkraft" ist, wie die Genesungskraft, eine innere Fähigkeit de menschlichen Natur. Wie der Arzt kann auch der Lehrer nicht meh tun als der Natur zu ihrer „Selbstverwirklichung" zu helfen (306— 314). Die Heilkunst wie die Lehrkunst können nur die Natu nachahmen. Der Lehrer führt auf keinem anderen Weg zum Wisse als auf dem, über den der Lernende aus eigener Kraft das Wisse findet (315—324).

Der Vergleich des Lehrers mit dem Arzt lenkt den Blick vorers vom Lehrer weg. Er ist nur Helfer, Diener der Natur („ministe naturae", 296), die Natur wirkt im Lernvorgang hauptsächlic (*principaliter operatur*, 296): sie, das heißt der Lernende selbs Aus der Frage nach dem Lehrer wurde die Frage nach dem Ler nenden. Thomas wird deshalb auch zurecht den Lehrer zuers selber als Lernenden betrachten: wie kommt er selber zum Wisse wie entdeckt er selber, was er dann andere lehrt? Damit sind w aber wieder bei der Frage nach den „Wissenskeimen". Wie komm Wissen zustande? Wieweit ist Wissen „angeboren", wieweit erwo ben?

Gegen die Angeborenheit des Wissens spricht die schlichte Erfah rungstatsache, daß wir vieles nicht wissen und meist nur mit Müh unsere Ignoranz in Wissen umwandeln können. Anderseits können wir nur Wissen erwerben, wenn wir schon „Inseln des Wissens" besitzen, von denen aus wir Unbekanntes verstehen können. Diese müssen uns immer schon verfügbar sein, damit wir überhaupt erkennend nach Neuem ausgreifen können. Sie sind daher nicht erworben, sondern „angeboren", sie gehören zu uns wie wir selber uns gehören. Was aber wissen wir mit ihnen? Welcher Art ist dieses „samenhafte Wissen", ohne das wir keine Lernenden sein können, das wir aber selber nicht zuvor erlernt haben?

5. *Was wir beim Lernen wissen, ohne es gelernt zu haben*

Wir kommen zum Herzstück der thomasischen Lehre vom Lehrer: seine Lehre von den „prima principia". Wie wir schon weiter oben sahen, ist die Terminologie des hl. Thomas hier erstaunlich vielfältig und beweglich. Dies liegt wohl nicht an einem Mangel an begrifflicher Schärfe, sondern an der Schwierigkeit, das, worum es sich handelt, auf einen Nenner zu bringen. Die Lehre von den „prima principia" ist der originellste Beitrag des hl. Thomas zur Frage De magistro, sie nimmt unseres Erachtens in den Darstellungen der thomasischen Erkenntnislehre nicht den Platz ein, der ihr gebührt.

Erkenntnis gibt es nur „im Licht dieser ersten Prinzipien". Anderseits aber gilt, daß alle Erkenntnis von den Sinnen ausgeht. Wie vermittelt Thomas diese beiden Gesichtspunkte, die „Präexistenz" der allgemeinen Prinzipien des Erkennens und die Sinnenorientiertheit des Erkennens? In unserem Text erklärt Thomas dieses Verhältnis wie folgt: diese „primae conceptiones intellectus" erkennen wir s o g l e i c h im Licht der tätigen Vernunft durch die von den Sinnendingen abstrahierten Bilder („statim lumine intellectus agentis cognoscuntur per species a sensilibus abstractas", 268 f.). Das Erkennen der „Wissenskeime", der „prima principia", ist, so verstehen wir diesen Text, nichts anderes als das, was i m m e r geschieht, wenn wir w i r k l i c h erkennen: das Erkennen der „prima principia" ist nichts anderes als das wirkliche „Erkennbarwerden" der von den Sinnen empfangenen Bilder. In einem Text, der ein Jahr jünger ist als unsere *quaestio* De magistro, sagt Thomas das ausdrücklich: Die „prima principia", die wir nicht zu lernen noch zu entdecken brauchen, die uns vielmehr natürlicherweise bekannt sind, „werden dem Menschen offenkundig durch das Licht der tätigen Vernunft, durch welches uns nur insofern etwas offenkundig wird, als durch es (sc. dieses Licht) die Sinnenbilder zu wirklich Erkanntem werden. Das nämlich ist die Tätigkeit des tätigen Verstandes[19]."

Was aber ist dieses Wissen der ersten Prinzipien, das in jedem wirklichen Erkennen aufleuchtet? Es sind jene ersten und unableitbaren Grundsätze des Erkennens und des Seins, die in jedem Erkennen miterkannt und auch mitbejaht sein müssen, wenn es ein wirkliches Erkennen geben soll. Thomas nennt diese Erkenntnisprinzipien „dignitates", „axiomata", „conceptiones communes"[20]. Ihr Oberstes ist das „Nichtwiderspruchsprinzip": „Quod non est simul affirmare et negare." Auf diesem Prinzip beruhen alle anderen[21]. Dieses Prinzip ist unmittelbar einleuchtend, es ist unbeweisbar, da nicht nocheinmal begründbar, sondern vielmehr der Grund aller Begründungen, man kann es zwar verbal in Frage stellen, kann ihm aber nicht „interiori ratione" widersprechen[22], „niemand kann sein Gegenteil denken"[23], jeder, der etwas lernen will, muß ihm zustimmen[24].

Dieses Zustimmenmüssen ist freilich kein äußerer Zwang. Die Erkenntnisprinzipien beruhen auf den Seinsprinzipien[25]. Die Zustimmung zu den Ersteren ist immer schon eine Bejahung der Letzteren. Wir können gar nichts erkennen ohne zugleich das Sein mitzuerkennen und zu bejahen[26]. Alles, was wir erkennen, erkennen wir zugleich als Seiendes in allen seinen transzendentalen Eigenschaften, als *ens, unum, verum, bonum*.

Was bisher sehr abstrakt formuliert wurde, wird sofort anschau-

---

[19] In Boëtium de Trinitate, q. 6, a. 4 corp.: „... manifestantur ex lumine intellectus agentis,... quo quidem lumine nihil manifestatur nobis, nisi in quantum per ipsum phantasmata fiunt intelligibilia in actu. Hic est enim actus intellectus agentis."

[20] Vgl. dazu P. Wilpert, op. cit.

[21] Summa theologica, I[a] II[ae], q. 94, a. 2; In post. anal., I, Lect. v, n. 6: „affirmatio et negatio non sunt simul vera, cuius contrarium nullus mente credere potest etsi ore proferat"; In post. anal., I. lect. xix, n. 3: „... principium notissimum, quod non contingat idem esse et non esse".

[22] In Post Anal., I, lect. xix, n. 3: „Quaedam autem adeo vera sunt, quod eorum opposita intellectu capi non possunt; et ideo interiori ratione eis obviari non potest, sed solum exteriori, quae est per vocem."

[23] Ibid., n. 2: „Nullus potest opinari contraria eorum"; weitere Stellen bei P. Wilpert, op. cit. 168, Anm. 133.

[24] In Post. Anal., I, lect. v, n. 6: „maxima propositio, quam necesse est habere in mente et ei assentire quemlibet qui doceri debet".

[25] „Fundatur supra rationem entis et non entis" (Summa theologica, I[a] II[ae], q. 94, a. 2).

[26] „Illud quod prima cadit in apprehensione est ens, cuius intellectus includitur in omnibus quaecumque quis apprehendit" (ibid.).

lich, wenn wir die Anwendung auf unsere Frage nach dem Lehrer betrachten. Die „prima principia" sind nicht abstrakte Schemata, sondern sie sind jener i n n e r e M a ß s t a b, der uns nicht erst anerzogen werden muß, sondern den wir „angeboren" in uns tragen, und der mit unserer menschlichen Natur selber mitgegeben ist: er ist nichts anderes als d a s L i c h t u n s e r e r V e r n u n f t, das uns von Gott geschenkt wurde a l s e i n A b b i l d d e r u n g e s c h a f f e n e n W a h r h e i t i n u n s[27] und mit dem wir alle die vielen Botschaften, die unsere Sinne empfangen, erst entschlüsseln und beurteilen können. Wenn auch unser Lernen von der Sinneswahrnehmung und der Erfahrung ausgeht, so besteht es doch nicht in diesen. Wir lernen nur indem wir den Maßstab der Wahrheit anwenden, der uns in unserer Vernunft gegeben ist. Durch diesen Maßstab ist Gott selber unser „magister interior"[28].

Wie nahe Thomas in seiner Auffassung vom „inneren Lehrer" bei der Sicht des hl. Augustinus bleibt, zeigt seine Antwort auf den ersten Einwand, daß die Schrift es verbiete, einen anderen als den Herrn selber „Lehrer" zu nennen. Thomas macht deutlich, daß hinter diesem Einwand nicht nur ein falsches Autoritätsverständnis der „magistri" steht (das Magisterium als „honor", nicht als „ministerium"), sondern auch eine unreife Haltung der Studenten. Der Herr verbiete nicht einfach den Lehrertitel, sondern daß wir unsere ganze Hoffnung auf Menschenweisheit bauen, anstatt das, was wir von Menschen hören, am Maßstab der göttlichen Wahrheit zu messen, die in uns selber spricht, da uns ihr Abbild (in unserer Vernunft) eingeprägt ist und wir daher a l l e s selber beurteilen können[29].

Augustins Lehre vom i n n e r e n L e h r e r, dessen Erleuchtung erst jedem Erkennen die Gewißheit der Wahrheit gibt, und Thomas' Lehre von der menschlichen Vernunft und den „eingegossenen" ersten Prinzipien als Teilhabe am Licht der göttlichen Wahrheit

---

[27] „Huiusmodi autem rationis lumen, quo principia huiusmodi nobis sunt nota, est nobis a Deo inditum quasi quaedam similitudo increatae veritatis in nobis resultans" (De magistro, a. 1, corp., 353—356).

[28] Vgl. De veritate, q. 1, a. 4, ad 5: „A veritate intellectus divini exemplariter procedit in intellectum nostrum veritas primorum principiorum secundum quam de omnibus iudicamus. Et quia per eam non iudicare possumus nisi secondum quod est similitudo primae veritatis, ideo secundum primam veritatem de omnibus iudicamus".

[29] De magistro, q. 1, ad 1 (363—374): „... de his quae ab homine audimus divinam veritatem consulentes quae in nobis loquitur per suae similitudinis impressionem qua de omnibus possumus iudicare".

kommen im Entscheidenden überein: daß Gott allein der innere und hauptsächliche Lehrer ist (359 f.). Thomas sieht zwischen seiner Lehre und der des hl. Augustinus keinen wesentlichen Unterschied. Er sagt es ausdrücklich: „Non multum autem refert dicere, quod ipsa intelligibilia participantur a Deo, vel quod lumen faciens intelligibilia participetur"[30]: beiden Sichten ist das Wissen gemeinsam, daß Erkennen immer nur möglich ist im Licht der göttlichen Urwahrheit, ob diese uns nun durch die Gabe der geistigen Erkenntnisformen oder durch das Geschenk des Lichtes des „intellectus agens" erleuchtet. Beiden ist die hohe Auffassung von der geistigen Natur unseres Erkennens gemeinsam, und damit auch die höchst anspruchsvolle Sicht des Lehrers. Thomas unterscheidet sich also nach seinem eigenen Zeugnis von Augustinus nicht in der „intentio profundior"[31] der Illuminationslehre. Mit seiner Lehre vom Licht des „intellectus agens" und dem Wahrheitsmaß der „prima principia" hat er freilich dem Wirken der Zweitursachen, der Rolle des menschlichen Lehrers, ein deutlicheres Profil geben können. Das wird besonders deutlich in seiner im Vergleich zu Augustinus erheblich „optimistischeren" Sicht der Sprache im Lehrvorgang.

6. Der Lehrer und die Sprache

Augustins De magistro versteht sich selbst als eine schonungslose Entlarvung des „Unvermögens der menschlichen Lautsprache zur Vermittlung der Wahrheit"[32]. „Was ist denn Wissen? Doch nicht, was sich ein Lehrer denkt. Was ist denn Wahrheit? Doch nicht, was ein Lehrer sagt. Was ist denn Glauben? Doch nicht, was ein Lehrer kraft seiner Autorität verlangt"[33]. Thomas stimmt mit Augustinus darin überein, daß die Gewißheit unseres Wissens nicht von den Sinnen alleine kommen kann. Die Frage ist nur: gehört die Sprache, das Instrument des Lehrers, ausschließlich in die Welt der (sinnlichen) Zeichen und damit in den Bereich, der kein sicheres Wissen vermitteln kann? Thomas stellt diese Frage in den weiteren Rahmen der Erkenntnislehre. Die Sprache ist ein Sonderfall sinnlicher Zeichen. Kann die Sprache uns keine Erkenntnis vermitteln, so gilt das

---

[30] De spiritualibus creaturis, a. 10, ad 8, ad fin.
[31] Ibid., ad 8.
[32] C. I. Perl, Vorwort zu Augustinus, Der Lehrer (Paderborn, 1974), s. xv.
[33] Ibid., S. xiv.

generell von allen sinnlichen Zeichen. Augustins „Sprachpessimismus" steht im größeren Zusammenhang seiner negativen Einschätzung der Rolle der Sinneswahrnehmung im Erkenntnisprozeß. Thomas' Lehre vom „intellectus agens" erlaubt es, mit einer Neubewertung der Sinneserkenntnis, die Rolle der Sprache, und damit des Lehrers, positiver zu fassen.

In der Antwort auf den 4. Einwand faßt Thomas diese Sicht knapp zusammen: „Aus den sinnlichen Zeichen, die in der Sinneskraft empfangen werden, schöpft die Vernunft die geistigen Gehalte (*intentiones intelligibiles*), mit deren Hilfe sie zum Wissen gelangt" (398—402). Thomas stimmt Augustinus insofern zu, daß nicht die Zeichen unser Wissen hervorbringen können. Er ist auch darin mit Augustinus einig, daß die Gewißheit des Wissens nicht von Außen, sondern nur von Innen kommen kann, und daß insofern der Lehrer nicht Quelle des Wissens sein kann:

Die Gewißheit des Wissens entspringt ganz der Gewißheit der Prinzipien: dann nämlich ist das Wissen der Schlußfolgerungen gewiß, wenn sie auf die Prinzipien zurückgeführt werden (506—510).

Daher stammt die Gewißheit des Wissens aus dem Licht der Vernunft, das Gott unserem Inneren eingegeben hat, und durch das Gott in uns spricht, nicht aber von einem äußerlich lehrenden Menschen (510—513)[34].

Soweit folgt der hl. Thomas der „intentio" des hl. Augustinus. Doch dann fügt er eine wichtige Einschränkung an:

... es sei denn, (der betreffende Lehrer) führe die Schlußfolgerungen (die er vorträgt) auf die (ersten) Prinzipien zurück. Daraus können wir freilich nur deshalb die Gewißheit des Wissens gewinnen, weil in uns die Gewißheit dieser Prinzipien ist, auf die die Schlußfolgerungen zurückgeführt werden" (513—517)[35].

Lernen ist letztlich nur möglich, weil wir in uns selber den Maßstab der Wahrheit tragen. Nur was wir selber an ihm gemessen haben, haben wir auch erkannt und somit erlernt. Hierein geht Thomas mit Augustinus einig. Er geht aber einen Schritt weiter. Damit dieses innere Richtmaß unseres Geistes „aktiv" werden

---

[34] „Et ideo hoc quod aliquid per certitudinem sciatur, est ex lumine rationis divinitus interius indito quo in nobis loquitur Deus, non autem ab homine exterius docente..."

[35] „... nisi quatenus conclusiones in principia resolvit nos docens, ex quo tamen nos certitudinem scientiae non acciperemus nisi inesset nobis certitudo principiorum in quae conclusiones resolvuntur"; vgl. auch die Antwort auf den 17. Einwand (543—549).

kann, damit wir also tatsächlich lernen, müssen wir suchend und fragend ausgreifen nach der Wirklichkeit, müssen das, was sich uns zeigt, seiner wirren Vielfalt entkleiden, es vergleichend und ordnend vereinfachen, die geistigen Gehalte („intentiones intelligibilies") aus der Fülle der Sinnenbilder „abstrahieren". In diesem Sinne heißt lernen nichts anderes als erkennen.

Was aber unser Geist der Wirklichkeit der Dinge gegenüber vermag, nämlich ihre Sinn- und Wahrheitsgehalte zu erfassen, das kann er auch den Worten eines anderen gegenüber, die ihn als sinnliche Zeichen erreichen: Wir können aus den Zeichen der gesprochenen oder geschriebenen Worte die Sinngehalte („intentiones intelligibiles") „schöpfen". Thomas sagt ausdrücklich: das Wort des Lehrers ist hier vergleichbar mit den Dingen der Wirklichkeit: aus beiden kann unser Geist das Wissen gewinnen (465—469)[36]. Kann er die Sprache der Wirklichkeit lesen, so auch die Sprache des Lehrers. In dieser Sicht bekommt nun aber der Lehrer eine überraschend große Bedeutung. Denn gegenüber dem eigenen Lernen an der wirren Vielfalt der Wirklichkeit hat das Lernen bei einem Lehrer einen unleugbaren Vorteil: Wenn wir selber durch Forschen und Entdecken, durch Ordnen und Bewerten mit dem eigenen „intellectus agens" unsere Erkenntnisse sammeln, so ist das ein langer und mühevoller Weg. Wir bringen zwar selber die Gewißheit der Wahrheitsregel der „prima principia" mit, doch garantiert uns das, wie die Erfahrung zeigt, noch nicht die richtigen Folgerungen, durch die erst Wissen zustande kommt. Das Wort des Lehrers hingegen bietet mir nicht erst ungeordnetes, ungesichtetes „Erkenntnismaterial", sondern bereits „gelungene" Erkenntnisse, geistige Sinngehalte („intentiones intelligibiles"), die ich sozusagen bereits fertig aus der Lehre des Lehrers schöpfen kann. Sie können mir als wahr und gut nur einleuchten, wenn ich sie im Licht der in mir sprechenden göttlichen Wahrheit als wahr und gut beurteile, ich kann sie aber bereits als geistige Erkenntnisformen („species intelligibiles") vom Lehrer empfangen.

Thomas setzt hier freilich ein Verständnis der Sprache voraus, das sich von Augustins De magistro unterscheidet. Die Sprache besteht zweifellos aus Zeichen (*signa*), die zur Sinnenwelt gehören und als solche nicht Erkenntnis vermitteln können. Doch sind sie noch

---

[36] „Unde ipsa verba doctoris audita, vel visa in scripto, hoc modo se habent ad causandum scientiam in intellectu sicut res quae sunt extra animam quia ex utrisque intellectus agens intentiones intelligibiles accipit."

mehr als sinnliche Zeichen: sie sind „signa intelligibilium intentionum"[37]. Die Sprache drückt das Denken aus, doch meint sie die Wirklichkeit. Die Sprache vermittelt daher erkannte Wirklichkeit. Die klare Sprache eines großen Lehrers fesselt uns deshalb, weil wir in den sinnlichen Zeichen seiner Rede ein klares geistiges Bild von der Wirklichkeit vermittelt bekommen, von der er zu uns spricht und die er selber schaut. Je klarer ein Lehrer denkt, je klarer er sein Denken ins Wort faßt, desto tiefer wird uns die „intentio intelligibilis" seiner Rede berühren, desto klarer wird sie im Licht unserer eigenen Erkenntnis uns „einleuchten". Thomas, dessen Rede nicht glanzvoll war, tat sich wohl leichter als Augustinus, in der Sprache jenes transparente Medium zu sehen, in dem wir einander die Einsichten unseres Geistes mitteilen können. Seine „realistische" Sicht der Sprache ist ein Hinweis auf seine eigene Art, den Dienst des Lehrers auszuüben. Dieser wenden wir uns abschließend zu.

7. Die „angeli doctores" und der „doctor angelicus"

Wer würde heute in einem Traktat über Lehren und Lernen die Frage erwarten, die Thomas in seinem De magistro (Artikel 3) stellt: „Ob der Mensch vom Engel belehrt werden kann"[38]? Daß Engel Menschen sichtbar erscheinen, zu ihnen sprechen, ihnen himmlische Botschaften bringen können, ist Thomas ebenso selbstverständlich wie der biblischen Welt. Als Leser und Kommentator des großen und geheimnisvollen Dionysius vom Areopag nimmt Thomas zudem an, daß die Engel ihrer lichten Natur entsprechend „Erleuchter" der Menschen sind. Doch welcher Art ist dieses Erleuchten? Diese Frage gibt Thomas die Gelegenheit, in didaktisch meisterhafter Art die Ergebnisse seiner bisherigen Darlegungen zusammenzufassen. Der Engel steht zwischen Gott und Mensch. Sein Einfluß ist also von dieser Mitte her zu ermessen. Er kann nicht, was Gott alleine vermag: dem Menschen in dem überragenden Sinne Lehrer sein, daß er ihm sowohl das Licht der Vernunft als

---

[37] Vgl. ad 14: „Homo exterius docens non influit lumen intelligibile sed est causa quodam modo speciei intelligibilis in quantum proponit nobis quaedam signa intelligibilium intentionum quas intellectus noster ab illis signis accipit et recondit in seipso" (518—524); vgl. auch ad 11: „Verba doctoris propinquius se habent ad causandum scientiam quam sensibilia extra animam existentia in quantum sunt signa intelligibilium intentionum" (469—473).

[38] „Utrum homo ab angelo doceri possit": Titel des 3. Artikels.

auch die „Wissenskeime", die „prima principia" schöpferisch ein-
stiftet (242—248). Er kann aber in gewisser Weise mehr als der
menschliche Lehrer: dieser kann das, was im Wissen der „prima
principia" implizit enthalten ist, durch seine Lehre in explizites
Wissen überführen. Dabei ist er aber auf die äußeren Sinneszeichen
der Sprache angewiesen. Der Engel kann dagegen in einem dem
Menschen nicht möglichen Sinne, „von innen" lehren, und zwar auf
zweifache Weise: durch die Bildung von bestimmten Bildern in der
Vorstellungskraft (*imaginatio*) des Menschen, etwa wenn in biblischen Berichten der Engel des Herrn im Traum erscheint (275—
289); vor allem aber dadurch, daß die Engel das natürliche Licht der
Vernunft in seiner Erkenntnistätigkeit stützen und stärken („lumen
infusum confortare ad perfectius inspiciendum"; 265—275).

Der Gedankengang wirkt heute befremdlich, und doch kommt in
ihm etwas vom tiefen Humanismus des Aquinaten zum Ausdruck:
der Engel lehrt den Menschen, das höhere Geschöpf hilft dem nied-
rigeren „lumen intellectus confortando" (ad 15; 417 f.), indem es
das Höchste des Menschen, die Tätigkeit seines eigenen Geistes,
stützt und stärkt. Thomas denkt sich das Lehren der Engel nicht als
eine Art Vermittlung fertigen Wissens, in der das höhere Geistes-
licht der Engel die Tätigkeit des menschlichen Geistes überflüssig
machen würde. Im Gegenteil: die Einstrahlung seines Geisteslichtes
in unseren Geist ermächtigt diesen, wirksamer s e l b e r zu wirken,
klarer s e l b e r zu erkennen[39].

In dieser Sicht kommt so etwas wie die G r u n d ü b e r z e u g u n g
des hl. Thomas zum Ausdruck: Je vollkommener ein „Einfluß",
desto vollständiger erweckt er die E i g e n a r t des Beeinflußten. Gott
ist im vollkommensten Sinne Lehrer nicht etwa dadurch, daß er uns
das eigene Lernen abnähme und uns ein fertiges Wissen eingösse,
sondern gerade dadurch, daß er uns in schöpferischer Souveränität
als solche geschaffen hat, die s e l b e r lernen können. Mit dem Licht
der Vernunft, mit dem Gott uns ausgestattet hat („ipsam animam
intellectuali lumine insignavit", 244), und mit den „Wissenskeimen" („seminaria scientiarum", 246), die er uns eingeprägt hat,
lehrt uns Gott, indem er uns lernfähig macht. Alle geschöpflichen
Lehrer, ob es die uns so fremd gewordenen Engel oder die
menschschlichen „magistri" sind, sind in dem Maße g u t e Lehrer,

---

[39] Art. 3, ad. 12 (388—390): „Per continuationem luminis eius [sc. angeli] cum
lumine intellectus nostri noster intellectus potest efficacius phantasmata illustrare".

als sie diesem Urbild des Lehrers nahe kommen, als sie zum e i g e-
n e n Lernen verhelfen.

Die gesamte E t h i k des hl. Thomas, die monumentale „Secunda
pars" der theologischen Summa, steht unter dem Vorzeichen der
Gottebenbildlichkeit des Menschen, deren höchstes Kennzeichen
die F r e i h e i t ist: daß der Mensch das „dominium sui actus", die
Herrschaft über sein Handeln hat[40]. Von dieser Schau des Menschen als Bild Gottes her durchzieht auch die thomasische Erkenntnislehre ein ethisches Motiv: nur wenn wir s e l b e r erkennen, wenn
Erkennen (und damit Lernen) u n s e r e i g e n e r Akt ist, ist er ein
wirklich menschlicher Akt; nur wenn wir s e l b e r erkennen, sind
wir auch s e l b e r für unser Tun verantwortlich.

In dieser Freiheitsperspektive sieht Thomas von Aquin auch die
Autorität des Lehrers. Und damit können wir versuchen, auf unsere
Anfangsfrage zu antworten: warum gerade Thomas von Aquin in
der katholischen Kirche eine solch hohe Lehrautorität zugesprochen wird. Der wahre Lehrer stellt gerade nicht seinen „honor",
seine „dignitas" als Lehrer in den Vordergrund, er wird nicht die
Schüler durch intellektuelles „Imponiergehabe" (K. Lorenz) oder
durch komplizierten Fachjargon beeindrucken wollen. Dadurch
würde er sie nur blenden und damit unmündig und unfrei machen.
Er kann dem Schüler nicht sein Wissen sozusagen „eintrichtern", er
kann nur helfen, daß der Schüler s e l b e r ein ähnliches Wissen
erwirbt wie er selber es erworben hat[41].

An den Lehrer richtet sich daher der Anspruch, nicht nur selbstlos die W a h r h e i t zu lehren, sondern sich selber selbstlos an die
Wahrheit hinzugeben. Er muß sich von ihr erfassen und leiten lassen. Gerade die Armut der Mendikanten, so argumentiert Thomas
im Bettlerordensstreit, hilft zu einer solchen Haltung[42]. Die Lehre
erfordert aber auch die *vita contemplativa*, denn „die Schau des
Lehrers ist der Ursprung der Lehre"[43]. Nur als einer, der von sich
selber weg und auf die Wahrheit hinschaut, wird der Lehrer auch
f r e i sein, frei von sich selber, frei, „das Geschaute anderen zu über-

---

[40] Vgl. den Prolog zur „Secunda pars"; vgl. auch Iᵃ, q. 29, a. 1 corp., wo die Person von der Freiheit her bestimmt wird.

[41] Der Lehrende könne nicht „transfundere scientiam in discipulum quasi illa
eadem numero scientia quae est in magistro in discipulo fiat", vielmehr gehe es
darum, daß „per doctrinam fit in discipulo scientia similis ei quae est in magistro":
De magistro, a. 1, ad 6 (417—422).

[42] Vgl. das 2. Kapitel von Contra impugnantes (s.o., Anm. 7 und 8).

[43] De magistro, a. 4, ad 3: „Visio docentis est principium doctrinae" (98 f.).

geben"[44] und damit die Freiheit der Lernenden zu achten und zu wecken.

Der hl. Thomas wird gerne der „doctor angelicus" genannt. Von den Engeln heißt es, daß ihr ganzes Wesen im Schauen Gottes, der ewigen Urwahrheit, besteht, und daß sie deshalb ungeteilten Sinnes der Wahrheitserkenntnis der Menschen dienen. Thomas gilt als der „engelgleiche Lehrer", weil er in einem selten zu findenden Maße ein Schauender war, der zudem in selten hohem Grade die Gabe hatte, das Geschaute in begrifflicher Klarheit der Einsicht anderer darzubieten. Thomas sagt einmal mit Gregor dem Großen: „Das kontemplative Leben heißt: F r e i h e i t[45]." Was Thomas vom Lehrer lehrt, vermittelt seine eigene Lehre: daß die Wahrheit Freiheit bedeutet.

[44] „Contemplata aliis tradere": Summa theologica II^a II^{ae}, q. 188, a. 6. Dieser Satz gilt als eine Art Devise des Ordens der Predigerbrüder.

[45] Summa theologica, II^a II^{ae}, q. 182, a. 1, ad 2, mit Bezg. auf Gregor, Super Ezech., hom. 3.

8

William Thorpe and the Question of Authority

ANNE HUDSON

Aτ the beginning of his trial before Archbishop Thomas Arundel in 1407 the Wycliffite William Thorpe offered to explain his beliefs. Arundel accepted and Thorpe proceeded to a series of tenets, based in their order and largely in their content upon the Apostles' Creed. He paraphrased some and embroidered others, largely by adding statements concerning the life of Christ from the Gospels, but for a considerable while Arundel must have thought his prisoner amenable to correction; if a few statements were awkwardly ambiguous, the general drift appeared unexceptionable. Thorpe's most significant addition, however, came towards the end, in his elaboration of the clause expressing belief in Holy Church.

He started in mild enough fashion: 'I bileue holi chirche: that is, I bileue that there hath ben and that ther yit now is, and alwei to the worldes eende schal be, a peple whiche schulen bisie hem for to knowe and to kepe the heestis of God, dredinge over al thing to offende God, and louynge and sechynge moost to plesen him.' Those who practise such virtues 'have her names writen in the book of liif. ...therfore I bileue that the feithful gederinge togidre of this people, lyuynge now here in this liif is the holi chirch of God, figtinge here in erthe agens the fend and the prosperite of this world and her fleischli lustis.'

To 'the hool gederinge togidere of this forseid chirche' Thorpe was prepared to remain obedient, to the ordinance and governance of this Church and of every member of it. 'Forthi I knowleche now, and everemore schal if God wol, that of al myn herte and of al my migt I wole submitte me oonli to the rule and governaunce of hem aftir my knowynge whom, bi the hauynge and usynge of the forseide vertues, I perceyue to ben the membris of holi chirche.'

The last sentence of the creed should, despite the scriptural echoes of the previous statements and the evident orthodoxy on many items of Christian belief, have warned the questioner of the problems that lay in the path of Thorpe's return to the fold of the

English Church.[1] Though Thorpe avoided at this point the use of Wyclif's abrupt formulation of definition, that the Church is the *congregatio predestinatorum*, this seems plainly implied in the periphrases; more alarmingly, his reservation of submission 'after my knowynge' reveals that the only absolute source of authority to Thorpe was the judgment of his own conscience. Thorpe's reiteration towards the end of his trial, 'i wole be now redy to obeie ful gladli to Christ, the heed of al holi chirche, and to the lore and to the heestis and to the counseilis of euery plesyng membre of him',[2] is even more explicit: only to a 'plesyng membre' will Thorpe submit, and Thorpe will be the judge of that status.

Thorpe's account of his investigation is the only record of the event that survives. The immediate impression made by it is of a fictionalized narrative, an attempt perhaps to provide a Lollard 'saint's life' to supersede the hagiography of which the movement disapproved; the persecuted suspect is confronted in his isolation by the combined power and unscrupulous deviousness of the Established Church, but manages through the superior wisdom afforded by knowledge of Scriptures to win through, if not to a happy release, at least to a confident imprisonment and hope of eternal reward.[3] The discovery of material in a collection of documentary model letters which relates to Thorpe's earlier history has, however, necessitated some reassessment of Thorpe's own narrative, since this hostile evidence bears out many of the statements that Thorpe makes. Looking again at other observations on which the new evidence does not impinge, it is clear that the facts of Thorpe's account are almost all verifiable.[4] Thorpe's origins are probably to be sought

[1] Thorpe's account of his trial is quoted from the only surviving medieval English MS, now Oxford, Bodleian Rawlinson C. 208, of which I am preparing an edition. A modernized version of the print put out, probably in Antwerp, about 1530 (STC 24045), appears in A. W. Pollard (ed.), *Fifteenth Century Prose and Verse* (Westminster, 1903), 101–67. The material there attached to the account, pp. 99–100, 168–74, has no counterpart in any medieval version of Thorpe's story. Quotations here are fos. 12ᵛ–13ᵛ (Pollard, pp. 110–11).

[2] Rawl. fo. 84 (Pollard, p. 162).

[3] Cf. the later provision of a Protestant hagiography surveyed by L. P. Fairfield, 'John Bale and the Development of Protestant Hagiography in England', *JEH* 24 (1973), 145–60. Bale knew the previous work by Thorpe, and indeed translated it into Latin; his version, now incomplete, in his own hand, is entered into 'Fasciculi Zizaniorum', Bodleian e Mus. 86, fo. 105ᵛ and following five inserted and unnumbered leaves.

[4] *John Lydford's Book*, ed. D. M. Owen (London, 1974, jointly published by HMC as vol. 22, and the Devon and Cornwall Record Society as vol. 19), documents nos. 206 and 209, a draft letter concerning Thorpe, drawn up for Bishop Braybrooke

in north Yorkshire: at one point he is described as 'capellano Ebor'dioc.', and it has been suggested that he is to be identified with a man of the same name who was instituted to the vicarage of Marske, Cleveland, in March 1395. Arundel refers to Thorpe's pro-seletyzing 'in the north lond'.[5] By Thorpe's own evidence, he left home for Oxford, agreeing with some reluctance to the demands of his family that he should become a priest.[6] How well he knew Wyclif personally there is not entirely clear from his account, though he was fully aware of Wyclif's reputation. If Thorpe's assertion in 1407 that he had followed Wyclif's teaching 'this thritti yeer' is accurate, this would put his stay in Oxford in the late 1370s when Wyclif was at the height of his powers in the university. Certainly he knew Nicholas Hereford, Philip Repingdon, and John Aston amongst the first generation Wycliffites, at a time when all three were still firm in their allegiance to their master's teaching. Thorpe joined the Wycliffite camp at Oxford, and maintained his position thereafter.[7] He fell foul of the ecclesiastical authorities for the first time, so far as is known, in London before the end of the 1380s.[8] There is no record of this in Braybrooke's London register, but the two letters provide considerable detail. The charges brought against Thorpe at that point do not impinge directly upon the questions of the identity of the Church or of the location of final religious authority; amongst other things Thorpe had, however, allegedly preached that a cleric in mortal sin does not and cannot consecrate the Host any more than a layman, and that the laity's power over the clergy extended to a right to imprison them for offences and to remove tithes. He had argued that the contemporary clergy were perverters, not con-verters, of the people.[9] The charge about the rights of laymen over

of London, together with a reply by Thorpe to accusations made against him by the bishop. Lydford, an Oxford graduate and canon lawyer, held many ecclesiastical positions and undertook various legal tasks, notable amongst them being his time as assessor at the Blackfriars Council in May 1382. I have added line-references to the edition.

[5] Lydford no. 206, 2; M. Aston, *Thomas Arundel: A Study of Church Life in the Reign of Richard II* (Oxford, 1967), 326 n. 2; MS Rawl., fo. 8 (Pollard, p. 107).

[6] MS Rawl., fos. 19ᵛ–20ᵛ (Pollard, pp. 115–16).

[7] MS Rawl., fos. 21–26ᵛ, 85–6 (Pollard, pp. 116–20, 162–3).

[8] Owen dates no. 206 as *c.* 1395. C. Kightly, 'The Early Lollards; A Survey of Popular Lollard Activity in England, 1382–1428'. DPhil. thesis, York, 1975), p. 438, n. 1, observes that this is substantially too late since one of the clergy mentioned, William Chestre, rector of St Martin's Orgar (no. 209/42) had been replaced in that position by January 1388; see *Calendar of Close Rolls 1392–6* (London, 1925), 524.

[9] Lydford no. 206, ll. 23–46.

the clergy was briefly answered by Thorpe's assertion that to deny his view is to deprive the king of his royal prerogative, though he volunteered that he would argue its correctness through canon law, as he would support his view concerning consecration by a cleric in mortal sin.[10] The outcome of this investigation is uncertain. A colophon at the foot of Thorpe's reply in the Lydford notebook appears to indicate that Thorpe refused to recognize his heresy or to abjure, and that Braybrooke therefore excommunicated him. This is in a different hand from the rest of the document.[11] As a conclusion to the case it is manifestly incomplete, since there is no indication of the sentence given; the sentence must inevitably have been imprisonment. But Thorpe in his later narrative gives a different version of the conclusion: he claimed that he was released and that Braybrooke demanded no recantation from him, and appears to suggest that his release was in some way connected with Arundel's banishment in 1399—implying that Braybrooke only held him because of the archbishop's insistence and not because the bishop himself thought there to be a valid case against him.[12] Thorpe's claim has an obvious relevance to his later position when he was again under investigation: if he had been forced to abjure before Braybrooke, the only way in which he could have escaped further imprisonment, he could have been faced by Arundel with the penalties of relapse. His story to Arundel was therefore obviously to his own advantage. But in view of the doubtful nature of the colophon in the notebook, it may actually have been true.[13]

The second investigation of Thorpe came on 7 August 1407.[14] No

---

[10] Lydford no. 209, ll. 61–78; note 67–8 '*aufferre a domino rege regaliam suam*'. Cf. the text found in three Bohemian MSS, which argues that the clauses of the coronation oath sworn by the king are contravened unless he has power to correct the clergy; since the oath is that of the English coronation, and closely similar to that sworn by Richard II, the text must be English despite the present provenance of the MSS.

[11] Lydford no. 209, ll. 88–93.

[12] MS Rawl., fo. 88–88ᵛ (Pollard, p. 165), 'whanne ye weren gon, the bischop of London, whos prison ye putten me and lafte me, fond in me no cause for to holden me no lengir in prisoun. But at the preers of my freendis he delyuerede me to hem, axynge of me no manere of submittinge.'

[13] The colophon could have been added by a later user of the notebook, which was clearly intended as a precedent manual, realizing that no formula for sentence had been included. The precise formulation of the penalties for relapse were not refined until Chichele's tenure of the Canterbury chair; see the account by E. F. Jacob, *The Register of Henry Chichele*, i (Oxford, 1943), pp. cxxxii–cxxxv.

[14] MS Rawl., fo. 8 (Pollard, p. 107).

record of it is found in Arundel's register, and for what follows we are entirely dependent upon Thorpe's own words. He had been arrested in April of that year in Shrewsbury by the civil authorities, and was sent to Arundel with five accusations against him, all of which related to his preaching in the town on 17 April.[15] Thorpe had taught, it was claimed, that the sacrament on the altar remained material bread after the consecration, that images should not be worshipped, that men should not go on pilgrimage, that priests have no claim to tithes, and that it was not lawful to use oaths. These charges were investigated by Arundel, and two further issues were discussed largely at the instigation of Thorpe himself: those of the nature of the Church, and hence the claims of the contemporary hierarchy to authority, and the prime obligation on the priest to preach even without licence.[16] There is some overlap here with the accusations brought previously in London, but Thorpe's position seems to have become more overtly heretical in the interval.[17] Thorpe's offending sermon had been preached in St Chad's church, which presumably means that the rector was sympathetic or had anyway been persuaded to provide him with a pulpit.[18] The outcome of the investigation by Arundel is unknown: Thorpe's narrative ends with his relegation to the archbishop's prison to cool his heels, but his own determination to continue the fight.[19] He expressed a desire to put himself under the better instruction of the Church for amendment, but made no modification to his definition of that Church.

After this episode there is no certain information about Thorpe.[20]

[15] MS Rawl., fo. 27–27ᵛ (Pollard, p. 121); the charges are mentioned repeatedly in the text, but no further information about the circumstances of Thorpe's presence in the town is given.

[16] MS Rawl., fos. 12ᵛ–13, 38ᵛ–39, on preaching fos. 27ᵛ–38ᵛ (Pollard, pp. 110–11, 128–9, 121–8).

[17] Particularly on the subject of the Eucharist Thorpe's position is more clearly Wycliffite: cf. Lydford, no. 206/25–6, no. 209/72–8 with MS Rawl., fos. 39ᵛ–44ᵛ (Pollard, pp. 129–33).

[18] MS Rawl., fo. 39ᵛ: 'thou prechedist there opinli in seint Chaddis chirche' (Pollard, p. 129).

[19] MS Rawl., fo. 90ᵛ (Pollard, p. 167).

[20] The *Testament* that appears in the 1530 print following the autobiographical account (and consequently in Pollard (1903), pp. 168–74) is not present in either the English or the Latin MSS. The date given in the final colophon to that *Testament*, 19 or 20 Sept. 1460, is difficult to reconcile with the other dates known for Thorpe; it would make Thorpe about 100 in 1460. In fact it seems to me unlikely that the *Testament* has anything to do in origin with Thorpe; there is certainly nothing in it that is in any way distinctive.

In a manuscript in Prague is a list of opinions on the eucharist, attributed to a disciple of John Wyclif. This attribution is enlarged by another hand interlinearly 'prout ferunt de secta illa Wylhelmi Torp cuius librum ego habeo'.[21] But, though the opinions are certainly Wycliffite, they are not particularized in any way that would allow identification with Thorpe. The existence of two Latin manuscripts of Thorpe's autobiography in Bohemia makes it tempting to speculate that Thorpe, like Peter Payne, found safety from enquiry by fleeing to the Continent and eventually to Prague.[22] This must remain speculation unless firmer evidence to support it is found in Hussite sources. If Thorpe did leave the country, however, he was certainly not forgotten: the *book of William Thorpe* is a title frequently mentioned amongst the books owned at the end of the fifteenth and beginning of the sixteenth centuries by Lollard suspects.[23]

As has been said, the accusations from Shrewsbury against Thorpe did not specifically raise the issues of the Church or of the location of authority. Explicitly, however, the question was discussed just before Arundel interrogated Thorpe about those accusations. Thorpe professed his willingness 'to be gouerned bi holi chirche'. Arundel, unable to resist this bait, asked for Thorpe's definition of 'holi chirche'. Thorpe's first response was uncompromising: 'I clepe Christ and his seintis holi chirche.' Arundel took this to refer to the Church in heaven and demanded that Thorpe define the Church on earth, but Thorpe only differentiated between those who 'regneth ioifulli in heuene' and those 'pilgrymes of Crist wandrynge towardis heuene'.[24] Again, though the English equivalents of the term *congregatio predestinatorum* were not used, there can be no doubt that Thorpe's Church is just that.

It seems fair to say that the notion of the Church as the *congregatio predestinatorum* is an abstract one, involving concepts of some obscurity and in the Wycliffite formulation of no apparent immediate application. Wyclif had admitted the coexistence on earth of this Church with a Church where the predestined and those foreknown

[21] Prague Metropolitan Chapter Library MS D.49, fos. 179^v–181^v.

[22] For Payne see A. B. Emden, *An Oxford Hall in Medieval Times*, 2nd edn. (Oxford, 2nd 1968), 133–61; the MSS are Vienna Österreichische Nationalbibliothek 3936, fos. 1–22^v, and Prague Metropolitan Chapter o.29, fos. 188–209.

[23] See *The Acts and Monuments of John Foxe*, ed. S. R. Cattley and J. Pratt (London, 1853–70) iv. 235, 259, 679, v. 39.

[24] MS Rawl., fos. 38^v–39 (Pollard, pp. 128–9).

to damnation mingled indistinguishably. He had repeatedly insisted that man in this life is ignorant of his own state, let alone of that of others.[25] The frequency with which Wyclif's definition of the real Church is faithfully reproduced in Lollard texts is therefore something of a surprise. That the academic author of the *Opus arduum* of 1389/90 should specify that 'ecclesia est numero predestinatorum' is not remarkable; the Latin sermons of Laud Misc. 200, though undated, show by their language the learning of their author, and extend this definition in equally comprehensible fashion to 'tales qui sunt de familia electorum cognoscencium Deum'.[26] But it is more surprising to find John Godesell, 'parchemenmaker' though he may have been, and a dominant member of the East Anglian group investigated between 1428 and 1431 by Bishop Alnwick, stating 'ecclesia catholica est congregacio solum salvandorum.' Godesell's own words were doubtless in English; so were those of Thomas Bikenor in 1443, when he described the Church as 'the congregacion of trewe men wiche only shul be saued.'[27] The first definition given by the *Lanterne of Liyt* of the Church is 'the chosun noumbre of hem that schullen be saued'. The long English sermon cycle parallels this frequently: 'the chirche is taken . . . first for men that shulen be saved', or 'yif we shulen not be saved, we ben not men of holi chirche.'[28]

With the gradual shifting of the concept of 'the predestined' to 'the saved', or even further to 'the congregacion of juste men for whom Jesus Crist schedde his blood',[29] I am not here primarily concerned. But, as Thorpe's trial shows, the theological concept did not remain a purely theoretical issue for the Lollards. Before the

[25] Wyclif's most extended treatment comes in the first part of his *De Ecclesia*, written probably between early 1378 and early 1379 (for the evidence see W. R. Thomson, *The Latin Writings of John Wyclif* (Toronto, 1983), no. 32). For a discussion of his view see G. Leff, *Heresy in the Later Middle Ages* (Manchester, 1967), ii. 516–45, and A. Kenny, *Wyclif* (Oxford, 1985), 68–79.

[26] Brno University MS Mk. 28, fo. 173ᵛ, Oxford Bodleian Laud Misc. 200, fo. 76; for the first text see *Lollards and their Books* (London, 1985), 43–65, for the second C. von Nolcken, 'An Unremarked Group of Wycliffite Sermons in Latin', *Modern Philology*, 83 (1986), 233–49.

[27] *Heresy Trials in the Diocese of Norwich, 1428–31*, ed. N. P. Tanner (Camden Society, 4th ser. 20; 1977), 61; Salisbury reg. Aiscough, fo. 53ᵛ.

[28] *The Lanterne of Liyt*, ed. L. M. Swinburn (EETS 151; 1917), 23/3; *Select English Works of John Wyclif*, ed. T. Arnold (Oxford, 1869–71), ii. 209/20, 210/20.

[29] Arnold, iii. 273/13. I have discussed this shift, and the evangelical problem of the function of preaching in a predestined/foreknown world, in my forthcoming book *The Premature Reformation*, ch. 7.

interrogation proper began, Thorpe announces in his account that 'I was moued in alle my wittis for to holde the archebischop neithir prelat ne preest of God', his conviction arising from Arundel's responsibility for the burning of the first Lollard martyr, William Sawtry, and from Arundel's evident willingness to follow that execution with others like it.[30] Later Thorpe speaks of 'preestis whos preesthode Crist acceptide either now acceptith, and 'euery preest . . . whos presthode Crist appreueth'.[31] He reveals his hand unashamedly when he describes those men of Shrewsbury who accused him to the archbishop as 'out of the feith' of Christ, whilst those who are favourable towards him as 'in the feith of Crist'.[32] Thorpe here appears to controvert Wyclif's conviction that certainty concerning a man's final salvation or damnation was inaccessible on earth. But, whilst this was Wyclif's theoretical position, his abhorrence for the ways of life practised by many contemporaries led to numerous anticipations of divine condemnation. Thorpe had good precedent from his master. If Thorpe is pictured as brazen, Arundel is shown as unintelligently limited by his own conventional vocabulary: the archbishop repeatedly demands assent to the determination, or the ordinance, of Holy Church. One such instance arises in the questioning about the eucharist, where Thorpe delightedly points out that the wording to which Arundel demands conformity had been formulated as recently as Thomas Aquinas.[33]

Does Thorpe provide any criteria for his decisions on membership of the Church, or is it just an arbitrary division into friends and foes? The latter may seem the more probable when Thorpe counters the archbishop's exhortation that he should follow the example of Purvey and the others in recantation by observing that they should revoke their abjuration 'last thei ben sodeynli vomed [vomited] out of the noumbre of Goddis chosen peple.'[34] Can man know the priest 'whos preesthode Crist appreueth', and if so how? A minor spat between the two opponents comes with the question of the legitimacy of music in church services: the archbishop defends the consolations of song and instruments in church, but the suspect

---

[30] MS Rawl., fo. 18ᵛ (Pollard, p. 114); for Sawtry's case see D. Wilkins, *Concilia Magnae Britanniae et Hiberniae* (London, 1737), iii. 254–60.
[31] MS Rawl., fos. 60ᵛ, 64 (Pollard, pp. 144, 146–7).
[32] MS Rawl., fo. 29–29ᵛ (Pollard, p. 122).
[33] MS Rawl., fos. 42–44ᵛ (Pollard, pp. 131–3).
[34] MS Rawl., fo. 24 (Pollard, p. 118).

loftily scorns 'mannes ordinaunce' which allows organs, whilst 'the ordynaunce of God' prefers a good sermon.[35] Though the issue is a minor one, the terminology is crucial. The ordinance of God, for Thorpe and for his fellow sectaries, is coterminous with Holy Writ. At one point Thorpe takes over the questioning, and gains Arundel's unwilling acceptance that God's word and God are identical; from this he leads the archbishop to admit that only teaching 'groundid in Cristis lyuynge and techinge' should be accepted.[36] This is not, however, a simple biblical fundamentalism. Though Thorpe, like his allies, cites Scripture frequently—as Arundel testily observes, they delight to pick out hard sayings of Scripture to reproach the ecclesiastical establishment—he also uses in his own support the Fathers. In so far as saints and doctors write 'acording to holi writt' they are to be credited, and no further. Is Chrysostom, he asks Arundel, 'an autentike doctour'?—Chrysostom, following the Gospel reinforcement of Exodus 20, forbade the swearing of oaths, so how can the archbishop maintain that oaths are lawful?[37] More surprising perhaps, though it is common Lollard practice, is Thorpe's use of canon law to bolster his claims. The most interesting instance comes in a discussion of the dilemma faced by a man under an unrighteous ruler. Thorpe distinguishes between 'vertues souereynes' and 'vicious tirauntis'; to the second, he claims, citing 1 Peter 2: 18 with his own gloss, obedience is due but not in 'ony thing that is not plesinge to God'. Arundel counters this with the usual interpretation that the subject is bound to obey, whilst the sovereign carries the responsibility for any evil committed. Thorpe's answer is that anyone consenting to sin must bear the moral responsibility for that sin. He cites the biblical stories of David, and also Gregory and canon law to support his view.[38]

In some of the Lollard definitions of the Church there is a muddled, if comprehensible, weakening of the concept of the predestinate to the morally virtuous, and a parallel tendency to equate those of evidently reprehensible life with the foreknown. Arundel was

---

[35] MS Rawl., fo. 57–57ᵛ (Pollard, pp. 141–2); cf. Arnold, iii. 203/18, 479/27; *English Works of Wyclif Hitherto Unprinted*, ed. F. D. Matthew (EETS 74; 1902), Liyt. 77/25, 191/4; *Lanterne of Liyt*, pp. 51/2, 57/15, 59/5.

[36] MS Rawl, fos. 72ᵛ3, 83–83ᵛ (Pollard, pp. 153, 161).

[37] MS Rawl. fo. 72–72ᵛ (Pollard, p. 153); cf. other citations of Augustine, Jerome, Gregory, fos. 50, 50ᵛ, 58 (Pollard, pp. 136, 137, 142), etc.

[38] MS Rawl., fos. 34ᵛ–36 (Pollard, pp. 125–7); citing Prov. 17: 15, PL 77. 30, and *Decret.* II, c. 11 q. 3, c. 93.

well aware of this tendency. He puts to Thorpe an extreme case: if
Thorpe knew a priest guilty of numerous sins, including that of
notorious fornication, would Thorpe consider the man damnable?
Arundel, since he points out that the sinner may quickly repent, is
evidently here interested in the issue of the possibility of sin in the
predestinate. Thorpe skilfully evades this trap: he refuses to damn
any man, whatever his sin, though he condemns the sins; his only
demand, and one he regards as specially acute for a priest, is that the
repentance should match in publicity the original offence.[39]
The comment of William Emayn in 1429 'thoo that be in dedly
synne be out of the church of Goddes ordinance and on the sinagog
of Sathanas' is much less astute. Emayn could well have been responding to the question which appeared in the list of enquiries formulated about 1428 'an mali sint pars ecclesie catholice?'[40] The fact
that this is the only question in that long list that concerns the definition of the Church perhaps reflects the difficulty even the legists
found in devising an enquiry on this issue that was bound to separate
orthodox from Lollard. Indeed, even this seems dubiously satisfactory. Whilst John Burell's other opinions would certainly have been
sufficient to damn him, the record of his account of the Church
(again translated from its original language) as 'anima cuiuslibet
boni Christiani', whilst it has transmuted the negative into a positive, is scarcely manifest heresy.[41]

It was unwise of Arundel to allow Thorpe to stray from the familiar challenges of the Eucharist, images, pilgrimages, tithes, and
oaths onto the more treacherous ground of the Church and authority at the start of the investigation. Arundel's ineptitude, and
Thorpe's matching skill, obviously lose nothing in Thorpe's telling.
Thorpe's reservations about Arundel's membership of the Church
underlie the whole of the remaining debate. Though it is clear that
Thorpe's views and the archbishop's on the five issues are irreconcilable, less is made of this than of Arundel's demand that Thorpe
swear obedience. When the fifth issue of the men of Shrewsbury is
reached, Thorpe explains one of the problems: he will not swear an
oath by a creature, a refusal which extends to swearing on a copy of
the Gospels 'euery book is nothing ellis, no but dyuerse creaturis of

---

[39] MS Rawl., fos. 66ᵛ–67ᵛ (Pollard, pp. 148–9).
[40] See my paper 'The Examination of Lollards', in *Lollards and their Books* (London, 1985), 134; for Emayn Bath and Wells reg. Stafford op. 53b.
[41] Tanner, pp. 73, 77.

whiche it is made; therefore to swere upon a book or bi a book is to swere bi creaturis, and this sweringe is euer unleeful.'[42] In this Thorpe followed Wyclif's rejection of such oaths, as he did in his reluctant agreement, if forced, to swear to Arundel. In Thorpe's reconstruction of the affair, Thorpe happily plays cat to Arundel's mouse: after much sophistical argumentation Thorpe agrees to swear to Arundel, only to withdraw his agreement as soon as the book is produced on which he should make his oath.

Even if, however, we discount the rose-tinted spectacles through which Thorpe sees his encounter with the archbishop, and the 'Boys' Own Paper' presentation of our hero's escapades, it is clear that major issues are at stake in the trial. Obviously the issue of the Eucharist, as well as being the rubicon which separated Wyclif's earlier radicalism from his condemned heresy, became the article on which Lollardy might most readily be recognized; if it appears less frequently in the episcopal records than the matter of images and pilgrimages, that is probably only because questions that required a simple positive or negative answer were more easily devised on the latter. But Thorpe is too astute an author to allow his account to proceed as a series of anticlimaxes: the Eucharist may come first in the accusations of the men of Shrewsbury because they thought it the most significant, just as they set oaths last as least important, but Thorpe was prepared to leave them so because in his presentation the emphasis has shifted from these five accusations to an issue more fundamental. Is Arundel a member of the Church? If he is not, then what authority has he over Thorpe, or indeed over any person in his province? If authority does not lie with Arundel, the Primate of England, then where does it reside? To Thorpe, as to any Christian, the ultimate answer had to be 'in God'; but for Thorpe, as for many later Puritans, the only access to divine judgement was through the Bible, or more particularly through the Gospels. Thorpe proclaimed, and his words were echoed many times in later generations, 'the lettre that is touchid with mannes hande is not the gospel.'[43] Implicit in this is the insistence that the only possible interpreter of the Gospel is the believer's own conscience. As Arundel evidently perceived, the logical outcome of such a view in practical terms is anarchy.

---

[42] MS Rawl., fo. 70 (Pollard, p. 151); in one of the Latin MSS a marginal reference is given to Decret. 11, c. 22, q. 1, c. 14, in support of this view.
[43] MS Rawl., fo. 73–73ᵛ (Pollard, p. 153).

9

Luther und die Autorität Roms im Jahre 1518

BERNHARD LOHSE

Summary

A good deal has been written on the development of the quarrel between Luther and Rome, and in particular on Luther's growing criticism of the Roman authorities in the years 1517–21. I consider here some texts, principally from the year 1518, whose implications have not yet been fully explored. During this period Luther moved within a few months from a limited, but far-reaching, acknowledgement of papal authority to the view that the Pope was Antichrist.

1. The Ninety-Five Theses of October 1517 contain some critical remarks on the power of the Pope. It was these statements that were taken up by the leading defenders of the Curia and sharply rejected, while those on penance and indulgence occasioned far less discussion. In his *Resolutiones Disputationum de Indulgentiarum Virtute* of the spring of 1518 Luther made some important statements on the papacy. He still recognized the authority of the Pope, but emphasized with regard to indulgences that the Pope was able to come to the aid of the souls in purgatory, not by virtue of the *potestas clauium*, but only by intercession. Especially important is the emphasis that it does not lie with the Pope alone to establish new dogmas; he can give an opinion on, and decide, questions of faith only according to the articles of faith already laid down. New articles had to be decided by a Council.

2. The Roman theologian Silvester Prierias's *De Potestate Papae Dialogus* appeared in June 1518, and its exaggerated emphasis on papal authority proved provocative to Luther. Prierias expressed the view that the teaching of the Roman Church and of the Pope was the infallible rule of faith, from which Holy Scripture derived its authority. By the summer of 1518 Luther was strongly emphasizing the authority of Holy Scripture over against this view. Where Prierias saw the Pope as the Church's representative, Luther contended that such representation was possibly only for a Council.

3. Luther's meeting with Cardinal Cajetan in Augsburg in October 1518 was of signal importance. The question of the papacy was brought up several times in the course of Luther's interrogation. Cajetan had of course some appreciation of Luther's reforming theology, but he appears to have been essentially of Prierias's opinion. Cajetan's cross-examination was conducted on the Pope's orders and he explained that there could be no appeal

to Scripture against papal infallibility. Luther was driven to the conclusion that at least on the question of indulgences Scripture and the authority of the Church were at odds.

It may be that fresh examination of the texts will show that in the autumn of 1517 Luther did not actually intend to criticize the papacy. Rather, the question of the papacy became central during the course of the ensuing controversy, and with it the question of the authority of Scripture.

IN den Jahren von 1517 bis 1521 hat sich die Auseinandersetzung zwischen Luther und Rom Schritt um Schritt verschärft. War Luther, als er am 31. Oktober 1517 seine 95 Thesen an Erzbischof Albrecht von Mainz sandte, noch der Überzeugung, im Grunde den Papst auf seiner Seite zu haben, so mußte er bald erkennen, daß jedenfalls führende Theologen sowohl in Rom als auch an verschiedenen Universitäten seine Thesen ablehnten. Einen ersten Höhepunkt erreichte die Debatte um das Papsttum auf der Leipziger Disputation im Juli 1519, wo Luther die Unfehlbarkeit von Papst- und Konzilsentscheidungen bestritt und insbesondere das Urteil des Konstanzer Konzils gegen Johannes Huß in Frage stellte. Als Leo X. im Sommer 1520 die Bannandrohungsbulle gegen Luther unterzeichnete und zu Beginn des Jahres 1521 Luther exkommunizierte, hat Luther auch seinerseits das Papsttum mit den schärfsten Worten verworfen. Luther war nunmehr überzeugt, daß das Papsttum vom Antichristen beherrscht sei.

Das Jahr 1518 ist im Verlauf dieser Kontroverse für Luthers Haltung zu Rom insofern von besonderem Interesse, als Luther damals zwar schon ein sehr umstrittener Theologe war, aber die Frage der päpstlichen Autorität sich noch nicht zu äußersten Konsequenzen zugespitzt hatte. Luther ist, wie auch immer man seine Stellung zur Autorität Roms im Jahre 1518 sehen und bewerten mag, damals zunächst noch der Meinung gewesen, dem Papst gehorsam zu sein. In gewissem Sinne war er auch bereit, das zu erwartende Urteil des Papstes zu akzeptieren. Noch konnte er manches Positive über die Autorität des Papstes sagen. Auf der anderen Seite hat sich seine Haltung in der Auseinandersetzung des Jahres 1518 in wichtigen Punkten geändert: Ende des Jahres 1518 hat Luther in einem Brief an seinen Freund Wenzeslaus Linck zum ersten Mal vorsichtig den Verdacht geäußert, daß der wahre Antichrist in der römischen Kurie herrsche[1]. Das Jahr 1518 führte also bei Luther von der Über-

---

[1] WA Briefwechsel 1, Nr. 121, 11–14 (18.12.1518).

zeugung, den Papst auf seiner Seite zu haben und dem Papst gehorsam zu sein, zu der beginnenden radikalen Ablehnung des Papsttums durch Luther.

Diese Entwicklung ist oftmals untersucht worden[2]. Trotzdem dürfte eine erneute Behandlung dieser Thematik nicht unnütz sein. Denn einmal ist es bislang noch nicht gelungen, über die wichtigsten Aspekte bei Luthers Haltung zum Papsttum seit 1517 einen Consensus unter den Forschern zu erreichen. Zum anderen sind, wie es scheint, manche wichtigen Äußerungen Luthers noch nicht gebührend herangezogen worden. Insbesondere dürften sich Luthers Resolutiones disputationum de indulgentiarum virtute vom Frühjahr 1518 dazu eignen, Luthers Haltung zu Rom in einem etwas größeren Zusammenhang zu sehen. Im Folgenden sollen aber auch die wichtigsten anderen Äußerungen Luthers zum Papsttum in der Zeit des Jahres 1518 mitberücksichtigt werden.

I

Luthers 95 Thesen über den Ablaß vom 31. Oktober 1517 enthalten eine Reihe von Äußerungen über die Gewalt des Papstes sowie auch manche kritischen Anfragen zu dem Gebrauch, den der Papst von seiner Vollmacht in der Praxis macht. Das Gewicht, welches diese Aussagen über das Papsttum innerhalb der 95 Thesen haben, wird in der Forschung bis heute unterschiedlich gesehen. Auf der einen Seite wird die Ansicht vertreten, daß die eigentliche Intention der 95 Thesen die Kritik an der Veräußerlichung der Bußübungen sowie die Bemühung um eine Wiedergewinnung des neutestamentlichen Sinnes der Buße als „Umkehr" gewesen sei[3]. Auf der anderen Seite

---

[2] Folgende wichtige Untersuchungen seien genannt: E. Bizer, Luther und der Papst (Theol. Existenz Heute, 69; München, 1958); H. A. Oberman, „Wittenbergs Zweifrontenkrieg gegen Prierias und Eck: Hintergrund und Entscheidungen des Jahres 1518", Zschr. f. Kirchengeschichte, 80 (1969), 331—358; R. Bäumer, Martin Luther und der Papst (Kath. Leben u. Kirchenreform im Zeitalter der Glaubensspaltung, 30; Münster 1970, 3. Aufl. 1982); Sc. H. Hendrix, Luther and the Papacy: Stages in a Reformation Conflict (Philadelphia, 1981); K. Aland, Luther und die römische Kirche, Luther und die politische Welt (Wissenschaftl. Symposion in Worms vom 27.—29.X.1983, ed. E. Iserloh u. G. Müller, Akademie der Wissenschaften und der Literatur Mainz, Hist. Forschungen, 9; Wiesbaden–Stuttgart, 1984), 125—172.

[3] So u.a. M. Brecht, Martin Luther: Sein Weg zur Reformation 1483—1521 (Stuttgart, 1981), 173; Sc. H. Hendrix, op. cit., 26 ff; B. Lohse, Martin Luther: Eine Einführung in sein Leben und sein Werk, 2. Aufl. (München, 1982), 55.

gibt es aber auch die Auffassung, daß diejenigen Aussagen in den 95
Thesen, welche die Potestas des Papstes eingrenzen und auch eine
bestimmte Kritik an der Ausübung der päpstlichen Gewalt vor
bringen, die eigentliche Absicht der 95 Thesen gewesen seien⁴.
Diese bis heute noch nicht hinreichend geklärte Kontroverse kann
hier nicht weiter verfolgt werden. Soviel dürfte freilich wohl fest-
stehen, daß die kritischen Töne gegenüber dem Papsttum, auch wenn
man sie nicht für das eigentliche Thema der 95 Thesen hält, nicht zu
überhören waren⁵. Wichtig ist zudem, daß die damaligen Leser der
95 Thesen begreiflicherweise keine Kenntnis von Luthers früher
Theologie haben konnten. Für sie betrat Luther mit den 95 Thesen
die Arena der Öffentlichkeit. Unter dem Aspekt der Wirkung dürften deshalb die kritischen Bemerkungen in den 95 Thesen gegenüber dem Papsttum vermutlich eine größere Bedeutung gehabt
haben, als es Luthers Absicht bei Abfassung der Thesen entsprach.
Insofern ist es nicht erstaunlich, daß in den frühen Gegenschriften,
welche insbesondere von Tetzel und Wimpina, von Eck sowie von
Prierias gegen Luthers 95 Thesen verfaßt wurden⁶, übereinstim-
mend gegen Luther die Autorität des Papsttums herausgestellt
wurde. Es ist freilich eigenartig, daß Luthers geistliche Bemühung
um eine Erneuerung des Bußgedankens von keinem seiner frühen
Gegner aufgegriffen und als solche gewürdigt wurde.

Wenn in den 95 Thesen über den Ablaß Luthers Stellung zum
Papsttum nicht mit letzter Deutlichkeit hervortritt, so finden sich in
den Resolutiones disputationum de indulgentiarum virtute derart
zahlreiche Aussagen, daß jedenfalls für das Frühjahr 1518 Luthers
Haltung zu Rom deutlich gewürdigt werden kann. Luther hat das
Manuskript dieser Resolutiones vermutlich schon im Frühjahr 1518
fertiggestellt; erst im August 1518 sind die Resolutiones erschienen.
Die Resolutiones sind zwar gedacht als ein Kommentar zu den 95
Thesen. Tatsächlich hat Luther in ihnen jedoch an manchen Stellen

---

⁴ So u.a. J. Lortz, Die Reformation in Deutschland, 6. Aufl. (Freiburg–Basel–
Wien, 1982), 202 („Angriff gegen das Papsttum... die Quintessenz der Ablaß
thesen“); R. Bäumer, op. cit. 15.

⁵ E. Kähler, „Die 95 Thesen: Inhalt und Bedeutung“, Luther. Zschr. der Luther-
Gesellschaft, 38 (1967), 114—124, S. 121: „Der Papst ist... im Grunde das zweite
große Thema der Thesen.“

⁶ Die wichtigsten Stellen dieser drei Gegenschriften sind zusammen mit Luthers
95 Thesen und den Resolutiones am besten zugänglich gemacht durch W. Köhler,
Luthers 95 Thesen samt seinen Resolutionen sowie den Gegenschriften von Wim-
pina-Tetzel, Eck und Prierias und den Antworten Luthers darauf (Leipzig, 1903).

seine Ansichten unter dem Eindruck der frühen Kritik gegenüber den 95 Thesen etwas modifiziert.

Die Tatsache, daß Luther den Resolutiones Widmungsbriefe an seinen Ordensvater Johannes von Staupitz und an Leo X., datiert am 30. Mai 1518, vorangestellt hat, ist zumindest ein Zeichen dafür, daß Luther sich der Hoffnung hingab, nicht im Gegensatz zu seinen kirchlichen Oberen zu stehen. Was Staupitz betrifft, so konnte Luther damals nach wie vor ziemlich sicher sein, dessen Wohlwollen zu besitzen[7]. Staupitz hat Luther im Jahre 1518 in vielfältiger Weise unterstützt, ohne darum freilich sich auch Luthers Positionen in allem zu eigen zu machen. Was den Papst angeht, so verweist Luther in seinem Widmungsbrief sicher nicht ohne Grund darauf, daß man ihn gegenüber dem Papst bereits verdächtige, die Befugnisse des Papstes bei der Ausübung des Schlüsselamtes herabzumindern. Wie Luther weiter hervorhebt, wird er schon als Häretiker, als Abtrünniger, ja als Verräter angeklagt. In seinem Widmungsbrief versucht Luther, seine eigene gute Absicht bei der Abfassung der 95 Thesen zu betonen.

Es sind vor allem zwei Passagen in dem Widmungsbrief an Leo X., die immer wieder die Aufmerksamkeit der Forschung gefunden haben, ohne daß es freilich gelungen ist, diese beiden Abschnitte mit der wünschenswerten Sicherheit zu interpretieren. Einmal, inmitten dieses Briefes an den Papst finden sich die drei Worte: „Revocare non possum"[8]. Die Erörterung dieser Stelle dürfte wohl so viel klar gemacht haben, daß sowohl die Übersetzung „Widerrufen kann ich nicht" als auch die andere „Zurückrufen kann ich sie [sc. die 95 Thesen] nicht" vertretbar sind. Es ist möglich, daß Luther sich hier absichtlich doppeldeutig ausgedrückt hat.

Die andere Stelle in dem Widmungsbrief an Leo X. lautet:

Quare, Beatissime Pater, prostratum me pedibus tuae Beatitudinis offero cum omnibus, quae sum et habeo. Vivifica, occide, voca, revoca, approba, reproba, ut placuerit: uocem tuam uocem Christi in te praesidentis et loquentis agnoscam. Si mortem merui, mori non recusabo. Domini enim est terra et plenitudo eius, qui est benedictus in saecula, Amen[9].

R. Bäumer hat die Ansicht vertreten, daß Luther mit diesen Worten

---

[7] Näheres s. bei D. C. Steinmetz, Luther and Staupitz: An Essay in the Intellectual Origins of the Protestant Reformation (Durham, NC, 1980).

[8] WA 1, 529, 3.

[9] Ibid. 22—27.

die bevorstehende Entscheidung „als eine himmlische Eingebung"
bezeichne, „ganz gleich, ob der Papst erkläre, daß Luthers Schriften
zu verbrennen oder zu bewahren seien"[10]. Luther sei zu jener Zeit
einer der schroffsten Papalisten gewesen; selbst Theologen wie
Cajetan oder Prierias seien in ihrem Papalismus nicht so weit gegangen wie Luther in diesem Widmungsbrief an den Papst[11]. Im übrigen wertet Bäumer diese Aussage als einen Beleg dafür, daß der
Gedanke der Unfehlbarkeit des kirchlichen Lehramtes, wie er in der
modernen katholischen Theologie begegnet, bereits in der Zeit des
frühen 16. Jahrhunderts vorhanden gewesen sei. Bäumer erwähnt
zwar, daß sich in den Resolutiones selbst einige wenig schmeichel-
hafte Äußerungen über die schlechte Amtsführung von Päpsten finden; allerdings erörtert er die Aussagen in den Resolutiones nicht
im Zusammenhang. Wichtig ist, daß nach Bäumer, der Luther nicht
gerade in dem besten Licht erscheinen läßt, Luthers Aussagen nicht
lediglich taktisch bedingt sind, sondern seiner wirklichen Meinung
entsprechen.

Zur Interpretation von Luthers Äußerung in dem Widmungsbrief
an den Papst müssen unbedingt seine Ausführungen in den Resolutiones zu These 26 herangezogen werden. In der These 26 hatte
Luther gesagt: „Optime facit papa, quod non potestate clauis (quam
nullam habet), sed per modum suffragii dat animabus remissio-
nem[12]." Luther nimmt hier also Bezug darauf, daß die Päpste im
späten Mittelalter den Ablaß für Verstorbene nicht kraft ihrer
Schlüsselgewalt, sondern auf dem Wege der Fürbitte gewährt
haben. Die recht komplizierte Differenzierung zwischen der potestas clavium und dem modus suffragii besonders im späteren 15.
Jahrhundert braucht hier nicht erörtert zu werden, zumal Luther
auf diese Entwicklung nur kurz eingeht. Luther benutzt jene Differenzierung nur zu dem Zweck, die Gewalt des Papstes einzuschrän-
ken.

In der Resolutio zu dieser These sagt Luther u.a. Folgendes:

Dagegen [sc. gegen Luthers Betonung der Tatsache, daß der Papst den Seelen im Fegefeuer „per modum suffragii" zu Hilfe kommt] wird nun
eingewendet: ... es gilt als eine anerkannte Sache, was ein Pariser Gelehrter
in einer Disputation behauptet hat: der Papst habe Gewalt über das

---

[10] R. Bäumer, op. cit. 21.
[11] Ibid. 25.
[12] WA 1, 234, 27 f.

Fegefeuer. Und der Papst habe davon Kenntnis genommen und jenem Magister nach seinem Tode den Erlaß, wie er von ihm behauptet worden war, erteilt und ihn damit gewissermaßen bestätigt. Hierauf antworte ich: Ich kehre mich nicht daran, was dem Papst gefällt oder mißfällt. Er ist ein Mensch wie andere auch. Es hat viele Päpste gegeben, denen nicht nur Irrtümer und Laster, sondern auch ganz ungeheure Dinge gefallen haben. Ich höre auf den Papst als Papst, das heißt, insofern er im kirchlichen Recht seinen Vorschriften gemäß sich äußert oder gemeinsam mit einem Konzil eine Entscheidung trifft, nicht aber, wenn er nach seinem Kopf redet, damit ich nicht etwa gezwungen werde, mit gewissen Leuten, die die Lehre Christi schlecht kennen, zu sagen, das entsetzliche Morden, das Julius II. unter dem christlichen Volk angerichtet hat, sei die Wohltat eines frommen Hirten, die er den Schafen Christi erwiesen habe[13].

Etwas später äußert Luther in demselben Zusammenhang zu These 26, daß „es dem Papst allein nicht zukomme, neue Glaubenssätze aufzustellen, sondern nur die Glaubensfragen nach den bereits festgesetzten Glaubensartikeln zu beurteilen und zu entscheiden". Neue Glaubensartikel müßten von einem Konzil beschlossen werden[14].

Diese beiden Aussagen in der Resolutio zu These 26 machen deutlich, daß jene Passage in dem Widmungsbrief an den Papst nicht in dem Sinne eines bedingungslosen Gehorsams gegenüber der zu erwartenden päpstlichen Entscheidung verstanden werden darf. Für sich genommen, könnte jene Stelle in dem Widmungsbrief zwar so verstanden werden; in Verbindung mit den Resolutiones muß man jedoch sagen, daß die päpstliche Entscheidungsgewalt für Luther insofern eingegrenzt ist, als sie gebunden ist an das Kirchenrecht. Luther hat, als er dies schrieb, noch nicht den Grundsatz „Sola Scriptura" in einem ausschließlichen Sinne vertreten, vielmehr hat er sich häufig auch auf die Kirchenväter, das Kirchenrecht sowie die Ratio berufen[15]. Zweifellos hat dabei für Luther die Hl. Schrift

[13] Ibid. 582, 14—26 (eigene Übersetzung). Die wichtigsten Aussagen lauten lateinisch (Zeilen 21 — 23): „Ego audio Papam ut papam, id est ut in Canonibus loquitur et secundum Canones loquitur aut cum Concilio determinat, Non autem, quando secundum suum caput loquitur."
[14] WA 1, 582, 38—583, 1: „cum solius Papae non sit nouos fidei statuere articulos, Sed secundum statutos iudicare et rescindere quaestiones fidei..."
[15] Hierzu s. insbesondere K.-V. Selge, Normen der Christenheit im Streit um Ablaß und Kirchenautorität 1518—1521 (Theol. Habil.-Schr. Heidelberg 1968/1969, Maschinenschrift). Besonders wichtig ist in diesem Zusammenhang Luthers einleitende Äußerung in den Resolutiones (WA 1, 529, 33—530, 3): „Primum protestor, me prorsus nihil dicere aut tenere uelle, nisi quod in et ex Sacris literis primo, deinde

schon bei weitem die größte Autorität; eine Lehre, die sich nicht auf die Hl. Schrift stützt, könnte für ihn keineswegs durch die anderen Autoritäten hinreichend begründet werden. Insofern muß man sagen, daß der Papst, wenn er nach Luthers Meinung durch das Kirchenrecht gebunden ist, indirekt und in letzter Instanz durch die Hl. Schrift selbst gebunden ist.

Aber auch die Aussage, daß es dem Papst nicht zustehe, neue Artikel des Glaubens aufzustellen, daß er vielmehr strittige Fragen nach den bereits festgesetzten Glaubensartikeln zu entscheiden habe und daß neue Glaubensartikel von einem Konzil zu beraten und zu entscheiden seien, engt im Sinne Luthers die Autorität des Papstes gegenüber bestimmten Praktiken im späten Mittelalter ein. Da Luther in demselben Zusammenhang erklärt, daß eine extensive Auslegung der Formel „per modum suffragii" einen neuen Glaubensartikel darstellen würde, ergibt sich als Luthers Meinung zwingend, daß eine päpstliche Entscheidung, wenn sie rechtens und im Einklang mit Schrift und Tradition sein soll, Luthers Meinung über „potestas clauium" und „per modum suffragii" bestätigen soll. Anders gesagt: es ist für Luther unvorstellbar, daß der Papst Gewalt über die Seelen im Fegefeuer haben sollte.

Liest man Luthers Äußerung in dem Widmungsbrief an den Papst im Zusammenhang mit diesen Ausführungen in den Resolutiones zu These 26, dann ist es nicht möglich, Luther zu dieser Zeit als Papalisten oder als einen Vertreter der päpstlichen Unfehlbarkeit zu bezeichnen. Gewiß, die Formulierung in dem Widmungsbrief geht sehr weit; sie ist auch nicht gegen Mißverständnisse abgesichert. Luther konnte aber doch wohl annehmen, daß man in Rom nicht nur den Widmungsbrief, sondern auch die Resolutiones selbst lesen würde, wie es tatsächlich ja auch etwa durch Cajetan geschehen ist. Insofern konnte er annehmen, daß man auch in Rom verstehen würde, in welchem Sinne er eine päpstliche Entscheidung akzeptieren würde.

Neben dieser wichtigen Stelle müssen für Luthers Haltung zu Rom im Frühjahr 1518 auch einige andere Äußerungen in den Resolutiones herangezogen werden, um das Bild zu vervollständigen.

Ecclesiasticis patribus ab Ecclesia Romana receptis, hucusque seruatis et ex Canonibus ac decretalibus Pontificiis habetur et haberi potest. Quod si quid ex iis probari uel improbari non potest, id gratia disputationis duntaxat pro iudicio rationis et experientia tenebo, semper tamen in hiis saluo iudicio omnium superiorum meorum."

Immer wieder sagt Luther, daß der Papst, wenn er Ablaß erteilt, ganz offenbar lediglich diejenigen Strafen erlassen will, die er nach dem Kirchenrecht oder nach eigener Entscheidung jemandem auferlegt hat[16]. Luther ist sich völlig sicher, daß der Papst keine Gewalt über die Hölle hat[17], was freilich auch nicht behauptet wurde. Zeigen will Luther jedoch, daß der Papst ebenfalls über das Fegefeuer keine Gewalt hat[18].

Weiter, die oft erörterte Aussage in These 6 und der dazugehörige Kommentar in den Resolutiones müssen wenigstens erwähnt werden, daß nämlich der Papst die Schuld nur in der Weise erlassen kann, daß er erklärt, sie sei bereits von Gott erlassen worden[19].

Der Vorrang, welchen für Luther das Wort Christi vor der Gewalt des Papstes hat, kommt unmißverständlich zum Ausdruck in der Feststellung:

Nec Iuristae... segnes sunt authores, qui, dum nimio studio extollunt potestatem Papae, plus foecerunt aestimari et mirari potestatem Papae quam uerbum Christi honorari fide, Cum docendi sint homines, ut non in potestatem Papae, sed in uerbum Christi Papae promittentis confidere discant, si modo uelint esse pacati in conscientiis suis. Non enim quia Papa dat, aliquid habes, sed si credideris te accipere, habes: tantum habes, quantum credis propter promissionem Christi[20].

Aus dieser Äußerung kann man wohl schließen, daß für Luther der Papst, wenn er sein Amt recht ausübt, gewissermaßen das Sprachrohr ist, dessen sich Christus bedient. Freilich ist dabei für Luther stets schon die Hl. Schrift als kritischer Maßstab vorausgesetzt, an dem sich die Aussagen des Papstes messen lassen müssen.

Unter den mancherlei weiteren Gedanken, die Luther über den Papst und die päpstliche Potestas äußert, ist folgender von besonderem Interesse. In These 69 hatte Luther gesagt: „Tenentur Episcopi et Curati ueniarum apostolicarum Commissarios cum omni reuerentia admittere[21]." In den Resolutiones erklärt Luther hierzu:

Man muß nämlich der päpstlichen Autorität in allem mit Ehrerbietung nachgeben. Denn „wer sich der Gewalt widersetzt, widersetzt sich der

---

[16] WA 1, 534, 20 f.
[17] Ibid. 25—28.
[18] Ibid. 29 f.
[19] Ibid. 538, 37—39.
[20] Ibid. 543, 3—9.
[21] Ibid. 236, 35 f.

Ordnung Gottes" (Röm. 13, 2); die sich aber Gott widersetzen, ziehen sich selbst die Verdammnis zu. Und der Herr selbst sagt: „Wer euch verachtet, der verachtet mich" (Lc. 10, 16). Deshalb muß man auch in kleinen Dingen nicht weniger als in großen der Autorität nachgeben. Daraus folgt nun auch: selbst wenn der Papst ein ungerechtes Urteil fällt, muß man dieses Urteil fürchten, wie auch Kaiser Karl sagt: „Was er auferlegt, wenn es auch schwer sein sollte, muß man tragen." Wie wir auch aus der Erfahrung sehen, daß es von der Kirche geschieht, die gewiß heute durch unendliche Lasten bedrückt wird und es gleichwohl ruhig trägt mit Ehrerbietung und Demut. Das muß man jedoch recht verstehen, damit man nicht in den Irrtum des Gewissens gerate, als ob man ungerechte Urteile deshalb befolgen müsse, weil sie für gerecht gehalten werden müßten von denen, die sich ihnen fügen sollen[22].

In diesem Text wird deutlich, daß Luther an dem Gehorsam gegen den Papst auch dann festhält oder wenigstens festhalten möchte, wenn der Papst ein ungerechtes Urteil fällen sollte. In solchem Fall darf man ein derartiges Urteil nicht etwa für gerecht halten. Es fällt auf, daß Luther die Notwendigkeit des Gehorsams auch in einer solchen Situation nicht aus Mt. 16, 18 f., sondern aus Röm. 13 ableitet[23]. Die Frage, ob man daraus schließen kann, daß der Papst für Luther vornehmlich nur noch Obrigkeit ist wie andere Obrigkeiten auch, kann hier nur gestellt, nicht jedoch näher erörtert werden. Auf jeden Fall macht aber dieser Text deutlich, daß Luthers Aussage in dem Widmungsbrief an Leo X., er werde jedes Urteil des Papstes hinnehmen, nicht die Ansicht einschließt, daß das zu erwartende Urteil des Papstes unbedingt auch gerecht sein wird. Luther würde vielmehr auch ein offensichtlich ungerechtes nicht — noch nicht! — verwerfen. Man spürt freilich gewissermaßen zwischen den Zeilen, daß diese Haltung Luthers sich dann ändern könnte, wenn er zu der Überzeugung gelangen sollte, daß es sich in einem bestimmten Fall nicht lediglich um ein Fehlurteil handeln sollte, sondern daß in Rom der Antichrist herrscht.

Sieht man die Äußerungen Luthers in dem Widmungsbrief an den Papst nicht isoliert, sondern im Zusammenhang mit den Resolutiones, dann dürfte sich im ganzen ein geschlossenes Bild von

---

[22] Ibid. 618, 24—34 (eigene Übersetzung).
[23] Hierauf hat insbesondere hingewiesen J. Heckel, Initia iuris ecclesiastici Protestantium (Sitzungsber. der Bayer. Akad. der Wiss., phil.-hist. Kl., Jg. 1949, 5; München, 1950), 120 ff.

Luthers Haltung zu Rom ergeben. Freilich sah Luther sich nicht mehr für längere Zeit in der Lage, seine Bereitschaft zum Gehorsam beizubehalten.

II

Es war insbesondere die Schrift des römischen Theologen Silvester Prierias De Potestate Papae Dialogus (erschienen im Juni 1518), welche die Frage der päpstlichen Autorität in dem Streit um Luther in verschärfter Form stellte. Wichtig war schon die Tatsache, daß Prierias als Magister Sacri Palatii eine beratende Funktion für den Papst innehatte; der Dialogus ging auf den Auftrag zurück, ein Gutachten zu erstatten. Obendrein hatte Prierias den Wunsch, als Dominikaner seinem Mit-Ordensmann Johannes Tetzel zu Hilfe zu kommen.

Prierias hat sein Gutachten zu Luthers 95 Thesen in der Weise angelegt, daß er zunächst vier Fundamenta mitteilt, in denen er seine Ekklesiologie zusammenfaßt, um erst darauf Luthers 95 Thesen anzugreifen. Die schroffe, papalistische Ekklesiologie, die sich hier findet, muß kurz umrissen werden, weil Luther in seiner nächsten wichtigen Äußerung hierauf Bezug nahm.

Die vier Fundamenta des Prierias sind die folgenden. Das erste fundamentum besagt: die universale Kirche ist wesensmäßig die Versammlung aller an Christus Glaubenden zum Gottesdienst. Die universale Kirche ist virtuell die römische Kirche, das Haupt aller Kirchen, und der Papst. „Ecclesia Romana repraesentatiue est collegium Cardinalium, uirtualiter autem est Pontifex summus, qui est Ecclesiae caput, aliter tamen, quam Christus." Das zweite fundamentum bedeutet: wie die universale Kirche bei Entscheidungen in Fragen des Glaubens und der Sitte nicht irren kann, so kann auch ein Konzil, das alles in seinen Kräften Stehende tut, nicht irren. So kann auch die römische Kirche und auch der Papst nicht irren, wenn er alles in seinen Kräften Stehende tut, um die Wahrheit zu erkennen. Das dritte fundamentum — für den Streit mit Luther war dieses von besonderer Bedeutung — heißt: „Wer nicht der Lehre der römischen Kirche und des römischen Papstes als der unfehlbaren Glaubensregel anhängt, von der auch die Hl. Schrift ihre Kraft und ihre Autorität erhält, der ist ein Häretiker." Das vierte fundamentum schließlich meint, daß die römische Kirche in gleicher Weise durch eine Entscheidung wie auch durch faktisches Verhalten

(„sicut verbo ita et facto") Fragen des Glaubens und der Sitten regeln kann[24].

Es ist zwar richtig, daß Prierias ebenso wie auch Cajetan insofern ein gewisses Gegengewicht gegen diese papalistischen Argumente schuf, als er der Meinung war, daß der Papst gegebenenfalls Häretiker werden könne. Aber das war doch eigentlich nur eine theoretische Erwägung, wie sie in der Kirchenrechtswissenschaft und auch in der Dogmatik schon seit langem angestellt worden war[25]. Nur wenige Theologen wie etwa Ockham oder Marsilius von Padua, ganz zu schweigen von Wyclif oder Huß, hatten es gewagt, daraus auch praktische Konsequenzen zu ziehen und etwa gar einen bestimmten Papst für häretisch zu erklären. Was das frühe 16. Jahrhundert betrifft, so haben jedenfalls Prierias wie auch Cajetan Luthers Aussagen über die Autorität des Papstes bei weitem übertroffen. Es kann keine Rede davon sein, daß Luthers „Papalismus" weiter gegangen sei also derjenige von Prierias oder Cajetan, wie R. Bäumer behauptet[26]. Insbesondere die Auffassung des Prierias, daß die Lehre der römischen Kirche und des Papstes die unfehlbare Glaubensregel sei, von welcher auch die Hl. Schrift ihre Kraft und ihre Autorität erhalte, bedeutet letztlich die Überordnung der päpstlichen Autorität über diejenige der Schrift.

Es dürfte ziemlich sicher sein, daß es wesentlich dieser Gedanke des Prierias war, der in Luther die Ansicht wachsen ließ, daß die Stimme des Papstes die Stimme Christi zum Schweigen zu bringen droht[27].

---

[24] Der Dialogus des Prierias ist vollständig am bequemsten zugänglich in der Erlanger Luther-Ausgabe: EA, Opera uarii argumenti, Bd. 1 (Frankfurt–Erlangen, 1865). Hier finden sich die vier fundamenta SS. 346 f. Die wichtigsten Aussagen lauten: „... Fundamentum secundum. Sicut ecclesia uniuersalis non potest errare determinando de fide aut moribus, ita et uerum concilium, faciens quod in se est (ut intelligat ueritatem) errare non potest, quod intelligo incluso Capite, aut tandem ac finaliter, licet forte prima facie fallatur, quousque durat motus inquirendae ueritatis, imo etiam aliquando errauit, licet tandem per spiritum Sanctum intellexerit ueritatem, et similiter nec ecclesia Romana, nec pontifex summus determinans ea ratione, qua Pontifex, id est, ex officio suo pronuncians, et faciens quod in se est, ut intelligat ueritatem. Fundamentum tertium. Quicunque non innititur doctrinae Romanae ecclesiae, ac Romani Pontificis, tanquam regulae fidei infallibili, a qua etiam sacra Scriptura robur trahit et auritatem, haereticus est. Fundamentum quartum. Ecclesia Romana sicut uerbo ita et facto potest circa fidem et mores aliquid decernere... Corollarium. Qui circa indulgentias dicit, ecclesiam Romanam non posse facere id quod de facto facit, haereticus est."
[25] Hierzu s. insbesondere B. Tierney, Foundations of the Conciliar Theory (Cambridge, 1955).
[26] R Bäumer, op. cit. 25.
[27] H. A. Oberman, op. cit. 340.

Die Erwartung oder Hoffnung, die in Luthers Widmungsbrief an Leo X. zum Ausdruck gekommen war, wurde damit für Luther, als er den Dialogus des Prierias vermutlich Anfang August 1518 in Händen hatte, gegenstandslos. Luther lernte also den Dialogus ungefähr zu der Zeit kennen, als seine Resolutiones im Druck erschienen.

Luther hat zunächst auf diese Publikation in der Weise reagiert, daß er den Dialogus einfach ohne irgendeine kommentierende Bemerkung nachdrucken ließ[28]. Er war der Meinung, daß die Argumentation des Prierias derart fragwürdig sei, daß sie keiner Widerlegung bedürfe. Dabei hatte er nicht nur die vier Fundamenta im Blick, sondern auch die einzelnen Gegenargumente des Prierias gegen seine eigenen 95 Thesen. Als aber dieser Nachdruck in kurzer Zeit vergriffen war, hat Luther noch im August 1518 unter dem Titel Ad Dialogum Silvestri Prieriatis de Potestate Papae Responsio eine Entgegnung verfaßt, die noch im August 1518 im Druck vorlag.

In dieser Entgegnung behandelt Luther die vier Fundamenta mehr am Rande. Er sagt zu ihnen lediglich: „Ich übergehe deine Fundamenta, deren genauen Sinn ich mehr vermute als begreife.“ Statt dessen nimmt Luther sich die Freiheit, seinerseits ebenfalls drei Fundamenta aufzustellen, aus denen seine Gegenposition deutlich wird[29].

Luthers erstes Fundamentum ist

jenes Wort des seligen Paulus: Prüfet alles, was gut ist, behaltet (1. Thess. 5, 21), sowie Gal. 1(, 8): Wenn ein Engel vom Himmel euch anderes verkündigte, als ihr empfangen habt, so sei er verflucht. Das zweite Fundamentum ist jenes Wort des seligen Augustin an Hieronymus: Ich habe gelernt, allein den kanonischen Büchern die Ehre zu erzeigen, daß ich ganz fest glaube, keiner von ihren Verfassern habe geirrt. Bei den übrigen aber, wie bedeutend sie auch durch ihre Lehre und Heiligkeit sein mögen, glaube ich nicht, daß ihre Aussagen nur deshalb wahr sind, weil sie eben in dieser Weise gedacht haben. Das dritte Fundamentum ist jenes Wort aus den Dekretalen (Clementinen, Tit. IX „de poenitentiis et remissionibus“, cap. II „Abusionibus“, ed. Friedberg 1190): den Quästoren ist bei der Ablaßpredigt nichts gestattet, dem Volk zu predigen, als was in ihren Vollmachtsbriefen enthal-

---

[28] Eine kurze Übersicht über die Entstehungsgeschichte von Luthers Antwort an Prierias findet sich in WA 1, 645 f.

[29] Ibid. 647, 17 f.: „Omitto fundamenta tua, quorum intelligentiam magis suspicor quam capio, et more exemploque tuo mihi quoque fundamenta iaciam necesse est.“

ten ist. Das ist dasjenige, was du sagst mit der Bemerkung über das, was die Kirche de facto tut[30].

Luther ist der Meinung, daß mit diesen seinen eigenen Fundamentalsätzen der gesamte Dialogus des Prierias vollkommen widerlegt ist. Luther verweist darauf, daß Prierias sich im wesentlichen nur auf die Meinungen des Thomas gestützt habe, daß er dabei jedoch nicht die Hl. Schrift, die Kirchenväter, die Canones sowie Vernunftgründe berücksichtigt habe. Luther kann seinen Spott nicht unterdrücken: wenn es schon unter Juristen das Sprichwort gibt, daß ein Rechtsgelehrter, der ohne Text redet, eine Schande sei, dann könne man ja leicht sehen, wieviel Ehre ein Theologe einbringe, der ohne Text rede. Wenn dies beherzigt worden wäre, dann hätte man gegenwärtig in der Kirche weniger an „quaestiones et opiniones" und dafür mehr vom Evangelium und der christlichen Wahrheit[31]. Es ist deutlich, daß Luther damit der Hl. Schrift bei weitem den Vorrang vor allen anderen Autoritäten einräumt, auch wenn er deren Geltung und Bedeutung noch nicht in Frage stellt. Besonders wichtig ist dabei, daß Luther sich für die Betonung der Schriftautorität auf Augustin, an anderen Stellen seiner Schrift Ad Dialogum aber auch auf andere Kirchenväter oder die Kirchenväter insgesamt beruft[32].

Wenn also auf seiten von Luthers Gegnern gegen Luthers 95 Thesen die Autorität des Papstes herausgestellt wird, dann hat Luther im Gegenzug dazu die Autorität der Schrift stärker betont. Für Luther beginnen die Autorität Roms und die Autorität der Schrift sich voneinander zu unterscheiden, ja in Gegensatz zueinander zu treten. Tatsächlich konnte Luther in seiner Antwort an Prierias nicht mehr wie in dem Widmungsbrief an Leo X. sagen, daß er aus den Worten des Papstes die Stimme Christi selbst hören und beherzigen werde. Es mutet wie eine Korrektur jener zugespitzten Formulierung aus dem Widmungsbrief an, wenn er jetzt zu Prierias sagt: „Hunc [sc. Christum] autem in te loquentem non audio, sed Aristotelem et hominem[33]."

Die Argumentation Luthers gegen Prierias braucht hier nicht im einzelnen dargestellt zu werden. Immer wieder weist Luther auf den

---

[30] Ibid. 19—28; s. hierzu K. Aland, op. cit. 153, wo auch der Fundort des Zitates aus den Dekretalen nachgewiesen ist.
[31] WA 1, 648, 2—9.
[32] Ibid. 649, 14 ff.
[33] Ibid. 648, 38.

Unterschied oder auch Gegensatz hin, der zwischen bestimmten kirchlichen Ansprüchen oder Praktiken im Ablaßwesen einerseits und Worten Jesu in den Evangelien andererseits besteht. Auch wenn Luther den Grundsatz „Sola Scriptura" hier noch nicht formuliert, folgt er praktisch bereits dem sog. reformatorischen Schriftprinzip[34].

Im weiteren Verlauf seiner Argumentation kommt Luther dann freilich doch noch auf die Fundamenta des Prierias zu sprechen, die er zunächst hatte übergehen wollen. Es sind besonders dessen beide erste Fundamenta, auf die Luther eingeht. Luther macht hier geltend — ein Jahr vor seiner berühmten Kontroverse mit Eck auf der Leipziger Disputation —, daß sowohl der Papst als auch ein Konzil irren können, und beruft sich auf den bekannten Kirchenrechtler Panormitanus. Aus der Irrtumsfähigkeit von Papst und Konzil ergibt sich für Luther, daß die Unterscheidung des Prierias zwischen „ecclesia essentialis", „repraesentativa", „virtualis" nichtig ist: diese Distinktion stützt sich nicht auf die Hl. Schrift. Luther äußert dagegen: „Ego ecclesiam uirtualiter non scio nisi in Christo, repraesentatiue non nisi in Concilio[35]." Etwas später fragt Luther: wenn der Papst virtuell, die Kardinäle repräsentativ und die Versammlung der Gläubigen essentiell die Kirche sind, welche Bezeichnung bleibt dann noch für ein Konzil übrig? Ist das Konzil etwa nur „accidentalis, nominalis et uerbalis" Kirche[36]?

An anderer Stelle greift Luther das dritte Fundamentum des Prierias an, nämlich vor allem die Aussage, daß die römische Kirche die Glaubensregel sein solle. Luther sagt hiergegen: „Ego credidi semper, quod fides esset regula Romanae Ecclesiae et omnium Ecclesiarum[37]." Nach Luther stellt Prierias die Dinge hier auf den Kopf. Nicht Rom, sondern der Glaube, den die römische Kirche bekennt, ist die Richtschnur[38].

---

[34] Cf. etwa ibid. 651, 12—20. Hier weist Luther auf folgendes Problem hin. Wenn man Jesu Wort „Tut Buße" (Mt. 4, 17), wie Luthers Gegner wollen, auf die sakramentale Buße und insbesondere auch auf die Satisfaktion bezieht, wie kann man dann den Ablaß rechtfertigen; denn einerseits ist ja Jesu Wort für die Kirche verbindliche und unveränderbare Autorität, andererseits wird durch den Ablaß eben die Satisfaktion umgewandelt. Luther schließt hier (ZZ. 19 f.): „Non enim remittere potest homo, quod deus praecepit et ligauit."

[35] WA 1, 656, 26—37.

[36] Ibid. 657, 10—12.

[37] Ibid. 662, 25 f.

[38] Ibid. 27—31: „Rogo, eousque digneris adulari Romanae Ecclesiae, ut eam permittas discipulam esse fidei, quae reguletur fide, non regulet fidem. Sed forte haec

In diesem Zusammenhang kann Luther freilich eine Äußerung tun, welche die Bedeutung Roms stark herausstellt. Er sagt:

Denn auch ich danke Christus, daß er diese eine Kirche auf Erden durch ein gewaltiges Wunder, welches allein unseren Glauben als wahr erweisen könnte, so bewahrt hat, daß sie niemals durch irgendeines ihrer Dekrete vom wahren Glauben abgewichen ist, und auch der Teufel hat durch noch so viele Abgründe schlechtester Sitten nicht bewirken können, daß bei ihr nicht von ihrem Ursprung her die Autorität der kanonischen biblischen Bücher und der Kirchenväter und Interpreten erhalten blieb[39].

Diese Aussage kann, wenn sie in ihrem ganzen Zusammenhang genommen wird, nicht als papalistisch gelten[40]. Was Luther betont, ist vielmehr die Tatsache, daß auch in Rom die Autorität der Bibel und der Kirchenväter erhalten geblieben ist. Nicht die Irrtumslosigkeit Roms oder gar der Päpste, sondern die Bewahrung der Schriftautorität in Rom und insofern die Bewahrung Roms vor Irrtum ist der Tenor dieses Gedankens.

An anderer Stelle äußert Luther Folgendes. Prierias hatte gegen Luthers 20. These die Ansicht vertreten, daß der Papst eine auferlegte Strafe ebenso gut erlassen könne wie eine noch nicht auferlegte Strafe; die gegenteilige Behauptung sei häretisch. Auch hier findet sich eine Loyalitätserklärung Luthers: Wenn die Kirche hier eine Entscheidung gefällt haben wird, werde er dieser folgen[41].

Luther muß selbst das Gefühl gehabt haben, daß die verschiedenen Äußerungen, mit denen er die Autorität des Papstes bejaht, für römisches Empfinden nicht ausreichend sind. Gegen Ende seiner Entgegnung an Prierias erklärt er jedenfalls ein für alle Mal, daß er die Gewalt des Papstes ehre, aber die Meinungen und Schmeicheleien von Prierias und anderen verachte. Luther geht sogar so weit, Auffassungen, die mit seiner eigenen nicht übereinstimmen — Luther denkt hier an seine These, daß der Papst nur die von ihm bzw. von der Kirche auferlegten Strafen erlassen könne — , für häretisch zu erklären; denn der Mensch könne keinesfalls von sich aus die Versöhnung mit Gott herbeiführen. Auch könne der Papst nicht

uerbi est controversia. Quia regulam fidei improprie locutus uocas, quod ad eam fidem, quam Romana Ecclesia profitetur, omnium fides debet conformari."

[39] Ibid. 31—36.
[40] S. hierzu die Kontroverse zwischen R. Bäumer, op. cit. 24, und K. Aland, op. cit. 130 f.
[41] WA 1, 665, 12 f.

die rechtfertigende Gnade Gottes von sich aus schenken. Nach Luther stimmt hier die ganze Kirche mit ihm überein[42].

Grenzt Luther auf diese Weise die Gewalt des Papstes in folgenschwerer Weise ein, so wird in einer weiteren Aussage seine Auffassung von den Aufgaben des päpstlichen Amtes deutlich: „Der Papst ist Diener der Kirche. Was auch immer er den Gläubigen zum Heil tun kann, das muß er heilsnotwendig umsonst tun. Wenn er das nicht tut, wird Gott das Fehlende, wie ich hoffe, durch seine Barmherzigkeit ergänzen, was der Mensch durch seine Unachtsamkeit versäumt hat[43]."

Zum Schluß seiner Antwort an Prierias geht Luther noch einmal auf die Frage der Irrtumslosigkeit der Kirche ein. Hier betont er, daß die virtuelle oder repräsentative Kirche, wie Prierias sie nennt, irren könne, daß aber die universale Kirche nicht irren könne; im übrigen könne sich Prierias für seine Auffassung von der Irrtumslosigkeit der Kirche nicht auf eine päpstliche Entscheidung stützen[44].

Man mag finden, daß Luthers Stellung zu Rom, wie sie in seiner Entgegnung an Prierias sich äußert, noch der letzten Klarheit entbehrt. Luther befindet sich insofern deutlich in der Defensive, als er die von ihm schon in den 95 Thesen vorgenommene Eingrenzung der päpstlichen Gewalt gegen harte Angriffe verteidigen muß und seine in dem Widmungsbrief vom 30. Mai 1518 ausgesprochene Erwartung über den Papst als Christi Sprachrohr nicht mehr aufrechterhalten kann. Luther möchte nach wie vor gegenüber dem Papst botmäßig und loyal sein. Er meint sogar, daß die römische Kirche bislang vor Irrtum bewahrt geblieben ist, bezieht dies freilich auf die in ihr nach wie vor geltende Autorität der biblischen

---

[42] Ibid. 670, 3—8: „Respondeo tibi semel pro omnibus: Summi Pontificis potestatem honoro, sicut decet, uestras autem uel opiniones uel adulationes contemno: ideo huius conclusionis meae (hanc enim non disputo) contrarium libera fronte haeresim pronuncio. Non est in manu hominis reconciliari hominem deo, nec Papa potest gratiam dei iustificantem donare, ut tota sentit Ecclesia. Cuius contrarium nullus fuit tam foedus haereticus qui doceret."

[43] Ibid. 671, 34—36: „Papa minister est Ecclesiae: quicquid potest facere fidelibus in salutem, debet sub necessitate salutis etiam gratis, quod si non fecerit, deus supplebit, spero, per misericordiam suam, quod homo neglexit per incuriam suam."

[44] Ibid. 685, 18—25: „Ad quartam mihi pro regula tradis factum et dictum Ecclesiae Romanae. Respondeo: Si de uirtuali et repraesentatiua tua Ecclesia loqueris, nolo tuam regulam. Quia, ut supra dixi, ex c. Significasti, talis Ecclesia potest errare. Uniuersalis autem Ecclesia non potest errare, ut doctissime etiam probat Cardinalis Cameracensis in primo Sententiarum. Deinde: Nec Papa usquam hoc dicit aut facit, quod tu factum et dictum Ecclesiae vocas: promptulus es aequiuocator huius nominis ‚Ecclesia‘, ideo maxime mihi suspectus."

Schriften. Auf der anderen Seite kann er die papalistische Ekklesiologie des Prierias nur ablehnen. Insbesondere verwirft er die Meinung, als wäre Rom selbst die Glaubensregel. Daß Päpste und Konzilien irren können, spricht er deutlich aus, hält aber doch an der Irrtumslosigkeit der universalen Kirche im Sinne von Mt. 16, 18 f. fest.

Die Frage, die sich früher oder später stellen mußte, war, ob Luther seine Loyalität gegenüber dem Papst würde aufrechterhalten können. Von dem im August 1518 erreichten Diskussionsstand her muß man sagen, daß Luther das dann nicht würde tun können, wenn sich die papalistische Ekklesiologie des Prierias in Rom durchsetzen würde. Luther hingegen war der Meinung, daß die höchste Autorität in der Kirche dem Konzil zukomme[45].

III

Von den vielfältigen weiteren Fragen und Aspekten, die für Luthers Haltung zu Rom in den letzten Monaten des Jahres 1518[46] an sich zu behandeln wären, sei hier lediglich kurz auf das Augsburger Verhör Luthers durch Kardinal Cajetan in den Tagen vom 12. bis 14. Oktober 1518 eingegangen[47]. Dieses Verhör hatte für die weitere Entwicklung des Streites um Luther ganz erhebliche Bedeutung. War ursprünglich vorgesehen, daß Luther entweder Widerruf leisten oder sofort verhaftet werden sollte, so hatte der sächsische Kurfürst Friedrich der Weise es erreicht, daß der Kardinal Luther lediglich väterlich verhören sollte; die Kurie hatte wegen der anstehenden Nachfolgeregelung für Kaiser Maximilian I. und der Bedeutung von Friedrichs Stimme dabei diesem Wunsch aus Kursachsen nachgegeben. Wichtig ist das Augsburger Verhör vor allem aber auch durch die Person Cajetans selbst. Cajetan kann mit Recht als einer der fähigsten Theologen gelten, welche die gesamte Kirche damals überhaupt hatte[48]. Dabei war Cajetan durchaus nicht ohne Blick für manche Aspekte, auf die es Luther ankam. Das Gespräch zwischen Cajetan und Luther ist von daher eine der wichtigsten

---

[45] Hierzu s. ibid. 674, 29—32.
[46] Näheres s. hierzu insbesondere bei K. Aland, op. cit., der freilich auf das Augsburger Verhör Luthers durch Cajetan nur knapp eingeht.
[47] Hierzu s. M. Brecht, op. cit. 237—255.
[48] Zu Cajetan s. insbesondere J. Wicks, Cajetan und die Anfänge der Reformation (Kath. Leben u. Kirchenreform im Zeitalter der Glaubensspaltung, 43; Münster, 1984); B. Hallensleben, Communicatio: Anthropologie und Gnadenlehre bei Thomas de Vio Cajetan (Reformationsgesch. Studien u. Texte, 123; Münster, 1985).

Auseinandersetzungen zwischen Luther und Rom. Wenn überhaupt ene Chance für eine Verständigung oder wenigstens für eine
gewisse Annäherung bestand, dann war dies wohl im Oktober 1518
der Fall.

Bei dem Augsburger Verhör ging es an sich nicht unmittelbar um
die Frage des Papsttums. Vielmehr beanstandete Cajetan einmal
Luthers Auffassung über den Schatz Christi, zum anderen Luthers
Ansicht, daß für den heilsamen Sakramentsempfang die glaubende
Gewißheit der Rechtfertigung notwendig sei. Gleichwohl ist auch
die Frage der päpstlichen Autorität zwischen Cajetan und Luther
zur Sprache gekommen, wie Luther in seinen Acta Augustana berichtet.

Allerdings dürfte Luther Cajetans Meinung schärfer wiedergege-
ben haben, als es dessen wirklicher Meinung entsprach. Nach
Luther hat Cajetan geäußert, daß die Gewalt des Papstes größer sei
als die eines Konzils; sie stehe auch über der Schrift, ja schlechter-
dings über der ganzen Kirche[49]. Man kann vermuten, daß Cajetan
sich in dieser Frage wohl ähnlich ausgesprochen hat, wie es Prierias
in seinem Dialogus getan hatte[50], also wohl der Meinung war, daß
die Hl. Schrift ihre Autorität erst durch die Lehre der römischen
Kirche erhält. Dabei hat Cajetan kaum gemeint, daß die Autorität
des Papstes über der Autorität der Schrift stehe. Aber Cajetan hat,
wie besonders aus seinen Augsburger Traktaten von 1518 deutlich
wird[51], a limine ausschließen wollen, daß irgendjemand sich auf die
Schrift gegen den Papst berufen könnte. Von da aus reicht im Zwei-
felsfall für Cajetan die Autorität der römischen Kirche oder des
Papstes zur Entscheidung einer strittigen Frage aus; sie bedarf nicht
der Ergänzung oder Bestätigung durch einen Konzilsentscheid[52].

---

[49] WA 2, 8, 10 f.: „Tunc cepit [sc. Cajetan] aduersus me potestatem Papae com-
mendare, quoniam supra Concilium, supra scripturam, supra omnia Ecclesiae sit."
Cf. Lohse, „Cajetan und Luther", Kerygma und Dogma, 32 (1986), 150—169.

[50] S. oben im Text bei Anm. 24.

[51] Hierzu s. insbesondere G. Hennig, Cajetan und Luther: Ein historischer Beitrag zur Begegnung von Thomismus und Reformation (Arbeiten zur Theol.,
2. Reihe, 7; Stuttgart, 1966).

[52] Für diese Fragen sind zwei Bemerkungen in den Augsburger Traktaten Cajetans besonders aufschlußreich. Siehe Cajetan, Opuscula Omnia (Lyon, 1581),
col. 113ᵃ, 30—36 (zur Frage des „thesaurus ecclesiae"): „nulli in materia sacramen-
torum licere dissentire ab eo quod Romana ecclesia facit et praedicat: credendum est
igitur, in dubium aut opinionem uertendum sic esse. Nec somniauit aut finxit sibi
Romana ecclesia thesaurum istum indulgentiarum, sed ex Scripturae sacrae autoritate, certaque inde ratione sacrorum doctorum sententia probata id habetur." Ferner
ebd., col. 115ᵇ, 17—21 (ebenfalls mit Bezug auf die Frage des „thesaurus ecclesiae"):

Für Luther bestand freilich die Harmonie zwischen Kirchenautorität und Schriftautorität nicht mehr. Insofern konnte Luther von seinem eigenen Standpunkt aus Cajetan vorhalten, er stelle den Papst über die Schrift, obwohl dies nicht Cajetans Meinung war. Der Satz, den Luther in den Acta Augustana wiedergibt, zeigt also die Wirkung, welche Cajetans Position angesichts der fortgeschrittenen Kontroverse auf Luther hatte und wohl auch haben mußte, nicht jedoch die Meinung, welche Cajetan selbst hatte.

Im weiteren Verlauf des Verhörs hat Luther versichert, er sei sich nicht dessen bewußt, irgendetwas gegen die Hl. Schrift, die Kirchenväter, die päpstlichen Dekretalen oder gegen die „recta ratio" gesagt zu haben[53]. Außerdem verweist er auf seine Bereitschaft, sich einer legitimen Entscheidung der hl. Kirche zu unterwerfen[54].

Ein letzter Nachklang von Luthers Ansicht, wie sie in dem Widmungsschreiben an Leo X. vom 30 Mai 1518 ausgedrückt worden war, findet sich in Luthers Acta Augustana, freilich mit einer näheren Differenzierung, die der fortgeschrittenen Kontroverse Rechnung trägt. Luther sagt nämlich, daß man die Dekretalen des Papstes hören müsse „wie die Stimme des Petrus", fügt jedoch hinzu, daß dies nur von denjenigen Dekretalen gelte, welche mit der Hl. Schrift übereinstimmen und von früheren Dekreten der Kirchenväter nicht abweichen[55]. Das gilt für Luther deswegen, weil der Papst nicht über, sondern unter der Schrift steht[56]. Trotz dieser

---

„Et si solius Romanae ecclesiae autoritate diffinitiua diceretur, sufficeret ad rationem reddendam de ea, quae in nobis est fide, non minus, quam si autoritate generalis concilii diffinitum esset. Haeretici autem sicut refutare possunt Romanam ecclesiam, ita et concilium."

[53] WA 2, 8, 37—40: „hodie protestor, me non esse mihi conscium aliquid dixisse, quod sit contra sacram scripturam, Ecclesiasticos patres aut decretales Pontificum aut rectam rationem, sed omnia quae dixi hodie quoque mihi sana, uera, catholica esse uidentur."

[54] Ibid. 9, 1—3: „Nihilominus tamen sum homo potens errare, submisi me et etiam nunc submitto iudicio et determinationi legittimae sanctae Ecclesiae et omnibus melius sentientibus."

[55] Ibid. 10, 7—11: „Vexabat etiam, quod fieri posse constat, decretales aliquando erroneas esse et contra sacras literas et charitatem militare. Nam licet decretales Romani Pontificis tanquam uocem Petri oportet audire, ut dicitur dist. XIX, tamen hoc ipsum intelligitur de hiis solum (ut dicitur ibidem), quae consone sunt sacrae scripturae et a prioribus patrum decretis non dissentiunt."

[56] Ibid. 11, 2—4: „cum Papa non super, sed sub uerbo dei sit iuxta illud Gal: i. Si angelus de celo aliud uobis euangelisauerit quam accepistis, anathema sit."

Einschränkung ist Luther freilich auch jetzt noch bestrebt, dem Papst mit Ehrerbietung zu begegnen[57].

Das Verhör vor Cajetan verlief für Luther enttäuschend. Er hatte gehofft, mit Cajetan über sein eigentliches Anliegen, das er in den 95 Thesen vorgebracht hatte, zu sprechen, nämlich über die Erneuerung der Buße und über den Mißbrauch im Ablaßwesen. Sicher hatte Luther hier übertriebene Erwartungen gehabt. Das schon in Gang gekommene kirchliche Verfahren gegen ihn ließ eine solche Erörterung nicht mehr zu. Fast noch bedrückender war für Luther, daß die Berufung auf die Hl. Schrift bei dem Streit offensichtlich nicht zählte. Selbst Cajetan ließ sich dadurch bei dem Verhör nicht beeindrucken, obwohl seine Augsburger Traktate zeigen, daß er von Luthers theologischer Argumentation doch auf bestimmte Schwächen der damaligen Kirche und Theologie hingewiesen worden war; auf jeden Fall hat sich Cajetan seit 1518 immer wieder mit den durch Luther angeregten Fragen befaßt[58].

Was Luther betrifft, so haben Prierias wie auch Cajetan bei ihm die Auffassung hervorgerufen und bestärkt, daß kirchliche Entscheidungen u.U. nicht mit der H. Schrift übereinstimmen, daß es aber gleichwohl nach Meinung der kirchlichen Autoritäten niemandem erlaubt sei, sich gegen solche Entscheidungen auf die Hl. Schrift zu berufen. Luther gelangt von daher zu der Auffassung, daß man, falls kirchliche Entscheidungen der Schrift widersprechen, nicht der Kirche, sondern der Hl. Schrift folgen muß. In Augsburg ist Luther zu der Überzeugung gekommen, daß ein solcher Widerspruch zwischen der Hl. Schrift und päpstlichen Entscheidungen im Fall der Ablaßlehre tatsächlich vorliegt[59]. Von da aus war es kein großer Schritt für Luther, die Befürchtung zu hegen, daß an der Kurie in Rom der Antichrist herrscht.

Die Äußerungen Luthers zur Autorität des Papstes im Jahre 1518 zeigen somit, daß in Luthers Kritik am Papsttum an sich jegliche Programmatik fehlt. Mag Luther in seinen 95 Thesen nun den Papst schon attackiert haben oder nicht, im Zentrum seines Auftretens in der breiten Öffentlichkeit stand sein Bemühen um die geistliche

---

[57] Ibid. 18, 2—6: „Veritas diuina est etiam domina Papae: non enim iudicium hominis expecto, ubi diuinum iudicium cognoui: sed quia oportuit reuerentiam seruare ei, qui uice summi Pontificis fungebatur, tum quod etiam uerissime dicta oporteat cum humilitate et timore asserere et tueri."

[58] Hierzu s. insbesondere G. Hennig, op. cit., passim.

[59] WA 2, 19, 22—26.

Erneuerung der Buße; Motiv und Maßstab dieser Bemühung war die H. Schrift. Die verstärkt gegen Luther vorgebrachteln papalistischen Argumente machten es ihm unmöglich, den Gehorsam gegenüber dem Papst bedingungslos zu leisten. Nicht aus grundsätzlichen Erwägungen, sondern aufgrund bestimmter Erfahrungen und Argumente kam Luther im Jahre 1518 von seiner anfänglich noch bewährten Loyalität gegenüber dem Papst zu der Ansicht, in Rom herrsche der Antichrist.

10

The Lutheran *forma ecclesiae* in the Colloquy at Augsburg, August 1530*

IN an ecumenical age such as our own we read the history of the Reformation with different leading questions from those asked by our forebears. The promising dialogues between our Churches today, such as the Anglican–Roman Catholic dialogue, on which Henry Chadwick has served with distinction, stir a natural interest in the colloquies of the sixteenth century. These are less well known than the disputations, for example at Leipzig in 1519 and Zürich in 1523. But there were dialogues as well, at which appointed spokesmen worked, briefly but unsuccessfully, to prevent the emerging religious divisions from hardening into fixed ecclesial and political oppositions.[1] Beginnings seem to exercise a special fascination, and consequently a small, but notable, body of literature has developed around the first such Reformation-era bilateral colloquy. This took place between Lutheran and Catholic representatives at the German imperial Diet of Augsburg in 1530, after the submission of the Lutheran *Confessio Augustana* on 25 June and the reading of the imperial *Confutatio* on 3 August.[2]

My earlier study of Lutheran–Catholic relations in the decisive months of 1530 attended to the immediate preparations for the Diet and to the exchange of argument into early August. That study investigated the conflicting assessments made by the participants

* The author gratefully acknowledges his indebtedness to the Newberry Library, Chicago, for a fellowship grant in support of research on this topic and for continuing access to its collections and services.
    [1] The papers of the Wolfenbüttel Symposium of March 1979 reflect recent scholarship on these bilateral colloquies. See the edition, under Gerhard Müller, *Die Religionsgespräche der Reformationszeit* (Gütersloh, 1980). Also, more recently, M. Hollerbach, *Das Religionsgespräch als Mittel der konfessionellen und politischen Auseinandersetzung* (Berne–Frankfurt, 1982).
    [2] The basic narrative is Herbert Immenkötter, *Um die Einheit im Glauben: Die Unionsverhandlungen des Augsburger Reichstages im August und September 1530* (Münster, 1973). Immenkötter advances the prior research of G. Müller, E. Honée, and V. Pfnür. The contributions of these researchers will be noted in the pages that follow.

regarding concrete forms of religious practice, such as mass stipends, private masses, communion under one form, ritual blessings of objects for devotional use, clerical celibacy, integral confession of sins, fasting laws, and the institution of religious and monastic life under vows. The Lutherans offered a searing indictment of this complex of practices and structures, making evident just how imperative was their call for reform, a reform which the bishops had not undertaken. The Catholic *Confutatio* offered defences of selected practices and institutions as not being abuses, but instead being fully warranted and having hierarchical approval.[3] The present essay considers the colloquy of August 1530, giving special attention to the give-and-take of discussion on these controverted practices and structures of church life.

Philip Melanchthon gave a useful point of focus to the earlier study, when he wrote in the confession of 25 June that, since the Lutheran faith is orthodox and in continuity with past ages, the real argument lies elsewhere: 'The dispute and dissension are concerned chiefly with various traditions and abuses.'[4] For the middle phases of the Diet, especially for the colloquies of 7 to 31 August, another phrase penned by Melanchthon can serve to name the central issue. On or about 12 August, Melanchthon proposed that the Lutheran leader, Johann, Elector of Saxony, request the naming of a relatively small joint commission to work toward greater agreement between the Lutheran and Catholic positions on doctrine and rites. The Saxon and Lutheran goal in such an exchange would be to show that the real differences were—or could be brought—within the bounds of what the other side could tolerate, at least until the convocation of a General Council. Dogma will not be critical, since Melanchthon is sure that the Lutherans can make patent their essential orthodoxy. In the service of doctrinal continuity and good order, the Lutheran side would accept the restoration of episcopal jurisdiction. From the other side the specific concessions to request are the chalice for the laity, marriage for the clergy and religious, and 'our mass' (that is, only the reformed, communitarian celebration, with private masses being suppressed). In fact, if the other side granted only the chalice

[3] J. Wicks, 'Abuses under Indictment at the Diet of Augsburg 1530', *Theological Studies*, 41 (1980), 252–302.

[4] *Confessio Augustana*, Conclusion to Part I, cited from T. G. Tappert *et al.* (eds.), *The Book of Concord* (Philadelphia, 1959), 48, translating the German. In Melanchthon's Latin: 'Tota dissensio est de paucis quibusdam abusibus'; *Die Bekenntnis-*

and clerical marriage that could suffice, for 'thus our *forma ecclesiae* would remain.'⁵ The colloquies of August 1530 were, in fact, a lively exchange over the continuation, in certain territories and cities of Germany, of the *forma ecclesiae* recently constituted by reforms, inspired by Luther, for which responsible established authorities were asking tolerant recognition from the Emperor Charles V, the papal legate Lorenzo Cardinal Campeggio, and the majority block of princes and prince-bishops attending the Diet.

Before we attempt an assessment of the elements of the Lutheran *forma ecclesiae*, let us attempt a brief evocation of the mood or climate of the colloquy of 1530. Then our account of the actual dialogue will follow its three phases, at the end of which our reflection will probe the contributing causes of the final impasse at Augsburg in 1530.

The Climate of Dialogue

Two small details suggest something of the partial openness of Catholic authorities to some concessions to certain German Protestants. In May and October 1529, Miguel Mai, the imperial ambassador to the court of Pope Clement VII, reported how Clement expressed a readiness to grant certain Lutheran demands and to condone some at least of their practical and liturgical innovations, if thereby he could avoid having to convoke a General Council.⁶ The Emperor Charles V did not share the Pope's abhorrence of a Council, but he had other motives for magnanimity. In late July 1530 he was once discussing religious policy with his brother, Archduke Ferdinand, and the legate Campeggio. Ferdinand gave vent to his forthright disapproval of Lutheran doctrine,

---

schriften der evangelisch-lutherischen Kirche, 4th edn. (Göttingen, 1959), 83 C. The German text was read before the Diet on 25 June 1530, in the name of five princes of the Empire and the free cities of Nuremberg and Reutlingen, but both German and Latin texts were submitted to the Emperor Charles V.

⁵ Cited from the essential source collection, K. E. Förstemann (ed.), *Urkundenbuch zu der Geschichte des Reichstages zu Augsburg im Jahre 1530*, 2 vols. (Halle, 1833; repr. Osnabrück, 1966), ii 239. For the dating near 12 Aug., we follow H. Scheible, *Melanchthons Briefwechsel*, i (Stuttgart-Bad Cannstadt, 1977), 423.

⁶ Cited in P. de Gayangos y Arce (ed.), *Calendar of Letters, Despatches, and State Papers Relating to the Negotiations between England and Spain*, iv/1 (London, 1879), 23 f. and 283. Karl Brandi cited Mai's original Spanish of the first such utterance by Clement: *Kaiser Karl V*, 2 vols. (Munich, 1937–9), ii. 198.

to which Charles reportedly responded with a reproof and a reminder that kings should be outstanding for mercy and sympathy in dealing with their subjects. And Campeggio took Charles's side in admonishing Ferdinand.[7]

Clearly, the notoriously irresolute Clement VII was not firmly set on a policy of accommodation with even a small group of German Protestants. But there was a setting in which such accommodation was the lesser of two evils for the second Medici Pope. And in July 1530 Charles V was not determined on some form of peaceful coexistence with Lutheranism. But a susceptibility was present, if toleration of Lutheran doctrine and worship could be integrated into Charles's larger dynastic and imperial aims. Some form of negotiated settlement with the Lutheran party was not out of the question when the colloquies began in August 1530.

Looking to Charles V, one can point to three political and personal factors which favoured dialogue and negotiation with the Lutherans in 1530. First, Charles was not ready to make the outlay of funds required for the use of military force to suppress heresy and compel obedience to his edicts in Germany. Other goals, especially the defence of Austria and Hungary against the Turk, ranked ahead of securing religious unity in Germany.[8] Second, Charles was open to persuasion by the Lutheran protestation of orthodoxy. He was impressed by their confession of central Christian truths, while at the same time apparently not informed in detail about the doctrinal issues which had engaged Catholic theologians in controversy with Luther in the 1520s, such as the divine right of the papacy, eucharistic sacrifice, and the coexistence with divine grace of free choice and merit.[9] Charles's concentration on the

---

[7] Related in a letter of the Wittenberg theologian Justus Jonas to Luther, 27 July 1530: *D. Martin Luthers Werke: Briefwechsel*, 18 vols. (Weimar, 1930–86), xii. 120. Earlier Jonas had reported how observation convinced him of Charles's humane and generous manner, contrasting with Ferdinand's harshness (ibid. v. 427).

[8] W. Reinhard, 'Die kirchenpolitische Vorstellungen Kaiser Karls V.: Ihre Grundlagen und ihr Wandel', in E. Iserloh and B. Hallensleben (eds.), *Confessio Augustana und Confutatio* (Münster, 1980), 86–94. The Diet of 1530 became a watershed for church history, but one does well to ponder the fact that Augsburg was chosen as the site in order to facilitate Charles's negotiation of loans from the Fugger Bank to fund war against the Turk and to defray the cost of votes for his brother Ferdinand as king of the Romans and thus to secure the Habsburg dynasty.

[9] Some time early in the Diet, Charles told his sister, Queen Mary of Hungary, that his earlier information about the diabolical errors of the Lutherans had been proved false, since they hold to all the twelve articles of the Apostles' Creed. He is

foundational truths may well have been due to the third factor, his Latin Secretary, Alfonso de Valdés.

Valdés was a devoted Erasmian and the protégé of Charles V's recently deceased Chancellor, Mercurino Gattinara. Valdés wanted to see his master sponsor peace within Christendom and a spiritually based reform of Church and society.[10] Shortly after the Emperor's solemn entry into Augsburg on 15 June, Melanchthon and Valdés began discussions of the issues facing the Diet. For Melanchthon this was not an unwelcome distraction from the final revisions of the *Confessio Augustana*. Instead, this personal contact with the Emperor's entourage allowed Melanchthon to pursue a line of action and argument already thought out among the Saxon policy-makers, including Luther. Valdés received earnest assurances that an easy resolution of the Lutheran problem was within reach. The formula for peace would have the Catholic authorities accepting Lutheran requests for the chalice, clerical marriage, and only community masses, while the Lutherans would re-establish episcopal jurisdiction.[11] Valdés related this proposal to Charles even before the Lutheran confession was read out on 25 June. The prospect pleased the Emperor, and when Campeggio was informed he too evinced interest and willingness to explore Melanchthon's offer.[12] The legate assured his Lutheran visitor that he had delegated authority to grant some parts of Germany communion under both forms and a relaxation of celibacy for the diocesan clergy. Rome had provided, clearly to forestall if need be clamours for a general council. But the initial movement toward such a settlement came to a halt by decision of Campeggio in early July, because of the obstruction of princes such as the dukes of Bavaria and Duke Georg

thus ready to hear what the theologians say about the controverted externals. Cited in P. Rassow, *Die Kaiser-Idee Karls V.* (Berlin, 1932), 38 f.

[10] On Valdés, a fundamental interpretation is M. Battailon's chapter, 'El erasmismo al servicio de la politica imperial . . . ', in *Erasmo y España*, 2nd edn. (Mexico City, 1966), 364–431.

[11] Earlier, on 3 June, Melanchthon had written in the same vein to the Prince Elector of Mainz, Archbishop Albrecht: *Melanchthons Werke in Auswahl* (Gütersloh, 1951–), vii/2. 163–7.

[12] Melanchthon wrote to Luther on 19 June that Valdés had informed Charles and Campeggio about the proposal. *Philippi Melanchtonis Opera*, ed. C. G. Bretschneider, 28 vols. (CR; Halle, 1834–60), ii. 119. A fuller report went out in the dispatch of 21 June from the Nuremberg delegates to the Diet (ibid. 122–3). On 12 July Valdés wrote to the Cardinal of Ravenna about his exchanges with Melanchthon: G. Bagnatori, 'Cartas inéditas de Alfonso de Valdés sobre la Dieta de Augsburgo', *Bulletin hispanique*, 57 (1955), 362–4.

of Albertine Saxony.[13] However, a seed had been planted which could sprout again, and Valdés remained a force for moderation in the circle around Charles V. The Latin Secretary had the advantage of advocating an inexpensive and magnanimous solution to the problems posed by Luther and his protectors.

As papal legate, Campeggio influenced policy-making all through the Diet of 1530, but he showed some flexibility. In early May he had offered Charles V a lengthy memorandum on the Emperor's duty to apply a range of sanctions, and even military force, against the German heretics, but in late June, when he informed the Pope of Melanchthon's proposal of reconciliation by mutual concessions, Campeggio brought forth warrants for granting at least the chalice and a married clergy.[14] Campeggio, however, worked closely with a group of theologians, headed by Johann Fabri and Johann Eck, who were fresh from the front lines of doctrinal warfare with Luther. Here were men determined to catalogue publicly the Lutheran heresies and subversive notions. Fabri served the Archduke Ferdinand, and Eck the Bavarian dukes; along with the Duke Georg, this group constituted a force quite unfavourable to a dialogue of understanding with the Lutherans over doctrine and church reforms. The Catholic Estates, however, were not a solid phalanx against the Lutherans. Some, like the bishops of Augsburg and Mainz were more tolerant. On the other hand, the Estates were not ready to support Charles V in any measures likely to reinforce his power in the Empire. Even the opposition between him and the Lutherans could have its political usefulness.[15]

On the Lutheran side, the Saxon Elector had come to the Diet well prepared to make a case for his reformation. Since mid-1529 he had been insisting on adherence to the Schwabach Articles, enshrining

---

[13] Melanchthon on his conference with the legate (8 July): 'Summa fuit orationis illius, se nihil posse discernere, nisi de uoluntate Principum Germaniae: tametsi quarundam rerum relaxandarum potestatem habeat, qua inuitis Principibus uti non sit utile' (ed. cit. ii. 174 f.). A letter earlier in the same day had named the chalice and celibacy as matters for possible concessions by Campeggio (ibid. 174). E. Honée treated this in 'Die römische Kurie und der 22. Artikel der Confessio Augustana', *Nederlands archief voor kerkgeschiedenis*, 50 (1969–70), 148–59.

[14] *Nuntiaturberichte aus Deutschland, 1533–1559, Ergänzungsbände 1530–1531*, ed. G. Müller, 2 vols. (Tübingen, 1963–9), ii. 457–71 (8 and 12 May), i. 70–3 (26 June).

[15] A. Kohler, 'Die innerdeutsche und die außerdeutsche Opposition gegen das politische System Karls V.', in H. Lutz (ed.), *Das römisch-deutsche Reich im politischen System Karls V.* (Munich, 1982), 112–16.

Luther's affirmation of the Real Presence, as a condition for any Protestant alliance including Electoral Saxony. After the *protestatio* of Speyer in 1529, Saxony, along with Nuremberg, Hesse, and Brandenburg, sent a delegation to Charles to make clear the intent of their protest, and to differentiate it from unchristian and rebellious behaviour. In early 1530 Johann gained his allies' adherence to the Schwabach Articles and commissioned a new delegation to inform Charles that this group anathematized Zwingli, while requesting respect for their efforts to reform intolerable abuses. The Schwabach Articles were even submitted to Charles in Innsbruck in March 1530 in the hopes of thereby demonstrating Lutheran orthodoxy and opposition to the outrageous teaching of the Swiss.[16] Furthermore, there is ample evidence that the recurring Saxon formula for concessions leading to unity had been worked out before Augsburg in lengthy consultations which included the Elector, the Chancellor Gregor Brück, and Luther.[17]

There was tension, however, in the Lutheran camp. Landgrave Philipp of Hesse remained attracted to Zwingli and thereby sowed doubts in the Saxon group about his constancy as their partner in the developing alliance.[18] The free city of Nuremberg would clearly not agree to a reintroduction of episcopal jurisdiction, and Melanchthon's diplomacy eventually came under sharp attack from this quarter.[19] In late June the Electoral Saxon theologian Justus

[16] W. Steglich, 'Die Stellung der evangelischen Reichsstände und Reichsstädte zu Karl V. zwischen Protestation und Konfession 1529/30', *Archiv für Reformationsgeschichte*, 62 (1971), 161–92.

[17] Melanchthon wrote on 31 Aug. that nothing had been conceded beyond what Luther had agreed to: 're bene ac diligenter deliberata ante conventum' (ed. cit. ii. 334). Brück wrote in 1537 about lengthy discussions on the papacy and episcopal jurisdiction which accompanied the composition of the *Confessio* (cited in *Luthers Briefwechsel*, xii. 116). A recent exposition of the Saxon plan and effort for a negotiated settlement is H. Scheible, 'Melanchthon und Luther während des Augsburger Reichstags 1530', in P. Manns (ed.), *Martin Luther 'Reformator und Vater im Glauben'* (Stuttgart, 1985), 40–5. Martin Brecht's new account of Luther's life from 1521 to 1532 views Melanchthon's attempts at mediation as Philipp's personal programme and judges them harshly (*Martin Luther*, ii. *Ordnung und Abgrenzung der Reformation* (Stuttgart, 1986), 374–90).

[18] Philipp did sign the *Confessio Augustana*, but he also expressed orally his reservations about its profession of the eucharistic Real Presence (*Luthers Briefwechsel*, v. 427). Melanchthon's early letters from Augsburg expressed recurrent worries over Philipp's steadfastness (ed. cit. ii. 39 (4 May), 60 f. (22 May), 92–6 (appealing to Philipp, 11 June), 101–3 (another appeal, mid-June), and 126 (25 June)).

[19] On 29 Aug. Melanchthon told Luther 'Valde reprehendimur a nostris, quod iurisdictionem reddimus Episcopis' (ed. cit. ii. 328). On 1 Sept. he identified the Nur-

Jonas had confronted Melanchthon with arguments against accepting the authority of bishops in Lutheran territories, and on 28 June Jonas joined with theologians of three other signatories of the Lutheran *Confessio* to propose the preparation of a short list of non-negotiable positions in order to set down clear limits for Melanchthon's conciliatory efforts.[20]

A further factor was Martin Luther himself, isolated at Castle Coburg. By 1530 the German Reformation was no longer the immediate product of Luther's explosive tracts of 1520–1, but instead a complex movement being implemented and institutionalized under considerable influence of territorial rulers. Doctrine and religious urgency had to coexist with, and at times suffer, the constraints of the political dynamics of governing and relating to other public authorities. In 1530 Luther could chafe under such restraints, and some of his tracts from Coburg were in tone, if not in content, out of harmony with the Saxon diplomatic appeal for recognition and toleration of the new form of church life.[21]

Thus, on both sides a *complexio oppositorum* generated tensions during the August bilateral dialogues of 1530. The span of viewpoints on the Lutheran side concerned ways of interpreting and further elucidating the eirenic *Confessio* of 25 June, with its concentration on fundamentals of doctrine and reform and its selected omissions.[22]

embergers as those accusing him of seeking the reintroduction of papal tyranny (ibid. 336). Gerhard Müller related the bitter protest of Lazarus Spengler of Nuremberg against Melanchthon's ecclesiastical diplomacy at Augsburg in 'Die Anhänger der Confessio Augustana und die Ausschußverhandlungen', in Iserloh and Hallensleben (eds.), *Confessio Augustana und Confutatio*, pp. 253–6.

[20] M. Liebmann, *Urbanus Rhegius und die Anfänge der Reformation* (Münster 1980), 273 f. Liebmann sketches well the span of different views in the Lutheran camp regarding possible concessions through negotiations (ibid. 265–302).

[21] Mark U. Edwards has written sensitively about Luther's relation to what his reform was becoming in this period. See 'The Older Luther, 1526–1546', in G. Dünnhaupt (ed.), *The Martin Luther Quincentennial* (Detroit, 1985), 48–62, and *Luther's Last Battles: Politics and Polemics 1531–46* (Ithaca, N Y, 1983), 20–67. On Luther's writings at the Coburg, see J. Wicks, 'Abuses under Indictment', pp. 272–7, 287–93. My account ended with the Elector Johann's request on 21 July that Luther desist for a while from polemical publications.

[22] Luther was basically very pleased with the confession's proclamation of Christ, as he wrote to the Elector on 9 July (*Briefwechsel*, v. 453 f.). But on that same day, in Augsburg, Melanchthon and the other Saxon theologians formulated an apologia for their confession's omission of such topics as predestination, freedom and necessity, the priesthood of all believers, the *ius divinum* of papal primacy, indulgences, and the number of the sacraments. These, 'die gehässigen und unnöthigen Artikel', are

The Catholic tensions were played out in July as Fabri and his theological team composed two draft responses to the Lutheran confession which Charles V's advisors rejected as too polemical.[23] By the beginning of August, a third text, restrained and for the most part well argued, was ready and found acceptable. This became the imperial *Confutatio*, an article-by-article assessment of the *Confessio Augustana*, which was read before the Diet on August 3.[24]

The *Confutatio* concluded by admonishing the Lutheran princes and cities to distance themselves from the errors pointed out in the body of the declaration and to return to obedient profession of the faith of the Catholic and Roman Church.[25] Charles V had this appeal repeated in afternoon meetings with the Lutheran leaders on 4 and 5 August. In response, the signers of the confession of 25 June asserted they were not convinced by what they had heard on 3 August and that they needed a copy of the *Confutatio* for examination. From the imperial side, a copy was in effect refused, since it was offered on condition that it should not be printed or subjected to any counter-arguments.[26]

Melanchthon had not been present at the reading of the *Confutatio*, but the reports he received on its allegedly poor content and

matters of academic disputation, while the *Confessio* is an account of what is being preached publicly in the territories of the signers (ed. cit. ii. 182 f.). Later, Luther noted that the confession avoided forthright rejections of purgatory, the saints, and the papal Antichrist (*Briefwechsel*, v. 496). In recent studies R. Bäumer has highlighted the Augsburg Confession's concealment of points on which the Lutherans differed sharply with Catholic convictions, especially on the mass as the sacrificial offering which benefits the living and the dead ('Vermittlungsbemühungen auf dem Augsburger Reichstag', *Theologie und Glaube*, 70 (1980), 308 n. 34, 312 n. 64, 330 n. 184). See also Bäumer's 'Bekenntnis des einen Glaubens? Zur Diskussion um das Augsburger Bekenntnis', *Theologie und Glaube*, 71 (1981), 364–7.

[23] Alfonso de Valdés was one critic of the draft responses of mid-July as 'mas invectiva que respuesta ny admonitión christiana' (Letter of 21 July to Accolti), and he had a hand in softening the final version of the *Confutatio* so that it conformed to the attitude of Charles V (Letter of 1 Aug.; Bagnatori, 'Cartas inéditas', pp. 364, 366).

[24] *Die Confutatio der Confessio Augustana*, ed. H. Immenkötter (Corpus Catholicorum, 33: Münster, 1979), in which pp. 34–48 describe the genesis of the imperial response. The *Confutatio* had been studied from a helpful point of view in B. Dittrich, *Das Traditionsverständnis in der Confessio Augustana und in der Confutatio* (Leipzig, 1983), esp. pp. 107–213.

[25] *Confutatio*, ed. Immenkötter, pp. 204–7.

[26] Förstemann, *Urkundenbuch*, ii. 179–81. H. Immenkötter traced the equivalent refusal of a copy of the *Confutatio* to the interventions by Campeggio, who wanted the refutation to have something of the character of an imperial edict requiring obedience, not counterargument (*Um die Einheit im Glauben*, pp. 14 f., 22 f.).

style only served to strengthen him and his associates in assurance about their cause.[27] Other information, upon reflective consideration, made Melanchthon realize that the Emperor's response had in fact conceded the correctness of the main doctrines professed by the Lutherans. Where the refutation accused them of error, it was calumniating them.[28] At this time, Melanchthon sought to reopen his dialogue with Campeggio over a negotiated set of mutual concessions to restore unity. Campeggio's reply was negative in tone and most of its substance, but did leave a door slightly ajar by referring to the remote possibility that Rome could tolerate married priests.[29]

What though was to be done to overcome the impasse created by the Lutheran refusal to accept the *Confutatio* as a judgement on their doctrine and rites?[30] The direct appeals by the Emperor to the Lutheran leaders were not succeeding, and so the Estates aligned with the Emperor proposed that they take up dealings with the Lutherans. On 6 August this was accepted and seventeen members of the Diet, Electors, princes, and bishops, were named to under-

[27] Letter of 6 Aug. to Viet Dietrich, who was with Luther at Coburg (ed. cit. ii. 253). Martin Bucer criticized the refutation's use of Old Testament texts as arguments for communion under one form and for the sacrifice of the mass and found the case for the saints' intercession quite weak (letter of 14 Aug. from Augsburg to Ambrosius Blaurer in Constance; *Briefwechsel der Brüder Ambrosius und Thomas Blaurer*, ed. T. Schiess, i (Freiburg, 1908), 214 f.).

[28] Memoranda to the Prince Elector, from c. 4 and c. 12 Aug. in which, for example, Melanchthon wrote, 'unsere Artikel, in effectu, die fürnehmen approbirt sind. Ob schon etlich zusätz daran gehängt sind, so sind doch die unsern nicht verworffen' (ed. cit. ii. 258). See also Förstemann, *Urkundenbuch* ii. 240, where he predicts that the Emperor will not contest Lutheran doctrine in the proposed colloquy, where it should be easy to refute the several calumnies by the *Confutatio*.

[29] Melanchthon wrote on 4 Aug. to the legate's secretary Luca Bonfio (ed. cit. ii. 248 f.). Campeggio described his response in his dispatch to Rome on 11 Aug.: *Nuntiaturberichte*, ed. Müller, i. 108–10.

[30] Luther had described for the Elector Johann the limits within which Charles V could be acknowledged as a proper judge concerning religious issues: 'so fern und ausgenomen das sein K[eyserliche] M[aiestät] nicht widder die schrifft odder Gotts wort richte' (Letter of 9 July: *Briefwechsel*, xii. 118). A verse of Ps. 118, 'Nolite confidere in principibus', should instil reserve *vis-à-vis* imperial claims (ibid. 119). When consulted again in Aug. Luther drew up a five-point memorandum that even noted the prohibition in Justinian's Code against judging one's own case, which seems to apply now that the *Confutatio* had been presented in Charles's name. (ibid. 122 f.). Charles was under no illusions, and had informed the Pope on 14 July that the dissidents would not accept him as rightful judge in the case before the Diet (*Corpus Documental de Carlos V*, ed. M. F. Alvarez, 5 vols. (Salamanca, 1973–81), i. 228).

take mediation between the Lutherans and the Emperor who was now identified with the *Confutatio*.[31]

The First Phase of Dialogue

The exchanges of 7–14 August were not, strictly speaking, a colloquy on doctrine and rites, but they did bring to the surface certain issues of fundamental importance. The committee of seventeen repeatedly admonished the Lutheran princes to submit to the refutation of their confession and to return to a relation of peace and concord with the Emperor. The Lutherans pleaded their inability, on grounds of conscience and Scripture, to do this. Each side called on the other to recommend some other means likely to move the discussion forward toward resolution, and finally, on 13 August, the Lutherans proposed the formation of a smaller commission, with equal representation of the two sides and including some theologians, which should review the controverted doctrines and practices with the aim of establishing greater agreement.[32]

In this first phase of the August negotiations, the Catholics urged the non-theological consideration of the likelihood of war, bloodshed, and destruction, if the Lutherans did not recant their errors. Charles V, they intimated, would not be derelict in his duty as guardian of the Church in the West. The seventeen promised as well that if agreement in doctrine were attained, then reform of abuses could come up for deliberation and common decision.[33] Responding to the Lutheran appeal to conscience, Joachim, Margrave of Brandenburg, spoke for the seventeen in warning that this leads to schism and the multiplication of sects, much to the detriment of the Church. The pointed question was posed whether the Lutheran theologians and preachers deserved to have more influence in the formation of the consciences of their rulers than the teachings and ordinances of the holy and universal Church. The dissenting leaders

[31] V. von Tetleben, *Protokoll des Augsburger Reichtages 1530*, ed. H. Grundmann (Göttingen, 1958), 102 f. Tetleben was counsellor of the Archbishop of Mainz. E. Honée reported on the number of members of the commission in 'Die theologische Diskussion über den Laienkelch auf dem Augsburger Reichstag 1530', *Nederlands archief voor kerkgeschiedenis*, 53 (1972–3), 54.

[32] Tetleben, *Protokoll*, pp. 103 f., 108–17; Förstemann, *Urkundenbuch*, ii. 183–91, 201–17. Meetings of the seventeen with the Lutheran princes and their advisers, e.g. Brück, Chancellor of Saxony, were held on 7, 9, 11, and 13 August, with the days between given to each side's preparation of proposals and responses.

[33] Opening statement of the seventeen; (Tetleben, *Protokoll*, p. 103).

should take care not to be led astray.[34] Thus, this side evinced notable concern for authority, unity, and broad consensus.

But the Lutherans retorted that their position, formulated in the written confession they had submitted, rested on solid biblical arguments, while the *Confutatio* had not been given them for reflective study of its validity. For them to change at this point would be to shift from firm ground to sandy uncertainty. And some future deliberation on abuses held little attraction, since they had already realized the needed reforms in notable areas.[35] If the present dissension is lamentable, the blame falls on those who omitted holding synods for the supervision of teaching and on the bishops who neglected their duty of regulating worship and devotional practices.[36]

After such counter-statements, the Reformation party broached the idea of a colloquy on specific doctrinal, ecclesiastical, and ritual issues. The idea came from Melanchthon, in his memorandum of c.12 August, which sketched a forum in which Lutheran orthodoxy would be demonstrated and at least interim tolerance gained for the reformed configuration of the Church's life. Campeggio might be persuaded to use his dispensing power, if only a dialogue of explanation and mutual understanding could dissipate the accusations of heresy. On 14 August this proposal was included in the report of the seventeen to the assembly of Catholic Estates, which approved naming a smaller body which would include some jurists and theologians.

The Second Phase of Dialogue

On the evening of 14 August, Charles V consulted Cardinal Campeggio about the new form of discussion and with his agreement gave approval for the formation of a joint commission of fourteen members, with seven representatives from each of the two major

[34] Intervention by Joachim, in the name of the seventeen, on 11 Aug. (Förstemann, *Urkundenbuch*, ii. 188–91).

[35] Ibid. 183–7, esp. 184.

[36] Ibid. 213 f. H. Lutz observed that the German bishops of this time, as a body, were so enmeshed in feudal power structures and financial arrangements as to be unsusceptible to real reform—in contrast with the Spanish bishops of the same age, with whom Charles V had just had seven years' contact. See 'Kaiser, Reich und Christenheit: Zur weltgeschichtliche Würdigung des Augsburger Reichstages 1530', in Iserloh and Hallensleben (eds.), *Confessio Augustana und Confutatio*, pp. 11–13, 21–4.

religious parties of the Diet. The competency of the commission was strictly consultative and the results of their work to narrow down differences and formulate agreements had to be reported to the respective groups of the Estates and to Charles V himself who would act only in concert with the papal legate. Meetings of the fourteen were held on six consecutive days, 16–21 August, followed by separate reporting sessions on 22 August. For the colloquy, each side mandated two princes, two high-ranking officials with legal expertise, and three theologians, for dialogue on specific controverted issues of doctrine and religious practice.[37]

The first two days of the colloquy, devoted to the twenty-one doctrinal articles of the *Confessio Augustana*, went amazingly well. The Council of Nuremberg heard from its envoys to the Diet that on 16 August the tone was friendly and peaceable, with the Catholic side behaving well. Eck and Melanchthon had begun on occasion to collide in heated argument, but the princes forced them to keep on track toward interpreting Lutheran faith and doctrine in a mutually acceptable manner.[38] Campeggio wrote to Rome on the 20th that, contrary to his own misgivings before the colloquy, good results had emerged so far, with the Lutherans turning back to the truth and the number of serious differences being considerably reduced.[39]

With historical hindsight, one can point to some causes of the initial successes of the colloquy at Augsburg. Shortly before the formation of the mixed commission, a memorandum by the Saxon theologians, Melanchthon, Spalatin, Jonas, and Agricola, insistently reminded Elector Johann of his Christian and princely duty to seek

---

[37] Tetleben, *Protokoll*, pp. 117–19; F. W. Schirrmacher (ed.), *Briefe und Acten zu der Geschichte des Religionsgespräches zu Marburg 1529 und des Reichstages zu Augsburg 1530* (Gotha, 1876), 211–13, 216–23, 229–40. The Catholics chose Duke Heinrich of Brunswick and Bishop Christoph von Stadion of Augsburg, the Cologne Chancellor, Bernhard Hagen, and the Chancellor of Baden, Hieronymus Vehus (spokesman), and the theologians Johann Eck, Johann Cochlaeus, and Conrad Wimpina. When Charles V commissioned Duke Heinrich to chase down the departed Philipp of Hesse, Duke Georg of Albertine Saxony took Heinrich's place. The Lutherans were Prince Johann Friedrich of Saxony and Margrave Georg of Brandenburg-Ansbach, the Saxon Chancellor Gregor Brück (spokesman) and Sebastian Heller, Chancellor of Ansbach, and the theologians Philipp Melanchthon, Johann Brenz, and Erhard Schnepf of Hesse. Fatefully, no member represented Nuremberg and the other cities, by now six in number, of the Lutheran group. The Catholic spokesman, H. Vehus, has been treated biographically in H. Immenkötter, *Hieronymus Vehus: Jurist und Humanist der Reformationszeit* (Münster, 1982).

[38] Ed. cit. ii. 288.

[39] *Nuntiaturberichte*, ed. Müller, i. 115.

peace by all possible means. On the one hand, the religious divisions have already occasioned mob violence and can lead to yet more disorder. On the other hand, a settlement would benefit immensely the spread of the true doctrine of justification and of Christ's Gospel. With peace, the needed discipline can be imposed on the common people. So, for their own later peace of conscience, the Lutherans must leave no means unexplored which can lead to peace. With steadfastness concerning the primary doctrines on faith and works, Christian freedom, and the meaning of the Lord's Supper, all as set forth in the *Confessio*, they should reduce their practical demands to the minimum allowable by Scripture and the good of souls. They should be ready to accept a degree of public conformity in ritual matters and a restoration of episcopal supervision over priests, over marriage cases, and over the discipline of excommunication against public sinners. The Emperor could well be asked to determine the disposition of former monastic houses and properties.[40]

While the Lutherans pondered the imperatives connected with public peace and Christian instruction, Johann Eck re-examined their profession of faith and apologia for reformed rites and structures. Two memoranda written between 4 and 13 August reveal his readiness to think beyond the *Confutatio* of 3 August. On sin, justification, and merit, Eck indicates some ways of interpreting the Lutheran position in an acceptable manner: for instance, by specifying that justifying faith is faith active in love. On sacramental penance, he admits that part of the dispute is little more than a terminological difference, a *lis verborum*. Still, integral self-accusation in confession is a value not to be discarded. Lutheran ecclesiology needs more explicitation on the Church as a *corpus mixtum*, and its doctrine of the saints, denying their invocation, stands in serious need of correction. Eck is ready to argue for the sacrifice of the mass and religious vows, but he makes clear that communion under both forms, married priests, and the mitigation of certain church laws

---

[40] Ed. cit. ii. 281–5; Schirrmacher, *Briefe und Acten*, pp. 287–91; Förstemann, *Urkundenbuch*, ii. 244–8. For the date of *c.*14 Aug. see Immenkötter, *Um die Einheit im Glauben*, p. 29 n. 4. Immenkötter remarks incisively that the final recommendation on property betrays the political *naïveté* of the theologians composing this memorandum. Anton Schindling gives an informative account of the application of former church and monastic properties to new purposes in cities where the Reformation scored successes. See 'Die Reformation in den Reichsstädten und die Kirchengüter: Straßburg, Nürnberg und Frankfurt im Vergleich', in J. Sydow (ed.), *Bürgerschaft und Kirche* (Sigmaringen, 1980), 67–80.

could be accepted under conditions one could work out.[41] Thus, a Catholic leader, concentrating on Melanchthon's eirenic confession of 1530, was well prepared for the give-and-take of dialogue in the service of broader agreement, both on the primary articles and on the *forma ecclesiae*.

As the dialogue began on 16 August, the Chancellors Vehus and Brück expressed their respective understandings of the limited mandate given the commission and agreed to deal peaceably with the issues. The Lutheran side first proposed an article-by-article comparison of their *Confessio* with the imperial *Confutatio*, but they then agreed to a simpler procedure, one less likely to ignite disputes, of reviewing just their *Confessio Augustana*. Articles 1–12 were discussed in the later part of the first meeting, and on 17 August the commission worked through to Article 21 and thus completed its review of Lutheran faith and doctrine.[42]

In the scattered documentation of the Augsburg Diet of 1530, reports abound on the outcome of the first two days of doctrinal dialogue.[43] Hieronymus Vehus presented the results to Charles V according to a four-part scheme: on eight articles, immediate and full agreement; seven articles required discussion and further Lutheran elucidation in order to bring about agreement; on three

[41] Both documents by Eck examine the *Confessio Augustana* article by article. 'Oblata confessione Augustensi Protestantium Eckius pacis amans hanc offert concordiam', for Campeggio, ed. G. Müller, in 'Johann Eck und die Confessio Augustana: Zwei unbekannte Aktenstücke vom Augsburger Reichstag 1530', *Quellen und Forschungen aus italienischen Archiven und Bibliotheken*, 38 (1958), 225–39; and 'Iudicium doctoris Eccii de Augustana confessione', for the Archbishop of Mainz and Duke Georg, ed. Schirrmacher, *Briefe und Acten*, pp. 203–8. G. Müller dates the first piece between 4 and 10 Aug., the second between 8 and 13 Aug. ('Johann Eck und die Confessio Augustana', pp. 216–18).

[42] Förstemann, *Urkundenbuch*, ii. 220–9; Tetleben, *Protokoll*, pp. 124 f.; 'Acta septem deputatorum', in the partial edition of S. Ehses, *Römische Quartalschrift*, 19 (1905), Section *Geschichte*, pp. 132–5. The latter report, sent to Rome by Campeggio, says the Lutherans were told, 'debeant ipsi proponere, in quibus articulis a nobis dissentirent, item in quibus punctis conscientiae eorum grauarentur, et quae media hic haberi possent, quibus nihilominus catholicae ecclesiae unitas conseruaretur' (p. 132). There is sensitivity to Lutheran appeals to the dictates of conscience. Soon the evaluation of *media* for preserving ecclesial unity will prove decisive for the outcome of the colloquy.

[43] In addition to the texts mentioned in the previous note, reports are in Förstemann, *Urkundenbuch*, ii. 230–3 (by Brück); in Melanchthon, ed. cit. 299 f. (Melanchthon to Luther, 22 Aug.); in a report by Eck for Campeggio, ed. G. Muller, 'Johann Eck und die Confessio Augustana', p. 239; in H. Vehus's report for Charles V, ed. E. Honée, *Quellen und Forschungen*, 42–3 (1963), 427 f.; and in a 'Summa tractatus', in Schirrmacher, *Briefe und Acten*, pp. 218–22.

articles, discussion was postponed for later treatment in the context of the reform of abuses; finally, on three articles, partial agreement was reached, but unresolved differences remain.[44]

The most startling result of this dialogue is undoubtedly the nearly complete consensus on the doctrine of justification, which emerged from the exchanges and elucidation of Articles 4, 5, 6 and 20 of the *Confessio Augustana*. Eck, with Wimpina seconding, had insisted that justifying faith is faith active in love, and that the graced actions of the justified person are meritorious before God. Melanchthon was open to further specification on faith, but maintained that *meritum* had a chequered history because of scholastic theses on the congruous merit of justification and theories of meriting forgiveness by acts of penitential satisfaction. Eck retorted with a small barrage of arguments against 'sola fide', in the face of which Melanchthon stated his case for faith alone, urging for example that it properly directs one's attention away from self to God's grace. Eck maintained that charity *is* God's grace. Brenz explained that 'sola' only meant to exclude merit of forgiveness, not the sacraments and not the good works done by the righteous out of loving gratitude. Eck then proposed an inclusive formula: 'Justification or forgiveness of sins is had formally by sanctifying grace and faith, but instrumentally by the word and the sacraments.' This clarification, with faith not standing alone, the Lutheran side acknowledged as a possible articulation of their faith. But the question of merit was not resolved.[45]

Further agreements emerged on ministry, on the Church's inclusion of sinners as members, and on the eucharistic presence of Christ. But Article 12, on the component parts of sacramental penance, gave rise to a first unresolved issue. The Lutheran two-part account would combine contrition, emphasizing fear and felt sorrow, with faith—that is, assurance of forgiveness through

---

[44] Vehus, ed. Honée, pp. 427 f.

[45] For the give-and-take of dialogue, Förstemann, *Urkundenbuch*, ii. 223–7. The consensus formula is from the 'Summa tractatus': 'Iustificatio seu remissio peccatorum fiat per gratiam gratum facientem et fidem formaliter, per uerbum et sacramenta instrumentaliter' (Schirrmacher, *Briefe und Acten*, p. 219). Melanchthon wrote to Luther on 22 Aug. that Eck had not condemned 'sola fide', but had argued that it confused and upset lay people. They had agreed to say we are justified by grace and faith, 'sed ille stultus non intelligit uocabulum gratiae' (ed. cit. ii. 300). V. Pfnür has made the fundamental study of this discussion, with all its antecedents in the development of Lutheran theology and its sequel in which the agreement did not hold (*Einig in der Rechtfertigungslehre?* (Wiesbaden, 1970)).

absolution. The Catholics urged the traditional three-part analysis: contrition, absolution, and satisfaction. After discussion, the Lutherans found they could live with a three-part account if it were open to their way of interpreting the component parts. On satisfactory acts of penance, however, there was continuing discord over whether they were essential or not for forgiveness.[46]

Article 20, on good works, posed no difficulty where it asserted both the necessity of good works in the life of the righteous person and that works proceeding from faith and grace do please God and lead to a recompense from him. But the Lutherans would not revoke their protest against ascribing 'merit' to such works and placing any trust in them.[47]

Finally, there were the saints, whose example Article 21 of the *Confessio* has commended. But prayer invoking the saints for help was declared to have no biblical warrant and to derogate from Christ's pre-eminent role as heavenly advocate. Discussion brought out that the Lutherans would even admit that the saints are active intercessors for us in heaven and that this should be celebrated on their feast days. However, for direct prayer to the saints, the Lutherans maintained reserve, at least in not accepting the practice for themselves because of Scripture's silence and the many abuses in popular devotions.[48]

How are we to assess the initial achievement of the committee of fourteen at Augsburg in 1530? It is tempting to construct, on the three remaining differences, the edifice of a fundamental *dissensus* over the human person's role in his or her own salvation and in the salvation of others. Do not the differences over merit and satisfactory works reveal profound differences that the 'peace offensive' of mid-1530 momentarily obscured? To be sure, the two sides were

---

[46] 'Summa tractatus', in Schirrmacher, *Briefe und Acten*, p. 220; Vehus, ed. Honée, p. 427. W. Köhler edited a note, possibly by Melanchthon, which interprets the three parts in an evangelical manner, e.g. 'in confessione magis respiciendum est ad fidem absolutionis quam ad ipsum opus confessionis' ('Brentiana und andere Reformatoria', Part IX, *Archiv für Reformationsgeschichte*, 21 (1924), 99).

[47] Eck, ed. Müller, p. 239; 'Summa tractatus', ed. Schirrmacher, *Briefe und Acten*, p. 221; Vehus, ed. Honée, p. 428. Melanchthon's report to Luther, written on 22 Aug. relates that Eck in fact ascribed very little to merit: 'quamquam est exiguum quod merito tribuit, nos tamen ne illud quidem recipimus' (ed. cit. ii. 300).

[48] 'Summa tractatus', ed. Schirrmacher, *Briefe und Acten*, p. 222; Vehus, ed. Honée, p. 428; Eck, ed. Müller, p. 239. W. Köhler also found brief notes by Melanchthon on what could and could not be ascribed to the saints ('Brentiana und andere Reformatoria', pp. 101 f.).

really different in the religious attitudes each wanted to inculcate, as the Catholics insisted on grace giving a new dignity to the actions of the righteous person, while the Lutherans stressed looking away from self in exclusive dependence on God and his word of absolution. Still, some of those close to the proceedings did not think that the parties were deceived about their agreement on the various inclusive formulae. A report apparently prepared for Charles V expressed hope for eventual agreement on the relation between forgiveness and satisfaction for past sins.[49] John Eck stated later in August that the differences ascertained early in the colloquy were more verbal than real.[50] On the Lutheran side, the discussion showed their movement away from blanket condemnation of invoking the saints, a view that would have prevented them from living in ecclesial concord with others who pray to the saints. In effect, the colloquy on Article 21 ended with a Lutheran 'non possumus nos', which posed the question whether a rite could be tolerated in the Catholic Church which omitted liturgical prayers to saints. We are reminded that participants in religious colloquy do not aim at remaking the mentality of the partner in their own image, but rather at discovering heretofore obscured points of contact and deeper grounds for compatibility and *communio*.[51]

Three doctrinal articles had been passed over, since they seemed to belong more logically among the practical reforms for which *Confessio Augustana*, Articles 22–8, offer a potent apologia. Article 11, on confession of sin, was to be included under Article 25, with its treatment of the discipline of confession, esteem for absolution, and ministry of the keys, as these were taught and practised in Lutheran parishes. Article 14, on reserving ministry exclusively to those 'regularly called', would be treated with Article 23 on the marriage of priests. And Article 15, on the binding power of ecclesiastical

---

[49] ' . . . tamen speratur ad concordiam' (Förstemann, *Urkundenbuch*, ii. 234 n. 12). Eck had said earlier that the difference over satisfaction is 'lis verbalis non realis differentia' ('Iudicium', for the Archbishop of Mainz and Duke Georg, in Schirrmacher, *Briefe und Acten*, p. 205).

[50] Förstemann, *Urkundenbuch*, ii. 292. Earlier Eck felt that agreement could be reached on merit if the Lutherans would introduce another *solum*, by saying merit arises 'solum ex Deo, ex misericordia Dei, ex gratia assistente, preveniente et cooperante,' ('Iudicium', ed. Schirrmacher, *Briefe und Acten*, p. 203).

[51] The paragraph extends the considerations offered by V. Pfnür, *Einig in der Rechtfertigungslehre?* pp. 267–70, where one also finds further utterances of those (even Johann Cochlaeus) who believed the colloquy did ascertain a wide-ranging agreement on justification.

ordinances, such as those on feast days, fasting, and vows, was to come up in the context of Articles 26–8, on the episcopate and its law-making authority.[52] Difficult issues concerning the *forma ecclesiae* and the norms of its institutional life were to dominate discussion in the last four days of the colloquy of the fourteen. Would this further discussion bring more moments of *rapprochement* and a more limited and workable formulation of the differences?

The two sides agreed initially to treat the Lutheran reforms as a global whole, presumably because a common issue underlay all of them, namely, the rightful and advantageous use of law-making authority in the Church. The particular reforms of alleged abuses concerned the introduction of communion under both forms (*Confessio Augustana*, Article 22), marriage of priests (Article 23), the reformed, communitarian, and evangelical, celebration of the Lord's Supper (Article 24), the discipline of confession with emphatic instruction on absolution (Article 25), non-meritorious observance of 'human traditions' such as the fasting laws (Article 26), restoration of a regime of freedom under divine law for monks and religious (Article 27), and the proper scope of episcopal governance of the churches (Article 28). In his memorandum of *c*.12 August, Melanchthon proposed that the Lutherans should seek toleration of the changes they had introduced in these areas, since none of the changes goes contrary to the divinely ordered structure of the Church and its life. What is *de iure divino* remains fully intact in Lutheran territories, since the new practices only affect a number of abuses introduced by papal law.[53]

So on 18 August the Lutheran seven submitted a written proposal that they should be allowed communion under both forms, marriage for their clergy, and the reformed celebration of mass, at least until a general council could make further regulations. To maintain unity and good order, the Lutheran leaders would work out agreements with the bishops on the other articles, namely, on fasting, ceremonies, and the details of the exercise of episcopal authority. This would ensure clerical obedience, episcopal jurisdiction, and a

---

[52] 'Summa tractatus', ed. Schirrmacher, *Briefe und Acten*, pp. 220 f.

[53] Förstemann, *Urkundenbuch*, ii. 239. My earlier study found the term 'abuse/ *Mißbrauch*', as the *Confessio* uses it, burdened with ambiguity, half-concealing five distinct modes of critical analysis. 'Abuses' include actions the recent tradition interprets wrongly, the marginalization of central catechetical themes, hierarchical overreach in governance, episcopal malpractice, and institutional practices that must be contested ('Abuses under Indictment', *Theological Studies*, 41 (1980), 282–6).

good degree of conformity in doctrine and practice.[54] Thus the Lutheran group placed on the table the earlier Saxon design of a negotiated settlement, with the implication that their *forma ecclesiae* could well include real authority for bishops, if only recognition be given to the reforms they felt were mandated by Scripture and the requirements of Godly worship in the Church.

The initial Catholic response, given orally, charged the Lutherans with failing to speak directly to the key issue of episcopal authority and offering no assurances on the restoration of church properties recently confiscated. After the Lutherans conferred among themselves, Gregor Brück, as Chancellor, reaffirmed the primacy of the first articles, because the bishops' past connivance in abuses concerning clerical morals and the mass, along with opposition to the Gospel, had brought about the collapse of their authority. A fruitful discussion of bishops and their power to make laws must build on a commitment to reform the clergy and worship. The Catholics conferred, and Vehus voiced their conviction that the latter points were decisive; agreement on them could lead to easy solutions concerning clergy and worship. To overcome the impasse between demands for reforms and insistence on hierarchy, the groups agreed to exchange full written expositions of their respective proposals in documents which came to be called 'media concordiae'.[55]

With one Lutheran proposal already made, the Catholic side was able by the next morning, 19 August, to produce and submit a document. A new Lutheran statement was finished on the morning of 20 August and submitted that afternoon.[56] These two proposals remained fundamental for the rest of the August colloquy, even

[54] Förstemann, *Urkundenbuch*, ii. 249; Tetleben, *Protokoll*, pp. 125 f.; 'Acta septem deputatorum', ed. Ehses, *Römische Quartalschrift*, 19 (1905), Section *Geschichte*, p. 135. The Nuremberg envoys had been apprised of the content of the proposal of 18 Aug. and had agreed to it as a starting-point in the colloquy on reforms, but they made no binding commitment to it as a design for settlement (Melanchthon ed. cit. ii. 290 f.).

[55] For the exchange on 18 Aug. of charges and defences: Tetleben, *Protokoll*, pp. 125 f.; Förstemann, *Urkundenbuch*, ii. 236–8; 'Acta septem deputatorum', pp. 136 f. E. Honée adds precisions from a manuscript report by Vehus: 'Die theologische Diskussion über den Laienkelch', *Nederlands archief voor kerkgeschiedenis*, 53 (1972–3), 67 f.

[56] Förstemann, *Urkundenbuch*, ii. 250–5 (Catholic) and 256–63 (Lutheran). Tetleben gives Latin summaries, *Protokoll*, pp. 126 f. (Catholic) and 128–30 (Lutheran). Eck and Vehus composed the Catholic *media* in the early hours of 19 Aug. The redactors of the Lutheran document are not known, but Melanchthon was surely involved. See Honée, 'Die theologische Diskussion', 70–2.

with the several elucidations and adaptations given after 19–20 August.

The Catholic *media* did include the substance of the concessions that Cardinal Campeggio was empowered to make, namely, the chalice for the laity and a married diocesan clergy. But these were to be granted by Pope and Emperor as dispensations hedged in with extensive restrictions. Furthermore, the Catholic proposal began by firmly stating that episcopal authority must be maintained and respected. No place was left for independent reforming activity by civil rulers. After referring to a council for the definitive regulation of the communion rite and marriage for priests, the proposal concluded, in words surely not approved wholeheartedly by Campeggio, with a ringing call for early convocation of a general council, to be held in Germany for the reform of the Church in head and members.

Among the stipulations hemming in the concession of the chalice, the Catholic side called on the Lutherans to have it taught that reception under both forms is *not* a divine command obligating every communicant. The people should learn that the whole Christ is received even under one form, and those wishing to receive communion in the traditional way should not be hindered by their clergy or others.[57] The tradition should be maintained of celebrating both community and private masses, with the usual prayers of the offertory and canon. Given the decade of controversy over sacrifice, the people should hear instructions on the true meaning of offering the victim to God. Although priests who recently married will not be subject to penalties, no permission is given for further marriages and the authorities should try to install celibate ministers as pastors. Civil authorities are not to interfere with the regular round of observances in monastic and religious houses and they should show no tolerance for renegade religious who do not regularize their status with church authority. Religious houses now standing empty, along with their properties and income, should come under ecclesiastical administration at least until the council.

---

[57] G. Müller published a draft by Johann Fabri of Vienna of ten stipulations which should govern concession of the chalice: 'Um die Einheit der Kirche: Zu den Verhandlungen über den Laienkelch während des Augsburger Reichstages 1530', in E. Iserloh and K. Repgen (eds.), *Reformata Reformanda: Festschrift Hubert Jedin*, 2 vols. (Münster, 1965), i. 425–7. Johann Cochlaeus had been very reserved toward granting the chalice, since it would signify a schismatic difference between nations professing the same faith. Reported by R. Bäumer in 'Vermittlungsbemühungen auf dem Augsburger Reichstag', *Theologie und Glaube*, 70 (1980), 315 f.

Thus the Catholic *media concordiae* called for considerable restoration of traditional order and form to the Church in the Lutheran territories. Concessions were offered for some adaptations, but a thoroughly unconciliatory attitude could be sensed in the initial negotiating posture.

The Lutheran counter-proposal was more specific on the discipline of fasting, holydays, and confession. It formulated several responses to the Catholic *media*, both warding off insinuations of negligence and already accepting some of the many conditions laid down. The document is on the whole forthcoming in the face of Catholic demands, but also fails in places to meet the stated issue directly. The Lutheran concern for public order and discipline is evident in points going beyond the Catholic statement. The proposal of 20 August also concludes with a call for a general council of reform to be held in Germany.

The Lutheran *media* agreed not to brand wrong those receiving communion under one form or to subject communicants to a coercion alien to the Gospel. However, the fundamental rightfulness of receiving both forms will be taught in a moderate, uncontentious way, since this agrees with Christ's institution. Confession of sins is to precede reception of communion, as Article 25 of the *Confessio* had stated, and of course reverential handling of the sacrament will continue. But the Lutherans left room for Catholic misgivings by failing to state the concomitant presence of the whole Christ under just one form, and by making no mention of private masses. The *media* spoke vaguely of 'the usual ceremonies according to Christ's institution', in response to the Catholic insistence on the prayers of the offertory and canon with instruction on offering sacrifice.[58]

The Lutheran proposal of 20 August repeated the conclusion of Article 22 of the *Confessio* that one should judge clerical marriage as

---

[58] Förstemann, *Urkundenbuch*, ii. 256 f.; Tetleben, *Protokoll*, p. 128, where the proposal is censured for being 'perplexum, amfibologicum et dubium', and thus deceptive. But the Lutheran circumspect choice of words had serious motives. On 20 and 21 Aug. Melanchthon drew up memoranda critical of the Catholics for not speaking openly on the mass. If they meant 'hoc opus dici sacrificium tale, quod ex opere operato mereatur aliis gratiam', then sharp controversy must ensue. But agreement can be had if the 'offering' is first the giving over of Christ's consolation to the believer which then leads to thanksgiving for the whole Church. Thus the prayers of the canon, which say 'nos offerimus corpus', need discriminating review. See W. Köhler (ed.), 'Brentiana und andere Reformatoria', Part XII, *Archiv für Reformationsgeschichte*, 24 (1927), 295–7. The dating is given by H. Scheible, *Melanchthons Briefwechsel*, i. 427.

Christian and correct, all the more because of the widespread corruption of priests not given the high grace of chastity. In Lutheran territories, when the present corps of married priests starts to die out, there will be need of able and learned replacements, and how will sufficient numbers be found among the celibates, especially if the bishops do their duty in suppressing concubinage? The ordered life of marriage would impose discipline upon an otherwise corrupt clergy and the coming council should consider admitting this. Monastic and religious houses still functioning will not be disturbed, but the council should consider giving greater freedom to their inmates regarding departure or remaining. The houses from which monks and religious have all departed are better left under the administration of their secular patrons, so that income from them may go to support their ex-members, pastoral ministers, and schools. The council should receive a full accounting of this interim administration, but their deliberation should ponder what disposition of these matters redounds most to God's glory.[59]

The Lutheran *media concordiae* speaks clearly to the question of episcopal governance of the Church, and to the ordering of fasts and feasts. No approval, of course, is given to past episcopal failure to supervise preaching and sacramental administration, to the bishops' careless selection of ordinands, and to their neglect of firm discipline with the clergy. But pastors and preachers, in the future, should be presented for approval by the local ordinary, should render him obedience and be subject to his penalties when guilty of certain transgressions. Bishops should be unhindered in laying down excommunications in cases falling within the rightful scope of their jurisdiction, but they also should not encroach on areas properly under the governance of the secular estates. Sale of meat will be prohibited every Friday and Saturday and on eight other days of abstinence annually. The Lenten fast should be mitigated out of consideration for the poor and manual workers. However, such observances are required as a Christian pattern of good order, not as a service of God imposing a serious burden on conscience. Thirty-four holydays are listed for retention, and assurance is given that confession of sin pertains to Lutheran popular religiosity, albeit with stress on the consolation imparted by absolution.[60]

---

[59] Förstemann, *Urkundenbuch*, ii. 257–9.
[60] Ibid. 259–63.

A critical exchange followed in the latter part of the session of 20 August and all through that of 21 August. The fourteen reduced some of their differences, but some intractable problems remained. Furthermore, the language became acrimonious on occasion, as charges were levelled and demands made which touched the lived religiosity of the colloquy's participant members.

After receiving the Lutheran *media* of 20 August, the Catholic seven conferred apart for an hour. Then the Chancellor, Vehus, gave voice to their dissatisfaction with the Lutheran proposal on the rite of communion and the mass.[61] It had not specified whether their required confession of sin before communion was confession as traditionally practised, with enumeration of all of one's sins. The Lutherans made no commitment to affirming the rightfulness of receiving communion under one form, a teaching which after all the Council of Basle had required of the Hussites when it granted them the chalice. Vehus warmed to his subject, presenting arguments serially much as had been done in books by Eck and Cochlaeus during the 1520s. Brück would later claim that the disputatious manner went against the guidelines for the colloquy. Vehus claimed that the Lutheran position on communion under both forms was tantamount to reserving rectitude for only their own small group while condemning all other nations and all their ancestors. Adopting a rhetoric more common to the Lutherans, he claims that their position is sure to disturb and burden the consciences of many good people who have long followed the rite set down by the Church. The Lutheran leaders should encourage their theologians to imitate St Augustine, who was not ashamed to publish his *Retractationes*.

On the mass, Vehus was more succinct. The Lutheran *media* had made no commitment to the offertory and the canon of the mass or to interpreting the meaning of sacrifice in popular instruction. Furthermore, they gave no assurances that private masses would not be outlawed. After questioning the Lutherans as to whether they were ready to replace their present married priests with celibates, as the Catholic proposal had laid down, Vehus concluded. He had made clear that the Lutheran proposal as it then stood, could not be further transmitted to the larger body of the Estates, who would

[61] E. Honée studied Vehus's critique in detail in 'Die theologische Diskussion', pp. 75–9.

surely find injurious the Lutheran rejection, or even condemnation, of religious rites they practised as traditional.[62]

Brück fended off Vehus's criticism by referring to the commission's agreement to work out *media concordiae*, not to engage in contentious argument. The Lutherans had set down, after conscientious review, that to which they would commit themselves, and their document should be taken seriously. Disputation is not a proper response. If wrangling argument is to be reintroduced, the Lutherans will not be found weak or unprepared, especially regarding their communion rite. Brück reminded the Catholics that they were facing a group which had worked out a solid position on the Lord's Supper—a reference to the recent long argument with Zwingli. He gave assurances that any Protestant irreverence toward Christ's body was something the Lutheran leaders lamented deeply. After a brief account of Lutheran confession as telling the priest the major matters burdening one's conscience so that he could give counsel and absolution, Brück proposed that the session should end, to give his side time to consider what more might be said about the mass and clerical marriage.[63] Vehus agreed to close the meeting, but gave a parting admonition that the Lutherans should reconsider the approach to Holy Communion by which they in effect condemn all who have communicated under one form and continue to observe this rite.

The last meeting of the fourteen, on 21 August, began with Vehus offering a brief résumé of the shortcomings the Catholic side found in the Lutheran proposal on communion. The essential lacunae were narrowed down to three: the concomitant presence of the whole Christ under only one form, the basic rectitude of reception under one form, and the assurance that pastors in Lutheran domains would readily accede to the wishes of persons desiring to receive communion under one form.[64]

In the discussion, the Lutherans first reaffirmed their own seriousness about the proposal submitted on 20 August, and indicated that if the Catholic seven would not transmit that document to the

---

[62] 'Acta septem deputatorum', ed. Ehses, *Römische Quartalschrift*, 19 (1905) Section *Geschichte*, pp. 139–41; Förstemann, *Urkundenbuch*, ii. 265 f.

[63] 'Acta septem deputatorum', pp. 141 f.; Förstemann, *Urkundenbuch*, ii. 267 f.

[64] Ibid. 263, for the reference to the brief résumé; but for the contents we are dependent on E. Honée's citation from a manuscript copy of Vehus's report to the Estates on 22 Aug. 'Die theologische Diskussion', p. 81, n. 278.

Estates then what remained was to appeal for a decision by a General Council. However, an oral elucidation was given to the effect that Lutheran doctrine does not divide Christ in a Nestorian manner, but teaches the presence of the whole Christ, body and blood, humanity and divinity, even under one form.[65]

A lengthy exchange on the rite of communion followed. The Lutheran side submitted a prepared sheet explaining that they did not mean to condemn people past and present who received communion under one form 'in cases of necessity'. The institutional provision by Christ does oblige both priests and laity to partake of both bread and cup. But when this precept of Christ cannot be observed, then those receiving under one form are not guilty of any wrongdoing.[66]

A long argument ensued over the meaning of a 'case of necessity' excusing one from blame for receiving under one form. In the give-and-take of explanation, questioning, and further elucidation, the Catholic side somehow came to think the Lutherans were moving away from their insistence on the obligatory character of reception under both forms. If this be the case, the Lutherans should not simply refrain from condemning users of one form, but also have it taught openly that this traditional rite is correct. The Catholic seven went apart to confer and brought back a written paragraph stating what the means of agreement seemed to be in the present, more advanced, stage of dialogue.[67]

The new proposal would have the Lutherans, in the interim until the next council, teaching that neither form is prescribed by divine command. The Catholics would undertake to instruct people on the rightfulness of the Lutheran rite, once permission for the chalice is given them. Thus, all imputations of blame would be ruled out. Also, the Lutherans are to teach, as agreed, that the whole Christ is

[65] Förstemann, *Urkundenbuch*, ii. 268 f. Melanchthon had jotted down a brief account of Nestorius's view of Christ's two persons, and recommended that the Lutheran side speak of the whole Christ in the sacrament so as to leave no room for suspicion that they divided Christ (ibid. 271 f). Actually, Zwingli was the sixteenth-century theologian most given to emphasis on the different components of the one Christ.

[66] Johann Brenz had prepared a short memorandum on the rite with both forms, stating that it is a 'ceremoniale preceptum' open to dispensation 'in casu necessitatis', and the Lutheran elucidation took this over (ibid. 272 f.). But if the necessity arises by reason of an abusive law of the unreformed Church, then a serious accusation remains, even if those coerced into the abusive practice are excused from guilt.

[67] Ibid. 269 f. The new Catholic *media* is given on p. 274.

present under each form, and their pastors are to refuse no one seeking communion under one form.

The Lutheran seven needed no time for reflection or consultation, but could respond straightway with a sharp rejection of this latest Catholic proposal. The Lutherans can confess the whole Christ under even one form, but this is all.[68] The text showed that the Catholic seven had heedlessly stumbled into challenging the fundamental Lutheran belief that a divine command, clearly stated in Scripture ('Bibite ex hoc omnes'), governed the administration and reception of Holy Communion. On such a clear imperative there could be no fudging by speaking of a neutral matter left to the Church to regulate, whatever leniency might be appropriate in judging ordinary people.

Further discussion on 21 August took up the canon of the mass, but the tone deteriorated and the sides let their annoyance with each other be felt. At one point, the Lutherans listed three objections to the canon: it is wrongly made a mortal sin to omit it from mass, the canon makes the mass a sacrifice, and it includes the invocation of saints. Some progress could be made on the last point, since the saints of the canon are commemorated, not invoked for aid. But the Lutherans remained firm in the face of a brief attempt to explain the 'mysterial' or representative nature of eucharistic sacrifice.[69] There was no time for further discussion of conditions for a relaxation of celibacy, but discussion was on a better level in the final moments as each side asked the other to report on the dialogue to their principals and to present the *media* and their amendments in a good light, so as to promote peace and unity.[70]

On 22 August separate meetings were held in which each group of seven reported to the larger groups of Estates and counsellors on the six days of dialogue. Sometime during the day, the Elector, Johann, had four wagons packed and he sent part of his entourage back to Saxony. This became known to the Catholic Estates, who quickly sent the Elector a message begging him to remain at the Diet and to allow dialogue to continue in the hope of reconciling the opposed demands which faced each other as the fourteen had con-

---

[68] Ibid. 270. The report on this decisive moment in the colloquy: 'Aber derselb begrif Ist Irn gnaden unnd zugewannten abgewendt, unnd um glimpfs willen.' A dishonourable retreat from duty before God had been proposed.

[69] Schirrmacher, *Briefe und Acten*, p. 235.

[70] Förstemann, *Urkundenbuch*, ii. 270 f.

cluded.[71] A petition also went from the Catholic Estates to the Emperor requesting his approval for the naming of a smaller commission to continue working toward an acceptable design for unity.[72]

In addition to the reports to those in Augsburg who had commissioned the fourteen, other reports were composed on 22 August or shortly thereafter, which cast light on the situation as the second phase of dialogue ended. The allies of Electoral Saxony had reacted critically over not being consulted on the specific concessions offered by the Lutheran seven in the *media* of 20 August. The delegates of Nuremberg and Hesse wrote immediately to their respective superiors for instructions on lines to be followed in any further negotiations.[73] Melanchthon wrote on 23 August to inform leaders in Reutlingen, so that they could articulate a position on the apparently central question of episcopal jurisdiction.[74]

Melanchthon also related the outcome of the colloquy of fourteen with accustomed lucidity to Luther in a letter of 22 August.[75] On both forms the other side made a concession contingent on the Lutherans' saying there was no precept that binds people to one rite of communion. While excuses can be made for those to whom only one form is offered, Melanchthon had refused to deny the Lord's imposition of a binding precept: 'Ego non potui hoc recipere.' One may not be obliged to receive communion, but are not those who do receive then bound to the *forma sacramenti* instituted by Christ? Would Luther please state his considered view of this particular

[71] The Nuremberg envoys reported the departures in their dispatch on 23 Aug. (Melanchthon, ed. cit. ii. 302). On the 26th they told of the Catholic Estates' request that Johann should continue the dialogue (ibid. 312). Tetleben also recorded the fact of the appeal to the Saxon Elector (*Protokoll*, pp. 130 f.).

[72] Ibid. 131.

[73] The Nuremberg delegates had protested at the reporting session of 22 Aug. If the colloquy continues, such proposals are to be agreed upon before being submitted to the other side. The Nuremberg council was asked to review the *media* of the 20th after the fact (Melanchthon, ed. cit. ii. 301). The Hessian report and request for instruction are implied by Philip of Hesse's responses of 29 Aug. (ibid. 323–7). On the ensuing protests by the Nuremberg Council and Philipp, see Immenkötter, *Um die Einheit im Glauben*, pp. 51–4.

[74] Letter to Matthew Alber (ed. cit. ii. 302 f.). W. Gussmann relates the sharply negative reaction of Alber and his colleagues in Reutlingen to the main concessions under discussion. See *Quellen und Forschungen zur Geschichte des augsburgischen Glaubensbekenntnisses*, 2 vols. in 3 (Leipzig–Berlin, 1911–31), i/1. 158–62. For the text of Alber's draft response, ibid. i/2. 315–19.

[75] Ed cit. ii. 299–300.

question? The colloquy, Melanchthon reports, did not have a real exchange over the mass, vows, and celibacy. The other side simply laid down conditions on these points which the Lutherans rejected. Still, the Lutheran seven, out of a sense of the urgency of preventing war, did offer to obey the bishops, accept their jurisdiction, and introduce the 'ordinary ceremonies'.

Also on 22 August the Elector, Johann, formally asked Luther's opinion on positions to be taken in further negotiations.[76] Copies of the two *media* of 19 and 20 August were sent to the Reformer, along with three questions on specific demands. (1) Can the Lutheran side admit that communion under one form is not a matter of precept? The other side insists on this, arguing that it is needed for maintaining order among their own people, that is, by a Lutheran admission of the licitness of the rite practised in Catholic lands. (2) Can the Lutheran authorities withdraw their prohibition of private masses? This would not be an order reinstituting such masses, but only the admission that princely authority does not extend to such a matter of liturgical practice. (3) Can the traditional canon of the mass also be permitted, along with appropriate explanatory comments? Thus the wider recognition of the reformed *forma ecclesiae*, as this was giving institutionalized density to Luther's teaching, came to depend on three quite specific issues of eucharistic practice and doctrine.

The Third Phase of Dialogue

From 23 to 30 August a smaller commission of six, with three members from each side, served as the forum for Lutheran–Catholic negotiations.[77] The six met on 24, 26, 28, and 30 August, devoting part of the meeting on the 28th to drafting a brief report on the latest conditions proposed by the Catholic side, but not accepted by the Lutherans. On 30 August letters from Martin Luther arrived, answering questions posed to him by Melanchthon and the Elector, Johann, by which the Reformer forcefully confirmed and consolidated Protestant resistance against the latest Catholic proposal. On

[76] *Luthers Briefwechsel*, xii. 124 f.
[77] The basic sources for this phase are in Förstemann's *Urkundenbuch*, ii. 290–313, with the narrative account being given in Immenkötter, *Um die Einheit im Glauben*, pp. 56–66. The Lutheran members of the committee of six were the Chancellors Brück and Heller, and Philipp Melanchthon. The Catholics were the Chancellors Vehus and Hagen, and Johann Eck.

31 August the Catholic Estates came to realize the intractability of the situation that had emerged, and they made this known to Charles V, which thereby signalled the end of the effort toward reconciliation begun on 6 August.

The failure of the commission of six was due first to the lack of any fresh proposals from the Catholic side by which to attract the Lutherans toward more accommodations. Also, the three Lutheran spokesmen were severely restricted from offering any further concessions, especially at the behest of Lüneburg, Hesse, and Nuremberg. This resistance against further adaptations of reformed practices then took on new strength from Luther's forceful intervention. From the Protestant perspective, all that then remained was to negotiate an arrangement for peaceful coexistence, at least until the council, of groups of territories which are divided over doctrine, ritual, and church order.

A lengthy discourse by the Chancellor, Vehus, occupied most of the first session of the six on 24 August.[78] Whereas Johann Eck had urged treatment of the three unresolved doctrinal points, satisfaction, merit, and invocation of the saints, Vehus insisted on attacking the larger complex of problems which had emerged in the earlier colloquy regarding the reform of abuses.

However, Vehus's actual demands on the 24th coincided both in content and in spirit with the Catholic *media concordiae* of 19 August. Familiar adaptations were called for to hedge in acceptance of the Lutheran rite of communion. One result of further reflection may be found in Vehus's reference to the *dissensus* over communion as involving matters of faith, and not simply liturgical practice. He appealed to the Lutheran visitation articles of 1528, with their provision of consideration for weaker consciences, as an authority for continuing to honour the request of those desiring communion under only one form.[79] Vehus specified that commitments to reverent use of the sacrament were needed because in certain cities people were receiving communion at evening celebrations of the Lord's Supper without concern for the eucharistic fast from food and

---

[78] Förstemann, *Urkundenbuch*, ii. 292–8.

[79] The text is 'Unterricht der Visitatoren an die Pfarhern ym Kurfurstentum zu Sachssen', in *Luthers Werke; Gesamtausgabe* (Weimar, 1883–), xxvi. 195–240. The instruction treats the accommodations to be made on both forms at pp. 214–16. This is presented as a temporary work of patient love for people not yet convinced of the Lord's precept. However, if they become vociferous in their opposition to the truth, they are to be excluded from communion.

drink. On the mass itself, Vehus repeated the demand put forward on 19 August for use of the traditional canon, along with instructions on sacrifice. However, the question of applying the benefits or fruits of the mass to specific persons and purposes could be remanded for doctrinal and practical settlement at the next council. This latter concession would have been made at the suggestion of a theologian with an acute sense of what was and what was not taught as already binding doctrine by the Church.[80]

Vehus repeated the already known conditions for temporary tolerance of married priests in Lutheran territories, adding some rebuttals of arguments advanced by the Lutherans against justification of obligatory celibacy. For instance, according to Vehus the 'high gift' of chastity can be sought in earnest prayer, and priests can dispose themselves for continence by greater self-discipline and care to avoid occasions of sin, such as dances. The Lutheran pastors who broke their vow of celibacy are, strictly speaking, not validly married, and they are canonically suspended from their office and benefice. However, such men may remain in their posts temporarily, until the coming council makes its determination.

Existing monasteries and religious houses in Lutheran territories are to be left intact and not be subjected to pressures such as those exerted by the Nuremberg reformers upon the convents of Saint Clare and Saint Catherine.[81] Renegade religious, desirous of returning to life under their rule, should be allowed, out of respect for their consciences, to rejoin a community without application of the canonical penalties. In a variation on earlier demands, Vehus proposed on 24 August that the Emperor should be asked to stipulate how local authorities are to handle vacated religious houses and their properties.

---

[80] Eck wrote to Melanchthon on 27 Aug. that he was personally certain about the doctrine of the Mass's benefits, but he had none the less argued before the Estates that it could be left undecided until the council (ed. cit., ii. 316 f.).

[81] See Gottfried Seebass, 'The Reformation in Nürnberg', in L. P. Buck and J. W. Zophy (eds.), *The Social History of the Reformation: Festschrift Harold J. Grimm* (Columbus, Ohio, 1972), p. 35. Before the Reformation the Nuremberg authorities had already imposed considerable restrictions on religious houses in the city. G. Strauss, *Nuremberg in the Sixteenth Century*, 2nd edn. (Bloomington, Ind.–London, 1976), 157 f. At St Clara's, however, the Reformation measures toward suppressing religious life met the tenacious resistance of the Abbess Caritas Pirkheimer. Gerta Krabbel gives extensive passages from Caritas's diary in her account of this struggle: *Caritas Pirkheimer: Ein Lebensbild aus der Zeit der Reformation*, 5th edn. (Münster, 1982) 86–208.

Vehus also called for wider powers of local bishops regarding pastoral appointments. Where the Lutheran *media* had spoken of an obligatory 'presentation' by patrons of nominees to the bishop, it should be added that the bishop may by right examine the candidate and then decide upon his admission to the post in question.[82] Also the Lutheran list of abstinence days in the proposal of 20 August is to be somewhat expanded, while striking the unacceptable teaching that these laws about 'ceremonies' do not bind the consciences of church members.[83] Indicative of Catholic doctrinal concerns were the final demands that Corpus Christi be added to the list of holy-days and that the season of Advent be specified as the time for instruction and preaching on Christ's coming in judgment.[84]

Understandably, Brück's opening remarks on 26 August were critical of the Catholics. They had already heard in the last part of the previous phase of dialogue why the Protestant side could not accept their demands. Why then did they even ask for a new round of discussion when they had nothing new to propose?[85]

This sharp rejoinder gave notice of a new spirit of resistance in the Lutheran camp. Melanchthon had already come under fire on 22 August for the concessions offered in the *media* of 20 August. On the 23rd, the Nuremberg delegates wrote home about their misgivings over what they perceived as Saxony's and Brandenburg's over-eagerness to reach some kind of agreement with the Catholic, imperial party.[86] One report of Lutheran provenance states that for the colloquy of the six Melanchthon was strictly enjoined to make

[82] The Nuremberg delegates related this part of Vehus's proposal (letter of 26 Aug. ed. cit. ii. 313).

[83] B. Dittrich calls attention to this significant Lutheran–Catholic difference as documented in the *Confessio* and *Confutatio*. The latter does not say that obeying church laws gains grace and salvation, but that such laws constitute a pedagogy needed by people desiring to walk in the way of godliness: *Das Traditionsverständnis in der Confessio Augustana und in der Confutatio* (Leipzig, 1983), 27–30, 180–5. The traditional warrant for such law-making authority was Jesus' promise of the keys and the power to bind and loose (Matt. 16: 19, 18: 19). Luther delivered a forceful rebuttal of such an argument, between 20 July and 25 Aug. 1530, in 'Von den Schlüsseln', *Luthers Werke* (Weimar, 1883–), xxx/2. 435–464 (in English: *Luther's Works* (St Louis and Philadelphia, 1955–), xl. 325–77). M. Brecht sees here the basic reason why Luther did not speak in favour of admitting episcopal jurisdiction (*Martin Luther*, ii. *Ordnung und Abgrenzung der Reformation* (Stuttgart, 1986) 386).

[84] H. Immenkötter supplies these details from a manuscript copy of Vehus's own report: *Um die Einheit im Glauben*, p. 61.

[85] For the source see below, n. 90.

[86] Ed. cit. ii. 301 f.

no more concessions, since his offers regarding episcopal jurisdiction had already exceeded what Lüneburg, Hesse, and Nuremberg would approve.[87]

These demurs did not, however, prevent Melanchthon from thinking out a decidedly forthcoming response to what Vehus had said on 24 August. For an inner-Lutheran conference on the 25th he sketched ways in which the Lutheran side could still stand on fundamental principles, such as Christ's ordinance of both forms and the inalienable freedom of clerics to marry, but still enter into further discussion on these points. For all practical purposes, the Lutherans had already said that in view of certain circumstances they excused from wrongdoing both those offering and those receiving communion under only one form. On the Mass, one may question whether princes are not encroaching upon priests' consciences by prohibiting private celebration of Mass. Also, the Catholic readiness to suspend discussion of the applied benefits of the mass was an opening for discussing the revision of the offertory and canon where these texts spoke of such benefits. If the Lutheran theologians are permitted to compose the requested 'glosses' on sacrificial terms in the canon, then there is room for negotiation.[88]

However, the Lutheran conference of 25 August was a decisive defeat for Melanchthon and the conciliatory wing of the Lutheran party. The Chancellor of Duke Ernst of Lüneburg attacked Melanchthon's proposal on several points. Erhard Schnepf of Hesse added his objections as well. The Nuremberg delegates took the position, along with Lüneburg, Hesse, and the other cities, that discussion should cease on accommodations such as Melanchthon envisaged. There is no sense in seeking Catholic approval for the reforms already undertaken, and no reason for letting the other side dictate adaptations. The one issue remaining is to work out some formal arrangement for living side by side as territories not at one in belief, worship, and church order.[89] Thus, the Lutheran three could not come to the meeting of 26 August with any constructive response to Vehus's proposals.

Because Vehus had repeated such well-known demands on 24

---

[87] Schirrmacher, *Briefe und Acten*, pp. 242 f.

[88] Melanchthon's sketch was edited by K. Schornbaum, 'Zur Geschichte des Reichstages von Augsburg im Jahre 1530', *Zeitschrift für Kirchengeschichte*, 26 (1905), 144–6.

[89] Letter of the Nuremberg representatives, 26 Aug. (ed. cit. ii. 313 f.).

August, Gregor Brück could respond with clearly grounded refusals on 26 August.[90] Those who implement reform will not admit into their Churches a divisive and confusing diversity in the communion rite. Private Masses contrary to Christ's institution are rightly prohibited, since they constitute acts of public blasphemy. The Catholic demand for such Masses would in effect shift attention toward priests' meritorious work of sacrifice and away from Christ's redemptive passion—a sinful act for those who know the true meaning of the mass. The offer to treat application of mass-fruits at the council reveals an uncertainty which undercuts private Masses, since these are celebrated only so that they can be applied to the needs of some stipend-giver. The canon cannot be made obligatory, because it adds many unnecessary prayers over and above the substance of the mass, which is found in Christ's words of institution.

Brück questioned whether those who broke vows by marrying are more guilty than the popes and bishops who impose such a vow contrary to Christ's word that not all receive the grace of chastity (Matt. 19: 11) and Paul's assertion that it is better to marry than to burn (1 Cor. 7: 9). Remanding to the Emperor the determination of how vacated religious houses are to be administered can be discussed, once the Lutherans are told what he might have in mind. Vehus's suggested elaborations on episcopal jurisdiction and ceremonies need not be answered, since the Lutheran position remains what was submitted on 20 August in their *media*.

The crucial passage in Brück's presentation of 26 August came at the end, as he recommended that a report on the unresolved problems should be given to the Estates, so that they in turn could address the Emperor on the urgent need to bring about an early convocation of a general council. If then the Estates also wanted to discuss an interim arrangement for peaceful coexistence of the two parties, the Lutheran group would gladly take up this complex of questions.

In the discussion following Brück's statement, John Eck spoke some key words.[91] The Catholic three has no mandate for negotiating

---

[90] Brück gave a text of his intervention in his own *Geschichte der Handlungen zu Augsburg*, ed. K. E. Förstemann, in *Archiv für die Geschichte der kirchliche Reformation*, i/1 (Halle, 1831), 109–18. We use the excerpt given in *Dr. Martin Luthers Sämtliche Schriften*, 2nd edn., ed. J. G. Walch, 23 vols. (St Louis, 1880–1910), xvi. 1438–55.

[91] Förstemann, *Urkundenbuch*, ii. 301.

practical ways of maintaining the peace. Now certainly the Emperor, along with the Electors and other Estates, wants a council, but these authorities also hold that the Christian world can proceed to a council only when heresy and disobedience have ceased in Germany. The innovations recently introduced must be suppressed and earlier doctrines and traditional practices must first be reinstituted.[92]

We are informed through the Nuremberg delegates about the inner-Lutheran consultation on 27 August, at which the three members of the commission of six made their report. After discussion, it was confirmed that the Lutherans would present no more *media* and would protest against the demand of a wholesale restoration of pre-Reformation conditions. Brück was to draft a written statement for submission the next day. Also, it was suggested that another paper should be prepared to answer the imperial *Confutatio*, to the extent that the Lutherans grasped its content during the reading of 3 August.[93]

The next day Brück handed over his statement.[94] It begins by ascertaining that the Catholics are demanding a number of specific changes which the Reformation party, after careful examination, finds unacceptable. Beyond this, the other side has broached a massive new demand as a condition for the long-awaited council. But this further imposition also has to be rejected. The Lutheran authorities have shown more than adequate justification for the doctrine they promote and the reforms they themselves were constrained to undertake, given papal and episcopal neglect in supervising the life of the Church. Past imperial diets have issued calls for a council, precisely to heal divisions over doctrine and church practices. A year ago, at the end of the Diet of Speyer, the Lutheran estates made a formal appeal related to these questions and directed it to both the

[92] Campeggio had stressed this provision earlier in his discussions with Charles V, as the Legate reported in dispatches of 14 and 29 July to Rome: *Nuntiaturberichte*, ed. Müller, i.83, 90. Charles V had spoken of such a rollback in his letter to Clement VII of 14 July, indicating that it was a condition for the granting of a council in the face of Lutheran demands: *Corpus Documental de Carlos V*, ed. M. Fernández Álvarez, 5 vols. (Salamanca, 1973–81), i. 228 f. Thus, an aura of unreality surrounds many of the references made in 1530 to the coming council.

[93] Melanchthon, ed cit. ii. 320 f. The last recommendation amounts to the commissioning of Melanchthon's *Apologia Confessionis Augustanae*, a first draft of which was ready in the second half of Sept. 1530. Publication followed, after revision and expansion, in spring 1531.

[94] Förstemann, *Urkundenbuch*, ii. 306–10.

Emperor and the next council. While such an appeal is pending, Brück maintains, it goes against tradition and law to demand suppression of that which the council is to review. The Catholics show no respect for this duly formulated appeal and are trying to impose a solution before the council makes its decisions. If this had been required in the past, hardly any councils would have been held. So the Catholics should make no more calls for wholesale suppression of reforms, but instead turn to the requirement of the hour, the interim arrangement of terms of peace. In this interim, the Lutheran princes and cities will hold to their confession, without additional glosses, in a manner for which they hope to give a good accounting to His Imperial Majesty and to Almighty God.

The Catholic three responded by once again insisting that they had no mandate from their principals authorizing them to negotiate terms of peace for the time until the council meets. The only point they can discuss in this regard is the specification of what the Lutherans must suppress and reinstate in order to prepare for the council.[95] But since the Lutheran three have just submitted a written formulation of their position, which includes arguments against this interim rollback to the pre-Reformation state of affairs, the Catholics would be willing to report on this to the majority of the Estates. However, the group of six also agreed that the declaration the Lutherans had brought to this meeting would not serve by itself for such a report, because it did not specify the particular conditions or demands over which the dialogue on reforms had run aground. And so the Catholic three offered to formulate a statement of these unresolved issues, so that the six could agree to this text before the meeting of the 28th ended.[96]

Thus, the final report on the theological colloquy intends to state the particular measures Vehus had called for on 24 August and Brück then refused on 26 August.[97] In the text, warrants and arguments are left out, so that the sticking points themselves stand in clear light. However, haste took a toll, and the resulting document

---

[95] Tetleben, *Protokoll*, pp. 135 f.

[96] H. Immenkötter has reconstructed the sequence of the deliberations on 28 Aug. (*Um die Einheit im Glauben*, pp. 64 f.).

[97] German texts are given in Förstemann, *Urkundenbuch*, ii. 274–6 (under the wrong date), and in Schirrmacher *Briefe und Acten*, pp. 244–6. E. Honée edited a Latin text sent to Rome in 'Die Vergleichsverhandlungen zwischen Katholiken und Protestanten im August 1530', *Quellen und Forschungen aus italienischen Archiven und Bibliotheken*, 42–3 (1963), 432 f.

is so incomplete that one observer even called it 'yet another *media.*[98]

Over and above the Lutheran confession of the concomitant presence of the whole Christ under each form of the Eucharist, the Catholics call for the affirmation that those receiving under just one form are guilty of no wrongdoing. Also Lutheran authorities must not hinder those so desiring from receiving under one form, at least until the coming council. Communion under both forms will also be administered only during mass, unless a serious case of necessity dictates otherwise.[99]

The traditional ceremonies, vestments, chants, and readings are to be observed during both private and community masses. The traditional prayers of both the offertory and the canon are to be used, conformably with a 'pius atque Christianus sensus'. Disputed questions in this area, such as the basis for applying masses to a given intention and their *ex opere operato* efficacy, can be remanded to the coming council.

Priests already married may be tolerated in Lutheran territories, if the Emperor sees fit to accept this. He should, however, give special consideration to the fact that a reimposition of obligatory celibacy would deprive the Lutherans of the pastors they need.[100]

Finally, religious and monastic communities still functioning in Lutheran territories must be left intact, with no hindering of ex-members from re-entering, should they so desire. Regarding houses which have been vacated, including their properties and the persons forced to leave them—on these points the Emperor should decide what provisions are to be made.[101]

[98] Tetleben, *Protokoll*, p. 136.

[99] From earlier discussion it is clear that the final provision intends to rule out reservation of the Eucharist under the form of wine and the carrying of it under both forms to the sick.

[100] The three texts (see above, n. 93) do not agree in their formulation of this condition.

[101] The omission of any treatment of episcopal jurisdiction, the binding power of fasting laws, and the calendar of fasts and feasts makes this a quite incomplete listing of the unresolved problems as of 28 Aug. One can surmise that the text was meant to be taken as an elucidation of selected points in the Catholic *media* of 19 Aug, while leaving unmodified the other conditions of the earlier *media*. The main fact not taken into consideration in the document of 28 Aug. is that the Lutheran position on bishops had broken down, and that their *media* of 20 Aug. was no longer representative. This appears most dramatically in a memorandum by the Hessian theologian Erhard Schnepf from around this time which gives the biblical warrants which seem to him to demolish Melanchthon's case for reintroducing episcopal authority in Lutheran lands: Förstemann, *Urkundenbuch*, ii. 311–13.

On 29 August the Catholic three made a full report to the majority block of Estates on the three sessions of dialogue on 24, 26 and 28 August.[102] The report, however, did not snuff out all hopes of agreement, in spite of its recital of rejections and appeals to a future council. It was agreed that Duke Heinrich of Braunschweig would make a personal princely appeal to Elector Johann at the supper they were planning to have together that evening. Concretely, Heinrich would propose the naming of a new commission of fourteen to take up the unresolved issues concerning liturgy and clerical and religious life. Would not the presence of some princes and bishops, in a fourth phase of dialogue, contribute to more fruitful negotiations?[103]

So another important day of decision for the Lutheran party was 30 August. A consultation reviewed the suggestion that further discussion might well overcome the impasse reached by the committee of six. On this day, also, the courier arrived from the Coburg, bringing from Martin Luther the awaited answers to questions sent to him on 22 August. Later in the day, the committee of six held their final meeting.[104]

Luther argued from basic principle in his response to the Elector.[105] The Reformation position on the cluster of practices now at issue rests on clear biblical norms. One is to teach nothing and institute no practice in a binding manner without the certainty given by God's word.[106] Once God's word has been spoken and heard, then a Christian has no authorization for accepting an alternative arising by human enactment. One after the other, Luther brands as human inventions what the Catholic side had demanded. Communion under one form is such an invention ('ein lauter Menschen-fund'),

---

[102] Tetleben, *Protokoll*, pp. 132–6. The Nuremberg delegates heard that several Catholic Estates found offensive the Lutheran position paper of 28 Aug., predicting that it would be sure to anger Charles V as well (Melanchthon, ed. cit. ii. 319).

[103] Schirrmacher, *Briefe und Acten*, p. 248, Tetleben, *Protokoll*, p. 136. For the Estates, the alternative was to refer the whole matter for settlement by the Emperor, entailing what for many of them would be an undesired increment in his power.

[104] The author of this article is, however, not certain that the mail from the Coburg arrived in time to affect the decision made and communicated at the meeting of the six on 30 Aug.

[105] *Luthers Briefwechsel*, v. 572–4.

[106] In a short note on the same day to Justus Jonas in Augsburg, Luther concluded, 'Sed uiriliter agite neque cedite aduersariis quidquam, nisi quod euidenti Scriptura probauerint' (ibid. 580).

which goes against an utterly clear word of Christ.[107] Private Masses are human inventions which must be banned from divine worship. A prince who is a believing Christian must give way to Scripture's prohibition of private celebrations. The sale of masses under the rubric of sacrifice and *opus operatum* makes them human enactments as well, and this the prayers of the canon clearly confirm. In no way may such a rite be allowed, which one cannot grasp as the biblically mandated memorial of Christ's passion.

In another letter arriving on 30 August, Luther expressed his satisfaction and gratitude over Melanchthon's refusals of the conditions laid down by the Catholics in the commission of fourteen. At the same time Luther was uneasy over what might follow from the restoration of episcopal jurisdiction, for instance, if cases arose in which Lutherans disobeyed their bishops.[108] The papacy is the real problem for Luther, and its continued existence means for him that the Reformation doctrine of justification and the Church has not in fact been acknowledged and agreed to. In a summary judgement on the Diet, Luther concludes that it was quite enough that his side gave its public account of their faith and then uttered their plea for peace. There is no sense extending oneself in an impossible attempt to convert the enemies of the truth.[109]

The joint committee of six met for apparently a brief session on 30 August.[110] The Lutheran three related that their principals had carefully examined the proposal for yet another round of dialogue. But they see no purpose in further negotiation. They have already

[107] In his letter of the same day to Melanchthon, Luther counters the Catholic insinuation that the small reformed party condemns the whole world for practising communion under only one form. The Protestant charge is rather that Catholic authorities have reduced the Church to captivity, much like the Jews in Babylon, where God's people were impeded from practising their religion in its integrity. The call for help in maintaining a tranquil Catholic people is to be countered by attacking theologians like Eck for their complicity in violating the sacrament and thus condemning God's word (ibid. 577 f.).

[108] In his letter to the Elector Johann, Luther had undercut an important component of the Lutheran offer to conform to the calendar of fasts and feasts obligatory in the Western Church. In his view, the ordering of such matters should be determined by secular authorities. God has placed such outward matters under the rule of reason, not his divine law, and in the realm of reason established government has the decisive word: ibid. 574.

[109] Ibid. 577 f.

[110] Schirrmacher, *Briefe und Acten*, p. 248; Honée 'Vergleichshandlungen', pp. 433 f. Melanchthon mentioned in a letter the next day that at the session on the 30th Eck had wryly lamented that Charles V had not instituted inquisitorial measures against the Lutherans immediately upon his arrival in Germany. Then he would have

deliberated with great care over the unresolved issues, and at present conscience will permit no further concessions. Their written declaration of 28 August stated the case against an interim restoration of pre-Reformation doctrine, worship, and church order, and thus an argument from allegedly prescriptive rights of possessors has no validity. When, however, discussion begins on provisions for peaceful coexistence, the Lutherans will gladly participate.

The Catholic three agreed to inform the Estates about this decision to break off the theological colloquy. This was done on the morning of 31 August, and the report was consolidated by a narrative of the specific Lutheran refusals.[111] An account which Johann Eck gave to Cardinal Campeggio about this time on the remaining difficulties may well have been of use in this final report before the Estates.[112] In his memorandum Eck gives an approving account of the Lutherans' readiness to accept bishops, introduce abstinence days and holydays, and promote confession of sin. But the sides disagreed on what disposition to make of monastic properties. This issue the Catholics could well remand to the Emperor for a decision. The Lutherans had not agreed to the limiting conditions under which existing marriages of their clergy are to be tolerated, but for Eck this also can be referred to the Emperor for further deliberation and regulation. But on the Eucharist, Eck listed five problems for which he could apparently offer no solution. The Lutherans refuse to teach the liceity of one form; they will not allow variations in the communion rite within the same community; they reject private masses; they oppose the canon of the Mass; and they are intractable when the Catholics show how sacrifice should be explained. And the last-named problem remains, even though questions about the benefits of the Mass and their application can be remanded to a council for decision.[113]

heard their monstrous heresies and responded by wiping them out. But now he is forming his view of them from Brück's feigned orthodoxy and Melanchthon's sweet reasonableness, and has become a very mild emperor. Melanchthon adds that he and Eck get along in a friendly way (ed. cit. ii. 335).

[111] Schirrmacher, *Brief und Acten*, p. 248.

[112] The text was edited by G. Müller, 'Johann Eck und die Confessio Augustana', *Quellen und Forschungen aus italienischen Archiven und Bibliotheken*, 38 (1958), 240–2. H. Immenkötter proposed that Eck's report was composed on 30 Aug. (*Um die Einheit im Glauben*, p. 94 n. 8).

[113] On these eucharistic issues Eck saw and stated the Lutheran–Catholic conflicts quite clearly. Thus, there is reason to moderate the negative judgments of H. Immenkötter and R. Bäumer on Eck's excessive penchant for reducing serious differences to

The Catholic Estates then agreed that no more could be done through dialogue with the Lutheran party. That afternoon, they met with Emperor Charles V to report on what had transpired since 7 August. Their colloquies had come to a dead end, and so it was left to Charles to take action in the service of unity in the Church and peace in Germany.[114]

Conclusions

The end of August 1530 marked the completion of a significant phase of the Imperial Diet of Augsburg. Further efforts in early September had no success in negotiating an accommodation between the Lutheran and Catholic parties.[115] On 22 September Charles V presented to the Diet a draft recess declaring the Lutheran *Confessio* refuted and demanding that its signers state within six months whether they accept the adaptations proposed to them in late August. And in their domains they are to introduce no further innovations in doctrine and worship.[116] The Lutherans' dissent from this recess sealed the failure of the 1530 attempts at religious reconciliation. Even the extensive doctrinal agreements on *Confessio Augustana*, Articles 1–21, did not receive the codification needed for them to serve later as a basis for further relations between the Catholic and Lutheran groups.

Reflection on the details of this first colloquy of the Reformation era indicates four major reasons why it failed in its quest for doctrinal consensus and a mutually acceptable pattern of diversity in the *forma ecclesiae* regarding worship, clergy, and church order.

(1) A notable difference made itself felt all through the August colloquy regarding the norms regulating religious practice. The

issues of variant terminology. So Immenkötter, *Um die Einheit in Glauben*, pp. 58 f., 70 n. 13; and Bäumer, 'Vermittlungsbemühungen', *Theologie und Glaube*, 70 (1980), 320 f.

[114] Tetleben, *Protokoll*, pp. 137 f.

[115] This effort centred on an eight-point plan, formulated at the behest of Archduke Ferdinand by Georg Truchseß von Waldburg and Hieronymus Vehus and revised by Cardinal Campeggio. A basic account is H. Immenkötter, *Um die Einheit im Glauben*, pp. 71–80. Recent studies include G. Müller, 'Duldung des deutschen Luthertums? Erwägungen Kardinal Lorenzo Campeggios vom September 1530', *Archiv für Reformationsgeschichte*, 68 (1977), 158–72, and E. Honée, ' "Pax politica" oder Wiedervereinigung im Glauben?', in R. Bäumer (ed.) *Reformatio ecclesiae: Festschrift Erwin Iserloh* (Paderborn, 1980), 440–66.

[116] Förstemann, *Urkundenbuch*, ii. 474 f.

Lutheran documents repeatedly appeal to the dictates of a conscience which was formed by Scripture. The Catholics, for their part, insist that regulations set down by church authorities do bind in conscience. Melanchthon, around 12 August, stated his assumption that the dialogue on reform of the abuses did not concern provisions of divine law. None the less his side argued that it was bound in conscience by what God had determined on the communion rite, marriage for priests, and the Mass. The Catholic response at one point (11 August) called in question the authority the Lutheran princes ascribed to their theologians as interpreters of Scripture and God's will. In forming consciences, more weight should be ascribed, according to the Catholic argument, to what the Church has determined. And in the face of this contention, Martin Luther countered with the powerful shibboleth 'human enactments', in reference to unacceptable ecclesiastical encroachments upon the area where God has determined how he is to be worshipped. The two parties differed notably over what serves as the immediate source of norms regulating liturgy, the clergy, and church order.

(2) Among the particular issues of unresolved controversy, the Lutheran insistence on the chalice is emblematic of the previous difference over norms. Communion under both forms could be granted in the reformed territories—this the Catholic side stated quite clearly. But the sticking point was the qualification of communion under both forms. Was it a precept binding all ministers of, and participants in, the sacrament (so the Lutherans)? Or was this left open by Christ, for the Church to regulate according to changing conditions (so the Catholics)? The Catholic gaffe on 21 August occasioned an especially sharp clash over this matter, as the Lutherans straightway refused to link the offering of the chalice to communicants with instruction that receiving under only the form of bread was also admissible. This Lutheran refusal then became a first fixed element in the emerging *dissensus*. This point of Lutheran contestation of a Catholic demand makes especially clear how the Lutheran leaders felt themselves bound by imperatives derived directly from Scripture (e.g. 'Bibite ex hoc omnes'). One senses little comprehension on the Catholic side for such a personal encounter with God's revealing word and for the solemn obligations arising from such a communication.

(3) The provisions recommended by the Catholics for the celebration of Mass, and the ensuing refusals by the Lutherans, reveal

an opposition which was in all likelihood much deeper than most of
the dialogue participants realized. There was a 'dissimilitudo ingens'
over the meaning of the Mass.[117] Melanchthon's memoranda of
20–1 August stated a view of the controversy which would be
widely shared on the Lutheran side.[118] Eucharistic sacrifice is taken
as an egregious case of a meritorious work before God, one running
counter to the primacy of Christ's consoling gift which believers
can only receive in gratitude. The Catholics would reject such an
understanding of the Mass as woefully inadequate because theologically ill informed. This would eventually have manifested itself in
the instructions or glosses on sacrificial terms in the canon, had
Catholic theologians got to the point of formulating them. Such
instructions would emphatically attribute the sacrifice primarily to
Jesus Christ, the eternal Priest, who makes present his once-for-all
offering, so that his people may incorporate themselves into his
action.[119] But the Lutheran doctrine of the Lord's Supper rested on
a perception of the people of the Church as those needing, and
recurrently receiving, Christ's testamentary gift of forgiveness
through the words, gestures, and gifts of communion. Thus, the
eucharistic *dissensus* was also ecclesiological.

(4) Finally, our attention falls on the way the Lutheran case for
the renewed *forma ecclesiae* recurrently appealed to elements of
incipient confessionalization and modernization.[120] The Saxon
theologians had urged accommodation, so as to maintain the proper
climate for catechizing the people in true doctrine and for imposing
Christian discipline on an otherwise unruly populace.[121] The Luth-

---

[117] Urbanus Rhegius said this in 1539, speaking of how far apart even in 1530 the
two sides were on the number of masses and the *intentio* of eucharistic celebration
(cited by M. Liebmann, *Urbanus Rhegius und die Anfänge der Reformation*, p. 279
n. 434).

[118] See above, n. 58.

[119] So K. Schatzgeyer in various works on the mass in the 1520s. See *Schriften zur
Verteidigung der Messe*, ed. E. Iserloh and P. Fabisch (Corpus Catholicorum, 37;
Münster 1984), 59 f., 82, 229, 462–5, 495, 582, 613; also Tommaso de Vio Cardinal
Cajetan, *De sacrificio missae* (1531), trans. J. Wicks, *Cajetan Responds* (Washington,
DC, 1978), 189–200.

[120] The classic article on confessionalization is E. W. Zeeden, 'Grundlagen und
Wege der Konfessionsbildung in Deutschland im Zeitalter der Glaubenskämpfe',
Historische Zeitschrift, 185 (1958), 249–99 (repr. in E. W. Zeeden (ed.), *Gegenrefor-
mation* (Darmstadt, 1973), 85–134). On modernization, W. Reinhard, 'Gegenrefor-
mation als Modernisierung? Prolegomena zu einer Theorie des konfessionellen
Zeitalters', *Archiv für Reformationsgeschichte*, 68 (1977), 226–52.

[121] See above, p. 173; also, 178 f. and 182.

eran *media* of 20 August showed evident concern for enforcing public order in reformed territories. The case for married priests stressed how lawful marriage would impose control on a lower clergy otherwise given to concubinage and random sexual excursions. Episcopal jurisdiction recommended itself to Melanchthon because he could foresee the eventual application by bishops of the sanction of excommunication on lay people and priests who proved obstinate in their unruliness. Furthermore, the Lutherans intended to legislate a unified rite of communion under both forms in their territories, as Brück stated on 28 August. As we noted early in this essay, by 1530 the Lutheran reformation was not simply the product of Luther's early broadsides.

The measures just indicated exemplify facets of a major historical process which unfolded in Europe in the sixteenth century. The Lutheran élite, both rulers and theological advisers, were, as early as 1530, promoting indoctrination in more conscious orthodoxy and the imposition of more disciplined behaviour upon their people. The Catholics did not perceive or acknowledge this process, which they would hardly have opposed in principle. Instead, the Catholics fixed on details in which the Lutheran programme departed from more recent tradition. The details were indicative of significant differences over Scripture, the Eucharist, and the Church. But they also obscured the Catholic perception of a Lutheran intention and of a process unfolding in Lutheran lands which some Catholics of 1530 could have appreciated.

But, we must also note, many German Catholics at the Diet of Augsburg in 1530 could give only lip service to the indictment of abuses and the clamour for reform of Church and society. A new Catholic generation had to emerge, and evangelical idealism had to be injected from Spain and Italy, before 'reform' ceased being a century-old cliché and began to motivate personal living and ecclesial service. Sad to say, the eventual Tridentine reform, also a confessionalizing and modernizing process, took place behind the barricades thrown up against later generations living according to the Lutheran *forma ecclesiae*.

11

Duplex iustitia
The Sixteenth Century and the Twentieth

EDWARD YARNOLD

IN 1984 Professor Henry Chadwick wrote for the Anglican–Roman Catholic International Commission a study paper entitled 'Justification by Faith: a Perspective'.[1] In the section of the paper dealing with the Council of Trent, he gives an account of the debate in 1546 concerning the theory of 'double justice', a theory which the council fathers pondered deeply and debated passionately, but decided not to endorse. One of the motives—but not the only one—which lay behind the development of the theory was the desire to find a theology of justification which would satisfy both Catholics and Reformers. Professor Chadwick suggests that the reason for the failure of the attempt was in part the 'comparative novelty' of the theory and the 'unfamiliar language' in which it was expressed.

I believe that the concept of double justice considered at Trent can still have a place in Catholic theology and may still be ecumenically useful, and shall develop this view in the last section of this essay. However, it seems desirable first to give a selective account of its history. Although a succession of scholars, including very recently A. E. McGrath (to whom I am happy to acknowledge a considerable debt),[2] have done much to establish the development of the idea of double justice, there is still room for such a historical study, for there exists considerable disagreement about what the authors meant and what the sources of the theory were. For example, J. Rivière traces the 'principles' to the Dutchman Albert Pigge (Pighius), and the first 'literary manifestation' to Pigge's disciple at Cologne, John Gropper;[3] R. Stupperich believes that the decisive influence is that of Erasmus;[4] R. Braunisch, convincingly

---

[1] Reprinted in *One in Christ*, 20–3 (1984), 191–225, esp. 204.

[2] In his two-volume work *Iustitia Dei: A History of the Christian Doctrine of Justification* (Cambridge, 1986).

[3] DTC 8. 2159–62.

[4] *Der Humanismus und die Wiedervereinigung der Konfessionen* (Leipzig, 1936), 11.

refuting Stupperich, argues instead that there is a clear break in the evolution of the term between Gropper's *Enchiridion* of 1538 and the Colloquy at Ratisbon in 1541.[5]

Before Trent

A clear distinction between two kinds of justice occurs as early as Rom. 10: 1–6, where Paul rejects 'righteousness from law' in favour of 'righteousness from God' and 'righteousness from faith'. However, this distinction has no direct bearing on the present investigation, which is concerned with two kinds of justice both of which are included in the process of man's justification before God.

The origin of the theory of double justice in this sense is sometimes found in St Augustine's anti-Pelagian work *De spiritu et littera*. Now, from one point of view, Augustine teaches a single justice. How, he asks (n. 45), can St Paul state that 'the doers of the law . . . will be justified' (Rom. 2: 13), when he later in the same epistle will maintain that 'a man is justified by faith apart from works of law' (3: 28)? His answer is that in Rom. 2: 13 Paul is describing a single process of justification: to be justified by faith means to be made just, so that one becomes a doer of the law.

However, from another point of view, Augustine does provide some of the elements of the double justice theory of the 1530s and 1540s with his distinction between the 'perfect justice' which is enjoined upon us in the first great commandment and will be realized in heaven, and the 'lesser justice' which consists in resisting temptation, and which is all that the just man who lives by faith ever achieves in this life. In this state of lesser justice one must always hunger and thirst for the perfect justice for two reasons: first, because in this life everyone has some sins for which he needs forgiveness; secondly, because one must not take credit for the righteousness one has, but attribute it to God's grace (*De spir. et litt.* 63–5).

Among the scholastic theologians, however, a quite different theory of double justice became commonplace. Thus, in the *Summa* attributed to Alexander of Hales there is said to be a duality in justice analogous to the double nature of sin. With regard to sin there is

---

[5] *Die Theologie der Rechtfertigung im 'Enchiridion' (1538) des Iohannes Gropper* (Münster, 1974), 427–8.

sin from oneself (personal sin) and sin from another (original sin). So too there is a *duplex iustitia*: one must distinguish between justice in practice (*iustitia in exercitu*), which a man does to or for himself ('quam sibi homo facit') when he has grace, and the justice which is done to a man ('quae sibi fit') through the mediation of Christ, as in a baptized baby.[6] Aquinas draws a similar distinction, only with greater precision than Alexander; he contrasts the justice which consists in the performance of good works with the justice by which one becomes just, acquiring the *habitus iustitiae*.[7]

This scholastic understanding of the two kinds of justice was still current in the early decades of the sixteenth century. For Erasmus the *duplex iustitia* consists of the innocence to which one is restored by faith and baptism, as contrasted with the second justice, which consists of faith working through love. Elsewhere he expresses the same distinction in more colourful terms, as that between the justice which restores the house of our mind to cleanliness ('repurgantem mentis nostrae domicilium'), and that which decorates it with good works ('ornantem ac locupletantem eam bonis operibus').[8] His friend John Fisher spoke of the same *iustificatio duplex* in more prosaic terms, distinguishing that acquired ('acquisita') through grace from that to be acquired ('acquirenda') through works.[9] The Dominican Cardinal Thomas de Vio (Cajetan), in a work of 1532 entitled *De fide et operibus*, while not using the language of double justice, affirms that the justified are doubly owed eternal life: first through Christ's merits, and secondly through the merits of good works accomplished by a person incorporated into Christ.[10] In 1541, the year of the Ratisbon colloquy, another Dominican, Ambrose Catharinus, made a similar distinction explicitly in terms of double justification. The first justification is admission to the Christian struggle, and a beginning (*inchoatio*) in Christ; the second is completed in the context itself ('ipso agone et cursu ipso perficitur').[11] Even Martin Luther still had one foot within the same tradition when in 1519 he distinguished between 'alien righteousness, that is the righteousness of another . . . instilled from without', and 'our proper righteous-

---

[6] *Summa Theologica*, 2. 2. 229 ff.

[7] *Summa Theologiae*, 1a 2ae 100. 12.

[8] *In Psalmum XXII enarratio triplex*, opp. (Leiden), v. 325 B; *De amabili ecclesiae concordia*, v. 500 D.

[9] *Assertionis Lutheranae confutatio* (Antwerp, 1523), fo. 65ʳ.

[10] *De fide et operibus*, ch. 9.

[11] *De perfecta iustificatione a fide et operibus liber* (Lyons, 1541), 201.

ness' according to which 'we work with that first and alien righteousness' and which consists in 'life spent profitably in good works'.[12]

To summarize the history up to this point, we can say that
whereas Augustine was concerned with the distinction between
imperfect and perfect 'justice of works', the later writers were
contrasting the justice of works with what came to be called
'infused' or 'imparted justice'. In the late 1530s and the 1540s,
however, a number of Catholic theologians combined these
Augustinian and scholastic strands, applying the language of
double justice to Augustine's conviction that even the justified
need further justification. While it is evident that these theologians
were reacting to the Reformers' doctrine of justification by faith, it
would be a mistake to interpret their version of the double-justice
theory as simply a search for a compromise formula. The theory
springs at least as much from the desire to find a theological basis
for the Christian's perpetual need for mercy. The key figure in this
development seems to have been the Cologne theologian John
Gropper.

In Gropper's early work, the *Enchiridion* (1538), the theory is not
yet fully developed. Taking justification to consist of both the
remission of sins and the interior renewal or cleansing of the mind,
and rejecting Melanchthon's idea of a purely 'forensic' justification
followed by regeneration, Gropper referred to St Augustine's *De
spiritu et littera* for confirmation of his belief that to be justified
meant 'to be made just' (163[r]). Remission of sin and renovation by
the Holy Spirit form 'altogether the same justice'; one cannot separate the 'imputative justice of God' from the 'justice of a good conscience' (163[v]). Nevertheless the justified, conscious of their
weakness, cannot avoid questioning their assurance that they are
truly sons of God. When that question comes into his mind, Gropper says, 'then above all I ought to remember the word of promise,
in which, O Lord, you have given me hope; then, O Christ, I must
look to the words you spoke to the woman who was an adulteress,
though not yet condemned: "Neither do I condemn you." . . . O
vocem misericordiae, o auditum laetitiae salutaris' (169[v]). Our
works of faith, performed through grace, are 'imputed to justice (*ad
iustitiam imputari*)' (176[r]), because they please God 'through Christ

---

[12] *Two Kinds of Righteousness* (American ed.) xxxi. 297–306 *De duplici iustitia*,
WA ii. 145–52.

from whose perfection we make up our imperfection (*nostram imperfectionem supplemus*), for we are members of his body . . . Through Christ (who alone fulfilled the law) we fulfil the law by imputation (*imputative*)' (132^r).

In this early work of Gropper's four points should be noted: (1) in addition to the justice of works and imparted justice, a third factor is introduced into the discussion, namely the *imputed justice* of Christ; (2) Gropper does not consider the imputation of Christ's merits to the justified as a mere forensic transaction, but rather as the sharing by the members of Christ's body in the merits of the head; (3) the imputation and the imparting of justice, though distinguished, are not regarded as two separate processes of justification; (4) the main contrast is between the justice of works and imputed justice; infused justice is the presupposition of both. However, if it is correct to see the hand of Gropper in the section on justification in the *Liber Ratisbonensis*, the text which formed the basis of the discussion and partial agreement between the Catholic and Protestant delegates at the colloquy at Ratisbon in 1541, Gropper had by now modified his views. Imputed justice is no longer linked with the doctrine of the body of Christ, and is contrasted with 'inherent justice'—a new term introduced with little explanation, and with no attempt to define the relationship between the two. It seems that inherent justice is understood as the justice of works: 'the faithful soul does not rely on this [inherent justice], but only on the justice of Christ which has been given to us, without which there is and can be, no justice at all' (CR iv. 200).

In 1544 Gropper focused his thoughts on justification more sharply in his polemical work entitled the *Antididagma*. Applying the traditional categories of cause to the concept of justification, he explains that there are two 'formal causes'.[13] The first and highest is the justice of Christ imputed to us; it is on this we rely 'principally'. The second formal cause is inherent justice, which is now described not only in relation to works but also as the infusion of charity. (This ambiguity in the term 'inherent justice' was to blur the discussion at Trent.) We do not rely on this inherent justice principally, but 'we are assured by it with, so to speak, a certain interior experience (*tanquam interiori quodam experimento*) . . . that our

---

[13] The formal cause is always intrinsic to the subject—e.g. the formal cause of the whiteness of a wall is the whiteness itself.

sins have been remitted to us, and Christ's perfect justice is imputed to us, and so Christ dwells in us through faith' (13ᵛ).

The common view that Gropper derived his views on double justice from his old master Albert Pigge has recently been overturned by Jedin, who argued that Pigge, who did not publish his views on the subject until 1541, is more likely to have been influenced by Gropper rather than vice versa, and in any event conceives justification differently from Gropper.[14] Writing in the aftermath of the Ratisbon colloquy, Pigge devotes one chapter in his second Controversy to the subject of faith and justification, and speaks there of 'duplex iustitia' (fo. opp. Gʳ). However, the distinction here is between justice before men and justice before God, and therefore does not reflect the two formal causes of Gropper's later thought. In fact, when applying the causal categories to justification, Pigge gives no consideration to formal causality at all (fo. Miiiʳ). Indeed, in his insistence on the unity of our justification in Christ, he comes closer to the understanding of the young Gropper in the *Enchiridion*. Against the Protestants, who believe in justification 'sola fide' and not 'charitate', Pigge maintains that 'we are justified before God neither by faith nor by our charity, if we are to speak formally and properly, but by the one justice of God in Christ, the one justice of Christ communicated to us, the one mercy of God which forgives us our sins' (fo. Iʳ).

In explaining how works performed after justification are meritorious, Pigge, even more emphatically than Gropper, dwells upon the need of the imputation of the merits of Christ. Whereas in the *Antididagma* Gropper allows the Christian to rely on inherent justice as evidence that Christ's justice has been imputed to him, Pigge does not consider even this evidential value of good works. His concern is to affirm that what merit they have is not

of themselves, or from us, but from the divine grace from which they proceed. This dignity of our works is measured (*aestimata*) from the merits of Christ, our head, God-man, with whose blood they are sprinkled—his merits, which are communicated to us as his members, and in which our works are wrapped and clothed (*involvuntur atque induuntur*), as this vital and lifegiving spirit flows to us from him who is the head, so that it is not from ourselves that these works of ours now derive their efficacy, energy

[14] H. Jedin, *Studien über die Schriftstellertätigkeit Albert Pigges* (Münster, 1931), 117–23; A. Pigge, *Controversiarum praecipuarum in comitiis Ratisponensibus tractatarum . . . explicatio*; in the Cologne edition of 1545 from which I have quoted not all the pages are numbered, so that page references cannot easily be given.

and dignity. Thus this dignity of our works comes from Christ, not from ourselves, although it is communicated to us through the grace of justification, by which we merit (*promeremur*). (fo. after Liii^r)

For it is not only the vine but also the shoot grafted (*incorporatus*) on to the vine which bears fruit, though not of itself, but from the virtue which it receives from the vine (fo. after Liiii^v)

The works of the justified performed in faith, hope, and charity are gratuitously imputed to us for justice ('gratis ad iustitiam imputat'), not because of their intrinsic worth, but because the divine goodness and mercy are poured into us in Christ and in his blood (Miii^r). Thus Pigge works out more clearly than Gropper's *Enchiridion* the dependence of imputed justice upon infused justice.

Nevertheless it is not without good reason that H. Jedin observes that, in formulating this theory, Pigge is coming down on the side of Luther.[15] However in the second Controversy Pigge's Lutheranism is more a matter of vocabulary than of theology, because imputation to the Christian of Christ's justice is not merely extrinsic, but 'efficacy, energy, and dignity' which flow to our good works from Christ our head. The Lutheran tendency seems more marked in a letter which Pigge wrote to Gaspar Contarini elucidating his teaching. Here he puts forward an interpretation of justification which seems to exclude infused justice altogether. The grace of justification 'is not any quality, or any act, habit (*habitus*), attitude (*habitudo*) or relation (*respectus*) in the one who is pleasing, beloved and accepted, but the lover's kind disposition itself and his love itself.' But even here Pigge may owe less to Luther than to the Scotist tradition, with its emphasis on God's free acceptance, rather than the intrinsic value of good works, as the basis of merit.[16]

Contarini himself figures prominently in the history of the doctrine of double justice. Made a cardinal while still a layman, he served as pontifical legate at the Ratisbon colloquy of 1541.[17] Since

[15] Jedin, *Pigge*, p. 115.

[16] Quoted in F. Dittrich, *Regesten und Briefe des Kardinals Gasparo Contarini* (Braunsberg, 1881), 389.

[17] For Contarini's career see H. Jedin, *Kardinal Contarini als Kontroverstheologe* (Münster, 1949). The importance of Contarini in the present narrative is pleasing, seeing that the Anglican–Roman Catholic International Commission, to whose work Professor Chadwick has devoted so much of his time and energy, has frequently met in the Istituto Cardinale Piazza, which is built on the ground where one of the Contarini palaces once stood, near Madonna dell'Orto, the church which contains Contarini's tomb.

the Book of Ratisbon was put before the participants at the collo-quy only after it had undergone revision at Contarini's hands (it is in this form also that it has come down to us), it is no surprise to find a similar theory of double justice contained in Contarini's own 'Letter on Justification' written a few days after the colloquy ended.[18] Expounding a doctrine which he believes will be accept-able to Catholics and Protestants alike (595), he defines *justificari* as 'to be made just and therefore also to be considered just' (*iustum fieri, ac propterea etiam haberi iustum)*' (588). This implies a 'double justice (*duplicem iustitiam)*, one inhering (*inhaerentem*) in us, by which we begin to be just and are made partners of the divine nature, the other not inhering but given (*donatam*) to us with Christ, i.e. the justice of Christ, and all his merit; each [justice] is given to us at the same time, and we attain each by faith' (591). This given justice is also described as 'imputed' (592). As with Gropper and Pigge, this imputed justice is not forensic, but is grounded on the fact that we are 'grafted (*inserti*) into Christ and put on Christ'. Inherent justice is not conceived simply in terms of works, for it consists of the 'infusion of grace' (591) and 'the charity and grace of God inhering in us' (592). Inherent and given justice together make us just 'formally', in the same sense as whiteness makes a wall white, though Contarini does not use the expression 'formal cause'; faith makes us just in the same sense that a wall is made white by paint-ing. This is faith which is 'efficacious through charity' (592).

However, Contarini, like Gropper, finds the source of the justi-fied Christian's confidence before God not in his inherent justice, but in the justice which is given and imputed. But unlike Gropper, who in the *Antididagma* allowed our inherent justice a part, though not the principal part, in grounding our assurance, Contarini will not allow the Christian to rely on inherent justice at all. For 'our justice is inchoate and imperfect, and cannot preserve us from offending in many things.' Accordingly we are reckoned ('haberi') just in God's sight only through the imputation of Christ's 'perfect' justice (592). In support of this view Contarini appeals to various scripture texts. We need to pray each day: 'Forgive us our tres-passes.' Christ's justice is the treasure in the field and the pearl. Paul thought all things loss so as to gain Christ, and to be found with a justice which was not his own, but was through faith (Phil. 3: 8–9).

---

[18] Printed in *Gasparis Contareni Cardinalis Opera* (Paris, 1571).

The Laodiceans were vomited from God's mouth because they thought they were rich, but were really naked (Rev. 3: 16–17). The white stone with the secret name promised to the victorious of Pergamum bears the name of Christ (Rev. 2: 17).

Contarini's teaching concerning the need of the justified to continue to rely on the imputed justice of Christ was neither unthinking repetition of a traditional Augustinian formula, nor simply an attempt to find a compromise with the Reformers. It seems to rest on a deeply felt conviction. As people advance in holiness, he affirms,

they become more perceptive and see more clearly how frail the sanctity and justice which inhere in them are. At the same time they observe many faults which offend their sight the more now that it has become clearer. For this reason they know from experience (*re ipsa*) that they must not rely upon the sanctity, charity and grace which inheres in them, but must fly to Christ and to the grace of Christ which is given them, and on which they may rely and rest.

Contarini illustrates this teaching with a parable of a king who received a peasant at court to please his son. Although the peasant acquired some of the ways of the court, his manners still grated on the king; but the latter treated him as a courtier and a friend 'because of the grace and merits of the son, and these he gave (*donavit*) to the shepherd' (593).

Light is thrown on the experience which lay behind Contarini's teaching by a letter which he wrote in 1511 to his friend Giustiniani, and which remained unpublished until 1959. Contarini recounts how, in making his Easter confession on the Holy Saturday of that year he spoke to his confessor about the anxieties of conscience he was suffering at the thought that he ought to follow Giustiniani in becoming a Camaldolese monk. Praying afterwards he experienced the conviction that, however many penances he performed, they would not suffice to earn the happiness of heaven or to make up for his past faults. But he suddenly saw that he should rely, not on his penances, but on the work of Christ.

Shall I not sleep soundly [he asks], even in the middle of the city, even though I have not cleared my debt I have contracted, seeing that I have such a one to pay my debt? I shall indeed sleep and travel about as securely as if all the days of my life had been spent in the Hermitage . . . I shall live just as securely, without any fear of my crimes, because his mercy exceeds all his other works.

Jedin has good reason to call this incident 'a tower-experience of the young Contarini'—one indeed which predates Luther's experience by perhaps as much as four years.[19]

In fact the sense that the converted Christian still needs to throw himself on the mercy of God seems to have been in the air independently of Luther. Ignatius Loyola, who in his cave in 1522 is hardly likely to have felt the influence of the Reformation, describes the following experience which he had when he thought he was dying of fever:

The thought came to him that he was a just man. This thought caused him so much anxiety that he could only fight against it and recall his past sins. He was more troubled by this thought than by the fever, but for all his efforts against it he could not get the better of the thought. Once he had recovered somewhat from the fever and was no longer close to dying, he began to utter loud cries to some ladies who came to visit him, asking them for the love of God, if they saw him on the point of death again, to shout at him at the top of their voices, calling him a sinner and reminding him of the ways in which he had offended God.[20]

The Council of Trent

When the theory of double justification made its appearance at the Council of Trent, its defenders seem to have been most influenced by concern for the right understanding of the justified Christian's confidence before God, although the desire to leave a door open for an agreement with the Lutherans was not absent. No trace of the theory is to be found, however, in the first, 'July' draft of the decree on justification, drawn up by four elected deputies in 1546. It is only in the two preliminary versions of the 'September' draft that double justification enters upon the stage.

The author of these preliminary versions was one of the most influential prelates at Trent, Cardinal Girolamo Seripando, General of the Augustinian Friars (of which Luther had been a member), and

---

[19] H. Jedin, 'Ein "Turmerlebnis" des jungen Contarinis', in *Kirche des Glaubens: Kirche der Geschichte*, 1 (Freiburg, 1966), 167–80. The letter was first published in *Archivo italiano per la storia della pietà* 2 (1959), 62–5.

[20] *Autobiography*, n. 32. For the Spanish text, see e.g. *Obras completas de San Ignacio de Loyola*, ed. C. de Dalmases (Madrid, 1963), 105–6.

later one of the papal legates who shared the presidency of the council. Exhibiting the same Italian combination of piety and humanism as Contarini, he had spent many years studying the works of the Reformers, and had even been commissioned by Pope Paul III to continue these researches in preparation for the Council.[21] He received the invitation to prepare a new draft from Marcello Cervini, one of the legates, who was dissatisfied with the July attempt.

Seripando had already expressed his views on justification in a treatise which he dedicated to Lattanzio Tolomei in 1543.[22] Although, unlike the Cologne theologians and Contarini, he makes no explicit allusion to double justice (though he distinguishes six 'modes of justification'), the two main elements of the theory are already present: (1) the defectiveness of the good works of the justified even when performed in grace, a defectiveness which Seripando, following his patron St Augustine, attributes to the influence of concupiscence or self-love; and (2) the consequent need for a further perfect justice to supplement the incompleteness of the justice of our works. This perfect justice is both reward and grace. In judging our good works God considers the fact that they are performed by a member of Christ, and for this reason accepts them as equivalent to the reward.

The same ideas reappear in July 1546 in a long paper which Seripando submitted to the council concerning the July draft. 'Whence', he asks, 'will a Christian man be justified before God's tribunal, from his works or from the justice of Christ communicated to him through the grace of God?.' Quoting various writings of Augustine, including the *De spiritu et littera*, he replies that God will reward the works of the just 'not from the dignity of the works, considered on their own (*praecise*), but from God's mercy regarding a Christian man, who through faith has been made a member of Christ and a sharer in Christ's justice.'[23]

Seripando handed his first draft to Cervini on 11 August 1546, and eight days later submitted a revised version incorporating certain modifications suggested by the legate.[24] The eighth chapter of

---

[21] H. Jedin (Eng. trans.), *Papal Legate at the Council of Trent: Cardinal Seripando* (St Louis–London, 1947), 102. For the study of the debates at Trent on justification indispensable help is to be found in H. Jedin (Eng. trans.), *A History of the Council of Trent*, ii (London etc., 1961), chs. 5, 7, 8.

[22] *CT* xii. 844.

[23] Ibid. 635.

[24] Ibid. v. 821–33.

the second draft carries the unequivocal title *De duplici iustitia*. (Most of the text of this chapter, though not its title, had already appeared in Seripando's first draft, though in the form of a canon and not as a separate chapter). It seemed as though the doctrine of double justice was to be accepted in explicit terms as Catholic dogma.

However, the theory of double justice as Seripando expounds it in this draft is far less sharply focused than that of the *Antididagma* or of Contarini. Seripando distinguishes between, on the one hand, 'that most pure and complete justice of Christ our Saviour and head which is diffused throughout his whole body, the whole Church, and is communicated and applied to all his members through faith and the sacraments', and, on the other hand, 'grace or charity', which 'by the merit of this same Saviour of ours is diffused in the hearts of the justified through the Holy Spirit who is given to them.' Seripando chooses not to speak expressly of imputed and imparted justice, though the two forms of justice he describes seem to correspond to these terms.[25]

Before Seripando's draft was submitted to the council in September, it was subjected to such radical scrutiny and revision by Cervini and a number of advisors that the original author felt he could no longer recognise his own work. In particular he was distressed at the omission of his chapter on double justice: indeed, the September draft included an express denial of the 'two justices'. As Jedin observes, Cervini's draft changed the substance of Seripando's document, even though many features of it were retained.[26] The justice of Christ is said to be 'communicated and imputed as if it were ours and we had performed what he has performed (*praestitit*) for us.' Nevertheless there is only one justice, given by God through the merit of Christ, by which we are both reputed (*reputamur*) justified and are truly just.[27] Cervini's compromise, however, 'pleased neither the defenders of the doctrine of twofold justice nor the opponents.'[28]

In the course of October Seripando made two pleas for the reintroduction of the doctrine of double justice. On the 8th[29] he pleaded before the General Congregation that the beliefs of dis-

---

[25] Ibid. 829.
[26] Jedin, *Seripando*, p. 355. The text of the Sept. draft is given in *CT* v. 420–6.
[27] *CT* v. 423.
[28] Jedin, *Seripando*, p. 355.
[29] *CT* v. 485–90.

tinguished and orthodox doctors in Germany and Italy should not be rejected. He then focused the problem on the source of the justi-fied Christian's confidence before God, and put to the Fathers the following question: Before the divine tribunal are we of one justice, the justice of works (*iustitia operum*) proceeding from grace, or of 'a double justice, viz. our own . . . and the justice of Christ, viz. when the passion, merit and satisfaction of Christ supplement the imper-fection of our own justice.' Seripando is evidently contrasting imputed justice with the justice of works rather than with infused justice. The Fathers are urged to answer this question with great ser-iousness, each placing himself in front of the judge who holds the key of death and hell. The objection had been raised that this doc-trine is incompatible with belief in purgatory. Seripando's reply is that, on the contrary, the doctrine of purgatory demands the doc-trine of double justice. Purgatory follows after acceptance for salva-tion, which is possible only if Christ's justice supplements our own—not indeed to the extent that we can be admitted at once to glory, but in sufficient measure for us to be judged saved and to pay the penalty for our sins in purgatory.[30]

About the same time Seripando developed his views at greater length in a written paper entitled 'A statement in support of the opinion of certain Catholics concerning double justice.'[31] Seripando chose not to state his own views directly, but to reproduce lengthy quotations from Pigge, Gropper and Contarini, and then to answer their opponents' objections. The most significant point about these answers is again his apparent identification of inherent justice with the justice of works: before the divine tribunal we will be judged not by our possession of habitual grace but by our good works. Because of human weakness there is therefore a 'diminution of our merits', which consequently need to be supplemented by Christ's justice.[32]

In his speech of 8 October Seripando had asked a question con-cerning man's need for one justice or two before the divine tribunal. A week later the presidents requested formal answers to the ques-

[30] Ibid. 486, 488. Seripando's identification of inherent justice with the justice of works done in grace is explicitly formulated in another version he wrote of the ques-tion concerning confidence before the divine tribunal (ibid. ii. 431).

[31] Ibid. xii. 664–71.

[32] Ibid. 669, 671.

tion, though they altered the case in two significant ways. First, by speaking of the tribunal of Christ rather than the divine tribunal and so focusing attention on the general judgement, they made the question refer to the just who appear for judgement after they had undergone the purifying experience of purgatory. Secondly, instead of considering a deficiency in works done in grace (as Seripando's version of the question defined inherent justice), the deficiency in question now seemed to be one in sanctifying grace itself, which would imply a shortcoming on God's part rather than on man's.[33]

From 15 to 26 October the consultant theologians one by one gave meticulous answers to these questions. At the end of this grinding process, Massarelli, the secretary of the council, noted thirty-two theologians who had spoken against double justice, and only five who had supported it (three of whom were members of Seripando's order).[34] Comments were also forthcoming from a number of theologians in Rome, including Cardinal Reginald Pole, one of the three papal legates at the council. He had left Trent on the plea of ill health, and now sent from Rome a statement supporting the double justice theory in language that sounded so Lutheran that it failed to influence the debate.[35] The speakers opposed to double justice deployed a variety of arguments, some of which clarified the question, while others missed the point. It was said that the theory was a novelty, and that it sounded Lutheran. It was rightly argued that Christ's merit could not be described as a formal cause of man's justification, as a form must inform its subject, like whiteness in a white wall—but then Seripando had not followed Gropper and Contarini in arguing that Christ's justice was a second formal cause alongside inherent justice. It was maintained that the imputation of Christ's justice to those already justified implied that the more meritorious received no better treatment than the less, and made purgatory superfluous. The theory of double justice was thought to imply a 'new application' of Christ's justice—a suggestion which was rejected as a novelty, and seemed to imply the insufficiency of first justification.

Seripando's feelings are revealed by an entry in his records:

[33] Ibid. v. 523.
[34] Ibid. 632.
[35] Ibid. xii. 674–6. The *CT* text gives at the foot of the page Seripando's comments on Pole's statement, written in the margins of the statement. Pole also addressed a private note to the legates at their request (ibid. 671–4).

'Almost everyone was striving to exclude the justice of Christ from the hearts of men.'[36] However, recognizing that church councils, like politics, call for the art of the possible, he now worked intensely over a new draft of the September version of the decree. Without inserting any explicit reference to the two justices, he deleted the affirmation that there was only one justice, and introduced a number of unobtrusive changes which he hoped would express the heart of his belief in a way which the council fathers would not find controversial.[37] For example, the September draft had stated that no one ought to be presumptuous concerning the hidden mystery of predestination; Seripando turned the phrase into an affirmation of the just man's continuing need of mercy, by writing that no one, 'however just, as long as he lives in this mortal condition', ought so to presume.[38]

Seripando seems to have set this new draft aside without submitting it to the council. Instead at the request of the president Cervini he began to work with Massarelli on another revision of the September version. Between 20 and 31 October there are only two days on which the secretary's diary does not contain such an entry as: 'Worked from 7 to 10 p.m. with the General of the Hermits on the decree.'[39] For the first time a section was included which, in predominantly Aristotelian terms, analysed the various types of causality involved in justification. Unlike Gropper and Contarini, who had regarded imputed and inherent justice as the two formal causes of justification, the document now stated that the formal cause is 'the one justice of God, by which we are renewed in the spirit of our mind [cf. Eph. 4: 23] and are not only reputed just, but are truly named and are just.' Christ's passion is categorized as the meritorious cause which made satisfaction to God the Father on our behalf.[40] In this official draft Seripando was able to achieve his own purposes more effectively than he had in his unofficial revision by setting as the conclusion of the draft the warning that the just should not cease from imploring God's mercy for their sins, offences and negligences, and from trusting in the merits of Jesus

[36] Ibid. ii. 432.

[37] Ibid. xii. 679–85.

[38] Ibid. 683.

[39] Ibid. v. 581. Seripando's own record reads: 'The secretary came to me every day very early' (ibid. ii. 430). The text of the draft is given ibid. v. 510–17.

[40] Ibid. 512. The assertion of a single formal cause is evidently not, as is sometimes said, intended as a denial of Seripando's position.

Christ, 'because the whole of men's life is to be examined and judged not by human judgement but by the secret judgement of God.'[41]

However, del Monte, the second president of the council—Pole's resignation was published on 27 October—was not as sympathetic to Seripando's views as Cervini, and succeeded in getting his way with his colleague. On 5 November, after several days of intensive consultation, del Monte laid before the council fathers a draft which, though based on that of Seripando and Massarelli, had undergone many significant changes. The analysis in terms of the various causes (including the identification of the formal cause as the one justice of Christ by which we are truly rendered just) was retained, but Seripando's ending asserting the just man's continual need of mercy was removed. A new conclusion was written stating the exact opposite: nothing is lacking to the justified to prevent them from fulfilling the divine law with the help of grace and meriting eternal life, 'provided they have worked with that charity (*caritatis affectu*) which is required in the course of this mortal life'.[42]

Seripando, feeling himself betrayed by Cervini and isolated, wrote in the margin of the last chapter of his copy of the November draft: 'This whole section seems to be the work of a man who does not know what he is talking about, or who is wavering in fear of falling into the teachings of the Lutherans.'[43] On 26 November he took the opportunity of making one last plea for his convictions. Dr Chadwick rightly describes this lengthy address—Seripando had to continue it on the following day—as a 'deeply religious speech', and 'one of the most moving and human documents of the entire conciliar record'.[44] Nevertheless it is not only religious passion, but also indignation, irony, sarcasm, and even contempt for his opponents which flash out from the densely printed folio pages.

Seripando protests that his speech of 8 October had been misinterpreted; his purpose had not been to persuade the council to accept any view of his own, but simply to plead that the double justice theory of so many orthodox theologians should not be

[41] Ibid. 515.
[42] Ibid. 634–41.
[43] Ibid. 663, n. 2. For a fuller account of Seripando's reactions see ibid. ii. 430–1: he would say nothing in public against the draft decree, 'although many things sit heavily on my stomach (cum tamen meo stomacho multa disciplicerent)'.
[44] Chadwick, art. cit. 204. The speech is contained in *CT* v. 666–676.

condemned. He saw now that he had been naïve in expecting his hearers to understand this.[45] He consequently tried to define with greater precision what the point at issue was.

Before the divine tribunal, i.e. not at the last judgement but in this life, a Christian, though justified, needs to be further effected (*alterum effectum*) by God's mercy and Christ's justice. 'Consequently in this matter I see a double justice, namely the justice with regard to which we shall be judged, i.e. the justice of works, and the justice on account of which this judgement will be made mercifully, i.e. the justice of Christ.' (Infused justice is thus left out of the equation, which is set out in terms of imputed justice and the justice of works.)

This does not apply to baptized babies or to any whom God's grace may make perfectly just and sinless.[46] But the rest of mankind are in constant need of mercy. Christ's justice is imputed to us not only extrinsically, as the heretics say, nor only by being communicated (*communicari*) to us so that it inheres formally, but in both ways. In making up their minds on this point theologians should remember that the question is not theoretical but practical. Each must speak for himself, because it is his own skin which is at stake, not somebody else's ('de proprio, non alieno, corio luderent').[47]

Seripando is not, however, totally consistent in stating his reason for holding this belief. On the one hand he seems to be influenced by the Augustinian doctrine of concupiscence in asserting that no Christians perform as many good works as they should, and that sins are mixed in with their good works. Our works are not found with 'that purity which is owed to God, and which with the help of God's grace we could show'.[48] On the other hand he states that this further effect of mercy is not needed by those who after justification commit only venial sins, but only by 'the great number of Christians who sometimes perform good works in grace, but often fall into graver sins'.[49]

The Augustinian General was aware of the need to try to win support from other theological traditions besides that of his own order. He consequently attempted to show that his conclusion

[45] Ibid. 666.
[46] Ibid. 668.
[47] Ibid.
[48] Ibid. 669.
[49] Ibid. 668.

would also follow from Scotist premises. The great Franciscan doctor's emphasis on the divine will had led him to base justification and merit on God's free acceptance of mankind. For Scotus God's free acceptance is logically prior to his communication of grace and his regard of our works as meritorious. Consequently the Scotist system implied a double effect of Christ's justice: grace to perform good works on the one hand, and God's merciful acceptance of these works on the other.[50]

There was nothing heretical, Seripando affirmed, in this exposition of the theory of double justice. If anyone disagreed, he must be a theological and literary ignoramus ('tamquam theologiae et bonarum omnium litterarum expertem'), and Seripando would not deign to reply.[51] Nevertheless he would not hold up the promulgation of the decree by insisting on his point. He would be satisfied if two additions were made in the concluding paragraph. The first was the more important: after the affirmation that nothing was lacking to the justified who performed good works under the influence of charity, he requested the insertion of the sentence: 'Those who know they have not performed good works under such an influence of charity, or who doubt about it, should do penance and invoke God's mercy through the merits of Christ's passion.' This would be a net full of large fish. The second proposed addition was to the same effect.[52]

The concluding section of Seripando's long speech was devoted to answering objections to the double justice theory. The last objection is to his own excessive vehemence. His defence was courteous and moving. 'I will be much more vehement in defending the truth as you will define it than I have been in arguing for the views which I have expounded, whether they are the views of others or my own.'[53] It is greatly to the credit both of Seripando's colleagues and of the Holy See that however isolated he may have been on the question of double justice, within fifteen years he was made one of the presiding papal legates.

The decree as eventually passed on 13 January 1547 incorporated neither of Seripando's proposed additions; but nor did it deny

[50] Ibid. 671. Seripando had appealed to the authority of Scotus in his October paper (CT xii. 671).
[51] Ibid. v. 671.
[52] Ibid. 671–2.
[53] Ibid. 676.

them. Indeed it was perhaps in deference to him that a few lines
were added recalling that, even if one were not aware of sin, every
detail of a person's life would be subject to the scrutiny and judgment not of men but of God. A phrase was even borrowed from the
Seripando–Massarelli draft. But no place is made for the statement
for which Seripando had fought so valiantly, namely that the just
man must continue to have recourse to the merit of Christ's passion
for the mercy he needs.   .

Double justice today

In the search for convergence between the reformation and the Tridentine positions concerning the doctrine of justification, there are
more points than one on which agreement can be reached. Perhaps
the most obvious of these points is the belief that the process of justification through the merits of Christ comprises not only God's
declaration imputing justice to man, but also his action in imparting
justice so that it becomes a quality of the person concerned. But
there is a second, more subtle point. According to Trent, man, once
justified, is now just in God's eyes *because* of the justice which God
imparts. On the other hand, a classical Anglican view, expressed for
example by Hooker, is that, although the justice by which we are
sanctified and which issues in good works is imparted to us, the justice by which we are justified is imputed and not imparted.[54] This,
Hooker argues, is the meaning of St Paul's hope to be 'found in him,
not having mine own righteousness, based on law, but that which is
through the faith of Christ, the righteousness which is of God
through faith' (Phil. 3: 9).[55] In other words, Hooker deploys
against the decree of Trent a theory of double justice. Could Seripando's own version of the double justice theory provide a way of
reconciling Trent with Hooker?

There are perhaps two answers to be given, one based on theory,
the other on experience and devotion.

Theoretically one must conclude that Seripando does not provide
the bridge. For him righteousness is due to inherent as well as to
imputed justice. This belief does not however mean that we are just
apart from the merits of Christ, for it is through Christ's merits that

---

[54] See esp. Hooker's Sermon 2, 'A Learned Discourse of Justification . . . ', in
Works, ed. J. Keble (Oxford, 1888), ii. 483–547.
[55] Ibid. 490.

God imparts the justice which makes us righteous. Seripando had no disagreement with the majority at Trent on that score. God makes us intrinsically righteous, even though our sins and imperfections make that righteousness incomplete. For Hooker, however, to make imparted righteousness even imperfectly the ground of our justification would be to make it no longer depend on the merits of Christ. Though Seripando is compatible with Trent, he is not compatible with Hooker.

But Seripando insisted that the issue was not one of theory alone, but of religion, and it is here that Seripando and Hooker can be reconciled. Each knew from his personal experience that the justified man must find his confidence before God not in his works or even in his infused justice, but in God's mercy. And though this belief finds no explicit mention in the Tridentine decree, Seripando was satisfied that his views were at least consistent with the teaching of the council.

We turn at last to the present day. The second Anglican–Roman Catholic International Commission has recently published an agreed statement on Justification entitled *Salvation and the Church*. The keen-sighted reader may be able to spot traces of Seripando's theory in the discussion of salvation and good works. After lying dormant for nearly four and a half centuries, a revived theory of double justice may be about to make a delayed contribution to ecumenical theology. It may even help to fulfil Seripando's hope of catching some large fish.

12

The Authority of Chalcedon for Anglicans

J. ROBERT WRIGHT

> Chalcedon is different. It has remained like Nicaea a great name—
> a mass of rock irreversibly diverting the course of the river. If in
> 1982 we ask what the Church of that great tradition believes about
> the person of Christ, at least in formal terms, we shall be pointed
> to this Council of 451 with its carefully articulated, lapidary defi-
> nition which retains classical status and authority not only for
> Roman Catholic, Orthodox, and Anglican, but also for the main
> traditions of Reformation theology.
>
> HENRY CHADWICK, Preface to *Actes du Concile de Chalcé-
> doine: Sessions III–VI (La Définition de la Foi)*[1]

NOT every modern Anglican theologian might agree with these
words of the eminent patristics scholar, magisterial ecumenist, and
senior friend whom these essays are intended to honour, that the
Christology of Chalcedon is irreversible, its definition retaining
classical status and authority. One has only to recall the oft quoted
opinions of another great theologian and former archbishop of Canterbury, William Temple, who in the 1920s and before assuming the
primacy had written that the formula of Chalcedon is 'a confession
of bankruptcy of Greek patristic theology', a 'definite failure'.[2]
Individual theologians must always be allowed to express their
opinions, Anglicans generally believe, for by such exploration the
mind can probe God's mystery. None the less, to assess the status
and authority of the fourth ecumenical council for Anglicans, one
must look to documents of a more official sort and cast a net that
has more breadth and depth than individual opinion generally
tolerates.

The purpose of this present essay, acknowledging gratefully that

---

[1] French trans., ed. A.-J. Festugière (Cahiers d'Orientalisme, 4; Geneva, 1983), 7.
[2] The first quotation is from William Temple, 'The Divinity of Christ', in B. H.
Streeter (ed.), *Foundations* (London, 1920), 230. Temple added, however, on the
same page, 'The Fathers had done the best that could be done with the intellectual
apparatus at their disposal.' The second quotation is from William Temple, *Christus
Veritas* (London, 1926), 134.

Professor Chadwick himself has already written on 'The Status of Ecumenical Councils in Anglican Thought',[3] will be first to offer a general historical survey of the Anglican reception of the Council of Chalcedon, then to ask in particular what authority has been accorded to Chalcedon by the long line of Anglican commentators on the Thirty-Nine Articles of Religion, and finally to sketch out the official Anglican attitude towards the so-called pre- or non-Chalcedonian churches which do not formally recognize its definition of faith. The major attention will be given to this definition itself, although some consideration will also be given to the canons and creed that this council endorsed as well as to the anathema attached to its definition. Throughout, my attempt will be to *ascertain* what authority Chalcedon may possess for Anglicans, not to *criticize* what authority it may have; the latter, I realize, could be done, but it would require another and different sort of essay.

From the outset it should be emphasized that the question of the reception of the Christology of the fourth ecumenical council within the Anglican Communion of Churches (and thus, in the USA, within the Episcopal Church) differs significantly from the situation of the Protestant Churches generally as well as from the positions of the Roman Catholic and Eastern Orthodox Churches. This will best be seen from the historical development and in the context of Anglican relations with the Oriental Orthodox Churches.

1. *Historical Development of the Anglican Reception of Chalcedon*

Both doctrinal and disciplinary reception of the council of Chalcedon by the English Church first come into focus during the late seventh century under the primacy of the Greek archbishop of Canterbury, Theodore of Tarsus. At the synod of Hertford in 672 over

---

[3] Published in D. Nieman and M. Schatkin (eds.), *The Heritage of the Early Church: Essays in Honor of the Very Reverend Georges Vasilievich Florovsky* (Orientalia Christiana Analecta, 195; Rome, 1973), 393–408. See also C. J. Fenner, 'The Concept and Theological Significance of Ecumenical Councils in the Anglican Tradition (Catholic University of America Ph.D. diss. Washington, DC, 1974); E. R. Hardy, 'Chalcedon in the Anglican Tradition', *Ecumenical Review*, 22 (1970), 412–23; S. L. Greenslade, 'The English Reformers and the Councils of the Church', in *Oecumenica: Jahrbuch für ökumenische Forschung* (1967) 95–115; and Nicodim, Metropolitan of Sliven, 'The Anglican Church and the Ecumenical Councils', *St. Vladimir's Seminary Quarterly*, 12 (1968), 17–29.

which he presided (Bede, *Ecclesiastical History*, iv. 5), Theodore produced and read from a book of canons which has been identified as the canonical collection of Dionysius Exiguus, which included canons approved at Chalcedon.[4] Then, Theodore having 'learned that the faith of the Church at Constantinople was greatly disturbed by the heresy of Eutyches', the synod of Hatfield in 680 under his presidency formally received 'the five holy and universal councils of the blessed fathers who were acceptable to God', specifically including Chalcedon 'which condemned the teachings of Eutyches and Nestorius' (EH iv. 17). Thus, when the English Church first began after Whitby to legislate formally on its own as one body under the presidency of the Archbishop of Canterbury, we find its first and second national synods receiving and confirming the actions and faith of the Council of Chalcedon. And canons of Chalcedon were still being cited as authoritative at the council of Westminster in May of 1175.[5]

The doctrine of Chalcedon was also received, and cited extensively, in the pastoral letters of Aelfric of Eynsham, the abbot and literary leader of the English monastic revival, which are dated to the late tenth and early eleventh centuries.

In 993/5, he wrote:

There were four synods for (establishing) the true faith against the heretics who spoke foolishly about the Holy Trinity and the Saviour's humanity. . . . And the fourth was in Chalcedon, consisting of many hundred bishops. And they were all unanimous among themselves about the ordinance which had been appointed at Nicaea, and they amended whatever of it had been broken. Those four synods are to be observed, just as the four gospels, in Christ's church. Many synods were held afterwards, but these four are nevertheless the foremost, because they extinguished the heretical doctrines which the heretics invented heretically against God, and they also appointed the ecclesiastical services.

Again, in 1006, Ælfric wrote:

The fourth synod was afterwards, consisting of six hundred bishops and thirty priests, in the time of Marcian, the glorious emperor; it condemned the diabolical abbot who said in his heresy that our Lord's body and his

---

[4] *Bede's Ecclesiastical History*, ed. B. Colgrave and R. A. B. Mynors (Oxford, 1969), 351.

[5] *Councils and Synods with Other Documents Relating to the English Church*, i. *A.D. 871–1204*, ed. D. Whitelock, M. Brett, and C. N. L. Brooke (Oxford, 1981), part II. *1066–1204*, p. 985.

godhead were of one nature. Then he was excommunicated by the great synod, because the Saviour is, as you have often heard, true man and true God, ever continuing. Afterwards there were very often other synods of wise bishops, but these (four) were the foremost, which with full teaching confirmed the faith and excommunicated the heretics who wished with their heresy to turn wrong to right and lead mankind astray from their Lord.[6]

And Chalcedon was clearly still accepted as authoritative in the great work of William Lyndwood, *Provinciale Anglicanum*, the fundamental pre-Reformation English Anglican work on canon law, composed in 1430, in which it was firmly asserted that 'such general councils may not be convened without the authority of the apostolic see.'[7]

At the time of the Reformation Cranmer's book, which was designed to replace the medieval canon law, but never became fully official, the *Reformatio Legum Ecclesiasticarum* (1551–3), states (cap. 14) that General Councils, although ranking 'far below the dignity of canonical Scripture', are to be regarded with honour and that the decisions of the first four in particular 'we embrace and receive with great reverence.' It also remarked that some councils sometimes have erred and contradicted each other, and that our faith is not bound by them except as they can be confirmed out of Holy Scripture.

In 1559, the Act of Supremacy (1 Elizabeth I, cap. 1, sect. 36) which inauguated the Elizabethan settlement of religion for the *Ecclesia Anglicana* (as it was still then called and had been for centuries) directed that no doctrines were to be considered heresy (then a legal offence) by the High Commission in the English courts, 'but only such as heretofore have been determined, ordered, or adjudged to be heresy, by the authority of the canonical Scriptures, or by the first four general Councils, or any of them, or by any other general Council wherein the same was declared to be heresy by the express and plain words of the said canonical Scriptures . . .' or such as might be declared to be heresy by the English authorities of Church and State. Although this act was cited by Hooker in his *Ecclesiastical Polity* (VIII. ii. 17) later in the same century, the High Commission was abolished in 1641 and the act is no longer regarded as of

---

[6] Ibid. part I. *871–1066*, pp. 215–16, 275.
[7] Lib. v, tit. 4 ('De Magistris'), cap. 1 ('Reverendissimae Synodo'), f ('per Ecclesiam') (Oxford, 1679), 284.

binding authority, even though it does indicate the standard of its own time.[8]

The Thirty-Nine Articles of 1563–71, while not mentioning Chalcedon by name, have been regularly interpreted by commentators as applicable to this council at several points, as we shall see in the second section of this essay.

John Jewel's *Apology of the Church of England* (1561–4), the classical statement of Anglican claims from the Reformation period, reckons a total of four councils, Chalcedon being the fourth, and receives its definition and canons with approval.[9]

In 1571 the Second Book of Homilies, which has held a certain degree of authority for Anglicans in view of its endorsement in Article 35, in its homily 'Against Peril of Idolatry' (part ii), written by Jewel, accepted the authority of the first six councils, the reason being that it wanted to deny authority to the seventh (which had sanctioned the veneration of images).

In 1597 Richard Hooker, in his *Ecclesiastical Polity* (v. liv. 10) made the classical Anglican statement whereby the Chalcedonian definition was clearly endorsed:

To gather, therefore, unto one sum all that hitherto hath been spoken touching this point, there are but four things which concur to make complete the whole state of our Lord Jesus Christ: his Deity, his manhood, the conjunction of both, and the distinction of the one from the other being joined in one. Four principal heresies there are which have in those things withstood the truth: Arians by bending themselves against the Deity of Christ; Apollinarians by maiming and misinterpreting that which belongeth to his human nature; Nestorians by rending Christ asunder and dividing him into two persons; the followers of Eutyches by confounding in his person these natures which they should distinguish. Against these there have been four most famous ancient general councils: the council of Nice, to define against Arians, against Apollinarians the council of Constantinople, the council of Ephesus against Nestorians, against Eutychians the Chalcedon council. In four words, ἀληθῶς, τελέως, ἀδιαιρέτως, ἀσυγχύτως, truly, perfectly, indivisibly, distinctly; the first applied to his being God, and the second to his being Man, the third to his being of both One, and the fourth to his still continuing in that one Both: we may fully

---

[8] It is, however, cited by several later Anglican commentators on the Articles of Religion, esp. when commenting upon Article 21: e.g. O'Donnoghue (1816), Hall (1868), Boultbee (1871), Jelf (1873), Green (1896), Gibson (1896), and Griffith Thomas (1930).

[9] Ed. J. E. Booty (Ithaca, NY, 1963), 48, 116, 118, 124.

by way of abridgement comprise whatsoever antiquity hath at large handled either in declaration of Christian belief, or in refutation of the foresaid heresies. Within the compass of which four heads, I may truly affirm, that all heresies which touch but the person of Jesus Christ, whether they have risen in these later days, or in any age heretofore, may be with great facility brought to confine themselves.

We conclude therefore that to save the world it was of necessity the Son of God should be thus incarnate, and that God should so be in Christ as hath been declared.

In this way, therefore, the authoritative status of Chalcedon for Anglicans was set in documents of an official or definitive sort both before and after the Reformation. It remains to be shown, now, how this reception continued in writings throughout the seventeenth century and beyond.

In 1609 King James I, in his *Premonition to All . . . Monarchs*, stipulated 'I reverence and admit the Four First General Councils as Catholic and Orthodox. And the said Four General Councils are acknowledged by our Acts of Parliament and received for orthodox by our Church.'[10]

Richard Field, Dean of Gloucester and author of the first and principal post-Reformation Anglican treatise on ecclesiology, *Of the Church*, termed Chalcedon as 'absolutely oecumenical, and wholly approved' (v. 1610). In the same book, he also wrote:

Of this sort there are only six. . . . The Fourth, defining the distinction and diversity of His natures, in and after the personal union. . . . These (*i.e. six*) were all the lawful General Councils (lawful, I say, both in their beginning and proceeding, and continuance) that ever were holden in the Christian Church touching matters of faith. For the Seventh, which is the Second of Nice, was not called about any question of faith, but of manners. . . . So that there are but Seven General Councils that the whole Church acknowledgeth called to determine faith and manners.

Still elsewhere in his treatise Field was concerned to note the relatively subordinate position of the bishop and see of Rome at this council and in its famous canon 28 on patriarchal status.[11]

In 1613 Lancelot Andrewes, successively Bishop of Chichester

---

[10] Quoted from P. E. More and F. L. Cross (eds.) *Anglicanism* (Milwaukee, 1935), 3.

[11] The first quotation of Field is from the Cambridge edn. (1850), iii. 385. The second is taken from *Anglicanism* (last n.) pp. 152–3. The final references may be found in the Cambridge edn. (1850), i. 101, iii. 262, iv. 71, 81, 466, 533.

(1605), Ely (1609), and Winchester (1619), in his *Concio* penned the famous Latin phrase: 'Duo Testamenta, Tria Symbola, Quatuor Priora Concilia, Quinque saecula',[12] although in his *Responsio* of 1610 he seemed to grant a limited acceptance even to the sixth council.[13]

And in the middle and later seventeenth century, there are significant statements from Jeremy Taylor, the Bishop of Down and Connor (1610) and famous author of *Holy Living* and *Holy Dying*: 'The Church of England receives the four first Generals (*i.e. General Councils*) as of highest regard, not that they are infallible, but that they have determined wisely and holily' (*Dissuasive from Popery*, 1664). And in another work he asks: what do Anglicans lack, when 'We have the Word of God, the Faith of the Apostles, the Creeds of the Primitive Church, the Articles of the four first General Councils . . . ?' (*Letter to a Gentlewoman Seduced to the Church of Rome*).[14] Earlier, speaking specifically of the manner by which Chalcedon had become authoritative, Taylor remarks:

That council both *ex post facto*, and by the voluntary consenting of after ages, obtained great reputation; yet they that lived immediately after it, that observed all the circumstances of the thing, and the disabilities of the persons, and the uncertainty of the truth of its decrees, by reason of the unconcludingness of the arguments brought to attest it, were of another mind.[15]

The consent of the Church, he thus indicates, is somehow necessary for authoritative reception.

It remains now to cite from modern times, first from William Palmer, fellow of Worcester College, Oxford, author of probably the most outstanding modern (albeit Tractarian) Anglican work on ecclesiology, *A Treatise on the Church of Christ* (2 vols., 1838) in which he held that there have been six ecumenical councils and that their final authority derives only from the subsequent consent of the whole Church.[16]

---

[12] Quoted from Hardy, op. cit. 414.
[13] Fenner, op. cit. 215.
[14] Quotations from *Anglicanism*, pp. 162, 15.
[15] *The Liberty of Prophesying* (London 1647), 109–10. For the opinions of other Anglican divines of the 17th century, such as Bramhall, Cosin, Hammond, Laud, Stillingfleet, and Thorndike, who generally held the number of general councils to have been four (or sometimes six, predicated upon the relationship of the last two to the first four), see Fenner, op. cit. 213–15.
[16] Third edn. (London, 1842), ii. 112–39.

The first Lambeth Conference, a meeting in 1867 of Anglican bishops from around the world, in a rather ambiguous phrase, declared its belief in the Christian faith as 'affirmed by the undisputed General Councils', and the third Lambeth (1888) declared the same as 'affirmed by the undisputed Œcumenical Councils'. No reason for the change from 'General' to 'Œcumenical' was given. The committee report appended to the resolution of the third Lambeth, not however part of the conference's official resolution, did go on to explain that 'With regard to the authority of the Œcumenical Councils, our Communion has always recognised the decisions of the first four Councils on matters of faith, nor is there any point of dogma in which it disagrees with the teaching of the fifth and sixth.'[17]

The Chicago–Lambeth Quadrilateral of 1886–8, which remains the most authoritative Anglican ecumenical standard even today, does not refer to Chalcedon as such, but it does recognize the Niceno-Constantinopolitan Creed, which the Chalcedonian fathers affirmed and claimed to be expounding.

A carefully nuanced evaluation of Chalcedon was given in 1938 in the report *Doctrine in the Church of England* from the official commission appointed by the Archbishops of Canterbury and York, at the end of its section on 'The Relation of Modern Christology to the Formula of Chalcedon': 'We believe ourselves to be affirming in our Report that which was affirmed in the language of its own time by the Council at Chalcedon. But we wish to assert that the Church is in no way bound to the metaphysic or the psychology which lie behind the terms employed by the Council.'[18]

For the Episcopal Church in the United States of America, one of the most influential textbooks in theology at the turn of the nineteenth into the twentieth century was the *Dogmatic Theology* of Professor F. J. Hall, which in its second volume (*Authority: Ecclesiastical and Biblical*, published in 1908) gave the opinion that 'Seven Councils have been generally received in the Church, and are to be reckoned as Ecumenical', adding (and citing Field) 'The first four covered impliedly the whole field of doctrine determined by the seven, and are often appealed to exclusively.' Hall often cites the

---

[17] *The Lambeth Conferences of 1867, 1878, and 1888*, ed. R. T. Davidson (London, 1889), 15, 97, 275, 355. The 1888 committee report, p. 355, cites in a footnote the Elizabethan Act of Supremacy.

[18] (London, 1938), 81.

Chalcedonian definition authoritatively in his writing, although he adds 'General Councils are not infallible in themselves. The infallibility of the Church resides in the whole catholic body; and no assembly of men whatever may impose its decisions upon the faithful independently of their subsequent acceptance by the Church.'[19]

The Christological thought of individual American Anglican theologians, as perhaps also of those in the Church of England, in the latter part of the twentieth century has become more interpretative and less 'scholastic' than it was in the days of Hall,[20] although it is significant that the newly revised *Book of Common Prayer* (1979) of the Episcopal Church in the USA has become the first official Anglican Prayer Book to include the Chalcedonian definition (without, however, its final anathema). It is quoted (in English, with some transliterated Greek terms) on p. 864, in a section near the end, just following the Catechism, which includes also the Athanasian Creed, the Preface to the First (1549) Book of Common Prayer, the Thirty-Nine Articles (in their American, 1801, version), and the Chicago–Lambeth Quadrilateral. This section is collectively entitled 'Historical Documents of the Church'. No introductions or explanations are given for any of these documents, and thus their precise authority is not stated, but it is safe to assume that their inclusion here signifies more clearly approval than disapproval.

[19] (New York, 1908), 137, 132. In the same school of thought as Hall, but known for still higher doctrinal views, was Henry Robert Percival, American Episcopal priest and rector of the Church of the Evangelists in Philadelphia, who concluded the Preface to his edition of *The Seven Ecumenical Councils of the Undivided Church*, with these words: 'I would add that nothing I have written must be interpreted as meaning that the editor personally has any doubt of the truth of the doctrines set forth by the Ecumenical Councils of the Christian Church, and I wish to declare in the most distinct manner that I accept all the doctrinal decrees of the seven Ecumenical Synods as infallible and irreformable' (A Select Library of Nicene and Post-Nicene Fathers, 2nd ser., 14; 1899), p. ix.

[20] The many works of individual modern theologians do not form the subject of this essay and cannot be treated here, but one especially perceptive American Anglican contribution towards a modern critical interpretation is that of R. A. Norris, jun.: 'Toward a Contemporary Interpretation of the Chalcedonian Definition', in id. (ed.), *Lux in Lumine: Essays to Honor W. Norman Pittenger* (New York, 1960), 62–79. The Chalcedonian definition, he concludes, 'becomes intelligible in its Christological use when it is understood not as a direct account of the constitution of the Person of Christ, but as a definition of the normative form of any statement about Christ, without consideration of the metaphysical framework which such a direct statement must inevitably presuppose' (p. 77).

2. The Authority accorded to Chalcedon by Anglican Commentators on the Thirty-Nine Articles

Still another method for assessing and determining the ways and degree in which the council of Chalcedon has been accorded authority within the Anglican tradition, since the sixteenth century, is to examine the long line of Anglican commentators upon the Thirty-Nine Articles of Religion (1563–71) with a purpose to determine what they say, if anything, about Chalcedon in their comments upon the pertinent Articles 2, 8, and 21. If they can be shown to demonstrate a consistency in their view of this council, it can at least be said that Anglicans have a tradition of interpreting their authoritative documents in a way that reveals their attitude toward the authority of the council itself.

There is little question about the authoritative status that the Articles have held for Anglicans since the time of the Reformation by setting the official standard of doctrine for both clergy and laity for well over 300 years. An Act of Parliament in 1571 provided by statute law (13 Elizabeth I), which was reinforced by supplementary act of Convocation, that for the future the Thirty-Nine Articles were to be 'subscribed' by all candidates for ordination as well as by any person admitted to any benefice with cure of souls. The form of subscription was set by the Thirty-Sixth Canon of 1604 (endorsing the form set by Archbishop Whitgift in 1584), and with certain variants it was retained until a less stringent declaration of 'assent' was approved by the two Convocations and confirmed under royal letters patent in 1865. More recent alteration has weakened considerably even this 'assent', but most (though not all) Churches of the Anglican Communion still retain the Articles in their constitutions and many of them still require some form of ministerial assent or subscription either explicit or implicit. (As of 1968, the only Churches that had actually revised the Articles were the church of the Province of New Zealand and the Episcopal Church in the USA.) The ancient universities of Oxford and Cambridge, moreover, as bodies of ecclesiastical foundation, also required subscription to them of all members well into the nineteenth century. Subscription was required at the time of matriculation at Oxford since 1581, and before proceeding to a degree at both Oxford (since 1576) and Cambridge (1616–23), such requirements being finally removed by formal legislation in 1854 and 1871. Thus for some

three centuries, from the later sixteenth to at least the later nineteenth, the Thirty-Nine Articles have defined the authorized doctrinal standard for the Church of England and implicitly for much
of the rest of the Anglican Communion, even though there have
been recurring disputes about their correct interpretation.[21]

These various disputes as well as the Articles' authoritative status
have, not surprisingly, given rise to a particular genre of book providing a comprehensive interpretation of all or most of the Articles,
of which about eighty such commentaries have been published in
England, Ireland, and the USA from the sixteenth to the twentieth
centuries. Of these, I have personally been able to examine a representative selection of fifty-six, representative both in chronological spread and in theological orientation, to each of which I have
asked questions about the authority accorded to Chalcedon as each
author proceeds to comment upon Articles 2, 8, and 21. Let us now
consider the results of this research, in order to ascertain how these
particular Articles relate to Chalcedon and what patterns or traditions of interpretation, if any, have prevailed whenever these commentators have remarked upon the Chalcedonian council.[22]

The language of Article 2, although based proximately upon the
Lutheran confessions of Augsburg and Würtemburg, is in large part
identical with that of the Chalcedonian definition and was intended,
in part, to exclude what Chalcedon excluded:

The Son, which is the Word of the Father, begotten from everlasting of the
Father, the very and eternal God, and of one substance with the Father,
took man's nature in the womb of the blessed Virgin, of her substance: so
that two whole and perfect natures, that is to say, the Godhead and Manhood, were joined together in one Person, never to be divided, whereof is
one Christ, very God and very Man . . .

No less than twenty-five of the fifty-six Anglican commentators,

---

[21] The Articles of the Church of England were adopted by the convocation of the
Church of Ireland in 1634, and the two Churches were united in 1801. My general
information on the Articles is summarized from E. C. S. Gibson, *The Thirty-Nine
Articles of the Church of England* (London, 1896), i. 30–68; *The Articles of the
Church of England*, ed. H. E. W. Turner (London, 1964); and *Subscription and
Assent to the Thirty-Nine Articles: A Report of the Archbishops' Commission on
Christian Doctrine* (London, 1968).

[22] The fifty-six commentators that will be considered in this section are listed in an
Appendix at the end of the chapter. The multitudinous page references will not be
given here for the information cited in each, but the appropriate reference may be
found in each commentary under the Article being discussed.

spanning the sixteenth to the twentieth centuries, and all approvingly, link this Article, especially the latter phrases quoted here, with the Chalcedonian council's condemnation of Eutychianism. In chronological order they are: Rogers (1579 and 1585–7), Beveridge (1710), Welchman (1713), Veneer (1725), Pretyman (afterwards Tomline) (1799), Cary (1835), Fowler (1839), Dimock (1845), Trollope (1847), R. B. P. Kidd (1848), Browne (1850–3), MacBride (1853), Forbes (1867), Jelf (1873), Ball (1877), Miller (1878), Baker (1883), Lightfoot (1890), Percival (c. 1895), Green (1896), Gibson (1896), B. J. Kidd (1899), Thomas (1930), Bicknell-Carpenter (1919, 1955), Graves (1965).

Article 8 specifies that the three Creeds, Nicene, Athanasian, and Apostles', 'ought thoroughly to be received and believed; for they may be proved by most certain warrants of Holy Scripture.' In a general way the three creeds received here contain the substance of the dogmatic decisions of the first four councils which is therefore by this Article given authoritative status, but more particularly it is to be noted that the Nicene Creed in the form Anglicans have received it (except for the 'Filioque') received its final authority from the council of Chalcedon. This Article's endorsement of the Nicene Creed, therefore, may be said to carry an implicit endorsement of the faith of Chalcedon, and no fewer than thirteen of these commentators make this point: Ellis (1694), Burnet–Page (1699, 1841), Adolphus (1852), MacBride (1853), Miller (1881), Baker (1883), Cloquet (1885), Lightfoot (1890), Gibson (1896), Tait (1910), Bicknell–Carpenter (1919, 1955), Thomas (1930), Wilson and Templeton (1962). (Dates are repeated for the sake of the chronological development.)

Article 20 asserts that 'The Church hath power to decree Rites or Ceremonies, and Authority in controversies of faith', and it may be remarked in passing that not one of the fifty-six commentators I have examined cites Chalcedon as an example of the Church's authority in controversies of faith, nor remarks that Chalcedon derives authority from a later decision of the Church, nor refers to Chalcedon in such a way as to distinguish its definition of faith from its disciplinary decrees.

Number 21 is the Article most pertinent to Chalcedon, and it must first be quoted in full:

General Councils may not be gathered together without the commandment and will of Princes. And when they be gathered together—forasmuch as they be an assembly of men, whereof all be not governed with the Spirit and Word of God—they may err, and sometimes have erred, even in things pertaining unto God. Wherefore things ordained by them as necessary to salvation have neither strength nor authority, unless it may be declared that they be taken out of Holy Scripture.

Many commentators of course begin their remarks on this Article with attention to 'the commandment and will of Princes' in its first sentence, presumably inserted to deny the papal claim that the Pope alone might summon a council[23] and probably the reason why this Article was omitted from the American revision of the Articles[24] and qualified in the New Zealand revision. But we pass on to what the Article may say about the Anglican reception of Chalcedon.

The first question to ask of the Anglican commentators on this Article is whether or not they regard Chalcedon as one of the 'General Councils' of which the Article speaks, and the answer is so overwhelmingly affirmative that those who say this need not even be listed but only counted. Forty-one of the fifty-six, commenting at this point, recognize Chalcedon as the fourth General Council, and not one of the others denies it. Three of them do question whether, strictly speaking, there has *ever* been a General Council, since (they say) there has never been a council at which all Churches were represented: Budd (?1813–53), Dimock (1845), and MacBride (1853). Not one of the fifty-six regards Chalcedon, specifically by name, as having erred even in things pertaining unto God. In fact, nine of them specifically or apparently state that Chalcedon did *not* err: Rogers (1579, 1585–7), Beveridge (1710), Pretyman (Tomline) (1799), Claughton (1843), Browne (1850–3), Ball (1877), Lightfoot (1890), Percival (*c.* 1895), Kidd (1899). Seventeen more give lists of councils that *have* erred, none of which includes Chalcedon, and these lists are all of councils subsequent to or other than the classical first four or six: Ford (1720), O'Donnoghue (1816), Newland (1829), Trollope (1847), R. B. P. Kidd (1848), Adolphus (1852), Beaven (1853), MacBride (1853), Forbes (1867), Hall (1868), Jelf (1873), Baker (1883), Cloquet (1885), Green (1896), Gibson (1896), B. J. Kidd (1899), and Wilson and Templeton (1962). As to the

[23] This is still a papal claim today: canons 338 and 341 of the new (1983) papal *Code of Canon Law.*
[24] It is now included, in italics, in the new (1979) American *Book of Common Prayer*, p. 872. On its omission from the 1801 American revision of the Articles see

Article's last sentence, nineteen of the fifty-six specifically regard Chalcedon as being proven from Scripture: Burnet–Page (1699, 1841), Beveridge (1710), Pretyman (Tomline) (1799), Newland (1829), Heathcote (1841), Claughton (1843), Dimock (1845), Trollope (1847), R. B. P. Kidd (1848), Browne (1850–3), MacBride (1853), Hall (1868), Jelf (1873), Cloquet (1885), Maclear and Williams (1895), Green (1896), B. J. Kidd (1899), Middleton (1900), and Thomas (1930). Not one denies that it is proved from Scripture.

A very high status is thus accorded to Chalcedon by this long tradition of Anglican commentators, and fifteen of these even go so far as specifically to state that the Church of England 'receives' or 'accepts' the doctrinal decisions of Chalcedon: Burnet–Page (1699, 1841), Pretyman (Tomline) (1799), Newland (1829), Claughton (1843), Dimock (1845), R. B. P. Kidd (1848), Hall (1868), Jelf (1873), Ball (1877), Green (1896), Gibson (1896), B. J. Kidd (1899), Bicknell–Carpenter (1919, 1955), Thomas (1930), Graves (1965). In addition, fifteen of the fifty-six emphasize that Chalcedon's authority comes from its subsequent reception by the consent of the whole church: Heathcote (1841), Dimock (1845), Browne (1850–3), Adolphus (1852), MacBride (1853), Ball (1877), Baker (1883), Lightfoot (1890), Maclear and Williams (1895), Gibson (1896), B. J. Kidd (1899), Tait (1910), Bicknell–Carpenter (1919, 1955), Thomas (1930), Wilson and Templeton (1962).[25] Not one commentator, however, holds that Chalcedon derives its authority from the subsequent consent of the Church *rather than* from consonance with Scripture, and in general they agree that Chalcedon is authoritative because it represents the Church's consensus about the correct interpretation of Scripture.[26] Some commentators emphasize consonance with 'the Word of God' rather than with Holy Scripture, but none distinguishes between the two. Not one of the commentators remarks upon how it is to be determined whether a particular

K. J. Woollcombe, 'The Authority of the First Four General Councils in the Anglican Communion', *Anglican Theological Review* 44 (1962), 155–81.

[25] The comment of E. H. Browne, writing in 1850–3, is to the point: 'Now, we can only know that they speak the language of the Church, when their decrees meet with universal acceptance, and are admitted by the whole body of Christians to be certainly true.' (London, 1865 edn., p. 488). His commentary was later translated into Spanish (1867) and French (1878).

[26] The reasoning is a bit circular, as is indicated in the remark on the inerrancy of the councils by W. E. Collins: 'It is a mere question of words; and just as it may be said that 'treason doth never prosper,' for 'when it prospers, none dare call it treason,' so it may be said that General Councils do not err; for when they err, they are

conciliar decision accords with Scripture or whether or when such a decision can be known to have received the consent of the whole Church, or whether such consent is merely tacit approbation without some formal and binding or permanent ecclesial act.

   Chalcedon, therefore, is clearly recognized as authoritative by virtually every one of these Anglican commentators on Article 21, although in so doing these writers implicitly set themselves, or at least the Church of England, as the determinators of this reception. Chalcedon for them does not possess authority by itself, but by the opinion of each writer who believes there is a consensus in the Church that it is consonant with Holy Scripture. There is a remarkable agreement among these commentators about the authoritative status of Chalcedon, even though they acknowledge no corporate Anglican mechanism for reaching such decisions and none of these writers seems to believe there is any need for one. In addition, their overall attitude towards Article 21 is for our own day faithfully reflected in the commentary on authority and reception of councils in the *Final Report* of the Anglican–Roman Catholic International Commission (pp. 71–2), published in 1982, of which Henry Chadwick has been a valued member.

   None of the fifty-six writers under examination comments at this Article on the canons of Chalcedon (as distinct from its doctrinal definition), nor does any of them remark upon the anathema which concludes its definition of faith:

Since, therefore, these matters have been determined by us with all possible precision and care, the holy and ecumenical synod decrees that it is not permissible for anyone to propose, write, compose, think, teach anything else. But those who dare to compose another creed or to bring forward or teach or transmit another symbol to people who want to turn to the knowledge of truth from Hellenism or Judaism or from any heresy whatever—such persons if they are bishops or clergy, are deposed, the bishops from their episcopate and the clergy from their office; but if they are monks or laity they are anathematized.[27]

Thus, whereas the reception of the Chalcedonian definition seems deeply embedded within the tradition of Anglican interpretations of

---

not recognized as general, by the true mind of the Church.' (*The Authority of General Councils*, iv (Church Historical Society, 12; London, 1896), 186.

   [27] Trans. R. A. Norris, jun., *The Christological Controversy* (Philadelphia, 1980), 159.

Article 21, there is no Anglican tradition of anathematizing or deposing those who dissent from it.[28]

3. Historical Development of Official Anglican Relations with the Non-Chalcedonian Churches

Anglicanism, I think it can be said, 'receives' the Chalcedonian definition of faith but does not 'receive' the anathema that concludes it. And if so, then a survey of the development of the Anglican attitude towards those Churches that officially do not 'receive' Chalcedon will itself be further revealing of the status and authority that Anglicans accord this council. In particular we shall now look at the official international Anglican relations with the group of churches known as pre- or non-Chalcedonian, or Oriental Orthodox: the Armenian, Coptic, Ethiopian, and Syrian Churches. These Churches, which officially do not accept the Christological definition of the fourth ecumenical council, generally do reject the teaching of Eutyches of a single divine nature and generally hold with St Cyril of Alexandria the formula of one divine-human nature after the Incarnation.[29] What is the Anglican view, if any, about these Churches and their doctrine?

Here I shall maintain that, although the Anglican tradition accepts the Chalcedonian definition of faith, it does not absolutely require it of other Churches for the purposes of closer ecumenical relationships and even the possibility of occasional intercommunion, especially when there is a basic Christological agreement and when much else is held in common. This section will focus chronologically upon the official resolutions and reports of the Lambeth Conferences, which are international meetings of all Anglican bishops from around the world that have been held about every ten years, since 1867, at the Archbishop of Canterbury's London palace called Lambeth.[30] The *resolutions* of Lambeth carry the collective

---

[28] The anathema, as has been noted above, is not included in the text of the definition quoted in the American *Book of Common Prayer* (1979).

[29] Cf. R. F. Taft (ed.), *The Oriental Orthodox Churches in the United States* (Washington, DC, 1986). The *Henoticon* of the Emperor Zeno (482), which repudiated Chalcedon, became the general position of the Armenian Church in the later 5th and 6th centuies (K. Sarkissian, *The Council of Chalcedon and the Armenian Church* (London, 1965), 51, 171, 207).

[30] A committee report of the 1930 Lambeth Conference even likened these meetings to the ecumenical councils themselves: 'If ever in the days to come a council of the whole Church were to be called together, it would be assembled on a plan of

authority of the bishops who vote for them, the *reports* no more than the authority of the committees who prepare and submit them. But although the authority of Lambeth, even of its resolutions, within particular Churches of the Anglican Communion is only consultative and advisory, having no legislative force until and unless particular resolutions or reports are endorsed by particular national or regional Churches, the Lambeth documents carry great weight in themselves and at least the Lambeth resolutions are regarded by Anglicans as having an authority which is highly normative. Overall, this material demonstrates the long history of friendly Anglican relations with the Oriental Orthodox Churches, as well as a considerable growth in theological understanding and convergence, especially in Christology.

The Lambeth material on these Churches spans the period from 1888 to 1968.[31] My analysis of it, in attempting to trace the evolution of an Anglican 'mind' about the status and authority of Chalcedon, will focus upon three points that indicate the developing Anglican attitude toward the non-Chalcedonian Churches: (1) the different names by which they have been collectively designated at each successive Lambeth Conference, (2) comments made by each conference about their doctrinal position, especially as it relates to the Chalcedonian faith, and (3) the attitude expressed by each conference, if any, toward the possibility of intercommunion or eucharistic sharing with these Churches.

Let us begin with a survey of the names by which these churches have been collectively designated. The committee report on 'Eastern Churches' of the Lambeth Conference of 1888 called this group 'the other Churches of the East'. Resolution 63 of Lambeth 1908,

---

autonomy and fellowship similar to that which is the basis of our Conference today' (p. 155).

[31] References for the early conferences are to be found in *The Lambeth Conferences of 1867, 1878, and 1888*, pp. 350–1, and (for 1908) in *The Lambeth Conferences 1867–1948* (London, 1948), 302–3. References to materials cited from the later conferences, 1920–68, are to be found in the official volumes published from each conference as follows: *Conference of Bishops of the Anglican Communion Holden at Lambeth Palace, July 5 to August 7, 1920: Encyclical Letter from the Bishops with the Resolutions and Reports* (London, 1920), 32–3, 148–51; *The Lambeth Conference 1930: Encyclical Letter from the Bishops with Resolutions and Reports* (London, ?1930), 50, 144–7; *The Lambeth Conference 1948: The Encyclical Letter from the Bishops, together with Resolutions and Reports* (London, 1948), part I, pp. 43–4, and part II, pp. 70–2; *The Lambeth Conference 1958: The Encyclical Letter from the Bishops together with the Resolutions and Reports* (London, 1958), 1.40, 2.50–2; *The Lambeth Conference 1968: Resolutions and Reports* (London, 1968), 44, 139.

with a bit more sophistication, called them 'the ancient separate Churches of the East'. Lambeth 1920 and 1930 both, in their resolutions called these Churches 'the Separated Churches of the East' and in their committee reports the name preferred was the 'Ancient Churches of the East'. The 1948 Lambeth, both in its resolutions and in its report, moved to a simpler term, 'the Lesser Eastern Churches'. In 1958, reflecting a growing appreciation of these Churches as distinct from the Orthodox churches that do recognize Chalcedon, the Lambeth terminology has changed still again, to 'Other Eastern Churches' both in the resolutions and in the committee report. By the Lambeth Conference of 1968, finally, the designation is updated to read 'Oriental (Orthodox) Churches'. The 1978 Lambeth was organized on rather different principles, and did not include any pertinent material. Thus, from 'Other' (1888) to 'Ancient Separate' (1908) to 'Ancient' and 'Separated' (1920 and 1930) to 'Lesser' (1948) to 'Other' (1958) to 'Oriental (Orthodox), (1968), I believe there is indicated by increasingly positive terminology a gradual development of recognition and appreciation of their unique position which will be even more clearly reflected in the evolution of the Lambeth doctrinal attitude shown in the following survey.

What have the Lambeth Conferences said about the doctrinal position of these Churches, especially as it relates to Chalcedon?

The committee report of Lambeth 1888 began rather soberly:

The Armenian Church lies under the imputation of heresy. But it has always protested against this imputation, affirming the charge to have arisen from a misconception of its formularies. The departure from orthodoxy may, perhaps, have been more apparent than real; and the erroneous element in its creed appears now to be gradually losing its hold upon the moral and religious consciousness of the Armenian people. In regard to the other Eastern communities, such as the Coptic, Abyssinian, Syrian, and Chaldean, . . . if these communities have fallen into error, and show a lack of moral and spiritual life, we must recollect that but for them the light of Christianity in these countries would have been utterly extinguished, and that they have suffered for many centuries from cruel oppression and persecution.

The resolution (no. 63) of Lambeth 1908 was quite optimistic:

The Conference would welcome any steps that might be taken to ascertain the precise doctrinal position of the ancient separate Churches of the East with a view to possible intercommunication, and would suggest to the Archbishop of Canterbury the appointment of Commissions to examine the doctrinal position of particular Churches, and (for example) to prepare some carefully framed statement of the Faith as to our Lord's Person, in the simplest possible terms, which should be submitted to each of such Churches, where feasible, in order to ascertain whether it represents their belief with substantial accuracy.

Apparently the steps recommended in 1908 were taken, because the Lambeth of 1920 resolved (no. 21) as follows:

The Conference has received with satisfaction its Committee's report of the investigations that have been made during the last twelve years with regard to the present doctrinal position of the Separated Churches of the East; and, without expressing an opinion as to the past, believes that these investigations have gone far towards shewing that any errors as to the Incarnation of our Lord, which may at some period of their history have been attributed to them, have at any rate now passed away.

The committee report of 1920 noted that these Churches had become separated from the rest of Christianity 'by reason mainly of the Christological dissensions of the Fifth century'. It added, 'These Churches have all at some period of their history been accused of theological error with regard to the Incarnation, and it is, therefore, necessary that we should examine with some care their doctrinal position at the present time.' The report called attention to the 'Statement of Faith' of the Syrian (West Syrian, Jacobite) Church which 'denies that the divine nature of our Lord was commingled with the human nature, or that the two natures became commixed and changed so as to give rise to a third nature, and asserts that the two natures became united in indissoluble union without confusion, mixture, or transmutation, and that they remained two natures in an unalterable unity.' It concluded that this Statement 'is quite free of Monophysitism.' And as for the Armenians, the Committee remarked,

This great and much-suffering Church has always repudiated charges of Eutychianism or of Monophysitism, and it is probable that their refusal to accept the decrees of Chalcedon is due to their having been prevented by political causes from being present at that Council, and to its decisions having reached them in a faulty version.

Overall then, the report concluded:

Your Committee would suggest that it is not necessary, even if it were possible, to determine how far the Separated Churches of the East have been in the past really implicated in the errors which have been attributed to them; but they think that the investigations of the last twelve years have gone a great way to shew that they have at any rate grown out of any errors they may have held on the Person and Nature of our Lord.

At the 1930 Lambeth Conference, the pertinent resolutions said nothing about doctrine, but the committee report did, and what it said was quite positive:

All the Churches with which we are here concerned have differed from the Orthodox faith, particularly with regard to the doctrine of the Person of Our Lord. In many cases a closer understanding of a particular Church and a sympathetic study of its liturgies has revealed that the ancient heresy has long since in fact passed away, though perhaps no formal abjuration of the heresy has been or could well be made.

And with regard to its enquiries about particular Churches, the committee reported it had been told 'that the Armenian Church, although it had never accepted the dogmatic conclusions of the Council of Chalcedon, was orthodox in its theology', and that the Syrian (West Syrian, Jacobite) Church had 'stated the Faith of the Church in such a way as to be entirely in accord with the Orthodox faith.' Overall, the 1930 report concluded, 'Doctrinal agreement as to the Person of Christ is at least within reach between us and certain of the Separated Churches with which we are concerned.'

Because of war and other conditions, no Lambeth Conference was held in 1940. A resolution (no. 68b) of the Conference of 1948 called upon the Archbishop of Canterbury to initiate discussions between theologians of the Anglican Communion and the Armenian Church, and the committee report noted 'the essential orthodoxy of the Armenian Church'. With regard to the Syrian Orthodox, the committee of 1948 noted that

This Church is in communion with the Armenian and Coptic Churches, and is thus one of the group regarded by the Greek Orthodox Church as Monophysite, though, as recorded by the last Lambeth Conference, the answers of the then Patriarch to the questions asked by the Archbishop of Canterbury were such as to remove any suggestion of heretical teaching.

Beyond these remarks, the first paragraph of the 1948 report quoted from the second paragraph of the 1930 report, adding, 'We have no information of any further progress since 1930 in the elucidation of their doctrinal position, but we reiterate the hope expressed by the

1930 Lambeth Conference that doctrinal agreement with some, if not all, of these Churches may be reached before long.'

The Lambeth Conference of 1958 spoke only of 'fellowship' and 'discussions' and 'conversations' with these 'Other Eastern Churches', its committee report adding that 'there is little to record in the way of advance in official contacts since 1948.' The report did repeat the recommendation of the 1948 report, earlier sketched in 1920 and 1930, that 'in all such negotiations the relations between the Anglican Communion and all the Eastern [i.e. Chalcedonian Orthodox] Churches should be borne in mind and that nothing should be done which is likely to prejudice those wider relationships.' And in 1968, finally, the Lambeth resolution (no. 57) recommended joint biblical study, and the report noted that the scope for theological discussion had been expanded by the vastly increased number of such Christians in Australia, Canada, Great Britain, and the United States.

Thus, to summarize the Anglican attitude toward the doctrinal position of these non- or pre-Chalcedonian Churches at the official, international level, especially as regards the Armenian and Syrian Churches, it can be said that by 1930 the following understanding had been reached. On the basis of several investigations into their present doctrine and liturgy, Anglicans no longer regard these Churches as heretically Monophysite, if ever they were, but rather as essentially orthodox.[32] And with regard to all the Oriental Orthodox Churches, the hope is expressed that complete doctrinal agreement may soon be reached even though they clearly do not formally accept the dogmatic conclusions of Chalcedon.

Two theologians whose writings were influential in the development of this Anglican doctrinal stance were W. A. Wigram and Charles Gore, and Gore's comment on Wigram makes the point quite well:

I have just read Dr. W. A. Wigram's *Separation of the Monophysites* (Faith Press, 1923), in which he pleads very earnestly (chap. xiv) that the nominally Monophysite Churches of to-day, who reject Eutyches and affirm the

---

[32] Only four of the above-mentioned fifty-six Anglican commentators on the Articles refer to these Churches as continuing the Monophysite heresy: Cary (1835), p. 40; Browne (1850–3), p. 63 of the 1865 edn.; Adolphus, (1852), p. 175 of the 1881 edn.; and MacBride, (1853), pp. 97–8.

permanent reality of two 'substances', divine and human, in the incarnate person, should not be required formally to accept the definition of Chalcedon with its term 'two natures,' but that the Orthodox Churches and ourselves should be satisfied with their acceptance, which they are willing to give, of the Christological clauses of the *Quicunque Vult*, wherein the 'two substances' are affirmed and which are identical in meaning with Chalcedon. I hope that this proposal will be met in the friendly spirit of Athanasius towards those who 'mean what we mean, and dispute only about the word' (*de Synod.*, c. 41).[33]

When we turn to the attitudes expressed by successive Lambeth Conferences toward the possibility of intercommunion with these Churches, a similar pattern of development may be seen. As early as 1908 Lambeth was envisaging the possibility of intercommunion with these 'ancient separate Churches of the East', and its resolution no. 64 stated:

In the event of doctrinal agreement being reached with such separate Churches, the Conference is of opinion that it would be right (1) for any Church of the Anglican Communion to admit individual communicant members of those Churches to communicate with us when they are deprived of this means of grace through isolation, and conversely, for our communicants to seek the same privileges in similar circumstances; (2) for the Churches of the Anglican Communion to permit our communicants to communicate on special occasions with these Churches, even when not deprived of this means of grace through isolation, and conversely, that their communicants should be allowed the same privileges in similar circumstances.

At the Lambeth Conference of 1920 the same possibility was envisaged, the term 'occasional intercommunion' being used (resolutions nos. 22 and 23). The Conference of 1930, in its resolution no. 36c, even expressed the hope that 'in due course full intercommunion may be reached', and its committee report, after repeating resolution no. 64 from the Conference of 1908, recorded very positive developments as regarding the Armenian and Syrian Churches. With respect to the Armenians, it was reported that 'Officially, there was no recognized intercommunion, but, if the need arises, they are prepared to admit members of both the Orthodox and the Anglican Churches to communion unofficially, and, similarly,

---

[33] Gore, *The Reconstruction of Belief* (London, 1926), 863 (from his earlier *The Holy Spirit and the Church*, 1924).

members of the Armenian Church would be prepared to receive the Communion in the Anglican Church', and the report concluded by urging 'friendliness on the basis of intercommunion already attained'. As regards the Syrian Church, the report concluded that correspondence to this end between the Canterbury archbishop and the Syrian (Jacobite) patriarch had 'advanced sufficiently in our judgment to allow of such occasional intercommunion as was recommended by the Lambeth Conference of 1908', even though a formal agreement could not yet be proclaimed because of political difficulties.

Resolution no. 68b of the 1948 Lambeth looked 'forward to the strengthening and deepening of spiritual fellowship with [these Churches], which may in God's providence lead in due time to full intercommunion'. With regard to the developing relations with the Syrian Church, the 1948 committee reported that 'No further steps have, however, been taken towards the implementation of the occasional intercommunion suggested by the Conference of 1908 and referred to in 1930.' Subsequent Lambeth Conference resolutions and reports have said nothing further about intercommunion with these Churches.

Overall, therefore, one can say that, just as Anglicans have been unwilling to accept the anathema that concludes the Chalcedonian definition of faith, so also they have been increasingly positive in terminology, in doctrinal understanding, and in the possibility of intercommunion, in their attitude toward the non- or pre-Chalcedonian Churches. There does not seem to have been much official development or progress since the Lambeth Conference of 1930, but neither has anything negative been recorded. From all this, I conclude that the Anglican tradition, while clearly accepting the Chalcedonian definition of faith, does not absolutely require it of other Churches for the purpose of closer ecumenical relationships, even of those who reject the definition of Chalcedon, especially when so much else is held in common as with the case of the Oriental Orthodox Churches. It should even be possible, on the basis of a common Christological agreement that does not verbally endorse the Chalcedonian definition itself, for the Anglican Communion to authorize formally the mutual sharing of some sacraments on an occasional basis with these Churches. A precedent has in fact been set by a similar agreement signed in 1984 by Pope John Paul II with the Patriarch of the Syrian Church and without endorsement of the text of the Fourth Ecumenical Council.[34]

Conclusion

Thus, from both official and unofficial Anglican sources both before and after the Reformation, from a large and representative selection of Anglican commentators on the Thirty-Nine Articles, and from the positions taken by the Lambeth Conferences towards the Oriental Orthodox Churches which officially do not recognize the dogmatic definition of the fourth ecumenical council, we have investigated and set forth the attitude of Anglicans towards the status and authority of Chalcedon.[35] It remains now to leave the final Anglican word to the one whom this essay is designed to honour:

In contending for the affirmation that Christ is both God and man the Council of Chalcedon was contending for that without which the shape of Christian faith would be utterly changed. The Definition's merit is to mark a sign of impasse against pathways which either so devalue nature and creation as to disparage man's capacity for God and aspiration for perfection, or so stress the human perfection of Christ as to discover in an individual man, and not in God, the crown towards which all creation moves.[36]

Appendix

The fifty-six Anglican commentaries on the Thirty-nine Articles of Religion that I have examined and upon which part of this essay is based, are in chronological order with earliest date of publication:

1. Thomas Rogers, *The Faith, Doctrine, and Religion, Professed, and Protected in the Realme of England, and Dominions of the same: Expressed in the Thirty-Nine Articles* (London, 1579; originally published 1579–87 as

---

[34] 'Common Declaration of Pope John Paul II and HH Mar Ignatius Zakka I Iwas, June 23, 1984.' The text in English is printed, among other places, in *L'osservatore romano* for 2 July 1984 and in the *Information Service* of the Vatican Secretariat for Promoting Christian Unity, no. 55 (1984).

[35] An earlier version of part of this paper was delivered as an address at a consultation 'Christological Concerns within the Apostolic Faith', sponsored by the Commission on Faith and Order of the National Council of Churches, USA, with the Oriental Orthodox Chuches, in New York City, 26–7 Apr. 1985.

[36] Festugière, op. cit. 16.

The English Creede . . . , *part* II and republished in 1854 for the Parker Society as *The Catholic Doctrine of the Church of England: An Exposition of the Thirty-Nine Articles*, ed. J. J. S. Perowne).

2. Henry Care, *Utrum Horum, or The Nine and Thirty Articles of the Church of England, at Large Recited, and Compared with the Doctrines of those Commonly Called Presbyterians on the One Side, and the Tenets of the Church of Rome on the Other* (1682).

3. John Ellis, *Articulorum XXXIX Ecclesiae Anglicanae Defensio* (1694).

4. Gilbert Burnet, *An Exposition of the Thirty-Nine Articles of the Church of England* (1699, revised by J. R. Page, 1841).

5. William Beveridge, *Ecclesia Anglicana, Ecclesia Catholica: or, The Doctrine of the Church of England Consonant to Scripture, Reason, and the Fathers, in a Discourse upon the Thirty-Nine Articles* (1710).

6. Edward Welchman, *The Thirty-Nine Articles of the Church of England . . .* (1713).

7. Thomas Bennet, *Directions for Studying,* i. *A General System or Body of Divinity*; ii. *The Thirty-Nine Articles of Religion* (1714).

8. James Boys, *A Practical Exposition upon the Thirty-Nine Articles of the Church of England* (1716).

9. Randolph Ford, *Christianae Religionis, sive Ecclesiae Anglicanae Articuli XXXIX* (1720).

10. J. Veneer, *An Exposition on the Thirty-Nine Articles of the Church of England,* 2 vols. (1725).

11. Martin Madan, *A Scriptural Comment upon the Thirty-Nine Articles of the Church of England* (1772).

12. George Pretyman (afterwards Tomline), *Elements of Christian Theology: Containing . . . a Scriptural Exposition of the Thirty-Nine Articles of Religion,* 2 vols. (1799).

13. Samuel Wix, *Scriptural Illustrations of the Thirty-Nine Articles of the Church of England* (1808).

14. H. C. O'Donnoghue, *A Familiar and Practical Exposition of the Thirty-Nine Articles of Religion of the United Church of England and Ireland* (1816).

15. William Wilson, *The Thirty-Nine Articles of the Church of England, Illustrated by Copious Extracts from the Liturgy, Homilies, Nowell's Catechism, and Jewell's Apology* (1821).

16. Edward Rutledge, *The Articles of Religion of the Protestant Episcopal Church, supported by Reference to the Scriptures: Together with a Short Address to his Parishioners* (1826).

17. Thomas Waite, *Sermons, Explanatory and Practical, on the Thirty-Nine Articles of the Church of England* (1826).

18. Thomas Newland, *An Analysis of Bishop Burnet's Exposition of the Thirty-Nine Articles, with Notes* (1829).

19. Henry Blunt, *Discourses upon Some of the Doctrinal Articles of the Church of England* (1835).

20. Henry Cary, *Testimonies of the Fathers of the First Four Centuries to the Doctrine and Discipline of the Church of England as Set forth in the Thirty-Nine Articles* (1835).

21. Andrew Fowler, *An Exposition of the Articles of Religion of the Protestant Episcopal Church in the United States of America* (1839).

22. John Henry Newman, *Tract 90: Remarks on Certain Passages in the Thirty-Nine Articles* (1841).

23. William W. Harvey, *Ecclesiae Anglicanae Vindex Catholicus, sive Articulorum Ecclesiae Anglicanae cum Scriptis SS. Patrum Nova Collatio*, 3 vols. (1841).

24. William Beadon Heathcote, *Documentary Illustrations of the Principles to be Kept in View in the Interpretation of the Thirty-Nine Articles* (1841).

25. Piers C. Claughton, *A Brief Comparison of the Thirty-Nine Articles of the Church of England with Holy Scripture* (1843).

26. James Francis Dimock, *The Thirty-Nine Articles of the Church of England, Explained, Proved, and Compared with Her Other Authorized Formularies, the Homilies and Liturgy, in a Plain and Popular Manner*, 2 vols. in 1 (1843–5).

27. Edward Bickersteth, *Questions Illustrating the Thirty-Nine Articles of the Church of England, with Proofs from Scripture and the Primitive Church* (1845).

28. Thomas Sworde, *An Exposition of the First Seventeen Articles of the Church of England* (1847).

29. William Trollope, *Questions and Answers on the XXXIX Articles of the Church of England* (1847).

30. Richard Bentley Porson Kidd, *Testimonies and Authorities, Divine and Human, in Confirmation of the Thirty-Nine Articles of the Church of England: Compiled and Arranged for the Use of Students* (1848).

31. Edward Harold Browne, *An Exposition of the Thirty-Nine Articles, Historical and Doctrinal* (1850–3).

32. Otto Adolphus, *Compendium Theologicum* (1852).

33. Henry Budd, *The XXXIX Articles of our Established Church: 1571 . . .* (n.d., ?c. 1813–53).

34. James Beaven, *A Catechism on the Thirty-Nine Articles of the Church of England, with Additions and Alterations Adapting it to the Book of Common Prayer of the Protestant Episcopal Church in the United States* (1853).

35. John David MacBride, *Lectures on the Articles of the United Church of England and Ireland* (1853).

36. Alexander P. Forbes, *An Explanation of the Thirty-Nine Articles, with an Epistle Dedicatory to the Late Rev E. B. Pusey* (1867).

37. John Hall, *Parochial Discourses on the Doctrine of Christianity Contained in the Articles of Religion of the United Church of England and Ireland* (1868).

38. T. P. Boultbee, *A Commentary on the Thirty-Nine Articles, Forming an Introduction to the Theology of the Church of England* (1871).

39. R. W. Jelf, *The Thirty-Nine Articles of the Church of England, Explained in a Series of Lectures*, ed. J. R. King (1873).

40. Thomas Isaac Ball, *The Orthodox Doctrine of the Church of England Explained in a Commentary on the XXXIX Articles* (1877).

41. Joseph Miller, *The Thirty-Nine Articles of the Church of England: A Historical and Speculative Exposition*, 4 vols. (1878–85).

42. William Baker, *A Plain Exposition of the Thirty-Nine Articles of the Church of England, for the Use of Schools* (1883).

43. Robert Louis Cloquet, *An Exposition of the Thirty-Nine Articles of the Church of England* (1885).

44. John Lightfoot, *Text-Book of the Thirty-Nine Articles of the Church of England, for Teachers and Students* (1890).

45. G. F. Maclear and W. W. Williams, *An Introduction to the Articles of the Church of England* (1895).

46. Henry Robert Percival, *The Thirty-Nine Articles Vindicated from the Aspersions of High Church Assailants* (n.d., c.1895).

47. E. Tyrrell Green, *The Thirty-Nine Articles and the Age of the Reformation: An Historical and Doctrinal Exposition in the Light of Contemporary Documents* (1896).

48. Edgar C. S. Gibson, *The Thirty-Nine Articles of the Church of England*, 2 vols. (1896).

49. B. J. Kidd, *The Thirty-Nine Articles: Their History and Explanation* (1899).

50. Frank Edward Middleton, *Lambeth and Trent: A Brief Explanation of the Thirty-Nine Articles* (1900).

51. Arthur J. Tait, *Lecture Outlines on the Thirty-Nine Articles* (1910).

52. E. J. Bicknell, *A Theological Introduction to the Thirty-Nine Articles of the Church of England* (1919; 3rd edn., rev. H. J. Carpenter, 1955).

53. W. H. Griffith Thomas, *The Principles of Theology: An Introduction to the Thirty-Nine Articles* (1930).

54. H. Edward Symonds, *The Council of Trent and Anglican Formularies* (1933).

55. Kenneth N. Ross, *The Thirty-Nine Articles* (1957).

56. W. G. Wilson and J. H. Templeton, *Anglican Teaching: An Exposition of the Thirty-Nine Articles* (1962).

13

The Influence of the Seventeenth Century on Contemporary Anglican Understanding of the Purpose and Functioning of Authority in the Church

H. R. MCADOO

I

THERE is a highly significant consensus sentence in ARCIC's agreed statement *Authority in the Church*, II. 31. It reads as follows: 'We agree that, without a special charism guarding the judgment of the universal primate, *the Church would still possess means of receiving and ascertaining the truth of revelation.*'

In the context in which the phrase occurs it aptly fits the theme being developed in that section of the statement. Taken by itself, it would be regarded by Anglicans, and no doubt by the Orthodox, as a majestic statement of the obvious or as the truism of the century. Yet it is sufficiently important, having been agreed by these particular conversationalists, to underline it here since, in my view, it is a fact which undergirds the Anglican understanding of what authority in the Church is for and how it functions.

The thrust of it becomes evident once one realizes that the primary purpose of authority is to maintain the Church in the truth. What we are talking about then is at once a service to the *koinōnia* and an aspect of authentic ecclesiality. Certain things immediately declare themselves as being of the essence in respect of authority in the Church; the lordship of Christ, the Spirit's abiding in the Church, the criteria of Christian truth, the organs or instrumentalities by which it is settled and established, and the question of legitimate development. We are made aware of a hidden agenda and questions of indefectibility and infallibility begin to surface.

Archbishop Wake spoke for seventeenth-century Anglicanism when he delivered the Cyprianic dictum that 'the chair of Peter . . . is preserved in all Catholic Churches.'[1] He was referring to episcopal

---

[1] See N. Sykes, *William Wake* (Cambridge, 1957), i. 274.

collegiality and its relationship to primacy and to the guardianship and declaration of the faith much as it was to be outlined by Lambeth 1968. We are thus saying in effect that authority does not create truth but witnesses to the truth, guards it and proclaims it. As an expansion then of these points and having taken as our *point de départ* the very significant phrase from the ARCIC agreed statement, I would include as a summation at this introductory stage a couple of paragraphs which I wrote elsewhere:[2]

What is fundamental in the Church is the authority of Christ as the living Lord of the Church who gave the Holy Spirit to form the relationship of the members of the Body to its Head and to create the common life in the Body of Christ and to guide its members into the truth. The Spirit both informs and impels the proclamation of Christ to the world through the members of the Church living and conveying this common faith and shared commitment.[2]

'I was determined that the full truth of the Gospel should be *maintained* for you', wrote St Paul (Gal. 2: 5) and the recurring New Testament phrases 'the truth of Christ' and 'the truth of the Gospel' underline the vital importance of maintaining the Church in the truth.[3] The inner dynamic of the apostolic community and the essential linking of the authority process with the truth are both clear in the promise to the post-resurrection Church; 'When he comes who is the Spirit of truth, he will guide you into all the truth; for he will not speak on his own authority, but will tell only what he hears . . . He will glorify me, for everything that he makes known to you he will draw from what is mine' (John 16: 13, 14).

The Church's life in Christ and its proclamation of 'the truth of the Gospel', in both of which the Spirit is continuously at work, necessarily involve the passing on to each generation of the record of the life of Jesus, of his words, and of the consequent conviction that his work was that of Saviour and Redeemer. Thus the Scriptural record of this early period became and remained the primary standard of assay for the truth of the Gospel, a foundation document through which the authority of the Word of God is formative and normative for the faith of the new community.

This highlights the second aspect of authority in the Church, that it is in its essence inextricably bound up with the truth of the faith 'once for all delivered' (Jude 3). In fact, the New Testament sees function and nature in this connection as inseparable for the right understanding of the Church

---

[2] H. R. McAdoo, 'Anglicanism and the Nature and Exercise of Authority in the Church', *New Divinity*, 7/2 (1976), 78–9.

[3] Cf. Rom. 1: 25, 3: 7, 15: 8; 2 Cor. 11: 10; Gal. 2: 5; Col. 1: 5.

which is 'God's household, that is, the church of the living God, the pillar and bulwark of the truth' (1 Tim. 3: 15, and hence my earlier remark that maintaining the Church in the truth is an aspect of authentic ecclesiality as we analyse what authority involves). The context in the epistle makes it clear that 'the truth' refers objectively to the Christian faith. This is reflected for Anglicans in Article XX where both the Church's function as 'testis et conservatrix' and the primacy of the scriptural criterion of saving faith are merged in the description of authority in the Church.[4] The deposit is to be guarded (1 Tim. 6: 20) but 'with the help of the Holy Spirit dwelling with us' (2 Tim. 1: 14), implying not a continuous revelation, but a continuous interpretation of 'what has been delivered'. Authority's judicial function is thus to be declarative of the truth. This operates in a variety of ways ranging from General Councils, synods, episcopates, to the consent of the universal Church and to a multiple authority, and all the time certain norms are operative to ensure that the 'deposit', the fundamental objective content and quality of 'the truth of the Gospel' is preserved undistorted.

Finally, authority in the Church is a derived or conferred authority: 'He that hears you hears me' (Luke 10: 16). Or as the Preamble to the Constitution of the Church of Ireland puts it:

The Church of Ireland, deriving its authority from Christ, Who is the Head over all things to the Church, doth declare that a General Synod of the Church of Ireland, consisting of the archbishops and bishops, and of representatives of the clergy and laity, shall have chief legislative power therein, and such administrative power as may be necessary for the Church, and consistent with its episcopal constitution.

Authority in the Church is Christ's, through the Spirit, and for Anglicans authority as truth-maintaining and authority as power to legislate and administer are linked and sited within the framework and structures of the *koinōnia*. This inseparable linking of the two

---

[4] Article XX (of the Thirty-Nine Articles) reads: 'The Church hath power (*ius*) to decree Rites or Ceremonies, and authority (*auctoritatem*) in controversies of Faith: And yet it is not lawful for the Church to ordain anything that is contrary to God's Word written, neither may it expound one place of scripture that it be repugnant to another. Wherefore, although the Church be a witness and a keeper (*testis et conservatrix*) of Holy Writ, yet, as it ought not to decree anything against the same, so besides the same ought it not to enforce anything to be believed for necessity of Salvation.'

aspects of authority comes through clearly in the reports of the Lambeth Conferences of 1948 and 1968. What we are talking about is authority in its internal and external aspect. I suppose this is another way of stating the distinction made by Article XX between *ius*, legislative power, and *auctoritas*, authority in controversies of faith. Of internal authority, R. P. C. Hanson writes: 'By this is meant authority in matters where it is not a case of doing what I am told and finding the right person to obey, but where the question is, what is my authority in arriving at the truth, in convincing my own mind of the truth?'[5] External authority is legislative authority, exercised at various levels of the Church's life by bishops having liturgical, cultic, and hierarchic authority as well as authority in matters administrative and doctrinal, and by synods in which bishops, clergy, and laity are representative of the whole Church, acting in concurrence, the bishops having, in view of their teaching office, an ultimate role or veto in respect of doctrinal issues.[6] It is as we contemplate authority in its primary function of maintaining the Church in the truth—internal authority—that we come face to face with the essential Anglican ethos which ultimately determines our understanding of what authority in the Church is about and how it should work.

One Greek disyllable has left an indelible mark on how Anglicans view the truth of the Gospel and consequently on the way in which authority arrives at and then maintains the Church in that saving truth. The word is *hapax*, 'the faith *once for all* delivered' (Jude 3), and it bears directly on the functioning of this internal authority. Attempts to enlarge the *hapax*, as for example, by adding on as *de fide* dogmas having no Scriptural warranty; or to subtract from it, as for example, by omitting baptism and the eucharist from the essentials of faith, are self-contradictory and unacceptable. Either procedure fails the test of the criteria by means of which authentic Christianity is ascertained and established.

These criteria are Scripture, tradition conformable to Scripture, and reason. Anglicanism in its formularies and theology accords the

---

[5] R. P. C. Hanson, 'The Anglican Conception of Authority', *Ekklesiastikos Pharos* (1970), LII. ii–iii. 83.
[6] Cf. *The Constitution of the Church of Ireland: Preamble and Declaration*, IV, and ch. I, part II, p. 21.

primary role to Scripture and sets store by tradition or antiquity (often seen, as in Church of Ireland formularies, in terms of the 'continued profession of the faith of the Primitive Church').[7] Inseparable from the whole approach is the importance of reason and its implications for a freedom which accepts authority and rejects authoritarianism. There is no source or part of this process which is immune to reason. Lambeth 1968 puts it this way:

To such a threefold inheritance of faith belongs a concept of authority which refuses to insulate itself against the testing of history and the free action of reason. It seeks to be a credible authority and therefore is concerned to secure satisfactory historical support and to have its credentials in a shape which corresponds to the requirements of reason.[8]

These three elements constitute the authority instrument by means of which Anglicans establish whether this or that doctrine is part of or consistent with the faith 'once for all delivered'.

This threefold appeal is the authority process though which Anglicans see the Church being maintained in the truth. The ARCIC statement, *Authority in the Church*, 1, notes this emphasis as characteristic of Anglicanism. The appeal to Scripture and to antiquity is written into the Preamble to the Constitution of the Church of Ireland and the very first Lambeth Conference spoke of 'maintaining the faith in its purity and integrity, as taught by the Holy Scriptures, held by the primitive Church, summed up in the Creeds, and affirmed by the undisputed General Councils'. But the appeal was actively operative well before the end of the sixteenth century and developed richly during the seventeenth. Just as the instrument, the means by which the truth of the Gospel is ascertained is this threefold appeal, so the instrumentality, or agency for so ascertaining in a situation of controversy or doubt, is the episcopate and the episcopate in synod.

This comes through for contemporary Anglicanism with great clarity in the deliberations of the Lambeth Conferences of 1948 and

[7] Cf. *The Constitution of the Church of Ireland: Preamble and Declaration*, 1 (1) and (3). See also the preface to the Irish revision of the Prayer Book in 1878, where the liturgical criteria are 'the true doctrine of Christ, and a pure manner and order of Divine Service, according to the holy Scriptures and the practice of the Primitive Church'.
[8] *Report of the Lambeth Conference of 1968*, p. 82.

1968.[9] The relevant sections of both conference *Reports* will repay careful study, bearing as they do directly on the matter which we are examining. Here it is enough simply to indicate the main thrust of both documents. The 1948 Report analyses this multiple authority, the elements of which are in organic relation to each other, mutually supportive and mutually checking and thus redressing errors or exaggerations. It is a concept of authority, 'resting on the truth of the Gospel',[10] alive to the Spirit's abiding in the Church, conscious of historicity and the *hapax* and the *consensus*, the living tradition and the role of the worshipping community. It seeks to serve both the corporate faith and the need for spiritual freedom, that inbuilt tension which exists in a living religion in a real world. This is a spelling out of how the threefold appeal works and a dissection of internal authority. It is an authority possessed of 'a quality of richness which encourages and releases initiative, trains in fellowship, and evokes a free and willing obedience'.[11] Something of the Anglican essence is crystallized here and one paragraph may be quoted:

Authority, as inherited by the Anglican Communion from the undivided Church of the early centuries of the Christian era, is single in that it is derived from a single Divine source, and reflects within itself the richness and historicity of the divine Revelation, the authority of the eternal Father, the incarnate Son, and the life-giving Spirit. It is distributed among Scripture, Tradition, Creeds, the Ministry of the Word and Sacraments, the witness of saints, and the *consensus fidelium*, which is the continuing experience of the Holy Spirit through His faithful people in the Church. It is thus a dispersed rather than a centralized authority, having many elements which combine, interact with, and check each other.[12]

We have already noted the 1968 Lambeth Conference's relating of the 'threefold inheritance of faith' to a concept of authority which has room for 'the free action of reason'. This interaction of corporate faith with spiritual freedom comes to the fore again in the Addendum as it speaks of multiple authority and ordered liberty:

The inheritance of faith which characterizes the Anglican Communion is an *authority of a multiple kind* and . . . to the different elements which occur

---

[9] See *Report of the Lambeth Conference of 1948*, pp. 84–6; *Report of the Lambeth Conference of 1968*, pp. 82–3, 63–4, 108.
[10] *Report* (1948), 84.
[11] Ibid. 85.
[12] Ibid. 84–5.

in the different strands of this inheritance, different Anglicans attribute different levels of authority. From this foundation arises Anglican tolerance, comprehensiveness, and *ordered liberty*.[13]

It is not without significance for the consistency of Anglicanism that the Lambeth Conference of 1888, concerned as it was with the overseas expansion of the Communion, had similarly affirmed the *hapax* and also defended the need for 'due liberty'.[14] Episcopal succession and 'substantially the same doctrine as our own' were laid down as essential for unity with the Spanish and Lusitanian Reformed Churches and it will be remembered that this was the Conference which enuntiated the Lambeth Quadrilateral. The 1968 *Report* reverts in another place to this mutual interplay of the *hapax* and freedom when it refers to the need for 'a deeper awareness of the deposit of the faith once delivered to the saints' and 'for an attitude and an approach that combine Christian assurance with a bold exploration of theology and society'.[15] The function of the bishop in this area is the safeguarding of the faith and the evocation of creative thinking among the people.[16]

Lambeth 1978 was preoccupied with the instrumentality of authority, a debate occasioned by the ordination of women in certain provinces. Reiterating the role of episcopate and synod in and for the People of God, the Conference insisted that neither bishop nor synod receives authority 'by any succession independent of the Church'.[17] The same point had been made centuries before by William Laud in his *Conference with Fisher* for this whole approach is entirely part of the Anglican heritage from earlier centuries.

Laud's name leads us straight to the seventeenth century, but the

---

[13] *Report of the Lambeth Conference of 1968*, pp. 82–3.

[14] The Conference proclaimed: 'We declare that we are united under one divine Head in the fellowship of the one Catholic and Apostolic Church, holding the one faith revealed in Holy Writ, defined in the Creeds, maintained by the Primitive Church and reaffirmed by the undisputed Ecumenical Councils.' This was expanded by Lambeth 1948 in its exposition of the multiple authority favoured by Anglicanism. The 1888 Conference then related this to the contemporary scene: 'It is of the utmost importance that our faith and practice should be represented, both to the ancient Churches and to the native and growing Churches in the mission field, in a manner which shall neither give cause for offence nor restrict due liberty . . . ' (*The Lambeth Conferences of 1867, 1878 and 1888*, ed. R. T. Davidson (1896), 274, 352–8).

[15] *Report* (1968), 63–4.

[16] Ibid. 108.

[17] *Report of the Lambeth Conference of 1978*, pp. 76–7.

shape or form of the Anglican answer before and after that golden age of Anglican theology has been consistently the same. We in the twentieth century have found it effective as we seek to maintain the Church in the truth of the gospel. Before Laud's time the canon of 1571 had directed the clergy to 'see that they never teach aught in a sermon to be religiously held and believed by the people, except what is agreeable to the doctrine of the Old and New Testaments, and what the Catholic Fathers and ancient bishops have collected from the same doctrine.'[18] A decade earlier, John Jewel in the Apology had insisted on Scripture as the primary criterion and had equally asserted the criterion of closeness to the Primitive Church: 'Surely wee have ever judged the primitive Churche of Christes tyme, of the Apostles, and of the holie Fathers to be the catholique Churche: neyther make we doubt to name it Noes arke, Christes spouse, the pillar and upholder of al trueth: nor yet to fixe therein the whole meane of our salvation.' Clearly also Jewel, as John E. Booty points out, 'made much use of reason in solving the problem of authority',[19] though an interesting investigation would be the kinds of reason Hooker or the Tew Circle or the Cambridge Platonists or the Latitudinarians visualized as compared with Jewel's view of 'an aided reason'.[20]

II

The purpose of the preceding introductory section has been to stress how close contemporary Anglicanism has kept in this matter to its theological sources, particularly as these had developed in the seventeenth century. There is a marked consistency as between Anglican understanding today of authority's chief function, of its instruments and instrumentalities, and the views expressed at the end of the sixteenth century and throughout the seventeenth century which saw the full flowering of these views as a distinctive theological method. Not that this attitude was a creation of the Reformation and subsequent periods. Henry Chadwick's contribution to *Mélanges Congar* (1974, pp. 163–75), entitled 'Some Reflections on Magisterium in the Early Church', drew attention to the

---

[18] H. Gee and W. J. Hardy, *Documents Illustrative of English Church History* (1896) 476.

[19] See J. E. Booty, *John Jewel as Apologist of the Church of England* (1963), 139.

[20] Ibid. 140.

growth in importance both of the individual bishop and of the Churches of apostolic foundation in respect of authority. It underlines the role of the local church as *guardian of truth*; stresses the primary role of Scripture as the source of doctrine and notes the differentiation between the rule of faith and fundamentals on the one hand and secondary matters which permit of divergence within the Church on the other. His conclusion is important, and for Anglicans it establishes the lineage of what their classical theologians have always maintained about the authority process and the authenticating process for Christian truth as this operated in the early Church. Chadwick writes of this process in the primitive Church that

> They judge by rational argument, and by the appeal to consensus. Both the bases of the teaching office and the very teaching office itself are multiple, never thought of as being concentrated in one community or one see. Moreover, a crucial part in the 'authority process' is played by subsequent reception by the faithful.

The threefold appeal endemic in the Anglican theological attitude to what constitutes Christian orthodoxy is exemplified by Irenaeus: 'Scripture is above all the charter of the community life and the source of its doctrine. But Irenaeus is also able to appeal to reason and to the paradosis of the apostolic churches within which the authentic meaning of scripture is guaranteed.'

Evaluation of contemporary Anglican documents shows that this threefold appeal remains a live option for the Church today. It is an inheritance of which seventeenth-century Anglicanism made much, in greatly varying theological contexts, and which was passed on to our own times, in contexts still more divergent. So Archbishop Ramsey could write that 'the times call urgently for the Anglican witness to Scripture, tradition and reason.'[21] It is only through such an instrument that the *hapax* and an ordered liberty can allow for a concept of genuine development under the guidance of the Spirit abiding in the Church. One cannot in fact discuss authority in the Church, (the main function of which is to maintain the Church in the truth), apart from the abiding of the Spirit who leads into all the truth, a point stressed in the ARCIC statements on authority. Furthermore, if development is to be authentic and necessary, it must be guided by the same Spirit, and clearly both it and the function

---

[21] A. M. Ramsey, *From Gore to Temple* (1960), p. ix.

of the *magisterium* must be subject to Scripture, to tradition and to what has been rightly termed 'intrinsic reasonableness'.[22]

III

How thoroughly all this was embedded in seventeenth-century Anglicanism may be seen not simply from the theological writings of the period but in a casual aside by that cultivated and charming layman, Sir Thomas Browne. In the *Religio Medici* he speaks of

The Church of England to whose faith I am a sworne subject, and therefore in a double obligation subscribe unto her articles, and endeavour to observe her Constitutions: whatsoever is beyond, as points indifferent, I observe according to the rules of my private reason, or the humour and fashion of my devotion . . . In briefe, where the Scripture is silent, the Church is my Text; where that speakes, 'tis but my Comment, where there is a joynt silence of both, I borrow not the rules of my Religion from Rome or Geneva, but the dictates of my own reason.[23]

Twenty years ago, in *The Spirit of Anglicanism*,[24] I endeavoured to show from an analysis of primary sources of the seventeenth century the way in which this threefold appeal lay at the heart of how Anglicans answered the questions 'What is my authority for asserting this or that to be part of authentic Christian truth, and, by what process is the Church maintained in this truth?' Throughout the seventeenth century which saw the Church both in prosperity and in exile and persecution, in theological controversy and political upheaval, facing the emergence of a new kind of rationalism and involved in the rise of the new science, this theological method (for want of a better term) continued to be part and parcel of the Anglican ethos. The period revealed differences of emphasis in its use by different individuals and groups. Thus, Hooker sought, as an alternative to a biblical authoritarianism, to establish a liberal method which in the event was indebted to the efforts of Aquinas to create a synthesis of faith and reason. His was a rationalism which brought a step forward Anselm's *fides quaerens intellectum*, but opposed that of the Latin Averroists. For Hooker, 'the light of Reason, wherewith God illuminateth every one which cometh into

---

[22] H. F. Woodhouse, 'The Holy Spirit, the Authority of the Church and Development in Doctrine', in *Directions* (Dublin, 1970), 57.

[23] *Religio Medici* (1642–3), i. 5.

[24] H. R. McAdoo, *The Spirit of Anglicanism* (London–New York, 1965).

the world' teaches us in part God's will and indeed natural law 'may be termed most fitly the law of reason'.[25] In his view, the source of all authority is law seen as an implanted directive through which all things attain their proper end. It is reason, inherent, governing the universe: law is 'a directive rule unto goodness of operation'; it is 'properly that which reason in such sort defineth to be good that it must be done'.[26] Anyone reading *Ecclesiastical Polity*, II. vii. 1–10, which is a discussion of the nature of authority and of the quest for the assurance of truth in religion, will understand how this liberal method and this intrinsic reasonableness came to be an indispensable element in the Anglican approach to questions of authority: 'such as the evidence is . . . such is the heart's assent thereunto'. When Lambeth 1968 related the 'threefold inheritance of faith' to a concept of authority which has room for 'the free action of reason' it was echoing Hooker's conviction 'that authority of men should prevail with men either against or above reason is no part of our belief'.[27] Later in the century, both the Tew Circle and the Cambridge Platonists would severally and in somewhat different contexts develop this emphasis. Neither group attached the same importance to the appeal to antiquity which in P. A. Welsby's phrase became 'the norm of Anglican apologetic'.[28] This was because, unlike such as Andrewes, Hammond, Laud, Bramhall, and Bull who used the appeal to establish continuity in faith and order with the Church of the first five centuries, the Tew Circle saw it in the light of their own preoccupation with liberating their thinking from systems and 'authorities' by means of rational enquiry. Yet, both Hyde and Chillingworth accepted a modified appeal to tradition in this Laudian sense, Chillingworth himself holding that the judgment of a General Council ought not to be refused and that 'they did best that followed Scripture interpreted by Catholic written tradition'.[29]

To Hooker, as to the whole of Anglican seventeenth-century theology, the Vincentian rule was, like the *hapax*, vital to the maintaining of the Church in the truth of the Gospel: 'Neither may

[25] See e.g. *The Laws of Ecclesiastical Polity*, I, viii. 3–10.
[26] Ibid. 4, 9. For a fuller discussion of law in Hooker's work see H. R. McAdoo, *The Structure of Caroline Moral Theology* (London, 1949), 18–26.
[27] *EP* II. vii. 6.
[28] *Lancelot Andrewes* (London, 1958), 156.
[29] For fuller references see *The Spirit of Anglicanism*, chs. IX and X, 'The Appeal to Antiquity'.

we . . . lightly esteem what hath been allowed as fit in the judgment
of antiquity, and by the long continued practice, of the whole
Church; from which unnecessarily to swerve, experience hath never
as yet found it safe.'[30] While General Councils may have been
abused 'by factious and vile endeavours' the principle of the council
is the preservation of unity in 'the chiefest things' and is 'a thing
whereof God's own blessed Spirit was the author; a thing practised
by the holy apostles themselves'.[31]

Scripture is of course the pre-eminent criterion and the control-
ling element in the triad for Hooker, as it was for his opponents and
for all theologians of the period. The difference lies in how they
handle it. Something perennial has passed into the theological make-
up of Anglicanism from passages (and they are many) such as this:

The truth is, that the mind of man desireth evermore *to know the truth
according to the most infallible certainty which the nature of things can
yield* . . . where we cannot attain unto this, there what appeareth to be true
by strong and invincible demonstration . . . thereunto the mind doth
necessarily assent. . . . Scripture with Christian men being received as the
Word of God; that for which we have probable, yea, that which we have
necessary reason for, yea, that which we see with our eyes, is not thought so
sure as that which the Scripture of God teacheth.[32]

The sufficiency of Scripture and its doctrinal force are everywhere
in the *Ecclesiastical Polity*[33] in company with the law of nature and
always attributing its full value to the gift of reason: 'Scripture
indeed teacheth things above nature, things which our reason could
not reach unto. Yet those things also we believe, knowing by reason
that Scripture is the word of God.'[34] To those who ask 'what Scripture can teach us the sacred authority of Scripture', Hooker adduces
the help of both tradition and reason to establish this authority. The
view of 'the whole Church of God' will weigh heavily with the
believer but if this be called in question by the non-believer 'this
giveth occasion to sift what reason there is, whereby the testimony
of the Church concerning Scripture, and our own persuasion which
Scripture itself hath confirmed, may be proved a truth infallible.'[35]

[30] *EP* v. vii. i.
[31] Ibid. i. x. 14. The reference is to the Jerusalem Council in Acts 15.
[32] Ibid. ii. vii. 5.
[33] Cf. Ibid. viii. 7, iii. iii. 2–3.
[34] Ibid. iii. viii. 12.
[35] Ibid. 14.

Certainly, we need 'the special grace of the Holy Ghost . . . to the enlightening of our minds', but this can be subjective in certain circumstances so that reason cannot be excluded.[36] Finally, Hooker has a word to say on the Church's authority in order and in doctrine. By 'order' he means 'the outward administration of public duties in the service of God' and this is 'ecclesiastical authority', what we have already characterised as external authority: 'All things cannot be of ancient continuance, which are expedient and needful for the ordering of spiritual affairs: but the Church being a body which dieth not hath always power, as occasion requireth, no less to ordain that which never was, than to ratify what hath been before.'[37] This conclusion however does not apply in matters of doctrine for here the *hapax* is all-important:

The Church hath authority to establish that for an order at one time, which at another time it may abolish, and in both may do well. But that which in doctrine the Church doth now deliver rightly as a truth, no man will say that it may hereafter recall, and as rightly avouch the contrary. Laws touching matter of order are changeable, by the power of the Church; articles concerning doctrine not so.[38]

This is the *ius* and *auctoritas* distinction set out in Article XX, the internal authority as distinct from external authority. The threefold appeal is the criterion and the test: 'Be it in matter of the one kind or the other, what Scripture doth plainly deliver, to that the first place both of credit and obedience is due; the next whereunto is whatsoever any man can necessarily conclude by force of reason; after these the voice of the Church succeedeth.'[39]

The stamp of Hooker is not simply on the theological writings of the century which he himself barely entered, but remains indelible on the manner in which Anglicans have subsequently done theology and understood the purpose and the functioning of authority in the Church. No theologian has exercised a magisterial role in Anglicanism as Calvin did for Calvinism or Luther for Lutheranism, but the 'poor obscure English priest' (as he was admiringly described to Clement VIII) has left a world-wide Church in his debt.[40]

Though the appeal to antiquity as a supplementary way of

---

[36] Ibid. 15.
[37] Ibid. v. viii. 1.
[38] Ibid. 2.
[39] Ibid.
[40] The incident is recorded in Izaak Walton's *Life* of Hooker.

establishing the truth of doctrine was an active and vital element from Jewel onwards, it was men like Andrewes and Hammond who wove it into the fibre of Anglican theology. It is not too much to say that Andrewes's writings are saturated with the Fathers as with the Scripture itself: 'This Booke chiefly; but in a good part also, by the books of the ancient Fathers, in whom the scent of this ointment was fresh, and the temper true; on whose writings it lyeth thick, and we thence strike it off, and gather it safely.'[41] He outlines the Anglican position in the same terms: 'One canon . . . two testaments, three creeds, four general councils, five centuries and the series of Fathers in that period . . . determine the boundary of our faith.'[42] The authority for Catholic orthodoxy is the Vincentian test: 'Let that be reckoned Catholic which always obtained everywhere among all, and which always and everywhere by all was believed.' The Spirit's abiding in the Church is central so that Andrewes can say succinctly 'No Dove, no Church.'[43] Yet, the Spirit in man being the candle of the Lord, as the Cambridge Platonists would insist, Andrewes will also assert that 'Prophecy can come from no nature but rational: The Spirit then is *natura rationalis*.'[44]

Henry Hammond's steady output of work in his enforced retirement (part of which was spent in prison) during the Interregnum was, as R. S. Bosher has put it,[45] a major contribution to the life of a persecuted Church. His theological range was enormous, his skill in patristics and in the schoolmen and in moral theology was notable and his whole approach is to establish the coinciding of 'the doctrine of the Anglican Church' (a very early use of the term?)[46] with the faith of the primitive Church. In his book *Of Fundamentals* (1654), Hammond makes full use of the familiar Anglican distinction between fundamentals and secondary truths, the former being contained in Scripture and the creeds and confessions of the universal Church. Significantly for our investigation, he holds that con-

---

[41] Lancelot Andrewes, Sermon X (Whitsunday Sermons).
[42] Id., *Opuscula* (LACT edn.), 91.
[43] Whitsunday Sermons, Sermon VIII.
[44] Ibid., Sermon XI.
[45] R. S. Bosher, *The Making of the Restoration Settlement* (London, 1951) 36: 'It is due in large measure to his efforts and his encouragement of others that the Interregnum became in fact a golden age of High Anglican theology and apologetic . . . Hammond set himself to the task of building an intellectual defence for the faith whose outward structure lay in ruins.'
[46] 'Of the Power of the Keys', iii.

cepts such as 'the infallibility of the Church' run counter to this establishing of the truth of the faith once for all delivered. We are back to the threefold appeal when he states that he cannot accept 'the practice of the present Church' when it is contrary to 'antiquity, or Scripture, or rational deductions from either'.[47] The Hookerian phrase 'as the affirmation is, such is the belief' (*Of the Reasonableness of Christian Religion*, C. i) is balanced by 'those three terms to which Vincentius Lirinensis . . . hath directed us . . . universality, antiquity, consent' (*A Paraenesis*, c. v. 5).

From among the great figures of the seventeenth century one may virtually pick names at random to illustrate our thesis. That gallant man, John Bramhall, Primate of All Ireland, comes to mind. Cromwell called him 'that Irish Canterbury' and narrowly missed capturing him. A penurious wanderer thereafter in France and the Low Countries, no less than seven books came from his pen during the years of exile. Positively and with simplicity his Anglicanism appears throughout his writings. As Bramhall sets out 'the infallible rule of faith, that is, the Holy Scriptures, interpreted by the Catholic Church', one meets the interplay of the idea of continuity with that of the finality of fundamentals and with a liberality of outlook in secondary questions as against the view, 'which will admit no latitude in religion, but makes each nicety a fundamental'. It is the classical Anglican approach by way of Scripture and antiquity and stemming as much from an attitude to reason and the reality of freedom as it does from the conviction that only fundamentals are authoritative.[48]

Even more striking is the great Jeremy Taylor whose Laudian affiliations kept company in his thought with the ideas of the Cambridge Platonists and Chillingworth. His mind was more complex than that of Bramhall and, time and again, one registers the impression that his theology is strangely modern, particularly in his view of reason and its relationship to faith.[49] He rejects any concept of authority which deprives authority of the possibility of being freely accepted nor will he agree that everyone is his own authority: 'I

---

[47] Ibid. xii.

[48] For an examination of Bramhall's theology, see *The Spirit of Anglicanism*, pp. 368–85.

[49] For Taylor's general theological position, see ibid. H. R. McAdoo, 49–80. See also 'Jeremy Taylor: An Essay on the Relationship of Faith and Reason', *Hermathena*, 107 (1968), 14–30.

affirm nothing but upon grounds of Scripture, or universal tradition, or right reason discernible by every disinterested person.' The 'desire to come to truth' and be 'secured' in it is the underlying theme of his *Liberty of Prophesying* and he knows of no other sure route, 'so that Scripture, tradition, councils, and fathers, are the evidence in question, but reason is the judge'.[50]

At the end of the century and well on into the eighteenth century, this familiar Anglican attitude to the truth of the faith witnessed to and guarded by the Church, the household of faith, the bulwark of the truth, was vigorously advanced in the context of unity discussions by William Wake, Archbishop of Canterbury, in his dealings with both the Gallican divines and the Lutheran and Reformed theologians.[51] With great theological acumen and perceptiveness Wake analyses the distinction between fundamentals and non-essentials,[52] the role of the Vincentian rule and the adherence to it of the Church of England,[53] the position of a universal primacy in a reunited Church and the nature of that primacy,[54] orders and eucharistic doctrine.[55] Throughout his correspondence with Continental theologians, the basis for Wake is the same as that of his predecessors, his heavy emphasis on fundamentals being at one with the expressed views of Taylor, Bramhall, and Hammond.

Not *dirigisme*, but direction—a sure sense of direction—is an essential component of seventeenth-century Anglicanism. The direction was that of genuine catholicity from which the Anglicans considered that the dogmatic constrictions both of Rome and Geneva caused the believer to be side-tracked. Thus Laud would not enclose catholicity in a 'narrow conclave' but desired 'to lay open those wider gates of the Catholic Church, confined to no age, time or place; nor knowing any bounds but that faith which was once (and but once for all) delivered to the saints'.[56] One could multiply names and extracts in support almost indefinitely, for this

[50] *A Discourse of the Liberty of Prophesying*, Sections VII and X.

[51] For a full account of Wake and his work, so far ahead of his times, see N. Sykes, *William Wake*, 2 vols. (Cambridge, 1957).

[52] e.g. op. cit. i. 262.

[53] e.g. op. cit. i. 282.

[54] e.g. op. cit. i. 312.

[55] For an examination of these areas in Wake's theology, see H. R. McAdoo 'Anglican/Roman Catholic Relations, 1717–1980: A Detection of Themes' pp. 147–95, in J. C. H. Aveling, D. M. Loades, and H. R. McAdoo, *Rome and the Anglicans* (Berlin–New York, 1982).

[56] Preface to his *Conference*.

quality was omnipresent in the period and has passed into the life-stream of the Anglican Communion. As one reviews the scene, past and present, it may be fairly claimed that Francis Paget in his *Introduction to the Fifth Book of Hooker's Ecclesiastical Polity* was not being unduly euphoric or overoptimistic when he wrote that 'The distinctive strength of Anglicanism rests on equal loyalty to the unconflicting rights of reason, Scripture and tradition.'

IV

Archbishop William Laud died on the scaffold, judicially murdered for his faith as some historians hold,[57] in the year 1645. Ten years before that happening was born Edward Stillingfleet who lived to the last year of the century and became the chief writer among the Latitudiarians. To bring them thus together is no scribe's trick for the Latitudinarian wrote a book about the only book produced by the father of the Laudians, completely agreeing with Laud's conclusions as to the authority by which we know that a Church is a true Church and holding the truth of the faith. The fact is only unexpected or unlikely if one forgets the deep and wide consistency of method which, with its varying applications and emphases, the seventeenth century reveals in Anglicanism.

So to round off this chapter it is illuminating to look in a little more detail at William Laud's *Conference (in 1622) with Fisher* (1639). The reason for this choice is twofold. In the first place, the book is really all about internal authority. Secondly, it represents the Anglican average since its author, though historically a most significant figure and obviously very widely read in theology, particularly in patristic studies, was not a leading theologian of the day. For these reasons and because the book is set in the form of argument and dialogue, it should enable us to discern how the Anglican approach fares early in the century and how it works out under pressure. The way in which, forty years on, Stillingfleet would handle the theme and the book in his *Rational Account* (1664) should throw further light on the nature of these seventeenth-century influences.

The book begins with the question of authority and whether

[57] e.g. W. H. Hutton, *William Laud* (London, 1913), and E. C. E. Bourne *The Anglicanism of William Laud* (London, 1947).

there is, or can be, an infallible visible Church. Laud is set to show that 'nobody is ever able to prove any particular Church infallible', asserting that the indefectibility of the Church, 'that it shall not fall away, doth not secure it from all kinds of errors'.[58] What Laud and Fisher are discussing is how to attain 'certainty in matters of faith' or how the Church can be maintained in the truth. While Fisher constantly attempts to move the argument towards infallibility, ecclesial and papal, Laud responds that certainty in fundamentals is established first by Scripture and then by tradition: 'we resolve our faith into Scripture as the ground; and we will never deny that tradition is the key that lets us in.'[59] This is, as he notes, virtually a quotation from Hooker. It was not Christ's intention, says Laud, to 'leave an infallible certainty in His Church . . . in things not fundamental, not necessary'.[60] 'All points of doctrine, generally received as fundamental are established by Scripture, Creeds, and the first four General Councils, and thus there is need for no other certainty and reason so asserts.' He is affirming a *confessio fidei* for the whole of seventeenth-century Anglicanism when he writes:

I admit no ordinary rule left now in the Church, of divine and infallible verity, and so of faith, but the Scripture. And I believe the entire Scripture, first, by the tradition of the Church; then, by all other credible motives, as is before expressed; and last of all, by the light which shines in Scripture itself, kindled in believers by the Spirit of God. Then, I believe the entire Scripture infallibly, and by a divine infallibility am sure of my object. *Then am I as sure of my believing*, which is the act of my faith, conversant about this object: for no man believes, but he must needs know in himself whether he believes or no, and wherein and how he doubts. Then I am infallibly assured of my Creed, the tradition of the Church inducing, and the Scripture confirming it. And I believe both Scripture and Creed in the same uncorrupted sense which the primitive Church believed them; and am sure that I do so believe them, because I cross not in my belief anything delivered by the primitive Church. And this, again, I am sure of because I take the belief of the primitive Church as it is expressed and delivered by the Councils and ancient Fathers of those times.[61]

Early on, Laud has set this out as the structure of the quest for

---

[58] *The Conference with Fisher the Jesuit*, i. 15, 22, and cf. x. 258, vii. 145: 'The whole Church cannot err in fundamentals.' The edition of the *Conference* used is that of the English Theological Library (1901), ed. C. H. Simpkinson.

[59] *Conference*, iv. 103.

[60] Ibid. xiv. 418, and cf. 379.

[61] Ibid. xiv. 385, and cf. 379.

certainty in fundamentals and certainty of salvation. This can neither be established simply by an infallible Book nor by an infallible Church, but by four arguments combined which cannot be taken separately: the testimony of the Church which leads us to Scripture, the light from Scripture and the testimony it gives to itself, the witness of the Holy Spirit and the proof provided by natural reason.[62]

His treatment of the major question of fundamentals is interesting in that it is bound up with the *hapax*. 'All points of the Apostles' Creed, as they are there expressed, are fundamental' but behind the Creed lies Scripture.[63] To these fundamental articles nothing can be added as *de fide*. The Church cannot make new articles of faith 'for the articles of faith cannot increase in substance, but only in explication', and this latter is a General Council's function.[64] With plainness he affirms that 'it is not in the power of the whole Church, much less of a General Council, to make anything fundamental in the faith that is not contained in the letter or sense of that common faith, which was once given and but once for all to the saints.'[65] This has been made clear as the operative element in the establishing of the Church in the authentic faith by Laud in his preface:

Salvation is not shut up into such a narrow conclave . . . therefore, I have endeavoured to lay open those wider gates of the Catholic Church confined to no age, time, or place; nor knowing any bounds but that 'faith which was once'—and but once for all—'delivered to the saints'.[66]

This theme of the distinction between fundamentals and non-fundamentals and its link with the *hapax* is everywhere in seventeenth-century Anglicanism. For Jeremy Taylor it is the only live option by which to achieve 'unity of faith'.[67] Archbishop Wake, seventy years later, in his letters on Christian unity to Reformed theologians and to the Gallicans alike, set out the same principle in either case. It is, in his view, an indispensable prerequisite to any effective discussion of unity.[68] The questions, What are the fundamentals, and, Where is doctrine to be found, exercised Wake as they

---

[62] Ibid. iii. 92: 'And, it seems, no one of these doth it alone.'
[63] Ibid. ii. 50–1.
[64] Ibid. 38.
[65] Ibid. 390.
[66] *Conference*, Epistle Dedicatory to King Charles I, p. xxx.
[67] *A Discourse of the Liberty of Prophesying* (1647), the epistle dedicatory.
[68] See e.g. Sykes, *William Wake*, i. 254, 262–4.

do theologians of today. Wake's perceptiveness here is keen and it is
strikingly matched by Laud. In a letter of 1719 to the Reformed
theologian Turretini, Wake wrote that he had 'come at last to this
opinion; that the peace of Christendom can no way be restored but
by separating the fundamental articles of our religion (in which
almost all churches agree) from others, which in their several
natures though not strictly fundamental, may yet be of more, or
less, moment to us in the way of our salvation'.[69] Wake sees a grada-
tion from fundamentals through matters 'not strictly fundamental'
but not to be lightly dismissed from 'the truths of faith'. This has
about it more than a suggestion of the hierarchy of truths which
would be set out in the Second Vatican Council's decree on ecumenism (II): 'When comparing doctrines, they should remember that
in Catholic teaching there exists an order or "hierarchy" of truths,
since they vary in their relationship to the foundation of the Christian faith.' More remarkable still is the similarity here of Laud's
wording on the same point:

And yet for all this, everything fundamental is not of a like nearness to the
foundation, nor of equal primeness in the faith. And my granting the Creed
to be fundamental doth not deny but that there are *quaedam prima credi-
bilia*, certain prime principles of faith, in the bosom whereof all other
articles lay wrapped and folded up.[70]

If one casts one's mind back to Hanson's observation that internal authority is concerned with the question, What is our authority
in arriving at the truth of faith, one can appreciate the force and
thrust of Anglicanism's heavy emphasis on the fundamentals/non-
essentials distinction linked with the *hapax*. Common coin though
it was in the seventeenth century, few made greater use of it than
Wake in his letters to Girardin, Du Pin and Quinot.[71] Writing to
the latter in 1720, the archbishop had once again reiterated this position which Quinot had accepted. But an earlier letter to Girardin in
1718 shows how Wake's theological acuity necessitates a closer look
at the content of the term 'fundamental':

It is indeed a work of greater difficulty, not to say danger, to distinguish the
essential articles of doctrine from the rest, in such wise that nothing in them

[69] Ibid. 253.
[70] *Conference*, ii. 50.
[71] e.g. *William Wake*, i. 262–3, 297.

is either superfluous or lacking; that nothing essential to salvation is omitted, nor anything non-essential included in the number of essentials'.[72]

What was he getting at and what was the difficulty? My own view is that Wake (and Laud) were affirming that fundamentals, still scripturally revealed, include certain scripturally warranted essentials in the life of the Church, namely the sacraments and a ministry to administer them. One has only to read Wake's correspondence and the great mass of seventeenth-century Anglican writing on these subjects, to see that for these men, without baptism, without the Bread and the Book, without a ministry, there could be no Church. 'Without these' wrote Ignatius 'there is no Church deserving of the name' (*Trallians*, iii) and the whole weight of Anglican theology and appeal to antiquity surely confirms that fundamentals must include that without which the household of faith could have no existence. To have inserted Wake here proleptically is, I believe, to do what he would have warmly approved since he would write to a French correspondent that it was Laud 'who beyond any other undertook the defence' of the standpoint they both shared.

A glance at the role of General Councils and the function of reason will complete a sketch of how Laud saw the Church to be maintained in the truth:

So to draw all together: to settle controversies in the Church, there is a visible judge and infallible, but not living; and that is the Scripture pronouncing by the Church. And there is a visible and a living judge, but not infallible; and that is a General Council . . . but I know no formal confirmation of it needful . . . but only that, after it is ended, the whole Church admit it, be it never so tacitly.[73]

It is of interest that Laud's estimate of the authority of General Councils matches that of Article XXI and that of the ARCIC statement, *Authority* I. 19, which says that 'only those judgements of general councils are guaranteed "to exclude what is erroneous" or are "protected from error" which have as their content "fundamental matters of faith", which "formulate the central truths of salvation" and which are "faithful to Scripture and consistent with Tradition" '.[74] Similarly, Laud, while holding that the whole

---

[72] Ibid. 262.
[73] Ibid. 222–4.
[74] *Elucidation 1981* (5), *Final Report*, p. 71.

Church cannot err in fundamentals,[75] agrees that General Councils may err. He emphasizes that the Spirit's abiding in the Church is the essential assistance in maintaining the Church in the truth and here again fundamentals and the Scriptural criterion are operative:

I consider that the assistance of the Holy Ghost is without error. That is no question; and as little there is, that a Council hath it. But the doubt that troubles is, whether all assistance of the Holy Ghost be afforded in such a high manner, as to cause all the definitions of a council in matters fundamental in the faith, and in remote deductions from it, to be alike infallible? . . . But 'into all truth', is a limited 'all': 'into all truth absolutely necessary to salvation'; and this, when they suffer themselves to be led by the Blessed Spirit, by the word of God; and all truth which Christ had before, at least fundamentally delivered to them.[76]

John Hales, known as the ever-memorable, asserted as the Anglican position that 'Infallibility either in judgement, or interpretation, or whatsoever, is annext neither to the See of any Bishop, nor to the Councils, nor to the Church, nor to any created power whatsoever.' P. E. More put his finger directly on the point when he wrote 'Evidently this does not exclude from infallibility those necessary truths which proceed directly from a divine and uncreated source. What Hales had in mind is exactly the addition to these fundamentals by tradition or their expansion by reason' (*Anglicanism*, London, 1935, p. xxviii), and this is precisely what Laud is saying. Perhaps it was all summed up in brief by Laud's friend and collaborator, William Chillingworth, converted to Roman Catholicism by Laud's opponent in the *Conference*, Fisher, but who later returned to the Church of England. He wrote that there is a large distinction to be drawn between 'being infallible in fundamentals and being an infallible guide in fundamentals' and 'that there shall be always a Church infallible in fundamentals, we easily grant; for it comes to no more but this, that there shall be always a Church'.[77]

'Grace', writes Laud, 'is never placed but in a reasonable creature',[78] and a final reflection on the *Conference* must note the surprisingly liberal strain of reason and tolerance in one still regarded

---

[75] *Conference*, vii, 145, x. 270–1, 279: 'but there is not the like consent, that General Councils cannot err.'

[76] Ibid. x. 265–6.

[77] Quoted in *Anglicanism*, ed. P. E. More and F. L. Cross, (London, 1935), p. xxviii.

[78] *Conference*, iii. 86.

by some historians as a rigidly doctrinaire High Anglican *pur sang*. Surprising only if one transposes modern labels and categories into Laud's century and ignores the unifying consistency created by the all-pervasive threefold appeal in seventeenth-century Anglicanism. Reason alone is not sufficient and faith is essential for man 'cannot have light enough to see the way to heaven but by grace . . . but this light, when it hath made reason submit itself, clears the eye of reason; *it never puts it out*'.[79] Like Hooker, Laud stresses the function of reason, holding that it has the right to challenge the decisions of Councils. Reconsideration may be necessary, as in the case of the Councils of Rimini and Ephesus.[80] But this is a function of the Church and 'I give no way to any private man to be a judge of a General Council.'[81]

Laud refused the proposition of contemporary Puritans that the Church of Rome was no true Church. He held (and was accused of this 'dangerous' moderation at his trial) that it was a 'true Church' because it accepts the Scriptures and the Sacraments but not a 'right Church' because it had not maintained the faith once for all delivered but had added to it.[82] This tolerance (in the terms of those times) is reflected also in a generosity of attitude to the intellectual problems of individual believers and his use of the word 'latitude' as against Fisher's claim of a 'one soul-saving faith' guaranteed by an infallible Church is prophetic and looks forward to his future admirer, Stillingfleet the Latitudinarian. At the close of his book, Laud writes:

There is a latitude in faith, especially in reference to different men's salvation; but to set a bound to this, and strictly to define it—Just thus far you must believe in every particular, or incur damnation—is no work for my pen . . . for though the foundation be one and the same in all, yet a 'latitude' there is, and a large one too, when you come to consider, not the foundation common to all, but things necessary to many particular men's salvation . . . for the gifts of God, both ordinary and extraordinary, to particular men are so various . . . nor will I ever take upon me to express that tenet or opinion, the denial of the foundation only excepted, which may shut any Christian, the meanest, out of heaven.

Significantly for our subject, the maintaining of the Church in the

---

[79] Ibid. x. 292.
[80] Ibid. x. ff.
[81] Ibid. xiv. 419.
[82] Ibid. vii. 145–6.

truth, Laud laments the 'miserable rent in the Church' and adds 'nor is he a Christian, that would not have unity, might he have it with truth'.[83]

As we take brief note of what is distinctive about the Latitudinarian approach we see Stillingfleet structuring his argument along the lines of the familiar threefold appeal but displaying a certain shift of emphasis indicated by the very title of the book, *A Rational Account*.[84] This agreed basis is common to Laudians and Latitudinarians alike, Stillingfleet pressing the appeal to antiquity as vigorously as does Herbert Thorndike. The standard of assay is 'Scripture, reason, or the consent of the Primitive Church'.[85] The shift of emphasis is discernible first in the style and Stillingfleet adopts that popularized by the Royal Society, 'to join clearness of expression with evidence of reason'.[86] In the second place, there is a subtle difference of handling the material in that he does not have recourse to the Fathers as to a dictionary of antiquity but in order to ascertain their method. His purpose is to show that they too proceeded by way of rational inference and by the use of Scripture as definitive for fundamentals. This he does by means of numerous patristic references, not hesitating to point out that 'nothing ought to be looked on as an article of faith among the Fathers but what they declare that they believe on account of Divine revelation.'[87] The difference as compared with Laud is that, while both he and Stillingfleet are desirous of showing that they and the Fathers held the same view of the relationship of Scripture to fundamentals and shared the same method of proceeding by way of rational inference from the evidence, the times in which Stillingfleet lived had made more urgent the mutual relationship of authority and reason. Thus Stillingfleet takes the question, discussed in the *Conference*, of 'the resolution of faith' as the major question in an unsettling age of new discoveries.[88] For him (and here

---

[83] Ibid. xiv. 422–3.

[84] *A Rational Account of the Grounds of the Protestant Religion: Being a Vindication of the Lord Archbishop of Canterbury's Relation of a Conference, and c. from the pretended Answer by T.C.* (1664).

[85] Stillingfleet, *A Rational Account* (1681 edn.), ii. 41. In what follows I depend on the fuller analysis of Stillingfleet's theology in my *The Spirit of Anglicanism*, pp. 387–94.

[86] *A Rational Account*, preface.

[87] Ibid. 595, and cf. the statement that it is not 'enough to prove that one or two Fathers did speak something tending to it, but that all who had occasion to mention it, did speak of it as the doctrine of the Church' (p. 596).

[88] Ibid. 188–9.

we see the Latitudinarian emphasis) no solution is possible which discounts the function of reason: 'when we speak thereof of the resolving of faith, we mean, what are the rational inducements to believe.' There is a confusion here, he insists, between the way in which 'saving faith is wrought in us' and the 'rational inducements which do incline the mind to a firm assent'—a confusion between the 'efficient cause' and the 'grounds of faith'. Any discussion of the resolution of faith implies that in this context faith means 'a rational and discursive act of the mind'. It is 'an assent upon evidence' and he concludes that 'this account which men are able to give why they do believe, or on what ground they do it, is that which we call resolving faith.'[89] True, tradition is validly part of the equation, but 'reason partly makes use of the Church's Tradition, not in any notion of infallibility, but merely as built on principles common to human nature.'[90] Hooker echoes down the intervening decades in the phrase 'But still as the assent is, so the evidence must be.'[91]

We are made aware that authority in religion is here being considered in a part of the century which is intellectually moving on from Bacon and Sir Thomas Browne, through Descartes and Hobbes, Glanvill, and Boyle, into the atmosphere and climate of opinion with which the Royal Society would become synonymous. In fact, one may recall that Thomas Sprat's *History of the Royal Society*, so illuminating in this respect, was first published only three years after Stillingfleet's *Rational Account*.

We discern also the ancestry of that view of authority as maintaining the Church in the truth by means of a threefold appeal in which reason moves freely, and decisively, and which was set down by Lambeth 1968:

To such a threefold inheritance of faith belongs a concept of authority which refuses to insulate itself against the testing of history and the free action of reason. It seeks to be a credible authority and therefore is concerned to secure satisfactory historical support and to have its credentials in a shape which corresponds to the requirements of reason.

Throughout the consideration of this subject it has to be kept constantly in mind as was stressed at the beginning of this essay that what is under discussion is authority *in the Church*. What is central

---

[89] Ibid.
[90] Ibid. 267.
[91] Ibid. 129.

to the Church is not authority but the life of Jesus, the risen Lord, which makes the Church his body, the members of which live through a Life not their own. Thus, the Christian life is the life of Christ continuing in the members of his body: 'I live, yet not I, but Christ lives in me.' Authority is explicable only as it relates to Christ from whom all authority in the Church derives, and as it relates to the spiritual formation of the members in Christ—hence the importance of authority's function in respect of the Church's proclamation of the truth of the Gospel. Without true doctrine which is the understanding and explication of the faith once for all delivered, that proclamation cannot be authentically made by the Church, the *testis et conservatrix*. To this end authority is the means through its human and ecclesial instruments and instrumentalities though these can never stand by themselves alone since authority in the Church is ultimately a function of the Spirit abiding in the Church, acting in and through the one body, 'the pillar and bulwark of the truth'.

Envoi

In 1979 Hans Küng published a theological meditation on aspects of the subject which we have been examining.[92] Not only the title, *The Church Maintained in the Truth*, but the approach and the handling of the problems involved commend themselves to Anglicans who are conscious of the tradition sketched in outline in this essay. Küng is asking the same questions, What is Christian truth and how is the Church established and maintained in that truth? His answers, for the large part, chime with those examined in the preceding pages. The normative criterion by which the people of God are maintained in the truth is Scripture and the second factor is tradition. There is the same assessment of Councils as that which we have been examining and the Spirit's abiding in the Church is central: 'The Church does not keep itself in the truth. It *is* maintained: by God, through Jesus Christ, in the Spirit.'[93] The whole meditation moves by the process of applying criteria in freedom, the process which we have been analysing in the Anglican tradition. It is a matter of verifi-

---

[92] H. Küng, *The Church Maintained in the Truth* (Eng. trans., SCM Press; London, 1980).
[93] Ibid. 21.

cation, of answering the question, What is our authority for the identification of true and authentic doctrine:

The first thing to be noticed is that recent teaching on infallibility is faced with quite serious difficulties when it comes to verification. Even if I accept infallible propositions as a fact, the question arises as to why these statements are true. Certainly their truth does not follow from their infallibility. Even according to the usual teaching, dogmas are not true because they have been defined; they are defined because they are true. Why then are they true?[94]

This is the question which is central to the purpose and functioning of authority in the Church.

[94] Ibid. 39.

14

Authority in Church and State
Reflections on the Coronation of Louis XVI

JOHN MCMANNERS

ON Friday, 9 June 1775, Louis XVI came to Reims for the *Sacre*, the ceremony of his coronation. The civilian militia paraded outside the city gates, where the provincial governor, the duc de Bourbon, and the municipal officers in scarlet gowns met him. The king changed over from his huge travelling coach to a gala carriage, all glass, paintings, and embroidery, surmounted by plumes. Salvoes of artillery were fired and the bells pealed as he was escorted to the cathedral square between the ranks of the Gardes Françaises in their blue, white, and red uniforms.[1] The bishops of the ecclesiastical province, led by the Archbishop of Reims, Cardinal La Roche-Aymon, met Louis in the shadow of the vast ornate façade of the cathedral. The cardinal was old and feeble, but he had girded himself to preside over the ceremonies of the coming days, when an Archbishop of Reims was the most prestigious figure in France after the king. A mediocre and compliant man ('on ne se brouille pas avec moi'[2]), he had risen to monopolize the greatest ecclesiastical offices and sinecures Versailles could confer: *grand aumônier du Roi*, holder of the *feuille des bénéfices* and the titular abbacy of Saint-Germain, as well as the prelacy of Reims. The king knelt before the bishops to receive aspersion with holy water and to kiss the Gospel book. A *Te Deum* was sung, then the royal cortège adjourned to the episcopal palace for loyal harangues. On the Saturday evening, the king attended a sermon. With apostolic rigour and fashionable reformist zeal, Boisgelin, Archbishop of Aix, preached on the duties of rulers; Louis commended him, though the Court did not allow his liberal sentiments to be published.[3]

---

[1] Blue coats, white breeches, red stockings, red facings on waistcoats, white belts ('Les Gardes Françaises à Versailles', *Rev. de l'hist. de Versailles et de Seine-et-Oise* (1915), 10). Other details in Claude Manceron, *Les Hommes de la liberté*, 2 vols. (1972), i. 208, and P. de Nolhac, *La Reine Marie-Antoinette* (1948), 97–102.

[2] Véri, *Journal*, ed. J. de Witte, 2 vols. (n.d.) i. 68. Cf. Mme du Deffand to the duchesse de Choiseul, 25 Feb. 1772.

[3] J. Gog, *A Reims, le Sacre des Rois de France* (1980), 95.

The coronation took place on 11 June, Trinity Sunday. The Gothic aspect of the cathedral interior was masked by tapestry draping the pillars, by statues and ornaments, and by a lofty wood-work of Corinthian orders with richly gilded fluting and grooving, encasing the walls of the choir. Above the royal throne was a cupola of violet velvet drapery. An orchestra of a hundred players was concealed behind the altar. The canons of Reims were in their stalls, for they had a prescriptive right to their own places. On the epistle side of the choir were packed ministers of state, high ecclesiastics and nobles of the robe; on the gospel side, peers, marshals of France, and wearers of the *Cordon bleu*. The duc de Croÿ made a quick check to ensure that no one had manœuvred into a higher place than his rank justified: 'qu'il n'y avait point d'embarras pour le rang:[4] Ensconced among the reverend canons was the twenty-one-year-old Charles-Maurice, abbé de Périgord, on the first stage of an ecclesiastical career forced on him by his family because of his lameness. His uncle, the coadjutor of Reims, had arranged a canonry for him five weeks before, barely a month after he had been made a subdeacon.[5] In his memoirs, the young abbé says nothing about the *Sacre* except that the festivities gave him the opportunity to cultivate the friendship of three influential ladies of the Court.[6] Within fifteen years of hearing the king at Reims swearing to defend the privileges of the Church, Charles-Maurice, now bearing the name of Talleyrand and Bishop of Autun, was to propose the sale of ecclesiastical property in the revolutionary assembly, and within thirty years he was to wear the splendid habit of *Grand Chambellan* at the coronation of Napoleon, and to parade in the same office at the coronation of the last Bourbon king twenty-one years later still.

Everyone was in place by 7 o'clock in the morning. Then, a procession set off down the newly constructed covered way to the archbishop's palace to bring back the king—the *grand maître des cérémonies*, the canons of Reims, players of music, and the Bishops of Laon and Beauvais. The precentor of the cathedral hammered on the door. 'Que demandez-vous?' 'Nous demandons le roi.' 'Le roi

---

[4] The maréchal de Croÿ, *Journal 1718–1784*, ed. Le Vicomte de Grouchy and P. Cottin, 4 vols. (1906), iii. 173.

[5] L. S. Greenbaum, *Talleyrand, Statesman-Priest* (1970), 18.

[6] *Mémoires du prince de Talleyrand*, ed. the duc de Broglie, 5 vols. (1891–2), i. 24. Otherwise, just the vague 'tout était amour! tout était fêtes!'

dort.' But at the third time of asking—'Nous demandons Louis XVI que Dieu nous a donné pour roi'—the door was opened.[7]

The king in a silver cloak over a crimson shirt and wearing a black velvet hat adorned with diamonds was brought to the cathedral and set before the altar. Holy water was sprinkled over him and the prayer was said: 'God almighty and eternal, who hast elevated to the kingdom thy servant Louis, grant that he may ensure the good of his subjects in all the course of his reign, and never depart from the paths of justice and of truth.'[8]

The *Veni Creator* was sung while the Archbishop of Reims proceeded to the cathedral porch to meet the procession of the *Sainte Ampoule*.[9] The holy oil for the king's anointing, brought down from heaven by a dove at the prayer of Saint-Rémy for the baptism of Clovis, was kept in the *Sainte Ampoule*, a tiny crystal flask silvered inside and carried, for safety's sake, in a golden holder shaped like a dove, enamelled white with red beak and claws. The revered object was brought to the cathedral by the *grand prieur* of the abbey of Saint-Rémy, riding a white horse and dressed in a golden cope. He was sheltered by a canopy borne aloft by the four *chevaliers de la Sainte Ampoule* (vassals of fiefs of the abbey), and at each corner rode the *barons otagers*, hostages for the safe return of the flask, dressed in cloth of gold, each escorted by a groom. Ahead of the *grand prieur* went his monks in white albs and the Minims with their cross, and ahead of them marched a military escort of musketeers with their band, and first of all, a rustic guard of the men of the parish of Le Chesne, dressed in blue, wearing gaiters, with cockades and oak leaves in their hats, muskets on shoulder. This was their peculiar privilege, for their ancestors in the village had preserved the *Sainte Ampoule* from destruction in the Hundred Years War.

The coronation service began with the king taking the oaths. He promised to 'preserve the canonical privilege, law and justice due' to the 'bishops and the churches committed to their charge', to preserve all Christian people in peace, to prevent rapine and iniquity, to

---

[7] Account in the *Corresp. secrète*, conveniently given in A. Chéruel, *Dict. historique des institutions, mœurs et coutumes de la France*, 2 vols. (1855), ii. 1118.

[8] Ibid. 1119.

[9] See 'Journal anonyme', ed. H. Jadart, *Trav. Acad. Nat. Reims*, 110 (1902), 269–315. For description of the sacred object and for its final fate, Laurent, 'Le Conventionnel Rühl à Reims: La destruction de la Sainte Ampoule', *Ann. hist. de la Révolution Française*, 3 (1926).

be merciful and equitable in judgement and to do all in his power 'to exterminate, in all lands subjected to my rule, the heretics declared to be so by the Church' ('nommément condamnés par l'Église').[10]

The Bishops of Laon and Beauvais then asked the congregation if it received its king, and respectful silence ensued; Louis then took the oath to preserve the two great Orders of Chivalry—that of the Saint-Esprit and that of Saint-Louis—and to enforce the edicts against duelling (a solemn gesture against aristocratic lawlessness introduced by Louis XIV).

The king had made his promises, and he was now invested with the first instalment of the panoply of office.[11] The spurs (which came from the early days of the Capetian monarchy), the sword (supposedly that of Charlemagne, though the oldest part, the hilt, with two winged heads guarding the tree of life, dated only from the eleventh century), the long sceptre (surmounted by an effigy of Charlemagne, though dating only from the high Middle Ages), lay on the altar. Between coronations, these regalia were kept in the Parisian abbey of Saint-Denis, whose abbot was in proud attendance, standing by his treasures. The senior lay peer affixed the spurs, and the archbishop girded on the sword, after solemnly consecrating it to noble deeds. The king held it, drawn, while an anthem was sung; thereafter it was borne before him by a nobleman for the rest of the ceremony.

Kneeling on a vast carpet of violet velvet scattered with golden fleurs-de-lis, the king received the seven unctions. A drop of resin from the *Saint Ampoule* was taken out on a golden needle and mixed with the *sainte chrême*, the oil used in the cathedral for baptisms, confirmations, and ordinations. What was left on the patten after the ceremony was returned to the flask, so the supply of the sacred balm would continue to be available at the coronations of kings of France for all time.[12] The six ecclesiastical peers stood around; the Archbishop of Reims, assisted by the Bishop of Laon, administered the unctions; the prelates of Beauvais, Langres, Châlons, and Noyon arrayed their monarch in a tunic and dalmatic, vestments of a priestly type. Then came the unctions on the palms, unctions appropriate for a bishop. The great ermine-braided mantle

---

[10] Full wording in Chéruel, ii. 1119.

[11] Gog, p. 65.

[12] Croÿ, iii. 184; A. N. Duchesne, 'Relation d'un voyage à Reims à l'occasion du Sacre', *Trav. Acad. Reims*, 108 (1902), 48.

was thrown over the king's shoulders, and he was then given the remaining symbols of office, the sceptre, the ring, and the *main de justice*.

It was time to call in the laity. The *Garde des Sceaux* invited the lay peers to assemble, summoning them for the occasion under the archaic titles of dukes of Normandy, Burgundy, and Aquitaine, and counts of Toulouse, Flanders, and Champagne—evoking the memories of the war lords who had built the West in distant centuries, oddly contrasting with the present luxurious generation: the king's two brothers, and the duc d'Orléans and his son the duc de Chartres, and the prince de Condé and his son the duc de Bourbon.[13]

Then came the actual coronation. The Archbishop of Reims took the crown from the altar and placed it on the royal brow. All the peers, ecclesiastical and lay, gathered round and put out a hand to steady it. Crowned and vested with the garments and insignia of office, Louis moved off to his throne. As he sat there, the archbishop, now mitre-less, paid him the homage of a kiss and cried 'Vivat rex in aeternum!'—a cry which was re-echoed by all the peers. This was the signal for unrestrained public rejoicing. The air thundered with fanfares of trumpets, the crash of artillery and the pealing of all the bells of the city, and the great doors of the cathedral were flung open to let the people surge in to catch a glimpse of their ruler on his throne, adorned with the diadem of Charlemagne.[14] Among them (or was he stranded in the throng in the streets outside?) was an ugly sixteen-year-old playing truant from school at Troyes; on his return, he was to write a well-informed essay on the *Sacre* for his teacher, an early venture into eloquence by Georges-Jacques Danton.[15]

There were lengthy prayers and the *Te Deum* was sung, a prelude to the celebration of the coronation mass—dramatically a quiet anticlimax to the ceremony, spiritually, the true heart of it. The king recognized his insignificance and mortality by taking off his crown

---

[13] Chéruel, ii. 1120. The archaic titles had been annexed to the Crown, and the king nominated the six relatives who were to bear them (*Encyclopédie, ou dictionnaire raisonné des Sciences, des Arts et des Métiers*, xiv (1765), 476, s.v. 'Sacre'). The sardonic comment is Manceron's, p. 215.

[14] In fact, a crown made in the late 12th century for a queen. An identical one for the king had been stolen.

[15] H. Destainville, 'La jeunesse de Danton', *Ann. hist. de la Révolution Française*, 5 (1928), 427–8.

when the Gospel was read, then the Church received him into the circle of its chosen ministry by giving him communion in both kinds, a prerogative of the clergy.

As the royal procession left the cathedral, hundreds of little birds were released from their cages to flutter under the vaults, and the heralds scattered commemorative medals among the people.

Though the comte d'Artois and some libertine nobles had laughed and gossiped,[16] the overwhelming impression was one of splendour, dignity, and rejoicing, a vast pageant of national loyalty. As she saw her husband crowned, Marie-Antoinette had broken down and wept. It was astonishing, she reflected, that the king should be so received by his people only two months after starvation had driven so many into riot; we must work for their happiness, she wrote to the Empress her mother. It had been a day she would never forget. 'Je sais bien que je n'oublierai de ma vie (dût-elle durer cent ans) la journée du Sacre.'[17] The royal couple were drawn together; Louis by the sight of her tears, Marie-Antoinette by the vision of his great calling; but the attraction lasted but a day, and desire failed.

Cardinal La Roche-Aymon, sustained through the rigours of the long ceremonial by coffee and stimulants, ended the day feeling fine. Solicitously, the king asked him if he was tired. 'O non, Sire! prêt à recommencer'; a fatuous answer which delighted the courtiers for long afterwards.[18]

From henceforth, Louis, the Lord's anointed, was endowed with the power of healing the victims of scrofula. Renan was to exaggerate when he described the 'touching' for 'the king's evil' as the 'eighth sacrament', but it was true enough that the monarch, once crowned, was regarded as the channel of divine mercy (he could act only if he was in a state of grace and had received communion). Three days after the *Sacre*, on 14 June, a procession[19] set off for the abbey of Saint-Rémy, a procession with a military flavour—the Musketeers, the Swiss Guards, the *Chevaux-légers*, and the royal Pages, with Louis on his famous horse 'Vainqueur' (a corpulent

---

[16] De Nolhac, p. 102; Duchesne, 'Relation', p. 47; Croÿ, iii. 188.

[17] Marie-Antoinette in *Corresp. secrète entre Marie-Thérèse et le Cte de Mercy-Argenteau avec les lettres de Marie-Thérèse et Marie-Antoinette*, ed. A. d'Arneth and M. A. Geffroy, 3 vols. (1875), ii. 343. For the queen's tears etc. see Mercy d'Argenteau's letter, p. 346.

[18] F. Masson, *Le Cardinal de Bernis depuis son ministère, 1758–94* (1884), 193 n.

[19] Manceron, pp. 223–5.

young man, but a fearless horseman, he looked his best in the saddle). The Benedictines of Saint-Rémy had gathered a multitude of sufferers from miles around into various hospitals awaiting the great day—there were many, alas, for the tumours massed behind ears and under jaws were the effect of malnutrition. The scrofulous were gathered together in the open air, 1,000, perhaps 2,000 of them. The task of touching was repulsive. The royal person was protected, in so far as the head of each scrofulous person was held by a doctor, and the supplicant hands were clasped within the gloved hands of the Captain of the Guard, but the day was hot and the vast assembly stank. Louis was relieved to complete the exhausting round and wash in vinegar and water scented with orange blossom.[20]

The message of the *Sacre* was: the king's power comes from God. His servants only open the door to the summons to attend the cathedral when the formula is used 'whom God has given us for king'. The symbols of office (the spurs excepted) are handed over by the ecclesiastical peers; even the sword is a gift from God. More than this, the king is a sacerdotal figure. The anointings, the priestly vestments, the reception of the sacrament in both kinds, the gift of healing and, perhaps, some minor details; the hands of the bishops outstretched to steady the crown, the sceptre as long as a bishop's pastoral staff—all imply that he belongs to the ranks of the clerical estate, those whose peculiar vocation comes intensely, uniquely and directly from heaven. Being called by God and instituted by God's servants, however, brings special obligations; the sovereign solemnly swears to preserve the privileges of the ecclesiastical order and to suppress heresy. Throne and altar are allied and interdependent. The prayers,[21] a richly layered historical accumulation, place the monarch in the lineage of Abraham, Moses, David, and Solomon; called by God, favoured by God and exercising power in the shadow of the Divine authority. The manifold intercessions have a threefold emphasis. First, the king is exhorted to fulfil his obligations, and God is implored to help him to do so. Louis is told that he must govern his passions, set a good example and be magnanimous. May he be a defender of the Church, a 'munificent patron' of ecclesiastical foundations; may he drive out 'false Christians, enem-

---

[20] Croÿ, iii. 203–5.
[21] Liturgy given in full in Gog, pp. 61–88.

ies of the name of Jesus Christ and heretics'. To all, he must give impartial justice, and he must wreak vengeance on the unjust. To the 'princes and seigneurs' of his realm, he must be 'liberal and kind', but his most especial solicitude must be shown to the poor, pilgrims, widows, and orphans. Secondly, the Church reciprocates by calling down on the king the blessings of heaven, in this life and the next. No less than twelve prayers ask for the boon of eternal felicity in the after life. But an equal number ask for the overthrow of his enemies in this (including the famous archaic supplication for the strength of the rhinoceros). Six petitions ask for the king to be granted a long life; others ask that he be given forgiveness for his sins, be delivered from infirmity, and that his descendants may reign for long after him. Thirdly, the prayers ask for material blessing to be shed upon the people of the kingdom. There are several references to the blessing of peace, one specific appeal for the multiplication of population, and two appeals (in the words of the blessings in the Old Testament) for the dew of heaven, the fatness of the earth, and an abundance of corn and oil for the consolation of the people.

The *Sacre* was too solemn a national institution to be ridiculed, but anti-clericals and lawyers were not prepared to allow the clergy to make capital out of the manifestly religious implications of the ceremonies. A journalist heaved a sigh of relief when he described how the lay peers were finally summoned to come forward: 'here is the moment when the clergy ceases to attribute to itself the right of conferring unlimited power on the king.' To his disillusioned eye, the unctions and the arrayal in sacerdotal vestments was the supreme moment for clerical pretensions—'symbols by which the order of clergy seeks, no doubt, to prove it is united to the royal power'.[22] He was right; the unctions could imply a certain subordination of the monarch—as the Epistle to the Hebrews had said, 'the less is blessed of the better'. And in France, as distinct from England, it was accepted that the king could not exercise his healing touch until he became the Lord's anointed.[23] Laymen, therefore preferred not to enthuse over this aspect of the liturgical observances. Scholars, in the safe obscurity of Latin, had doubts about the provenance of the *Sainte Ampoule* and the story of the dove.[24]

---

[22] Chéruel, ii. 1120.
[23] M. Bloch, *Les Rois thaumaturges*, Eng. trans. by J. E. Anderson, *The Royal Touch* (1973), 126–8.
[24] Jean-Jacques Chifflet, *Tractatus de sancta Ampulla Remensi*, cit. Gog, p. 20.

Voltaire could not see how 'a few drops of oil' made any difference to an essentially secular ceremony[25]—in fact, the clergy did not claim that they did in so far as the rights of sovereignty were concerned.[26]

Those who had reservations about the unctions went even further in their scepticism about the magical touch of kings.[27] Saint-Simon has a story, untrue and evilly sardonic, about Mme de Soubise being the mistress of Louis XIV, yet dying from scrofula. Montesquieu was ironical in the *Lettres Persanes*; the *Encyclopédie* expressed disbelief; Voltaire urged the French monarchs to follow the example of William of Orange and renounce the claim to work miracles.[28] At the beginning of the reign of Louis XV the formula was indeed changed, from the absolute 'Dieu te guérit' to the hopeful 'Dieu te guérisse', and from 1739 onwards, Louis XV's private life ensured that he was disqualified from exercising healing powers. On Christmas Day 1736 he communicated and touched for the king's evil according to usage; the next Christmas, 'illness' provided an excuse to do neither. His last Easter duty was performed in 1738, and there was scandal in 1739 when he did not call the scrofulous to appear before him on the Easter Saturday.[29] Thus there was a gap of 36 years before Louis XVI touched the sick after his coronation. Three or four certificates about people he had cured were welcomed at Versailles, but it is doubtful if he convoked any further ceremonies of healing.

To the lawyers, the essential, decisively anti-clerical point about the coronation was: whatever else the clergy bestowed upon the monarch in the name of God, they certainly did not make him king. From the end of the thirteenth century, the legal beginning of a

---

[25] Letter of 18 June 1740 to Frederick II, in *Corresp.*, ed. Besterman, x (1954), 161 (Letter 2110).

[26] B. Plongeron, *Théologie et politique au siècle des lumières, 1770–1820* (1973), 64–5.

[27] For a defence of the royal power see Regnault, *Dissertation touchant le pouvoir accordé aux Rois de France de guérir les Escroüelles, accompagnée de preuves touchant la vérité de la Sainte Ampoule* (1722). Regnault was a canon of Saint-Symphorien of Reims.

[28] Bloch, p. 224. See also Voltaire, *Mœurs*, Introduction. No less a celebrity than Jansenius had pointed out that the curing of King's evil demonstrated only God's gifts, not a king's right to rule. Balaam's ass had prophesied, but had no right to dominate other animals: R. E. Mousnier, *The Institutions of France under the Absolute Monarchy, 1598–1789*, i. Eng. trans. by B. Pearce (1974) 675.

[29] *Mémoires du duc de Luynes sur la cour de Louis XV*, ed. L. Dussieux and E. Soulié, 11 vols. (1860–5), i. 116–17, 154, 426. E.-J.-F. Barbier, *Chronique de la Régence et du règne de Louis XV, 1718–1763*, 8 vols. (1857–8), iii. 167.

royal reign was dated from the accession, not from the *Sacre*.[30] Skilfully taking the ceremonies as a whole and avoiding precise language
so as to give little opportunity for magnifying the role of the
Church, Chancelier d'Aguesseau defined what he supposed were
the religious implications: 'Kings protest publicly before the altar
that it is by God that they reign . . . the people, receiving the king in
a fashion (*en quelque manière*) from the hands of God, are more
disposed . . . to revere and obey him, not only by motives of fear or
hope, but by a sentiment and principle of religion.'[31] Similarly, the
Encyclopédie, welcoming the legal point that the king ruled already
by his birth and right of succession, treated the *Sacre* as a pictur-
esque parable to instruct the multitude. 'Doubtless, the object of
this pious ceremony is to teach the people, by a striking spectacle,
that the king's person is sacred, and threats against his life are forbidden because, as the Scripture says of Saul, he is the *Lord's
anointed*.'[32]

Apart from minimizing the importance of the religious aspects of
the *Sacre* in general, on two specific points men of the Enlightenment accused the clergy of impropriety. One concerned an omission—deliberate or accidental we cannot know—from the
traditional usages.[33] After the two bishops had asked the congregation if it received its king, the silence that ensued ought to have
been followed by the announcement of the Archbishop of Reims:
'quia populus acclamavit te, te sacro regem'—a formula transmitted
from prelate to prelate since Saint-Rémy. A substantial volume published later in the year, *Le Sacre royal ou les droits de la nation française reconnus et confirmés par cette cérémonie*, declared that the
omission was engineered by a 'party of reaction', a conspiracy
which included the higher clergy. Other pamphleteers took up the
theme, the monarchy they argued, was founded on a social contract,
to which the people in general gave formal assent. There were similar sentiments in the account of the *Sacre* given by a radical journalist at the point where he described how the peers, lay and

---

[30] Durand de Maillane, *Dict. de droit canonique et de pratique bénéficiale*, 3rd
edn. (Lyons, 1776), v. 225, s.v. 'Sacre'.
[31] D'Aguesseau, *Essai d'une institution du droit public*, ed. L. Rigaud (1955), 123.
[32] *Encyclopèdie*, xiv. 476.
[33] K. M. Baker, 'French Political Thought at the Accession of Louis XVI', *J. Mod.
Hist.* 50 (1978), 279–81. For Baker's view of the background, the 'new political culture' arising at the end of the *ancien régime*, see his 'On the Problem of the Ideological Origins of the French Revolution', in D. La Capra and S. L. Kaplan (eds.),
Modern European Intellectual History (1982), 197–219.

ecclesiastical, put out their hands to touch the crown—'a truly noble and expressive allegory, but one which would be much more appropriate if delegates of the people also joined in supporting the crown with the same allegorical implication'.[34]

The second point of criticism concerned the maintenance of a traditional observance which enlightened opinion regarded as no longer civilized—the oath to extirpate heresy. In the space of the three generations since Louis XIV, the persecutions had died away and the law courts had found ways and means of—virtually—giving civil rights to Protestants.[35] Turgot urged the young king to take a revised form of coronation oath: 'I promise God and my people to govern my kingdom with justice according to the laws; never to wage war except in a just and indisputable cause; to employ all my authority to maintain the rights of each of my subjects; and to work all my life to render them as happy as is in my power.'[36] Louis was sympathetic, but in the end he dared not do it—he mumbled the offensive formula almost inaudibly. The Assemblies of Clergy continued their hollow exhortations for action against heretics; 'under the government of a monarch', they argued, 'troubles are practically always inseparable from the diversity of religious opinions', and the coronation oath was 'the foundation of public peace', with its obligations to 'enforce morality and protect religion'.[37] When, in 1787, the long overdue grant of civil rights to Protestants was made, the clergy mostly acquiesced, though there were protests that Louis had betrayed his mission and broken his promises. In January 1788 the Bishop of Dol scandalously used the opportunity of a Breton delegation to Versailles to denounce his sovereign to his face. Constantine, Theodosius, and Charlemagne, he declared, would have convoked a National Council of the Church before embarking on a measure 'that threatened the collapse of the arches of the sanctuary'.[38]

---

[34] *Corresp. secrète* in Chéruel, ii. 1120.

[35] D. Bien, 'Catholic Magistrates and Protestant Marriage', *French Historical Studies* 2/4 (1962), 409–25. For the neat legal arguments used see Guyot, *Répertoire universel et raisonné de jurisprudence civile, criminelle, canonique et bénéficiale*, 64 vols. (1775–83)+14 vols. (1786), iii (1782), 318–39.

[36] D. Dakin, *Turgot* (1939), 217–21.

[37] M. Peronnet, 'Les Assemblées du Clergé de France sous le règne de Louis XVI, 1775–1788', *Ann. hist. de la Révolution Française*, 34 (1962), 29, 31.

[38] Ch. Robert, *Urban de Hercé, dernier évêque de Dol* (1900), 162–3, 183. Only one bishop, that of La Rochelle, forbade his clergy to assist with the application of the Edict of 1787: B. Plongeron, 'Recherches sur l'Aufklärung catholique en Europe

The coronation was the symbol of the indissoluble alliance between Church and State, an alliance that was a commonplace of ecclesiastical eloquence.[39] There was a long-established tradition in Christian political theory—which included Aquinas—authorizing resistance to tyrants; in 1663, the Sorbonne had defended the possibility of launching an excommunication against a godless, evil ruler. But by the end of the seventeenth century in France, this tradition had been repudiated. Memories of the murders of Henri III and Henri IV and the civil wars were never far from the minds of Frenchmen. The Third Estate of the Estates General of 1614 had declared that the king could not be deposed by the Church and subjects could not be released from their allegiance. This declaration was accepted by the Assembly of Clergy of 1682 as the first of its Four Gallican Articles, to be taught in all universities, colleges, and seminaries.[40] The Assemblies of Clergy in 1750 and 1756 renewed the formal statement that Christians were not entitled to revolt. In the Gallican Church, loyalty to the person of the monarch took precedence even over the sacredness of the confessional. In his oath of allegiance, a bishop swore he would not take part in any treasonable design, 'and if any such comes to my notice, I will make it known to your majesty.'[41] The law books define what was involved: the only case in which the seal of the confessional could be broken was when a crime of 'lèze majesté au premier chef' was involved.[42]

By contrast to their doctrine of unqualified loyalty, the clergy never ceased to proclaim—and the ceremonies of the Sacre were their warrant—that the king was under the judgement of God. God would judge him according to the way he fulfilled his obligations. The listing of these obligations, implicit in the coronation liturgy and formulated by Bossuet, carried on through the century. The

occidentale, 1770–1830', *Rev. d'hist. mod. et contemp.* 16 (1969), 580; A. Lods, 'L'attitude du clergé catholique à l'égard des Protestants en 1789', *Rev. française*, 33 (1897), 128–30.

[39] e.g. the Jesuit Charles de Neuville preaching before Louis XV: 'God subjects peoples to the authority of kings, and the authority of kings ought to keep the peoples submissive to God' (A. Bernard, *Le Sermon au xviiie siècle* (1901), 276–7). Pastoral letters of bishops greeting the birth of a new prince use New Testament phrases about the incarnation of the Saviour: A. Sicard, *L'Ancien clergé de France: Les Évêques avant la Révolution* (1912), 185.

[40] Mousnier, *Institutions*, pp. 312–31.

[41] Oath given in full in Durand de Maillane, v. 294; also in F. Masson, *Bernis* (1884), 37.

[42] Guyot, xiv. 254.

monarch had to obey Christian precepts, to observe the fundamental laws of France, to protect the Church, to defend the poor. As a mere man, no better than the others, he ought to be 'submissive to the prelates in the order of religion', and open-hearted to the misery of his fellows.[43] The language of adulation addressed to kings had its ambiguities. 'Vous êtes des Dieux' said Bossuet, but he is quoting the psalm in which God speaks to unjust judges: 'Ye are gods . . . nevertheless ye shall die like men and fall like one of the princes.' Ironically, Bossuet thunders on, 'Oh Gods of flesh and blood, Gods of dust and mud', you will die—the only thing that is godlike and continuous is your authority; 'the man dies . . . but the king, as we say, never dies, the image of God is immortal.'[44]

It is then, authority that endures, and is the true image of God. Much loyal rhetoric was devoted to declaring that 'Religion and the State fall with the king'—so Boisgelin proclaimed before Louis XVI in December 1790, with the shadow of revolution hanging over them.[45] But such statements were leaving a great theological truth unsaid: the Church had an eternal mission, and if the State lost its monarchical organization, the Church would go on. Bergier, the greatest French theologian of the century, answering the question 'what is the source of all authority', declared that God did not give power as a personal gift to a ruler; he created men with reciprocal rights and duties within a social nexus from the very beginning. From this nexus, systems of government arose, and we must accept them, since 'the harshest of governments is a lesser evil than anarchy.'[46] The argument from anarchy is strong, but ambiguous so far as monarchy is concerned; any port will do if the storm is wild enough. The difficulty becomes obvious if we ask why God should prefer monarchy. At the end of the seventeenth century, Quesnel, anxious to demonstrate to Louis XIV that his regal authority had nothing to fear from the Jansenist party, described how the divine Providence presides over the advent of monarchical rule, guiding men when they elect a sovereign, arbitrating on the battlefield when

---

[43] *Politique tirée des propres paroles de l'Écriture Sainte*, ed. J. Lebrun (1967), vi; F.-X.-J. Droz, *Histoire du règne de Louis XVI*, 3 vols. (1839–42), i. 94; P. Girault de Coursac, *L'Éducation d'un roi: Louis XVI* (1977), 37.

[44] Bossuet, *Œuvres oratoires*, ed. J. Lebarq, 6 vols. (1921), iv. 356. Cf. *Politique*, vii/1 (i). The Psalm is 82.

[45] Cit. A. Mathiez, *Rome et le clergé français sous la Constituante* (1911), 460. Cf. Massillon, *Sermon sur les écueils de la piété des grands* (Petit Carême).

[46] Plongeron, *Théologie et politique, 1770–1820* pp. 115–19.

a crown is won by conquest, and—above all—sending to hereditary kings the children destined to succeed them.[47] But what if an election is fraudulent? A victory mere brute force? What of a barren queen or an imbecile heir? Then, we are once more under the threat of the disintegration of society, when the theologian has to fall back on the argument from anarchy. Seventeen years after the coronation of Louis XVI, churchmen would have to dig into the dark, unspoken assumptions behind their political theory, and adjust to a world in revolution. Essentially, it was public order that was sacred; a *de facto* government had to be obeyed.[48]

In the last, unthinkable resort, fulsome loyal rhetoric was gilding a harsh, utilitarian proposition: obey, lest anarchy ensue. More than that, the political theory of churchmen—as also of their rivals, the Gallican lawyers and magistrates—was founded on a paradox. France was a monarchy at once absolute, yet hedged in by convention and vested interest—as was commonly said, it was not a 'despotisme à la Turque'. Taken as a whole, the ceremonies of the Sacre implied a qualification of royal absolutism, rather than an enhancement of it. The actors in the great pageant, from the peers ecclesiastical and lay to the abbots of Saint-Rémy and Saint-Denis, from the canons of Reims to the humble villagers of Le Chesne, played their parts by traditional right and privilege.[49] The lesson was improved by the spectacle of the monarch taking solemn oaths before he was crowned. Louis XV argued he had taken them 'to God alone'; according to the Parlement of Paris, they were taken 'to the nation'.[50] To the coronation oaths, the magistrates added other 'fundamental laws', 'traditions', and 'maxims', and their own right to register royal edicts and make remonstrances—their role, indeed, was to interpret the understandings between monarch and people. As Joly de Fleury declared in 1766, 'it is of the essence of a monarchy that there be intermediary bodies', and the chief of these was to be the Parlement of Paris.[51]

---

[47] R. Taveneaux, *Jansénisme et politique* (1965) 124–33.

[48] Summary of the problem in the Revolution in my *The French Revolution and the Church* (1969), 64–7, 125–9.

[49] Cf. the standard gifts of ecclesiastical ornaments the king was to give to the chapter of Reims, and to Aix-la-Chapelle for the tomb of Charlemagne: *Journal de Papillon de La Ferté (1756–1780)*, ed. E. Boysse (1887), 383–5.

[50] M. Antoine, *Le Conseil du Roi sous le règne de Louis XV* (1970), 7–8.

[51] Ibid. 15–17. On the question of the 'fundamental laws' see J. M. J. Rogister, 'The Crisis of 1753–4 in France and the Debate on the Nature of the Monarchy and

The claim of the Parlements, in the vein of Montesquieu, to be 'intermediary bodies' moderating the raw exercise of despotic power, could equally be echoed by the clergy. The Dauphin, son of Louis XV, was said to have derived this lesson from *L'Esprit des Lois*: 'le pouvoir du Clergé est très convenable; il sert de borne au despotisme sans y opposer de violence.'[52] In their quinquennial Assemblies, the clergy voted their own taxation;[53] they did the collection themselves, and had special tribunals to handle cases of disputed assessment. In the course of the century, they defied attempts of the Crown to subject them to ordinary impositions, and stood firm against royal attempts to influence the elections to their oligarchically constituted Assemblies. In the intervals between formal meetings, the two Agents General watched over clerical interests, and protested at Versailles against every infringement of clerical privileges. Usually, the clergy gave the king the money he asked for, though in a grave crisis of relationships or at a time of national discontent over royal policy, a refusal of supply was possible. The clergy of France, the First Estate of the realm, were at once a pillar of support to the royal absolutism and the most effective pressure group that moderated the exercise of royal power.

The jurists, who were so fond of intermediary bodies to hedge in absolutism, did not extend the benefits of the concept to churchmen. According to them, the secular power, established directly by God, was the sole judge of which matters fell into the temporal sphere, which in the ecclesiastical.[54] From the mid-century 'refusal of sacraments' crisis, the Gallican (and Jansenist) lawyers elaborated

of the Fundamental Laws', in R. Vierhaus (ed.), *Herrschaftsverträge, Wahlkapitulationen, Fundamentalgesetze* (Göttingen, 1977), 105–20.

[52] [Père Henri Griffet, SJ], *Mémoires pour servir à l'histoire de Louis, dauphin . . . avec un traité de la connoissance des hommes fait par ses ordres en 1758*, 2 vols. (1772), i. 124–6.

[53] The Assemblies have been the subject of comprehensive studies. For the 17th century see L. Serbat (1906), P. Blet, 2 vols. (1957), and A. Cans (1910). For the 18th, G. Lepointe (1923), M. C. Peronnet, *Les Évêques de l'ancienne France*, 2 vols. (1977), and E. Besnier, *Les Agents généraux du Clergé spécialement de 1780 à 1785* (1939). For the less well-known special courts, [Jousse], *Traité de la jurisdiction des Officiaux et autres juges d'église, tant en matière civile que criminelle* (1769), esp. pp. 46, 457–8.

[54] 'The temporal power, established directly by God, is absolutely independent . . . it is not the business of ministers of the Church, under whatever pretext, teaching or otherwise, to fix the boundaries God has placed between the two powers': *Parlement*'s formula in *Journal et mémoires de Mathieu Marais*, ed. De Lescure, 4 vols. (1863), iv. 288.

the grounds on which the State could intervene in what might have appeared to be spiritual matters—issues of fact, issues that are external, and those affecting public order are the affair of the secular magistrate.[55] Furthermore, church property was held in *usufruct*, not as ordinary, inalienable property;[56] churchmen constituted the First Estate only in so far as public opinion gave spontaneous admiration to their virtues;[57] their privileges in taxation were allowed by the Crown, rather than derived from fundamental rights.[58]

To these challenges, the Assemblies of the Clergy replied, more particularly in a major protest in 1765, claiming the right of the bishops to speak freely and enforce liturgical discipline, whatever the secular consequences.[59] A great pamphlet controversy followed,[60] Le Franc de Pompignan, Bishop of Le Puy, summarizing the clerical case in 1769 with a demonstration that if the bishops are silenced, doctrine goes by default, and if the State rules on the ecumenical status of Councils, the secular power is manufacturing Christian doctrine itself.[61] This was the high ground of the ecclesiastical argument, the citation of the Church's eternal mission. More prosaically, the clergy claimed a proprietorship, status and privileges existing before feudalism was invented, and before the monarchy itself was constituted;[62] the alliance of Church and Monarchy exemplified in the Sacre was the foundation of the French State. Further, the clergy put forward their own version of the view—as used by the *Parlements* and formulated by Montesquieu—that they themselves

---

[55] Masterly summary of the points at issue in Dale K. Van Kley, *The Damiens Affair and the Unraveling of the Ancien Régime, 1750–1770* (1984), 212.

[56] Guyot, ii. 74–5. A view urged by the *philosophes* (e.g. Voltaire, 'Biens d'Église', in *Dict. philosophique*; Montesquieu, *L'Esprit des lois*, xxv/5; and for Turgot see J. A. Clarke, 'Turgot's Critique of Perpetual Endowments', *French Hist. Studies*, 3 (1963–4), 495–501), and also by Jansenists (E. Mignot, *Traité des droits de l'État et du prince sur les biens possédés par le Clergé*, 6 vols. (1755–7, B. Nat. 8o Ld⁴ 2831).

[57] Guyot, lxix. 5–14. Was the 'First Estate' the clergy, or all 'churchmen', including the laity? See *Dict. de Trévoux*, cit. Berthelot du Chesnay, 'Le Clergé diocésain français au 18ᵉ siècle', *Rev. d'hist. mod. et contemp.* 10 (1963), 24.

[58] Guyot, i. 140–2; xxx. 139–49, 162.

[59] *P.V. Assemblée Générale du Clergé* (1765), viii/2. 425–9.

[60] See Dale K. Van Kley, 'Church State and the Ideological Origins of the French Revolution: The Debate over the General Assembly of the Gallican Clergy in 1765', *Journal of Modern History*, 51 (1979), 629–52.

[61] *Défense des Actes du Clergé de France concernant la religion* (1769); see Van Kley, *Damiens Affair*, pp. 213–4.

[62] Comprehensive statement of the standard arguments in *Mémoires pour le Clergé de France dans l'affaire des foi et hommages, et réponses de l'inspecteur du domaine* (1785, B. Nat. Fo. L⁵ d 529), esp. pp. 9–59, 73, 133, 249–296.

constituted the greatest, most respectable and traditional of the 'intermediary bodies' which supported the Crown and at the same time moderated the exercise of its power. That was why they held their privileges. 'Exemptions are the prerogative of the great corporations in the State. Abolish privileges and you will have either a popular State or a despotic one', said the Assembly of 1785, invoking the authority of *L'Esprit des Lois*.[63] In the second half of the century, the argument was reformulated in accordance with the rising tide of liberal opinions. In the Preface to the collected minutes of the Assemblies published in 1767, the clerical representative and taxation system was termed a 'reste précieux des États Généraux'.[64] In the crisis of 1788, the Assembly of the Clergy, refusing to give the king the enormous sums he was asking, claimed to be speaking for the 'national interest' until the day when the three Estates of the nation could be assembled.[65] It was dangerous to demand the calling of the long-defunct Estates General; like the magistrates of the *Parlements*—their new allies—the prelates of the Assembly of the Clergy were doomed to disillusionment[66] when the king turned to the Third Estate against the traditional 'intermediary bodies' confronting him in an aristocratic *Fronde*.

As a new, liberal epoch dawned, there were two prelates who were dreaming of a transformed role for the Gallican Church in a reformed State. Boisgelin of Aix secretly noted his view that Montesquieu was a fraud: 'intermediary powers in France are but instruments of arbitrary power, and not the safeguard of liberty.' Let churchmen give up all privilege and political power and become a 'corps national', with the sole duty of exhorting to moral conduct.[67] Openly, and less radically, Loménie de Brienne, in his *Mémoire sur les Assemblées Provinciales*,[68] followed Montesquieu in the view of

[63] Peronnet, 'Assemblées du Clergé', p. 30.

[64] *Collection des procès verbaux des Assemblées générales du Clergé de France depuis 1560 jusqu'au présent*, 10 vols. (1767–78), i, Preface.

[65] Peronnet, 'Assemblées du Clergé', p. 32.

[66] 'Tout va se perdre,' said the Bishop of Langres. For this and other gloomy views of the bishops see the brilliant thesis of Dr Nigel Aston, shortly to be published by Oxford University Press, 'The Politics of the French Episcopate, 1786–1791', pp. 179–182 (of the typescript). See also J. Egret, 'La dernière Assembleé du Clergé de France, 1788', *Rev. hist.* 119 (1958), 14–15. Throughout this essay I have benefited greatly from Dr Aston's advice.

[67] 'Réflexions sur l'Esprit des Lois' (1785), 1,200 fos. of manuscript, summarized in E. Lavaquary, *Le Cardinal de Boisgelin, 1732–1804*, 2 vols. (1920), i. 297–303.

[68] Printed in P. Chevalier, *Journal de l'Assemblée des Notables de 1787 par le comte de Brienne et Loménie de Brienne, archevêque de Toulouse* (1960).

France as a monarchy founded on 'honour'. 'Les grands', the great ones of the land, inspired by this principle, defend the people from the abuses of authority and uphold the throne against the fickleness of the people. So, in setting up the new Provincial Assemblies, there must be a clear recognition of distinctions of rank. True, in accordance with the spirit of the times, the Tiers État must have more than a third of the representation, and voting must be in common. 'Je repousse absolument les délibérations par ordres.' But the presidency must be given to 'les grands' and they must give leadership. These great ones are defined as the nobles and the clergy—all the clergy, irrespective of birth or rank. 'Properly speaking, there are only two Estates in France, nobles and non-nobles.'[69] The merits of the clergy, their good education, their hard work, their 'attachment to authority by interest and duty', their friendship with the people and their willingness to tell the truth to the king, and the 'excellency of their functions' generally, give them the right to noble privileges and to belong to 'the great', the leadership cadre of the nation.

This was a defence of the claims of churchmen on Enlightenment principles, but it was unrealistic in treating the clergy as a unified body standing solemnly by to play its role in the new constitutional arrangements. The *Sacre* had been an affair of the great ecclesiastical dignitaries—a procession of monks, and the canons of Reims in their accustomed stalls being a poor substitute for representation of the lower clergy, the *curés* and *vicaires* who did all the pastoral work of the Gallican Church. In 1789, the day of the *curés* came, and in the Estates General, they soon discovered that their place was not with 'les grands', but with the people.

[69] Cf. the same idea in the genealogist Maugard's pamphlet of 1787, cit. Y. Durand, *Les Fermiers généraux au XVIIIe siècle* (1971) 227.

15

Döllinger and Reunion

OWEN CHADWICK

THE Vatican Council decreed the infallibility of the Pope on 18 July 1870. The minority of bishops against the decree had been strong. For a time many people expected that quite a number of them would refuse to submit to the decree and the Council and that a schism was a likely outcome. A schism was the outcome, but it was not to be led by even a single bishop. They all submitted, one by one; some much more slowly than others; some with the maximum of torment in the conscience; some cheerfully making their own private reservations about the meaning of the decree of infallibility.

The theological leader of the opposition, though he did not go to the Council, was Döllinger, the professor of Church History at the University of Munich. He had dedicated many hours and much paper to proving that the Council could not define the Pope as infallible in the way proposed and still remain a Catholic Council. Therefore the eyes of the world were upon him. And the eyes of many Catholic professors in the German Universities also looked towards him. Many of them had fully accepted his opinion that the Council could not decree infallibility and remain a Catholic Council.

The Archbishop of Munich, von Scherr, demanded that Döllinger submit. Probably the demand never had a chance of being met. Döllinger was too committed, and publicly too committed. Nevertheless the interior struggle was long. In his view the bishops had put into the apostolical and traditional faith, to which he was pledged, a new dogma. Some of the best Catholics, even the historian Bishop Hefele of Rottenburg who had had agony over his own submission, pleaded with him to find some way of compromise, so that he might remain a strength to the Catholic Church and work upon it from inside.

Döllinger allowed the time to elapse by which the archbishop demanded his submission. Von Scherr was surprised and asked Rome what to do. Rome in effect refused to give him advice and made it into his decision. He acted high-handedly and too rapidly.

He was dealing with one of the leaders of the Catholic Church in Europe, however unpalatable that fact might be. Perhaps the subsequent history of the Catholic Church might have been different if a Hefele had been Archbishop of Munich at that moment. Von Scherr did not pause. On 17 April 1871 with all due solemnity he excommunicated Döllinger; from the pulpits of Munich cathedral and St Ludwig's Church. Such rapid rigidity was an extraordinary and embittering thing to do, to a priest of such eminent services.

Eight days before, on Easter Sunday, Döllinger assisted at high mass. He would not do so again. He knew himself to be, not a rebel priest, but an excommunicated priest, though wrongly excommunicated. He did not doubt the legal (as distinct from the moral or spiritual) authority of a Christian authority to behave wrongly. This attitude did not please the King of Bavaria and displeased still more his own Bavarian disciples. King Ludwig wanted him to stay on as provost and to continue to behave as if nothing had happened and the State would see that he was not disturbed. Some among his disciples believed that if he had consented to do this he would have carried with him most of the Bavarian Catholic people, with what consequences it would be hard to predict. Probably that judgement was quite mistaken. In any case, Döllinger did not think that he was the leader of a new Church. He thought that he was a wrongly excommunicated Catholic priest.

On 28–30 May 1871 a Munich gathering of Catholics, in majority laymen, met and repudiated the Vatican decrees. They repudiated also the demand of the German bishops from Fulda that they should submit, as an unlawful way of using Christian authority. And they asked for a reform of the Church in such a way that it would be able to reunite the now divided Christian denominations. Döllinger was not present. Confident that their better-known English backers would approve, even though they also were not present, someone added to the list of signatures—getting both signatures slightly wrong—Lord Acton-Dalberg and Sir Blennerhassett. Sir Rowland Blennerhassett promptly wrote to *The Times* to say that these were not authentic signatures. Acton decided to say nothing, lest he seem to repudiate the sentiments of the declaration. But he wanted the *Allgemeine Zeitung* to make the correction. Döllinger put this to the committee and found that they were stiff in their refusal to correct. A correction would help the Vaticanist side. They are satisfied that Blennerhassett had corrected for both names and therefore there could be no bad consequences for Acton in England. Acton, who could be very complicated, if not oversubtle, in such matters, denied that he had done any such thing as to withdraw his signature.[1]

By the summer of 1871 the Old Catholic Church was forming. Döllinger at least assented to the formation, so far, anyway, as persuading the King to allot a church in Munich for the use of the congregation. The moment the Old Catholic Church existed, even in embryo, it naturally began to seek ecumenical contacts. A still small group, set up against the might of Mediterranean and overseas Catholicism, it looked around for other Catholics not subject to Rome. Obviously it first thought of the Eastern Orthodox in Russia and Greece. Then it thought, not very enthusiastically, of the little Jansenist Church of Utrecht. It thought of the Church of England, as the Protestant Church which had preserved the episcopal succession, and valued it. This look towards the Anglicans was the more optimistic because Döllinger himself had been much affected by the reading of Dr Pusey's *Eirenicon* (1865), which had put for-

---

[1] Ignaz von Döllinger, *Briefwechsel*, ed. Conzemius, iii (Munich, 1971), 17 ff. No one can think about this whole area—Döllinger, Acton, Old Catholics, Liberal Catholicism generally in the 19th and 20th centuries—without being in debt to Conzemius. See the literature annexed to his *Katholizismus ohne Rom* (Zurich, 1969). The standard work on the Old Catholics is by U. Küry, *Die Altkatholische Kirche* (Stuttgart, 1966). The original documentation by J. F. von Schulte, *Der Altkatholizismus* (Glessen, 1887; repr. Hildesheim, 1965) is still needed. In English C. B. Moss, *The Old Catholic Movement, its Origins and History* (London, 1964), can be useful but is less satisfactory. R. Rouse and S. C. Neill (eds.), *A History of the Ecumenical Movement* (London, 1967), does not get the importance of Döllinger and his efforts at Bonn. Worthy of attention are the lives of Reusch by L. K. Goetz (Gotha, 1901)—cf. single address by J. E. B. Mayor (Cambridge, 1901); of Liddon by J. O. Johnston (London, 1904); of Pusey by Liddon and others, vol. iv (London, 1897); and of Harold Browne by G. W. Kitchin (London, 1895). F. Meyrick's *Memories* (London, 1905) are interesting, but occasionally his memory played him false. F. Meyrick edited (1877–99) the *Foreign Church Chronicle and Review*, in which much attention was paid to these questions. Meyrick also published an address about the second Conference at Bonn in an address which he gave at Lincoln Cathedral (London, 1875). In 1875 he published the correspondence, in two pieces, between the Anglo-Continental Society and the Secretaries of the Friends of Spiritual Enlightenment in St Petersburg; and in 1874 he had published correspondence between the Anglo-Continental Society and the Old Catholic and the Oriental Churchmen; more of the same in pamphlets of 1876 and of 1877. Bickersteth, the Dean of Lichfield (who was not, however, present at the Bonn Conference) together with Meyrick, published as a separate pamphlet the papers on the subject which they read to the Plymouth Church Congress. For the German literature see the bibliography in Peter Neuner, *Döllinger als Theologe der Ökumene*, for which see below, n. 5.

ward, from the Anglican point of view, a very Catholic hope of a reunited Catholic Church.

For the moment Munich was quite the centre of the ecclesiastical world. Paris was enduring the effects of the Commune, the city of Rome was under occupation from the Italian nationalists and full of an insecurity of outlook. Everyone looked to Munich to see what would happen in the revolt against the Ultramontane Papacy. Men from the great Churches interested in reunion came one after the other to see Döllinger who was now on a world stage—Liddon and Littledale and Beresford Hope from the high Anglicans, Gregorovius the anti-papal historian of Rome, Chauncy Langdon who had founded the Anglican episcopal church of St Paul's in Rome, Schaff the church historian from the United States, Friedberg the great German canonist, Pasquale Villari the Italian historian and statesman—these and others came to pay their respect to Döllinger and lend him such backing as they could give.

On the one side Döllinger was beginning to blame those—and none more than his favourite pupil Acton—who refused to stand up and be counted as open opponents of infallibility and the decrees. On the other side he was beginning to distance himself, at least a little, from the Old Catholic leaders like Reusch and Reinkens and von Schulte, the German Catholic professors who on their side blamed Döllinger, for they looked to him as their leader and found that he was reluctant to lead. They were confronted with practical and pastoral problems—people coming to them wanting to be married, or to be buried, or to receive the sacraments. They must therefore create Churches and a ministry to meet these pressing and justified needs. For Döllinger this was the road to lose influence and become a sect. For him they must be seen to be staying inside the Catholic Church, even if they were unjustly and perhaps illegally or uncanonically excommunicated. They had a chance, he believed, of focusing that vast body of Catholic opinion which was perfectly indifferent to the Vatican decrees and, if asked whether it believed in papal infallibility or in what sense it believed in papal infallibility, had not the least idea what was being talked about and certainly did not believe it when it was explained to them. Döllinger's idea was very theoretical. They must be seen to be in the Catholic Church, even though excommunicated. Therefore they must not set up altar against altar and ministry against ministry.

This was the professor in his study. People died. Who was to bury them? He recognized this practically and its most dramatic form when he himself died. He arranged that he should receive the sacrament, and have his funeral mass, from Johann Friedrich, who was one of the priests in the Old Catholic Church, the organizing of which he had preferred not to see. At that moment, the end of 1871, what he saw was that a sect would not influence the Catholic Church. The more separate from Rome they were, the less influence they would exert on Catholicism as a whole. Yet lots of Catholics all over the world were undoubtedly on their side. But such Catholics would have nothing to do with making a sect which would attempt to replace a historic Catholic Church. If the men of Munich acted gently, slowly, not too decisively, loud against the Vatican decrees, but not loud against the historic body of Catholicism, then large numbers of clergy, certainly in Germany, and perhaps all over the world, would be able to see in them a focus of an authentic Catholicity against innovation.

The climax of this difference of opinion between the main source of the Old Catholic movement and the Old Catholic leaders came at the 1872 Conference of Old Catholics in Cologne, 1872.

Still, they had to have a ministry. Therefore they had to have a bishop. Döllinger himself, inconsistently with what he had argued, came to see, and to agree, that it was absolutely necessary that they have a bishop. He had originally been confident that one of the Minority bishops at the Vatican Council would persist in his resistance to the decrees and therefore be their bishop without the necessity for any act of schism; someone like Strossmayer from Bosnia perhaps, or Kenrick from the United States. This hope faded quite quickly. When history looks back it must be seen as an extraordinary event that not a single bishop of the Minority persisted in resistance to the bitter end. Döllinger's optimism was not naïve.

So Döllinger not only agreed that they should make a bishop, but was willing to serve on the committee for choosing a bishop. The committee had difficulty. Döllinger wanted Reusch. Reusch refused. The committee tried Döllinger, who refused even to be considered. Not till 4 June 1873 was J. H. Reinkens elected bishop.

Here then was a body of Catholic priests; many of them scholars; with good relations across Europe by reason of the international community of Christian scholarship; with a lay following, but rather a small, and also rather educated, lay following, for this was in no sense a popular movement; being people with consciences sensitive to the informed tradition of the centuries and not being the heartfelt rebellion of a wave of simple faith among ordinary worshippers; who thought that they were the Catholic Church, but since that name would be confusing, were very soon the Old Catholic Church; with their own bishop and ministry and organization; and therefore in danger of becoming just another of the European sects, though exceptional in being the most academic and scholarly of all the groups of Christendom; refused by some very scholarly men who thought even worse of the Vatican Council than they did, like Lord Acton and the archaeologist F. X. Kraus—but with hopes of not being just another small denomination among others. They had these hopes for two main reasons: partly because they knew that inside the main body of the Roman Catholic Church there were lots of people who agreed with them in thinking nothing whatever of the infallibility of the Pope, at least unless it could be said to be only the focus or mouthpiece of the infallibility of the whole Catholic Church—which was not at all what the Vatican Council had said; and partly because their international friendships made them fully aware that in more traditional Churches divided from Rome there were many Christian leaders who would be drawn towards a Catholic Church if it could be presented to them purged of 'Vaticanism'.

The atmosphere any time from 1872 to 1876, is shown by language of the high Anglican and leading preacher of the Church of England, Henry Parry Liddon. Liddon visited Döllinger in Munich during 1872 and Döllinger took him for a walk. Döllinger there began to frame for Liddon's benefit a scheme for a great Church meeting or conference to discuss what were the problems which divided them. His motive was not anti-Vatican. As he put it to Liddon, he saw how disunity hindered the spread of Christianity among the nations and wanted to see whether he could do something about it. But Liddon reported, so far as he was afterwards able to remember the words, one sentence of Döllinger which showed great faith or optimism about what it was now possible to achieve:

When so many threatening forms of infidelity are attacking our belief on one side, and Vaticanism is putting forth its altogether new propositions about the constitution and faith of the Church of Christ on the other, ought not all we, who profess to follow the ancient Catholic Church as the keeper and unfolder of the Holy Scriptures, to be able to come to an understanding with each other? Surely this should not be impossible, unless we are rather stupid, or, perhaps, even self-willed.[2]

Döllinger had begun to think hard about the problem of Christian unity and disunity even in the last few years before the Vatican Council. Therefore this new situation after his excommunication, at a time when all the world hung upon what he would say, gave him a chance to be read across the world on the subject. He began to plan lectures on reunion almost at once, during the summer of 1871. His biographer Friedrich reports the occasion for the delivery of the lectures. During the winter of 1871–2 the future Old Catholic bishop Reinkens stayed in Munich with Döllinger and they planned a course by various lecturers, to be given in the Deutsche Museum. One of the chosen lecturers was Hyacinthe Loyson, and this can hardly have been Döllinger's choice. Loyson was a French priest strong against the Vatican Council, who was excommunicated, set up a rather Protestant sort of French-speaking Church, and married. Döllinger objected, not only to the rather Protestant Church, but to the marriage; for his attitude that they were still Catholic priests, though wrongly excommunicated, made him strong in maintaining the celibacy of the clergy. In the course of lectures at Munich Reinkens and Loyson both lectured.[3] These lectures were not a success. Loyson, though a popular speaker, would not be on a German wave-length. Reinkens had not the gifts of a popular orator. The course was in danger of failing.

Döllinger therefore gave a course of seven lectures on the reunion of the Churches, between January and March 1872 published as *Über die Wiedervereinigung der christlichen Kirchen*. They held crowds. They were reported, not always accurately, in the newspapers of other countries. Lord Acton complained a little about the reporting in *The Times*. 'Garbling', he called it. In Bavaria the *Allgemeine Zeitung* gave copious extracts. The Cardinal of Bavaria, Cardinal Hohenlohe (who was by now looked on with no favour whatever by the Curia in Rome), congratulated him on the lectures. The very same year 1872 the lectures were published in English and French translations; the English edition was translated by Acton's ally H. N. Oxenham who gave to the lectures what Döllinger regarded as rather too modest notes of explanation.

---

[2] Liddon's Preface to *Report of the Proceedings of the Reunion Conference Held at Bonn on September 14, 15 and 16 1874* (London, 1975), p. iii.

[3] Friedrich, *Döllinger*, iii. 632–3.

This book, when eventually it was published, made Döllinger's only systematic thoughts on Christian Reunion to be published in book form, though, as we shall see, not his only systematic thoughts on the subject. It was necessary to publish instantly in the foreign languages because of the garbled reports that circulated or faulty statements that were made in the press. But he did not like to publish the German edition. He was not satisfied with his text. It is not at all surprising that he was dissatisfied with the text. He took on a subject that was bound to survey most of history in a few lectures. He kept putting the lectures aside. They were not finally published in the German edition until sixteen years later, Nördlingen 1888. Some people thought that the failure to publish until the key moment had passed was the loss by Döllinger of one more chance.

There may have been a reason which made him discontented, which was not simply the scholar's desire to avoid superficiality. When he started giving the lectures, early in 1872, he had grounds for optimism. It was still possible that 'his' movement might 'carry' the Catholic Church—or those parts of it which he regarded as the parts most authentic and worth carrying. He could still think it possible that the great Eastern Orthodox Church might swing in behind a Western movement which eschewed an authoritarian papacy, for that had always been the fundamental Eastern complaint against the Western Church. His knowledge of Pusey's *Eirenicon* made him realize that among the Anglicans there were some who were closer to him, and indeed were in his view more Catholic in their outlook, than the reigning Pope. Not many months were to pass before he realized that he suffered from an excess of optimism and that Churches cannot or do not move so rapidly, even when there is crisis in Christendom.

Do we need to do anything at all about Christian reunion? The Churches always have been divided. A time never existed when they were not divided. They were divided from ancient times, sometimes on ethical grounds, sometimes on disagreements over order, sometimes from disagreements over doctrine. Is it certain that this is bad? If it is not bad we need do nothing about it. Is the whole history of the Church a great field or area of experiment in the building up different types of Christian societies? Do we test Churches by their staying power?—if it commands the assent of a lot of people and lasts, it must be of God, if it fails and vanishes it is not of God—is that a sufficient test?

We cannot think that wide acceptance and staying power are alone sufficient as a test of truth. That test would justify Islam. The fact is, Christians are disturbed when they watch Christian disunity and its consequences. Something in their conscience is troubled. They preach brotherly love, and hurl abuse at each other. They talk peace and behave as if they are at war, or at least as if they were cold and distant. Something deep inside Christian feeling bears witness to the truth that Christian disunity is a failure and that we need to work at its cure. And when we turn to St John's Gospel we find that this feeling of ours is apostolic. We have a commandment from the Lord to do what our conscience suggests ought to be done.

But is it sensible? Can it be done? Never have we been not divided. Is it practicable? Are we inevitably wasting time if we engage in trying to heal the divisions? Sometimes, as at the Reformation, the divisions have done a great deal of good, or, if not the divisions, at least the consequences of the divisions.

We are ordered to try to do it. Therefore it must be possible. It is not possible that we should be ordered to try to do what is impossible.

Döllinger identified Christian society with civilization.[4] Therefore—unite the Churches and you are helping to unite Christian society. The unity of the Church is the way to the unity of the world.

For example: the world is divided into blocs of power—one led by Russia the other by Germany. The collapse of the Ottoman Empire in that age is making these blocs menacing to each other. Russia sees that she has a political mission in the Balkan countries which is also a religious mission, the mission of uniting Orthodoxy. Orthodoxy regards all western Christianity as heretical and a departure from apostolic faith. If we could reunite Western Christendom

---

[4] Döllinger was brave enough to define civilization (*Über die Wiedervereinigung*, pp. 20–1): all men equal before God; all called towards the highest moral and spiritual perfection, and thereby called to blessedness; all to practise love of their brothers; no castes; no slavery; every man free; no man to be used as a mere means; free development of man's capacities and the legal right to exercise them; marriage which is consecrated by religion, monogamous, and rests on the equality of the woman with the man; parents' power over their children not absolute, but controlled by society; compulsory education; work a moral and religious duty; sexual restraint a moral and religious duty; governments bound by the law and the constitution, and not capricious despotisms; citizens with a sense of the moral duty to obey the law. Notice that he says nothing of the production of wealth, or artefacts, or communications, or music, or literature.

with Eastern Christendom we should have taken the greatest single step to making the two blocs of power realize that they belong to a common civilization as well as to a common Christendom.

The Russian Church is near the centre of the world's history at this moment. For Russia's vast power is still in the phase of expansion. Still it has a mission before it in North and Middle Asia. This task of civilizing a large part of Asia is 'the greatest and the hardest' that can be laid upon a modern nation. It is not certain that Russia has within its society the spiritual resources for this work. It has the power to conquer. We do not yet know whether it has the quality to rule, and to civilize what it has conquered. For this mission its Church is at the heart. Therefore it is very necessary, it is urgent, that the Russian Church should start to look outwards, and come out from behind its *zareba* (*Abgeschlossenheit*) and draw upon other Churches for a fresh strength in spirituality and a more varied use of the ecclesiastical structures which it possesses.

And, finally, the disunity of the Churches weakens their mission shamefully. We need only look at the conflict of Churches in India, and the disappointing results of the great evangelistic efforts in India; or look at Jerusalem and Bethlehem, where Turkish soldiers have to stop Christian sects from inflicting physical violence on each other.

Therefore we have to try—because it is a Christian commandment, and because this is the supreme way in which the Churches can serve mankind. And it happens that at this moment we have an unusual chance. The Churches are ready to learn from each other. They are ready now to share their heritage with others. We have a chance of better understanding. We must get groups of theologians together; get them talking in person over the old doctrinal formulas; discover where division is unnecessary and there is no matter of principle sufficient to divide; see whether we cannot get behind the formulas developed through history towards a more primitive shape; recognize the possibility that we can interpret formulas so that we understand them better and see that they do not imply all that rigidity makes them imply. No one will be so foolish as to think that we can create a new set of doctrinal formulas on which everyone might agree. But at least we can interpret them to each other, and perhaps discover that sometimes we are less far apart than anyone had supposed.

If we are to make progress, it is a necessary element that the endeavour be religious. That is, the formula must be set less in the context of logic or philosophy, and more in the context of its place in spirituality and the worshipping tradition. Formulas are hard if they are mere formulas. If they are the expressions of a deep religious spirit, they look very different.

You cannot unite everyone to everyone else in one operation. Therefore you must look about you for the areas where there is some hope; some measure of agreement already; some natural feeling of sympathy. Where are we to find such areas in this moment of time?

We shall not find them in the Latin-speaking Catholic countries. Their state as a society makes them uninterested in Christian unity. They are not divided between one religion and another, they are divided between religion and irreligion, and irreligion has no interest whatever in Christian unity. Nor shall we find promising areas in the Slav peoples. Because of the Ottoman Empire and its long centuries of rule or misrule, their religion is mingled strongly with nationality, and even with nationalism. Where religion is the expression of nationalism, it is being used as a way of dividing one's people from other peoples, not as a way of uniting one's race to other races. Nor shall we find a promising area in North America. There the sects proliferate. Their object is to prove their independence as sects. As sectarian they can have no kind of interest in the sort of Christian unity for which we are looking.

Therefore the hope of the future lies with the Germanic peoples—Germany and Britain. They are divided by religion; but the religions into which they are divided are sufficiently close to historic Christianity, and sufficiently close to each other, and are not sectarian in their temper. This hope for the future is specially true with England. For in England the Oxford Movement has helped the Church to recover the true sense of Catholicity and therefore revived the desire for Christian unity. But, at the moment, the Church of England is hampered in any work for Christian unity because it is legally established and has therefore certain links with the State which it cannot easily alter. Its establishment makes it simultaneously too narrow and too broad, too lax and too constrained, too free on one side and too dependent on the other. If the Church of England is to bear its proper part in the quest for unity, it must accept disestablishment as a necessary price for following this vocation. It is clear that this could not happen quickly. Döllinger seemed to think it specially monstrous that the Thirty-Nine Articles should assert (Article 21) that 'General Councils cannot be held without the orders and agreement of the princes' (*Wiedervereinigung*, p. 112). (His translator, Oxenham, p. 131, thought that the article 'is susceptible of a different interpretation, and cited Newman's *Tract* 90 to this effect. Oxenham also corrected an error of fact in Döllinger's original notes here and Döllinger took over the amendment when he published the German. Nevertheless it is not certain that Oxenham's own footnote of correction is in all respects a correct account of the ecclesiastical law in Victorian England.)

Döllinger had a great admiration for England. Sometimes his admiration rested upon judgements which were not totally informed. He admired England very much because the pornographic literature which circulated in Germany and France was not to be found there.

Germany is at the heart of all this because its divisions in religion lie at the heart of its national problem. The Germans started the worst of the modern divisions and they must expiate it by finding the remedy. 'Our weakness, political divisions, and humiliation before the world have a direct cause in Christian disunity.'

Despite what has been said about the Slavs and nationalism, we must nevertheless turn towards the Orthodox. They must be brought into these discussions. They are Catholics and near to Western Catholicism despite all their disagreements. We cannot make a unity with the Anglicans at a cost of deepening the chasm which divides us from the Orthodox. We cannot make a unity with the Orthodox at a cost of deepening the chasm which divides us from the Anglicans.

We already have a sort of unity and a true unity. This is a unity by baptism. By baptism all Protestants are members of the one Holy Catholic and Apostolic Church. All Protestants are agreed upon this. This also is official Roman Catholic doctrine.

It is also Catholic doctrine that you can err through invincible ignorance. You may still be a Catholic in the soul and heart even when your head has absorbed error or heresy.

Therefore it is impossible to identify the Catholic Church with any single denomination. And therefore a Catholic may say to members of other denominations—come, we are all brothers and sisters in Christ, beneath appearances we are members of the one visible Church. It is a great garden of God. Let us stretch out our hands towards each other, let us link hands across the fences so the we can embrace. These fences are differences in doctrine. We cannot both be right. Someone must be wrong. Nevertheless, let us not blame the other side for being (as we think) in the wrong, let us remember how these differences are caused by circumstances, and environment, and upbringing, and education. Let us remember that if a person sees a thing as right (even when we see that it is wrong) it is his moral duty to adhere to it until he can be persuaded of another opinion. Therefore, if we clasp hands across the fences, and do not blame each other for being on the other side of the fence from ourselves, what we can do is work together on the reason for the existence of the fence. We can talk, and examine, and test, and shed new light, and see if we can understand or interpret; to look at the end for the pearl of great price which is religious peace. Then we can work together in the Lord's garden, in a common endeavour to get rid of all the weeds at last.

One difficulty is formulas which people formally profess, but have not the least intention of believing wholeheartedly, perhaps no intention of believing at all.

For example, in Catholicism. Roman Catholics are now told that they must believe the decree of the Vatican Council of 1870 on the infallibility of the Pope. No other Church can possibly unite with a Church which really believes that doctrine and alleges that you cannot be a true Christian unless you believe that doctrine. It sounds rigid in the extreme. But the fact is that most Roman Catholics care nothing at all about this doctrine. And it is far from certain that in the long run the doctrine will come to be accepted within the Roman Catholic Church, since it contradicts all sane historical enquiry, and we are living in an age when the historical sense is becoming ever more widespread. The apparent rigidity of the doctrine does not really correspond to the deeper Catholic sense of the people who belong to the Church which at an outward level seem to profess this doctrine.

So with the Protestants of the Reformation. The Reformation was about justification by faith alone. This was finally enshrined, in a very rigid form, in the Lutheran Formula of Concord (1577). If everyone had to believe the apparent meaning of the Formula of Concord, no Christian unity would ever be possible; for, despite its name, it is, like the Vatican formulation on infallibility, a very divisive formula. But the fact is, hardly any Protestants, if any at all, nowadays believe in the obvious meaning of the Formula of Concord. Nearly all of them, if not all of them, now take a far wider view of the doctrine of justification, which can be easily reconciled with the teaching about justification by faith found in the ancient and undivided Church. The formula of Protestants is divisive, their meaning looks towards unity.

Döllinger regarded every other question as secondary and not too difficult to solve. (In saying this he made one weighty omission, whether consciously or not is not clear. He believed that no union was possible without a united ministry, and that must include the historic ministry of bishops. Other evidence shows that he found this problem not at all easy to see a way through. But here he mentioned it only, as it were, in passing.) Celibacy of the clergy is only a matter of church discipline and not a cause of division. The doctrine of purgatory takes various forms and would not now be a difficult matter for reconciliation. Lots of Protestants, at least Anglican and Lutheran, accept the practice of confession, and teach that in the eucharist there is a true sacrifice, and have begun to make the eucharist the centre of Christian worship, and have a growing understanding for the vocations of monks and nuns. As to the liturgy in the language of the people, it would be good if the Catholic Church had Mass in the vernacular. But this could hardly be thought a cause for mutual excommunication.

Despite all this optimism in the mood of 1872, Döllinger certainly did not expect reunion tomorrow. In any plan to change things, the number of people who do not want change is always greater than the number of people who do want to change. Some Protestants still think the Pope Antichrist, and imagine that it is impossible for the Roman Catholic Church to engage in any reform, it can only be repudiated. Vaticanists have no use for the Protestants, they regard their Churches as nothing, they are busy erecting ever higher barriers against them. Some Protestants have no use at all for the ancient Church, they want to free the Church from its origins; and it is certain that no form of unity could ever be achieved without respect for the ancient and undivided Church.

Therefore we cannot but go slowly.

Germany has a special responsibility. Germany started the worst of the Western Church divisions. And now in Germany the mixture of Roman Catholics and Protestants is more interwoven than anywhere else in the world. Germany is the heart of Europe. Its universities and their theological faculties give it more theologians than other lands. And since expertise is required—especially expertise in the study of the Bible and the ancient Church—languages are needed, and the German educational system is producing a better training in the necessary languages than can be found in any other country. Therefore the special responsibility of Germany is clear.

Yet you cannot do this just by theologians. You cannot achieve what the Church needs by meetings of theologians who represent the various denominations. You have to have these meetings of representative theologians. Such meetings are the discussion across the fence, the interpretation, the explanation, the seeking of a road to a mutual understanding. But they cannot achieve. For the consequences in practice are too great. There has to be a desire for unity in the heart of the people. The grass roots inside the Churches—they must have a longing. At the moment they do not, or most of them do not. They are content with the worship which they have, and hardly like to be disturbed. And yet we see in this age signs that the longing is growing among the people. It is like a few snow flakes falling, they are the foretaste of what will become an avalanche.

What can we do in practice at the moment?

The Eastern Orthodox: the education of their priests is of a low standard; they must attempt to create many more instructed priests. And they are too tightly bound to the State. They ought to seek more freedom from the State. And they ought to abandon altogether the link between nationalistic panSlavism and religion.

The Anglicans: they have found through the Oxford Movement a recovery of the sense of a Catholic inheritance and their feeling for the ancient and undivided Church as still in a measure authoritative. They ought to try to put forward these perceptions of the Oxford Movement more prominently. The Thirty-Nine Articles at first sight are like the Formula of Concord, divisive. But no Anglican believes every word of them literally, and they are easily understood in the sense of the ancient Church. They ought to try, like the Orthodox, to increase their freedom from the State. And they ought to reduce that element which wants to get rid of any authority in the ancient Church—Döllinger was not thinking of liberals or modernists, but what he regarded as 'the Calvinistic element'.

Rome: that is, Rome before the innovation of 18th July 1870: they have what is needed; they revere (or at least till July 1870 they did revere) the teaching of the ancient and undivided Church. They have the historic ministry. Some of the formulas of the Council of Trent in the Counter-Reformation might be thought to be divisive like the Formula of Concord or bits of the Thirty-Nine Articles. But in reality there is nothing in the formulations of the Council of Trent which cannot be interpreted in a moderate sense, and that is what should be done.

The Lutherans and Reformed in Germany: the original formula of the German Reformation, the Augsburg Confession, is a perfectly Catholic document, or is perfectly reconcilable with the Catholic inheritance. But the Formula of Concord, for the Lutherans, and the Heidelberg Catechism, for the Reformed, are not reconcilable. No amount of interpretation can make them into moderate statements. Some time these Churches must attempt to supersede these formulas in some official way. Döllinger did not overlook the difficulty of what he said. And the question of a common ministry in Germany he saw to be even more difficult. Catholicism has to have its structure of continuity with the ancient Church. That can only mean the sharing of bishops into the Lutheran and Reformed Churches. He pointed to various events of the past which did not make this so impossible a suggestion as it looked at first sight. He even mentioned the Anglo-Prussian bishopric set up in Jerusalem by the Church of England and the Church of Prussia in common. But Döllinger saw very clearly that this obstacle was not to be overcome soon or simply.

Meanwhile—till these things, or some of these things happen—what are we to do? Give up hostilities. Work together. Especially work together in our mission to the world. And while we begin to find ways of working together in common mission, let the theologians get on with their consideration; for it will be their task to find the ways to mutual understanding and more moderate interpretation of formulas, some of which are a dead hand from the past and do not represent the real mind of the Churches in the present.

Such were, in summary or paraphrase, the very influential lectures which Döllinger gave in the Deutsche Museum at Munich in the early months of 1872.

Reinkens took them up. In September 1872 he declared that the quest for reunion was a fundamental vocation of the Old Catholic movement. He also suggested a committee or commission to work at the different formulas and try to find interpretations or statements which the Churches could accept. And he was wholly in agreement with Döllinger that reunion cannot be got just because official representatives of different Churches get together and agree on some interpretation or restatement or better formula. The people must wish it. And, like Döllinger, he thought of the unity which was already possessed—how across the denominations the Christians love the Scriptures, and confess the ancient creeds, and value the Fathers of the Church, and understand the Scripture in the way the ancient Church understood it, and love the old martyrs, and unite in the objects of their prayers, and confess that the others are their brothers, and that charity unites us even when doctrine sometimes divides us.

But he had new emphases which were not quite those of Döllinger, though they proceed out of Döllinger's thought.

First, we cannot just return to the ancient Church, whatever its authority. As the Church is a living body, so its unity is a living thing; not static; a dynamic reality. We are not to think of the quest for unity as the quest for immobility. We must not deny the whole development of Christianity since the apostles. We must recognize the deepening apprehension through the centuries of the Gospel and its treasure-house.

Secondly, unity can never be uniformity. A nation is a natural entity. It has its own characteristics, its own way of life. This is true of its religious way of life. Germany is bound to develop customs or even practices suitable for Germany and not suitable for France. National particularisms are part of God's vocation, part of the way in which God made the world. A conception of unity as uniformity, in the sense of suppressing regional differences, would be contrary to the will of God. Therefore the unity that we have to aim for cannot mean agreement all round in everything. And therefore unity cannot proceed out of a single denomination. Freedom lies at the heart of what we seek, not regimentation or compulsion.

In this view of Reinkens, which drew heavily on Döllinger, unity is not a fixture. It is a developing process of agreement and harmony.[5]

---

[5] For the importance of Reinkens's address and comment, see P. Neuner, *Döllinger als Theologe der Ökumene*, (Beiträge zur ökumenischen Theologie, ed. H. Fries, 19; Paderborn etc., 1979), 171 ff.—an excellent guide to this whole theme, and to which I owe much help.

Döllinger's next important move was to create an ecumenical conference; in reality the first ecumenical conference, long before Faith and Order was heard of. He had to get rid of two rival plans. Some of his allies, for example Michelis, wanted an ecumenical conference set up consciously as a rival to the untrue ecumenical nature of the Vatican Council; that is, they wanted a council not so much directed towards unity as directed against Rome. That did not suit Döllinger, even though any move that he made must be seen in Rome as hostile since he was an excommunicated priest. Some of his allies wanted it to be an Old Catholic congress with many visitors invited from other Churches. For Döllinger that would have meant domination of the conference by a single denomination and one of which he was not sure that he could totally approve. Therefore the Conference of Bonn 1874, when it met, was not intended as an ecumenical Conference rival to the Vatican Council nor was it an official Old Catholic meeting where the Old Catholics were the hosts. It was Döllinger's conference.

He drafted the invitation. They would aim at union; but not a union where the resulting one body would absorb everybody and their different distinctive merits or practices. They would aim at the historic formula 'unity in what is essential', *unitas in necessariis*. They would not aim at a complete *Verschmelzung*, total fusion, of the different denominations. The measure or yardstick of their endeavours would be the creeds of the early centuries and the doctrines and institutions which were regarded as essential by both Eastern and Western Churches before the great separations.

Given the international stature at that moment of Döllinger, this invitation was very attractive indeed to two kinds of Christian leader.

The Eastern Orthodox had no strong sense of history as yet and imagined that they, the Orthodox, had preserved everything unchanged from the time before the Churches were divided. Therefore they had a fond hope that Döllinger's invitation was equivalent to a recommendation that we can find unity by all becoming members of the Orthodox Church. That was true especially of the narrower Orthodox, usually ex-Western Catholics who converted to Orthodoxy because they could not bear the Vatican Council or for other reasons, and as converts were filled with the conviction that Orthodoxy alone had the truth or even, in the most extreme case, that outside it no salvation was to be found.

Moreover the Eastern Orthodox Church was nothing like so

static in fact as some of its more austere members supposed. This was not so true of Greece, which looked towards the ecumenical patriarch in Constantinople, or even towards the monks of Mount Athos, over whom the tolerantly oppressive Ottoman regime ruled; and subjection to a non-Christian government, as always, bred a very strong conservatism in the still partly subject Churches; even though the kingdom of Greece, in the south of what is the Greece of today, had achieved independence. But in the third quarter of the nineteenth century the openness of Russia to the West was beginning to affect both sides: a Russian influence upon the West, especially in music and literature, a western influence upon Russia in political thought, philosophy, and even history. The natural outlook of the capital St Petersburg was westwards. And since Russia was the political hope of Orthodoxy everywhere, this new attitude meant a new hope for an openness of mind within Orthodoxy towards Western Christendom. The Russian Church had no use for the Pope. But it was less entangled than Constantinople, by the memories of history and crusades and mutual excommunication, with the more bitter sides of the historic schism. Under the Tsar Alexander II the educated of Russia clamoured for reform; and some aspects of reform naturally took on a western colour. An age in which the serfs were emancipated, the judicial system mended, and local self-government developed, was an age where the Church too must be affected. For the first time since the age when Greece was in a desperate plight before Constantinople fell to the Turks, some leaders of the Eastern Orthodox Church began to look to the Western Churches as though they might have something to give. With its eyes open to Germany through St Petersburg, Russian Church leaders were not disposed to neglect the chance which Döllinger offered. They even had a society with a liberal outlook which was consciously concerned—the Union of the Friends of Spiritual Enlightenment. It was a remarkable new thing in Russian history that the head of the theological academy at St Petersburg, then the most important, and indeed the best, of the Russian colleges for training clergy, should accept Döllinger's invitation to the conference at Bonn: Dr Janyschev, who was also confessor to the Tsar and his family.

The second group much attracted by the invitation were the Anglicans. All through the sixties they had been working towards ideas of Christian unity. Dr Pusey's *Eirenicon* was only the most famous book within a movement of ideas which was widespread among the Anglicans. The inspiration came from the high churchmen like Pusey. They had found liberal-minded Roman Catholics during the sixties, who were willing to discuss with them the possibilities for a form of reunion. These hopes, and the possibility of useful discussions, seemed to be shattered by the Vatican Council. After the infallibility decree Pusey at first felt that nothing more was to be gained by talking about such matters. Döllinger's initiative restored hopes to quite a number of frustrated people. We have seen that Liddon and Littledale were both at Döllinger's house not many months after the excommunication.

Döllinger had an amazing effect in restoring these Anglicans to the belief that something could be achieved and perhaps at no distant date. Liddon was a hard-headed man, neither naïve nor sentimental. Yet here is his optimism so lately as Easter of 1875:

The Old Catholic body seems to hold out to the English Church an opportunity which has been denied to it for three hundred years. Catholic, yet not papal; episcopal, with no shadow of doubt or prejudice resting on the validity of its orders; friendly with the Orthodox East, yet free from the stiffness and onesidedness of an isolated tradition; sympathising with all that is thorough and honest in the critical methods of Protestant Germany, yet holding on firmly and strenuously to the faith of antiquity—this body of priests and theologians, and simple believers, addresses to the English Church a language too long unheard, in the Name of our common Lord and Master. Once more the vision of a body which shall compass the world seems to rise however indistinctly before the mind's eye; a body which shall attract the many earnest souls whom we in our Anglican isolation cannot reach; a body through which one pulse shall throb at Constantinople, at Munich, at Lambeth, and to whose pleadings Rome herself, in the days that are assuredly before her, may not always be deaf. Is it irrational to hope that a body such as this, uniting all that is sincere in modern enquiry, with all that is deepest and most tender in ancient Christian self-devotion, may yet hope to win the ear of Europe, and to bring succour to the intellectual and moral ailments of our modern world?[6]

But this Anglican interest was not confined to the very high churchmen, nor to the high churchmen taken in a wider sense. Frederick Meyrick earned his living by being the rector of Blickling in Norfolk. He was a fierce opponent of Manning and Newman, and an

---

[6] Liddon, preface, pp. xxv–xxvi.

acid critic of some of the workings of the Roman Catholic Church in Spain. That is, he was an English Protestant with the traditional attitude of such Protestants towards European Catholicism. His interest in Christianity in Europe was partly, though not quite wholly, an anti-Catholic interest. In 1853 he founded the Anglo-Continental Society and became its secretary. The tone of this society was decidedly Protestant. But it encouraged better knowledge of the Church of England on the Continent, and encouraged the English to better knowledge of what was going on in Europe. It was of course very interested in the Old Catholic movement, not so much because it was Catholic as because it was a revolt from Rome and all revolts from Rome were exciting. Meyrick visited Döllinger soon after he was excommunicated. And yet Meyrick's interest in Döllinger's plans for a conference did not quite fit Döllinger's wishes. Döllinger, struggling to make his conference a real conference looking for Christian unity, and specially not a conference against anyone at all, was supported by some people who found in his conference a useful weapon in a campaign against the authority of the Pope. The largest number of visitors from any one part of the Church who came to Döllinger's in 1874 Conference at Bonn were Anglicans and Protestants.

The Conference at Bonn was impressive in its weight, as the first type of Faith and Order Conference (to use an anachronistic term) to exist in Christendom. More than fifty theologians attended. (This statistic is more impressive in appearance than in reality. Fifty-six persons were present in the minutes. But the minutes themselves, after providing a list of participants, say that 'all the above did not take an active part in the proceedings; many were present as hearers only'. In fact, if we deduct the theological students and the interested and the English chaplain at Düsseldorf and the Russian chaplain at Wiesbaden, the number of persons whom posterity would call theologians was much reduced; mainly, Reinkens, Döllinger, Langen, Reusch; the Frenchman Michaud, a friend and correspondent of Döllinger; the Russian Janyschev; Nevin the American; and six Englishmen headed by the Bishop of Winchester and Canon Liddon: the statistic 'more than fifty theologians' boils down in the realities to some thirteen or fifteen people with a lot of interested, and sometimes informed, spectators. We do not know, for example, much about the contribution of Baron Zwierlein, 'landed proprietor at Geisenheim-am-Rhein'). They came not only from the countries where there were Old Catholic movements in strength, like Germany and Switzerland, but from Russia, England, France, Denmark, and America.

The future pattern of the earlier, but not the later, twentieth century was laid down when no Roman Catholic clergy attended. There was however a Roman Catholic and it was not quite sure that he was not a clergyman; he always was addressed as 'the Reverend' and thought of himself as 'the Reverend': Henry Nutcombe Oxenham; a former Tractarian, son of an Anglican clergyman and nephew of the great Tractarian priest Thomas Thelusson Carter. Oxenham became a Roman Catholic in 1857 and was received by Dr Manning. He remained ever afterwards very hostile to 'Protestantism'. He took the four minor orders, but refused to be ordained priest because he was sure that Anglican orders were valid and therefore that he already was a priest. After a time he went to Munich to study under Döllinger and formed a veneration for him. He loved Dr Pusey's *Eirenicon* and hated the Vatican Council, and wrote fierce articles against the Vatican Council, and translated the even fiercer articles which appeared as the *Letters of Quirinus*, and in 1872 was the translater of Döllinger's lectures on Christian Reunion (to which he added a long viewy preface of his own which did not allow Döllinger to speak for himself). He regarded the present regime in his Church as a tyranny. Being a layman in the eyes of his Church he was never excommunicated and afterwards came to disapprove of the direction in which the Old Catholic movement travelled.

But it was inevitable that the Roman Catholics should be represented only by a rebellious liberal of their disreputable left wing who, like Lord Acton, wholly agreed with Döllinger, but were determined to stay inside the Church, and being a layman (though not in his own eyes) could survive in full communion with the Pope. It could hardly be expected that any priests whom Rome would regard as fully loyal would attend the invitation of an excommunicated priest, however high his reputation, only four years after his excommunication; the more so since Döllinger had made plain, in those lectures which were the direct cause of what was happening, that he had changed his mind not at all, over what had been decided on 18 July 1870.

The host of the Conference was Reusch as the Rector of the University of Bonn. Döllinger was made the chairman. No other chairman was possible. But Reusch expressed the motive for this selection in terms of statesmanship. They must not be seen to be official representatives of Churches or hierarchies. Therefore they must be presided over by someone who held no official post in a Church but was 'simply a learned man'. As chairman, Döllinger often intervened. If it is the job of a chairman not just to preside neutrally over debates, but to guide what is being done, then Döllinger was an excellent chairman. He had the considerable advantage that he could interpret the Germans to the English and the English to the Germans. But it was he who determined the direction which debates should take, he who did quite a lot of the actual drafting of formulas that was needed, and he who helped on the business to see that it did not end only in words. If it is the part of a good chairman not to talk rather too much, then Döllinger was not a good chairman.

It was moving to the visitors to see Döllinger's national status; how in the streets even the children would run to greet him, and how even the most Ultramontane of Roman priests would bare their heads as he passed. As a chairman he had one remarkable quality, apart from the bonus that everyone felt reverence for him, and apart from the range of his learning: no one ever saw him put out. Despite various sharp provocations at the Conference, no one ever saw him perturbed, or hurried, or other than serene. Perhaps he was not a very firm chairman always. At least we know that at the next Bonn Conference an ancient and simple-hearted and not well-informed Romanian bishop went on speaking so long, with only one sharp interruption from the chair, that eventually one of the Eastern Orthodox archimandrites next to him seized his flowing robes and pulled him back into his seat.

There were ten Old Catholics (counting Döllinger as one, and he so counted himself) of whom six were professors; ten German Protestants, but among them no name of weight in theology—the leading German Protestants were very reserved towards the Old Catholic Movement; only one Greek Orthodox, a Professor Rhossis from a Greek theological seminary at Rhizarion, but also a lecturer at the university of Athens; four Russians, but one of them was a real weight, hardly another man of that weight could be found, namely Johannes Janyschev, the rector of the Theological Academy at St Petersburg; seven Americans including Kerfoot, the Episcopalian Bishop of Pittsburgh, and the weighty theologian

Nevin, who was then the rector of the American Church in Rome, and a strong team of Englishmen, headed by Harold Browne who had lately become the Bishop of Winchester (but who had to leave after the first day); Liddon; Edward Stuart Talbot, the Warden of Keble College; and sixteen others including Oxenham.

It is not wholly easy to discover what happened at Bonn in 1874. No one provided a secretary to take the minutes. Various participants of course took notes. The common language, so far as there was one, was English, thus again anticipating the lingua franca of the ecumenical movement. Döllinger and Reusch and Janyschev spoke English well, but many of the participants had a hazy idea about what was being said part of the time. Almost all the papers which formed the agenda for discussion were written in English. But the participants who did not know English were not given a paper with a German text. They had to make do with a translation by Döllinger from the chair as they went along. This system or lack of it naturally affected the proceedings and outcome of the Conference. It made the chairman even more dominant than he would otherwise have been. And the English, who in any case had sent the weightiest delegation (theologically speaking) became even weightier because they did a lot of the drafting and could best understand the subtleties of the formulas which were put before the meeting.

Döllinger did not want publicity, at least not uncontrolled publicity. The hall was open to anyone and therefore any reporter could come in. A short communiqué was sent to the local Bonn paper. Döllinger asked Reusch to keep notes in German, and asked the English chaplain at Düsseldorf, G. E. Broade, to keep notes in English. But Döllinger's request was not for a complete record but for 'short notes'. Reusch in fact kept a lot of notes of what was said. The English chaplain also kept a lot of notes. Afterwards Broade provided Reusch with his notes, (the *Guardian* printed many of these notes, September 1874, columns 1221–3) and various speakers gave Reusch notes of what they thought they had said or perhaps what they meant to say, and especially Döllinger kept a lot of notes and handed them later to Reusch. On this vaguely haphazard basis Reusch afterwards drew up 'minutes' of the Conference. He took the liberty of altering the texts which he received from the 'So-and-so said' of the notes to the inverted commas of direct speech. That is, the minutes make someone talk as though we have his very words; but what we have is usually, or at least often, a turning into direct speech of notes of a summary or paraphrase of what was said, notes made by someone else in the chamber. Reusch himself was perfectly frank about this. 'That form is chosen for brevity and clearness, but a long speech is often comprised in a few sentences, of which none perhaps were literally spoken, but which are a faithful rendering of the substance and tenor of the speech.'

As soon as the Conference was over Reusch took all this material and made German minutes. He then showed it to Döllinger who revised it and pronounced it correct. Reusch then published it as *Bericht über den 14–16 September 1874 zu Bonn gehaltenen Unions-Conferenzen, im Auftrage des Vorsitzenden Dr. von Döllinger*. Some friends of Liddon then translated Reusch's German into English and published it in England. Thus, though English was the main language of the Conference, what we have are minutes in English only after they had passed through a German idiom. However, evidently we can sufficiently rely on what was recorded. For afterwards no one, certainly none of the English or Americans, protested that they were misrepresented in either of these publications. And this although none but Döllinger and Reusch saw the final text before it went to press.[7]

They all agreed at the start that only the universal undivided Church can make a Christian doctrine binding on all the ministry and all the faithful. That was part of Döllinger's original invitation. Therefore all accepted by implication the doctrines of the first six centuries of Christian history. All agreed that the later decisions of part of the Church do not thereby become binding outside the community or denomination which agreed them. The Church of England cannot make the Thirty-nine Articles bind anyone else. The Church of Rome cannot make the decisions of the Council of Trent bind anyone else. In answer to a question on the first day, Döllinger stated flatly that neither he nor his colleagues accepted the Council of Trent as an ecumenical Council, and from this no one, not even Oxenham, dissented. (Notice the phrase of Döllinger about Trent,

---

[7] No one should underestimate the inadequacy of minutes taken in the way they were taken at Bonn. I was present at the Anglican–Russian Conference in Moscow in July 1956 and when I read the summary minutes as published I realized that they gave a largely inadequate picture of either the depth or the atmosphere of the meetings.

'also in the name of my colleagues'. What colleagues? This can only be one of the not infrequent places at this period when Döllinger totally identified himself with the Old Catholic leaders.)

Perhaps the assent to the first six centuries, unchallenged, was more an assent for the sake of getting on than a general and heartfelt agreement. For it is difficult to imagine that some of the more Protestant delegates would accept with any enthusiasm that the authority of the first six centuries should in all weighty matters bind the Protestants. But in Bonn it seemed a remarkable consensus over the basic principle upon which Döllinger created the Conference.

The agreement instantly started the worst argument of the Conference. The first six centuries agreed the text of the Nicene Creed in the form that the Holy Spirit proceeds from the Father. After the six centuries were ended, the Western Church, first in Spain and later in Rome, added a clause to the agreed creed, that the Holy Spirit proceeds from the Father and the Son, 'Filioque'. Not the Eastern Orthodox, but Döllinger himself, was very quick to point out that on the principles just accepted the Western Churches must amend their form of the creed back to its original form, the only form which (as they had just agreed) had authority.

This preliminary proposal of Döllinger won the hearts of the Eastern Orthodox present. His language was strong enough fully to content them. The introduction of the 'Filioque', he proposed for agreement, was 'illegal'. He called it a 'disturbance of unity by a one-sided and illegally-effected alteration of that Creed, of which three successive General Councils had declared that nothing must be added to that concerning which it had been said, the faith thus expressed is perfect.'

Döllinger said a lot more to content the Easterners. He said that there were faults on both sides in the schisms between East and West, but by far the greater share of the blame rests with the Latins—forgeries and fictions, imperious despotism, ignorance of Christian antiquity and especially of the Greek tradition; followed then by the Latin occupation of the East. Döllinger's speech was a bitter attack on the long Latin maltreatment of the East. It was like a Western confession of penitence towards the Eastern Churches. The mistrust, he said, of the Greek tradition for the West was but too well founded. It was also a tribute of gratitude from a Westerner that the East had so gloriously maintained the Catholic faith through the centuries.

No wonder after this that the Orthodox present were positive in their attitude to what could be achieved through Döllinger and his Conference. 'The speech of the reverend President', said the arch-priest Janyschev, 'has made a most favourable impression upon me and doubtless upon the other members of the Eastern Church.'

The Anglicans present could not accept or like the resolution about Filioque and how it should be dropped from the Nicene Creed. Their senior representative was Harold Browne who had lately become the Bishop of Winchester and so one of the senior bishops in the Church of England. He had written a widely used commentary on the Thirty-nine Articles and was regarded as a truly representative and moderate Anglican theologian in that epoch. 'I own,' said Dr Browne instantly, 'I did not expect that this most difficult question would be discussed now. I thought we should have spoken rather of the theses proposed to us by the President, and of the possibility of intercommunion between the Old Catholics and the English Church.' The Anglicans were happy to allow that the 'Filioque' had been added to the creed without a universal authority in the Catholic Church. Dr Browne even conceded the word, that it was 'illegally' introduced. They were perfectly willing to say that the Eastern Orthodox were speaking the Christian truth when they professed the creed in its original form. But they were not willing to concede that the profession of the Filioque was error.

For this they had two grounds and probably all of them would have laid the emphasis differently. They believed that a long line of Catholic theologians showed that the clause 'proceeding from the Father and the Son' was faithful both to the New Testament and to the way in which the ancient Church understood the new Testament. They thought that when the Orthodox clause and the Western clause were interpreted in this light, they were seen to mean exactly the same thing and the argument was about nothing. And some of them were touched with the liberal scepticism about all doctrinal formulas and thought that to concede to the Orthodox what the Orthodox wanted was to be seen to make an absurd fuss about what did not matter. (One of the Danes agreed or went even further, that the Church hardly needed anything more than the Apostles' Creed and therefore the argument about the wording of the Nicene Creed was not important. Another of the Danes seemed to think that they were talking about nothing.) The more Catholic of them—as for example Dr Pusey, who, though not present at

Bonn, was heavily there in his influence (especially through the presence of his closest disciple and intimate friend Liddon—Liddon once explained one of his motives for voting for a Bonn motion thus: 'Dr Pusey would highly disapprove if I did not assent'[8]) were determined to do nothing which would widen the already wide gulf which separated the Anglicans from the Church of Rome and the Western Catholic tradition generally. If someone could prove that they were in error they would be prepared to listen. But since no one could possibly do that, they were not willing to concede. Therefore they wanted the Orthodox to allow what they freely allowed themselves, and indeed eagerly professed, that the difference in the form of the creed was not a bar to intercommunion.

The statesmanlike Bishop of Winchester therefore proposed a compromise. Döllinger had proposed that the original form of the creed be restored in the West. Browne devised a form thus: that in the interests of the peace of the Churches, the Churches should consider how they can restore the original form without loss to the truth contained in the form which the Western Churches professed. This weaker formula was agreed by the conference. This device was one of the first examples of those woolly, but not woolly-sounding, formulas by which an ecumenical conference pretended that it had a sort of agreement when it had none. If anyone thought about this formula even for a moment, he would have seen that what was being decided was a nothing; for they had recommended the Churches to do what no one could possibly do in practice, or even see a way of doing. And after a time it turned out that this agreement was no use anyway. The Russians refused to accept it. Their position was stiff. Take the 'Filioque' away or there is no point in talking any more.

Still, the Conference got a long way on other points. The Protestants accepted a statement about justification which contented the scruples of the Catholics about some of the language of the Reformation. The original draft jettisoned the phrase 'faith alone', but this was reworded to avoid the phrase. It was clear that the article on justification would no longer divide the Churches if other matters could be settled. They agreed that it was good that the worship of the people be conducted in the vernacular: and that no one should disagree about the administration of the eucharist in one kind or two. They accepted private confession, and were against the

---

[8] For Liddon's utterance on Pusey see Bonn minutes, Eng. trans., pp. 63–4.

doctrine of the Immaculate Conception. Everyone agreed that the Council of Trent was not an ecumenical council. The doctrine of a sacrifice in the eucharist did not seem to offer insuperable problems in the way of an agreement. There was a stiff argument about the celibacy of the clergy, but no one could think it would survive as divisive when it was fully examined. The Orthodox were determined that the sacraments are seven in number, neither more nor less, and repudiated the Anglican position that there are two sacraments of the Gospel and other rites also called sacraments. Döllinger pointed out that the number seven for sacraments was first settled during the twelfth century so that number did not have the binding authority of the Church of the first six centuries. The Russians refused this argument. They said that the seven was proved by the practice in worship of both Eastern Church and Western Church and was consistent with the teaching of the Fathers of the undivided Church. The Bishop of Winchester was again statesmanlike, about the way in which the Anglicans took the number of sacraments, and though the disagreement was strong, it did not seem to be one which would be a bar to intercommunion.

So the Conference had come very far, at least so far as the episcopalian Churches were concerned—Russian, Old Catholic, and Anglican. It was a remarkable feat. Something was due to the better mutual knowledge between Churches which modern railways and steamships had produced by their ease of travel. Something was due to Pope Pius IX, who shocked a large part of Christendom by erecting such a high barrier round the sanctuary of his own Church and therefore disturbed a lot of churchmen into seeing whether they could not do something to promote some Christian charity. Something was due to the revived English sense of Catholicity which was specially due to the Oxford Movement, above all to Dr Pusey. Something was due to the very rare opportunity of a Tsar openminded towards reform and some Russian churchmen prepared to look towards the West. But it was chiefly due to a single person: the international prestige, which the Pope and Archbishop von Scherr between them had created, of Döllinger.

There was another controversial matter which Döllinger threw into the arena. He said they would all agree, as a matter of historical fact, that the Church of England has maintained unbroken the episcopal succession.

Two of the Orthodox said that this was a controverted statement.

One of them quoted the learned Archbishop Philaret, 'a man of much note in Russia', who had given the opinion that the English succession in bishops is very doubtful. Döllinger promptly said that this was a purely historical question and that he as a historian and student of the documents had no doubt at all of 'the validity of the episcopal succession' in the Church of England. He then expounded the history of the controversy, Nag's Head fable and all. If the Anglican Orders were invalid, on precisely the same grounds Roman Orders were equally invalid. He implied, not in any veiled manner, that if the Eastern Orthodox thought the contrary, that only meant that they were ignorant of the facts.

And Reinkens said that he also had examined the question as a historian and agreed with Döllinger about the validity of Anglican Orders. Liddon said that he talked with Archbishop Philaret the year before he died, and Philaret then confessed that he had not studied the question of Anglican Orders for himself, but had relied on the arguments of Roman Catholic writers.

The doctrine of the Immaculate Conception gave a surprising amount of trouble. Döllinger wanted it rejected outright. Oxenham as a Roman Catholic, and two or three at least of the Anglicans led by Liddon, were only willing to condemn the erection of that opinion about our Lady Mary into a dogma of the faith. Döllinger wanted to condemn the dogma and the opinion; the Anglicans were only prepared to condemn the dogma and were freely ready to allow Catholics to hold the opinion. This was the point where the Conference came nearest to quarrelling. Bishop Kerfoot of Pittsburgh launched a savage attack upon the doctrine—savage especially in that there was a Roman Catholic present—and was personally discourteous to Oxenham, or was thought by some members of the Conference so to be. Oxenham later described it in the press as a 'violent and almost personal philippic'.[9] There was an actual vote, unique in the minutes. Döllinger defeated the other side by 25 to 9. The majority therefore believed the doctrine bad in itself, leading to error, and not simply bad if it were made a necessary part of the Christian faith.[10] Oxenham held that to declare the belief in

---

[9] *Guardian*, 1874, cols. 1238–9. *The Times* fiercely attacked Liddon on the subject (30 Sept. 1874); Liddon replied (*The Times* 2 Oct. 1874).
[10] On prayers for the dead there was a sort of vote; Döllinger, the Old Catholics, the Eastern Orthodox, the single Roman Catholic, and probably some of the German Protestants agreed that prayers for the dead were Catholic; though some of the

the Immaculate Conception heretical was just as much setting up a new dogma as Pope Pius IX declaring that everyone must believe it to be a true Catholic. Döllinger said that it was not the belief of the first thirteen centuries and, 'though it might be an opinion, it was not a pious opinion'. Döllinger, and all the Easterners, and most of the Anglicans, voted in the majority. Liddon, who did not believe the doctrine, was disturbed. Oxenham, who did believe the doctrine and had believed it before Pius IX told him that he must believe it, was very disturbed.

The next insoluble question after the 'Filioque' was the invocation of saints. Döllinger's doctrine was that this is not necessary for salvation; and was able to cite great Roman theologians like Cardinal Bellarmine in support of his thesis. He knew that he ran head on into Eastern Orthodox devotion and asked for their opinion. He expected them to protest and they did. They promptly said that the Church recommends the practice, and what the Church recommends amounts to a command; and secondly that the thesis that it is not necessary to devotion contradicts the decrees of the Seventh General Council on invocation. Liddon pointed out that the Seventh General Council was of the eighth century and the Conference of Bonn had agreed to take as a basis the Church of the first six centuries. This carried no weight at all with the Orthodox. And so Döllinger ruled that this was the second insoluble problem which must be left for further consideration.

The Conference at Bonn produced an astonishing amount of agreement between Eastern Orthodox, Anglicans of both England and America, all the Old Catholic leaders who after all believed themselves to be good Roman Catholics more faithful to Catholicism than modern Rome, one rebellious Roman Catholic, and a few Lutherans. The special conditions had helped to produce it: the confessor status of Döllinger, the momentary looking of Russia towards the West, the shock in Christendom of the Vatican Council, and the growing power of the Oxford Movement over English

Anglicans said that their Church was silent on the subject. But one Anglican low churchman, Howson, the Dean of Chester, abstained; and therefore it could be said that the thesis was carried by 'a large majority'. It is probable that one or two at least of the Protestants abstained with Howson, but of that we have no evidence. From the point of view of Liddon and the high churchmen, Howson behaved with great restraint throughout the conferences. That meant, however, that the more outspoken low-church-Anglican point of view was not so well represented at the conference as would perhaps have been desirable.

theology. But though the large measure of agreement was produced by the special conditions, it was a real series of agreements upon the most weighty and contentious issues. It proved that what Döllinger had undertaken with such hope need not be in the long run an impossibility.

The achievement was impressive. The press of the world was unimpressed; at least much was written rather contemptuously in the newspapers. Large numbers of the faithful in all Churches were not (and perhaps never will be) interested in Christian Union and therefore did not quite know what the bother was about. In England some Anglicans said (with truth) that local unity was far more important than unity with other countries and that the first effort of the Church of England ought to be with the English Nonconformists.

At the following Church Congress at Brighton that October (where Professor Mayor of Cambridge exhibited on the platform a photograph of Döllinger inadequately lit by a chandelier), Bishop Perry of Melbourne, a celebrated evangelical, won cheer after cheer for an attack upon the Bonn attitudes to Christian tradition; and he ranged—confession; eucharist; prayers for the dead—with cheers from one side and signs of disapproval on the other. Though the Tractarian Littledale answered him and also got cheer after cheer from a different part of the house, the feeling, or at least the noise, was more on the side of the Bishop of Melbourne. The vast Protestant communities across the world could not welcome some of the agreements which had been reached—the nature of the argument, for example, on the episcopal succession in the Church of England must have struck some of them as quaint. The present writer was once present at a committee of the Faith and Order Movement where an agreement about apostolic succession was reached between the Anglicans present and the Eastern Orthodox present. Two of the Anglicans, Professor Leonard Hodgson of Oxford and Professor Michael Ramsey, then of Durham, tried to explain to the Lutheran and Reformed what they were talking about. I happened to be sitting next to the well-known German divine Edmund Schlink. He could not understand what was being talked about. His lack of comprehension was total.

On the other side, it may easily be imagined what the writers in the Roman Catholic journals made of the Bonn Conference. And some journalists talked as though the affair was only a lot of amateurs in theology out for a holiday on the Rhine. Lastly, some Anglican high churchmen, including Dr Pusey himself, were anxious lest the Bonn Conference of 1874 might be manœuvering the Western Churches into a position where they would commit the error of removing the word 'Filioque' from the Nicene Creed as used in their Churches. They were conscious that the 'Filioque' of their creed had as much ecumenical authority as parts of the Apostles' Creed and they were determined that no negotiation with stiff Easterners would persuade them even to contemplate its omission. Dr Pusey, whose son Philip was on the point of publishing the Oxford translation, in the Library of the Fathers, of chapters 1–8 of the Commentary on St John by St Cyril of Alexandria, added a fat preface, proving how much evidence there was for the use of the phrase and the idea 'proceeding from the Father and the Son' among the divines of the Eastern Church in the centuries before the schism with the West.

Döllinger was not discouraged. They had planned a further meeting and they should have one. By the standards of modern planning, his methods could hardly expect to get all the people whom he wanted. On 20 July 1875 he issued an invitation to a second Conference at Bonn on 12 to 14 August, less than a month later. He did not invite selected persons. He invited everyone; actually he wrote in the invitation, 'everyone of sufficient theological knowledge, who is interested in the objects of the Conference': but it was left to the invited to decide whether their theological knowledge was sufficient.

This haphazard method was, however, compensated by a few personal letters first. In March he wrote a special letter to the theologians of Constantinople telling them of the plan for an August meeting and passing on the offer by some English 'men of rank' to pay their fares (they came without claiming the fares). He also asked the Secretary of the Friends of Spiritual Enlightenment in St Petersburg to do what he could to get other Orthodox theologians to the Conference in August. He also wrote specially to the excellent, though conservative, Anglican theologian, Christopher Wordsworth, the Bishop of Lincoln, in the endeavour to persuade him to come, but in vain.

Those who came were the same weighty group of German Old Catholics; but with an important addition, Herzog, the Professor of Theology at Berne who was the leader, and soon to be the bishop, of the strong Old Catholic movement in Switzerland; seven German Protestant pastors only; a much stronger Eastern Orthodox delegation—not dominated by the Russians, though the same good Russians were there. There were Greeks from the Aegean, a Romanian, a Serbian, two archimandrites and a deacon from Constantinople, a professor from Athens; and to their number we must add the mysterious landed proprietor of Geisenheim-am-Rhein, who seemed to have passed into Eastern Orthodoxy since he attended the Conference at Bonn the year before. The British and the Americans were also stronger in numbers though weaker in theological expertise; forty-six from England, and not all Anglicans, two from Scotland, and fifteen from the United States. There was a big gap. Not a single Roman Catholic was present. Oxenham did not come. After the performance of the Bishop of Pittsburgh at Bonn in 1874, that was inevitable.

Naturally under such conditions little useful could be done. One of the Orthodox was a German convert to Orthodoxy and an ex-Roman Catholic priest now living in England: J. J. Overbeck. He had all the militancy of a convert. He wanted to make all the West into Eastern Orthodox and was more uncompromising than any of the real Easterners. It was natural too that in the absence of Protestant weight apart from the British and Americans, the Eastern Orthodox question should dominate the proceedings.

That quite suited Döllinger. He wanted intercommunion with the East. The discussion of 1874 had seemed to show that a very small step divided them about the 'Filioque'; that the West was cheerfully ready to recognize the Orthodox as right on the legal matter and orthodox in what they said; but were only concerned to get the recognition that their own use of the clause, when explained, was also perfectly orthodox; and that a little more knowledge of history among Russians and Greeks would show to them that many of the Greek Fathers in fact accepted Western language and the Western idea of the true doctrine. He made a truly brilliant exposition of the old Greek doctrine of the procession of the Holy Spirit. He proved, in a way that they were bound to accept, first that the argument was partly a dispute about words; and secondly that their own great Father, St John Damascene, would have been satisfied with the Western doctrine. On their side the Orthodox had evidently been stirred by Döllinger's expression of Western penitence at their behaviour towards the Eastern Churches, and at his evident willingness, so far as he personally was concerned, to restore the Western Nicene Creed to its Eastern form. And they had come, after consideration, in a less uncompromising posture on this matter. They also wanted intercommunion if they could get it with truth, and were ready to talk.

They agreed, the two chief parties, that they would get further if they conducted the argument not in English but in German. For though the Russians at Bonn in 1874 spoke English fluently, the majority of the Orthodox of 1875 had German as their second language and knew no or little English. Therefore the most anxious discussions about the theology of the Holy Spirit had to be conducted in German. Since the Anglo-Saxon knowledge of the German language in those days was often very sketchy, that excluded most of the English. Döllinger said he would explain to the English-speakers what went on in the German discussions.

And on the last day of a conference of so few days in all, Döllinger took up the whole day in a speech of four hours (!—that is the best estimate, but another estimate is five hours—two and a half hours in the morning and the rest in the afternoon) which surveyed the entire history of the Christian Church in a manner not favourable to the adherents of the Vatican Council.

Therefore Bonn 1875 could not be compared with Bonn 1874 if the object of a Conference was to get something done. But something was nevertheless done and of lasting importance. It was the first time that informed Orthodox theologians had sat down with informed Western theologians and thrashed out the difference on the mystery of the procession of the Holy Spirit. The Westerners persuaded the Easterners that half the difficulty at least was a difficulty not of different doctrines but of different usages of language. The Easterners persuaded the Westerners, even more to their surprise, that they were well read and informed and that they were not simply being stiff but cared also about Christian unity. In the long and troubled history of the relations between East and West Döllinger and Bonn were not trivial.

At Bonn 1875 Döllinger announced that they would meet further next year at a Bonn 1876. No such meeting was ever summoned. The political sympathies between Russia and the West changed. During 1876 the Turks suppressed a rebellion in Bulgaria with the atrocities known as the Bulgarian massacres. Russia as official protector of the Orthodox intervened and moved towards the Russo-Turkish war of 1877-8 which cast all Europe into torment about balance of power, the Eastern Question, the German–Russian rivalry, and all the other tensions which were to lead in Eastern Europe to the war of 1914. Döllinger saw that the time was not propitious for more talk with Eastern theologians. At the end of the 1875 Bonn Conference he was an optimist. But afterwards things looked more gloomy, not only in the East. The tiresome or fanatical Overbeck issued pamphlets attacking Döllinger. These pamphlets perhaps had some effect upon the attitude to him of the Eastern Orthodox theologians. Certainly Overbeck's pamphlet of 1876, *The Bonn Conference and the Filioque Question*, written in English, was believed by several of the English to make the Eastern Orthodox feel cooler both to the Anglicans and to Döllinger. Overbeck hated the Anglicans and despised their Church. But he had come to realize that Döllinger was in fact nearer to the Anglicans, at least to the high Anglicans, than he was to the Eastern Orthodox. This was the real cause of Overbeck's enmity.

For the change towards pessimism, or at least towards more patience in Döllinger, we must also set the afflictions of the Old Catholic community. At Bonn in 1874 it still looked conceivable that the Old Catholics might in a not distant day carry German Catholicism. When Bishop Reinkens went round the Rhineland confirming, he was received everywhere by the Roman Catholic parishes as a true bishop, by mayors and corporations, by the ringing of bells. But that year Bismarck's anti-Roman May laws of 1873 began to bite. Roman Catholic bishops went to gaol on grounds of conscience, priests were arrested. The persecution swung the Catholic population of Germany in behind loyalty to Rome and the Pope. That meant, it was now certain that the Old Catholics would remain a small, even if highly educated and influential, denomination. It was as clear to Döllinger as to everyone else that now they had no great future in Germany.

Another great discouragement to Döllinger was the behaviour of Dr Pusey.[11] Here was the head of the Catholic movement in

---

[11] Best in J. O. Johnston, *Henry Parry Liddon* (London, 1904), 186 ff.; cf. H. P. Liddon *et al.*, *Life of Edward Bouverie Pusey*, iv (London, 1897), 294 ff. The press is well worth reading: e.g. *The Times*, 19 Aug. 1875; *Pall Mall*, 20 Aug. 1875; *Daily Telegraph*, 21 Aug. 1875; *Saturday Review*, 21 Aug. 1875; *Spectator*, 21 Aug. 1875; *The Times*, 21 Aug. 1875; *Tablet*, 21 Aug. 1875; Liddon's letter in the *Spectator*, 4

England, the author of the *Eirenicon* which Döllinger himself had so much admired as pointing the way towards Catholic unity. Dr Pusey was suspicious of the Old Catholics. No one yet knew where they were going or what sort of a body they would turn out or what would be their principles. Then he heard all the talk about the Western Church abandoning the 'Filioque' from the Nicene Creed and was horrified. He was a person who tended to a little horror at what he disagreed with on principle, and his principles always extended far. Some foolish person suggested that the Lambeth Conference of 1878 might recommend the alteration in the Nicene Creed as there was only one theologian in England who disagreed with the alteration, namely Pusey.

Dr Pusey wrote to *The Times* two very strong letters, almost as though he cared nothing for unity with the East, and very much cared that the Church or England should not do anything so appalling as fall into the heresy of dropping 'Filioque' from the Nicene creed (*The Times* 27 December 1875; 10 Jan. 1876). The climax of this emotional, rather than rational, upset came on 18 February 1876, when Pusey told Liddon that if the Church of England took 'Filioque' out of the Nicene Creed, he would either become a Roman Catholic, shutting his eyes to do so, or leave the Church of England and trust that he could be saved as a member of no Church.

Pusey saw that to take the 'Filioque' out of the Western creed would be a disaster. He also saw that it represented the truth of Scripture and of the Fathers, even most of the Greek Fathers, just as well as the shorter and canonical version used by the Greeks; in his opinion better than the canonical version used by the Greeks. He was also aware that to alter the Creed in this way would raise another barrier between the Church of Rome and the other Western Churches. And though after July 1870 he had given up all hope of Catholic union for the time being, the idea of raising one more barrier was to him not merely a mistake, it was abhorrent.

These three perceptions, which had much to be said in their favour, he surrounded, as was his way, with a vast array of learning, and other things for which there was less to be said, like points of principle, emotion, and even threat.

Sept. 1875. Döllinger walked with Liddon in Munich on 9 Sept. 1876. 'He said that reading Dr Pusey's letter to me had made him very sad. Pusey could not put himself in the position of the Orientals?' (Liddon's *Diary*, ad diem).

It was left to Liddon to attempt to diminish the effect. He must get Pusey to show the world that he really did care still about Christian unity, and did not only care about the particular form of a creed. And he must persuade Pusey that the calamity which he foresaw was not going to happen, and the programme was not to give way to the East, but to persuade them that each side could keep its creed and recognize the other side as Orthodox and on this basis allow intercommunion. Both these difficult ends he achieved. He achieved it by being allowed to publish in *The Times* letters (14 February 1876) of himself to Pusey and of Pusey to himself in which Pusey accepted an assurance that the Church of England would not give up the 'Filioque'; and stated that he understood (he was wrong) that the Anglicans did not say that the clause had been uncanonically introduced into the creed; and gave an assurance that he really did care deeply about Christian unity.[12]

So Liddon tried to save the situation for Döllinger. It was too late. The damage was done. Döllinger had been both hurt and disappointed that this should come from the person whom he had supposed to be the chief advocate of Catholic unity.

So Döllinger decided not to continue. The thing would take more time than he at first supposed. Some of the Anglicans were very disappointed. They all accepted that Döllinger was the only person who could create the opportunity and that he was already old and would not live for ever. The high-Anglican layman Beresford Hope collected an address of thanks to Döllinger for all that he had done, and got it signed by 8,000 lay-people and 3,800 clergy including thirty-eight bishops. The Lambeth Conference of 1878 expressed a special sympathy for the Old Catholics and, following the American lead, drafted the famous Lambeth Quadrilateral, the basic document for all future Anglican ecumenical endeavours.

The two Conferences at Bonn have been pooh-poohed in modern history as they were criticized by their contemporaries. The two chief criticisms in modern times have been these: first, that the discussion was so learned, so technical, so unintelligible to more than half the second meeting, that it betrayed an assumption that mere technical scholarship could solve the vast pastoral problem which lay before the Churches. This is the professor assuming that if he can agree on a footnote all will be well with the charity of the

[12] *Guardian*, 1876, 213.

Churches. Secondly, the meeting is criticized because the circumstances made it anti-Roman. The chairman's speeches, especially when he got carried away to inordinate length of utterance, (which was not seldom), betrayed strong hostility to the Vatican; and, it is said, you cannot build the peace of the Churches on a common hostility towards Pope Pius IX or the Jesuits or one of the Churches. Perhaps also you cannot build the peace of the Churches if the chairman, however wonderful a person and however the entire audience regards him as a wonderful person, takes up too much of the time allotted for debates. Even apart from Döllinger's one enormous speech, he started each day with a lecture of anything from one hour to two. Perhaps after all, for all his vitality, he was getting old. One of the English said, perhaps a little ruefully, 'We seem as if we have been listening to him the whole time.'

Both these criticisms have of course a measure of truth in them. But Döllinger had a defence to both. The first Conference achieved an extraordinary distance in diminishing misunderstanding and getting a large measure of agreement on certain vital matters. The second Conference was very badly organized, and Döllinger allowed the Eastern Orthodox to take command of the situation and talk about nothing except the two or three vital points which they considered essential to them. It was the Orthodox professors, not Professor Döllinger, who turned the argument into longwinded and arid philology. The second Bonn Conference, taken in isolation, was hardly successful in doing more than warn the future Faith and Order movement how thickly sown were the minefields ahead. But Döllinger never for an instant believed that the professors could solve the problems of the Church. As for the charge of anti-Roman speeches, it is justified: both as a charge in itself, and as a mistaken policy in view of what he was at that moment trying to achieve. Nevertheless, that is easy to say in later years. These were the years 1874 and 1875. No one must underestimate the shock to Christendom caused by July 1870.

Postscript

THE EDITOR

As this volume goes to press, Roman Catholics and Anglicans look towards a milestone in the reception process of the work of ARCIC I and of other commissions in 1988. What comes about within the formal structures of decision-making then is, however, only a part of the process of reception in which all the people of God take an active part. The action of those with a responsibility of oversight in the community is always carried out within the community, and as representing and focusing the action of the whole community; and at the same time it is complementary to an active embracing in individual hearts and minds.

Döllinger saw that 'you cannot achieve what the Church needs by meetings of theologians who represent the various denominations . . . They cannot achieve . . . There has to be a desire for unity in the heart of the people' (p. 310). These essays have encompassed a range of aspects of the question of Christian authority, but in the background of them all is a consciousness of the work of ecumenical commissions, and especially of the Anglican–Roman Catholic International Commissions on which Henry Chadwick has served. Döllinger in particular challenges us to think hard about their usefulness in a process of reception which is ultimately the work of the Holy Spirit through the structures of the visible churches and through the *consensus fidelium* together.

He saw the basics in terms strikingly in tune with those of the post-Vatican II world. We have to strive for unity because it is Christ's will for his Church and because it is through its unity that the Church can best serve the needs of mankind (pp. 304–5). We must always set doctrine 'in the context of its place in spirituality and the worshipping tradition' (p. 306). The Catholic Church cannot be identified with any single denomination (p. 307); we must recognise one another's ecclesial communities. Under the appearance of separation we are all members of one visible Church through baptism (ibid.). We live at a moment in the Church's history when the separated communions are ready to learn from one another (p. 305), and that is essential to the reception of common doctrine in unity, for only the universal and undivided Church can make binding decisions about the faith.

Döllinger's account is less modern when he describes the role of 'groups of theologians' meeting 'to talk over old doctrinal formulas' and discover where division is unnecessary (ibid.). He saw their task as fourfold: to try to get behind more recent formulae to a primitive stage; to try to understand the formulae; not to hope to create a new set of doctrinal formulae on which everyone might agree; but to interpret them to one another in the expectation that it will sometimes be discovered that 'we are less far apart than anyone had supposed' (ibid.). This endeavour is to be conducted in a spirit of mutual charity, on the assumption that 'we cannot both be right', but that need not make us enemies; making allowances for the circumstances which have placed us on opposite sides of a fence, we can then 'work together on the reason for the existence of the fence'. The end in view is 'the pearl of great price which is religious peace' (p. 308).

ARCIC and the other ecumenical commissions of recent decades have been seeking a pearl of even greater price: the consensus which Döllinger thought impossible. They have taken his conception of the task forward at its key points. They have sought not only to get behind the divisive formulae to a more primitive stage, but to understand those formulae themselves as stages in a growing understanding, partial then, but now often to be seen as complementary elements in a full statement of doctrine which can be made by everyone together. Interpreting their historic formulae to one another, the members of the commissions have begun to find words in which to express doctrine which is 'new' but in accordance with apostolic faith, 'primitive' but contemporary. In the process it has frequently turned out that the fence need not be there at all, for the members of the commissions commonly find themselves standing in mixed groups on both sides of it, with those they once thought to confront across it.

It is this achievement which we must set in the context of Döllinger's perfectly correct contention that commissions of theologians cannot achieve unity. Unity is an act of reception (p. 11, n. 25), and for reception authority is needed: the authority of the Holy Spirit guiding the Church; the authority of Christ in his Church; the formal authorization of the organs of the visible Church; the authorization of the whole people of God as they recognize the harmony of the faith which is being expressed with the apostolic faith. Reception is a corporate authorizing. But without the work of the commissions which are trying to give it expression, the 'desire for unity in the heart of the people' cannot easily speak. That is the contribution of an ecumenical theology, and it remains for us to communicate it in such a way that the longing for unity which is clearly to be seen in local churches all over the world can recognize its own voice and join in the affirmation of consensus.

A Bibliography of
Henry Chadwick's Writings

(Short Notices and brief Reviews [SN] in *JTS* are listed in the Index to NS, vols. 1–30, and thereafter noted here by page number only.)

1947

'Origen, Celsus and the Stoa', *JTS* 48. 34–48.

1948

'The Fall of Eustathius of Antioch', *JTS* 49. 27–36; repr. in 1982 Variorum volume (below).

'Athanasius De decretis xl. 3', *JTS* 49. 168–9.

'Origen, Celsus and the Resurrection of the Body', *Harvard TR* 41. 83–102.

1949

Review of Jean Daniélou, *Origène*, in *JTS* 50. 219–21.

1950

'The Silence of Bishops in Ignatius', *Harvard TR* 43. 169–72; repr. in 1982 Variorum volume (below).

σαίνεσθαι, 1 Thess. 3: 3', *JTS*, NS 1. 156–8.

1951

'Eucharist and Christology in the Nestorian Controversy', *JTS*, NS 2; repr. in 1982 Variorum volume (below).

1952

'An Attis from a Domestic Shrine', *JTS*, NS 3. 90.

1953

Origen: Contra Celsum (Cambridge University Press; rev. edn. 1965; further rev. 1980. repr. 1986).

'Notes on the Text of Origen, *Contra Celsum*', *JTS*, NS 4. 215.

Review of H. de Riedmatten, 'Les Actes du procès de Paul de Samosate', *JTS*, NS 4. 91.

1954

Alexandrian Christianity (with J. E. L. Oulton) library of Christian Classics, 2; (SCM Press: London, Fortress Press: Philadelphia).

1955

'The Exile and Death of Flavian of Constantinople: A Prologue to the Council of Chalcedon', *JTS*, NS 6. 17–34.

'All Things to All Men (1 Cor. ix. 22)', *New Testament Studies*, 1. 261–75.

1956

Lessing's Theological Writings (A. & C. Black: London, Stanford University Press, California).

'The Authorship of Egerton Papyrus no. 3', *Harvard TR* 49. 145–51.

Review of Carl Andresen, *Logos und Nomos*, in *Zeitschrift für Kirchengeschichte*, 67. 163–6.

'Der Einfluss der deutschen protestantischen Theologie auf die englische Kirche im 19. Jahrhundert', *Evangelische Theologie*, 16. 556–71.

1957

'St. Peter and St. Paul in Rome: The Problem of the Memoria Apostolorum ad Catacumbas', *JTS*, NS 8. 31–52; repr. in 1982 Variorum volume, (below).

'The New Edition of Hermas', *JTS*, NS 8. 274–80.

Review of J. Scherer, *Extraits des livres I et II du Contre Celse d'Origène*, in *JTS*, NS 8. 322–6.

'The Evidence of Christianity in the Apologetic of Origen', in F. L. Cross and K. Aland (eds.), *Studia Patristica*, ii (Texte und Untersuchungen, 64), 331–9.

Review of Marcel Richard, *Asterii Sophistae Homiliae*, in *Classical Review*, 71. 257–8.

Review of A. Grillmeier, *Der Logos am Kreuz*, in *JEH* 8. 266.

1958

'Ossius of Cordova and the Presidency of the Council of Antioch, 325', *JTS*, NS 9. 292–304; repr. in 1982 Variorum volume (below).

Review of H. Dörries, *De Spiritu Sancto*, in *Zeitschrift für Kirchengeschichte*, 69. 335.

1959

'Rufinus and the Tura Papyrus of Origen's Commentary on Romans', *JTS*, NS 10. 10–42; repr. in 1982 Variorum volume (below).

The Sentences of Sextus: A Contribution to the History of Early Christian Ethics Texts and Studies, 2nd ser., 5. (Cambridge University Press).

The Circle and the Ellipse, Inaugural Lecture, University of Oxford (Oxford University Press), repr. in 1982 Variorum volume (below).

1960

'A Latin epitome of Melito's Homily on the Pascha', *JTS*, NS 11. 76–82; repr. in 1982 Variorum volume (below).

'Enkrateia', in *Reallexikon für Antike und Christentum*.

'Die Absicht des Epheserbriefes', *Zeitschrift für die Neutestamentliche Wissenschaft*, 51. 145–53.

'Faith and Order at the Council of Nicaea: A Note On the Background of the Sixth Canon', *Harvard TR* 53. 171–85; repr. in 1982 Variorum volume (below).

'The Sentences of Sextus and of the Pythagoreans', *JTS*, NS 11. 349.

St. Ambrose on the Sacraments (Mowbrays: London, Loyola University Press: Chicago).

Review of J. Scherer, *Entretien d'Origène avec Héraclide*, in *JTS*, NS 11. 400.

1961

The Vindication of Christianity in Westcott's Thought, Westcott Memorial Lecture (Cambridge University Press).

'Justification by Faith and Hospitality', in F. L. Cross (ed.), *Studia Patristica*, iv (Texte und Untersuchungen, 79).

'St. Leo the Great', *Listener* (16 Nov. 1961), 813–14, 819.

1962

'Pope Damasus and the Peculiar Claim of Rome to St. Peter and St. Paul', in *Neotestamentica et Patristica: Eine Freundesgabe Oscar Cullmann überreicht* (Leiden: Brill, 1962), 313–18; repr. in 1982 Variorum volume (below).

Commentary on the Epistle to the Ephesians in the *New Peake Commentary* on the Bible.

Notice of E. Honigmann, *Trois mémoires posthumes*, in *JTS*, NS 13. 170.

1963

'The Bible and the Greek Fathers', in D. E. Nineham (ed.), *The Church's Use of the Bible*, (SPCK: London), 25–40.

'The Ring of a Musical Bishop of Ephesus', *Expository Times*, 74/7 (April), 213–14.

Obituary of Arthur Darby Nock (with E. R. Dodds), in *Journal of Roman Studies*, 53. 168–9.

1964

Articles for *Encyclopedia Britannica* on 'Celsus', 'Clement of Alexandria', 'John, Gospel and Epistles of', 'Origen', 'Philippians'.

1965

'Justin Martyr's Defence of Christianity', *Bulletin of the John Rylands Library*, 47/2 (March), 275–97; repr. in 1982 Variorum volume (below).

Review of Luise Abramowski, *Untersuchungen zum Liber Heraclidis des Nestorius*, in *JTS*, NS 16. 214–18; repr. in 1982 Variorum volume (below).

Review of Y. Azéma's edition of Theodoret's letters, in *JTS*, NS 16. 218.

Review of U. Wickert, *Studien zu den Paulus kommentaren Theodors von Mopsuestia*, in *JEH* 16. 262.

1966

Early Christian Thought and the Classical Tradition (Clarendon Press: Oxford; corrected reissue 1972; pbk. 1983; Japanese trans. 1984).

'St. Paul and Philo of Alexandria', *Bulletin of the John Rylands Library*, 48/ 2. 286–307; repr. in 1982 Variorum volume (below).

'Les 318 Pères de Nicée', *Revue d'histoire ecclésiastique*, 61. 808–11.

Review of K. Sarkissian, *The Council of Chalcedon and the Armenian Church*, in *Times Literary Supplement*.

1967

'Lessing, G. E.', in *Encyclopaedia of Philosophy*.

The Early Church (Pelican History of the Church, 1; corrected repr. 1968; translations in Portuguese, German (1972), and Korean).

'Philo and the Beginnings of Christian Thought', in A. H. Armstrong (ed.), *The Cambridge History of Later Greek and Early Medieval Philosophy*; repr. in 1982 Variorum volume (below).

Review of N. Hyldahl, *Philosophie und Christentum*, in *JTS*, NS 18.

1968

'The Discussion on Anglican Orders in modern Anglican Theology', *Concilium*, 4/4. 72–6.

'The "Finality" of the Christian Faith', in Michael Ramsey (ed.), *Lambeth Essays on Faith* (Lambeth Conference Papers).

Review of E. Klostermann, H. Dörries, and M. Kröger, *Die 50. geistliche Homilien des Makarios*, in *Zeitschrift für Kirchengeschichte*, 79. 93–6.

Revised ed. of Gregory Dix (ed.), *The Apostolic Tradition of Hippolytus* (SPCK: London).

1969

The Enigma of St Paul, Ethel M. Wood Lecture, University of London (Athlone Press).

Reflections on Conscience, Greek, Jewish, and Christian, Waley Cohen Memorial Lecture of 22 Oct. 1968.

'Romanticism and Religion', in *The Future of the Modern Humanities* (Publications of the Modern Humanities Research Association, 1), 18–30.

'Florilegium', in *Reallexikon für Antike und Christentum*, No. 56.

Review of D. J. Chitty (ed.), *Varsanuphius and John*, in *JTS*, NS 20. 644.

1970

'Some Reflections on the Character and Theology of the Odes of Solomon', in *Kyriakon: Festschrift Johannes Quasten*, i (Münster, 1970), 266–70.

'Einigkeit in den fundamentalen Glaubensartikeln', Lecture for the Catholic Faculty of Theology at Tübingen, *Theologische Quartalschrift*, 150. 396–402.

1972

Die Kirche in der antiken Welt, trans. G. May of *The Early Church* (1967), rev. and provided with references (de Gruyter: Berlin; corrected reissue, 1985).

'The Origin of the Title "Œcumenical Council"', *JTS*, NS 23. 132–5; repr. in 1982 Variorum volume (below).

'Prayer at Midnight', in *Epektasis: Mélanges patristiques offerts au Cardinal Jean Daniélou* (Beauchesne: Paris), 47–50.

'The Identity and Date of Mark the Monk', *Eastern Churches Review* 4. 125–30; repr. in 1982 Variorum volume (below).

Preface to second edn. of N. H. Baynes, *Constantine the Great and the Christian Church* (British Academy).

1973

'A letter ascribed to Peter of Alexandria' (with J. W. B. Barns), *JTS*, NS 24. 443–55.

'The Status of Ecumenical Councils in Anglican Thought', in *The Heritage of the Early Church: Essays in Honor of G. Florovsky* (Orientalia Christiana Analecta, 195), 393–408.

1974

'John Moschus and his friend Sophronius the Sophist', *JTS*, NS 25. 41–74; repr. in 1982 Variorum volume (below).

'Quelques réflexions sur le magisterium dans l'Église', in G. Philips (ed.), *Mélanges Yves Congar* (Paris), 163–75.

Betrachtungen über das Gewissen in der griechischen, jüdischen und christlichen Tradition, Vortrag G 197, Rheinisch-Westfälische Akademie der Wissenschaften (Westdeutscher Verlag: Cologne).

Review of S. Lancel (ed.), *Actes de la Conférence de Carthage en 411*, in *JTS*, NS 25. 532.

1975

'Christianity to 1054', in *Encyclopaedia Britannica*.

1976

Priscillian of Avila: The Occult and the Charismatic in the Early Church (Clarendon Press: Oxford; Spanish trans. by J. L. López Muñoz, Espasa-Calpe: Madrid, 1978).

'Gervase Mathew O. P.', *New Blackfriars*, 57. 194–5.

'The Unangelic Doctor', review of J. N. D. Kelly, *Jerome*, in *Times Literary Supplement*, 4 June.

Review of I. T. Ker's edn. of Newman's *Idea of a University*, in *Times Literary Supplement*.

Review of Irenaeus, *adv. Haereses*, ed. A. Rousseau and L. Doutreleau, in *JTS*, NS 27. 550.

SN: *JTS*, NS 27. 277.

1977

Truth and Authority, a commentary on the agreed statement of the Angican–Roman Catholic International Commission (with Edward J. Yarnold, SJ) (SPCK and Catholic Truth Society).

'A Brief Apology for "Authority in the Church" (Venice, 1976)', *Theology*, 80 (Sept.) (A reply to the critique of the ARCIC first statement on authority by Bishop Hugh Montefiore published in *Theology* for May 1977).

'Anglikanische Kirche' (written 1968) in F. Heyer (ed.), *Konfessionskunde* (de Gruyter: Berlin), 575–94.

Review of John Colmer (ed.), *S. T. Coleridge on the Constitution of Church and State*, in *Times Literary Supplement*, 16 Dec.

1978

'Gewissen', in *Reallexikon für Antike und Christentum* x. 1025–107.

'Conversion in Constantine the Great', in Derek Baker (ed.), *Studies in Church History* (Blackwell: Oxford).

'Anglican–Roman Catholic Relations', in *One in Christ* (Oct.) (a paper for the Lambeth Conference, 2 Aug. 1978).

Review of P. Canivet, *Le Monachisme syrien selon Théodoret de Cyr*, in *JTS*, NS 29. 560.

Review of M. Simonetti, *La Crisi ariana del IV Secolo*, in *JTS*, NS 29. 559.

SN: *JTS* NS 29. 314, 329, 631–5.

1979

'Messalianerne: En evangelisk bevegelse i det 4. århundre', in *Tidsskrift for Teologi og Kirke*, 3. 161–72.

'The Relativity of Moral Codes: Rome and Persia in Late Antiquity', in W. R. Schoedel and R. L. Wilken (eds.), *Early Christian Literature and the Classical Intellectual Tradition, in honorem Robert M. Grant* (Beauchesne: Paris), 135–54.

Review of H. Dörries, *Die Theologie des Makarios-Symeon*, in *JTS*, NS 30. 571.

Review of W. J. Malley, *Hellenism and Christianity*, *JTS*, NS 30. 563.

Review of C. Pietri *Roma Christiana* (Rome), *JEH* 30. 477.

SN: *JTS*, 30. 601.

1980

'The Authenticity of Boethius' Fourth Tractate *De fide catholica*', *JTS*, NS 31. 551–6.

'The Domestication of Gnosis', in B. Layton (ed.), *The Rediscovery of Gnosticism* (Brill: Leiden).

'Theta on Philosophy's Dress in Boethius', *Medium Aevum*, 49. 175–9.

The Role of the Christian Bishop in Ancient Society, Colloquy 35 of the

Center for Hermeneutical Studies in Hellenistic and Modern Culture, (Berkeley, California).

Review of Elaine Pagels, *The Gnostic Gospels* in *Times Literary Supplement*, 21 March.

SN: *JTS*, NS 31. 620, 698–9.

1981

Boethius: The Consolations of Music, Logic, Theology, and Philosophy (Clarendon Press: Oxford; Italian trans. by F. Lechi, Il Mulino: Bologna, 1986).

'Introduction', in Margaret T. Gibson (ed.), *Boethius: His life, Thought and Influence*, ed. (Blackwell: Oxford), 1–12.

'Pachomius and the Idea of Sanctity', in Serge Hackel (ed.), *The Byzantine Saint*, (Studies supplementary to Sobornost, 5); repr. in 1982 Variorum volume (below).

'The Church of the Third Century in the West', in A. King and M. Henig (eds.), *The Roman West in the Third Century* (British Archeological Reports, 109).

'Full Communion with other Episcopal Churches', *Churchman* 95. 218–26.

Why Church Music? Seventy-fifth anniversary lecture, The Church Music Society (London).

Review of M. Aubineau's *Hesychius of Jerusalem*, in *JTS*, NS 32. 529.

SN: *JTS*, NS 32. 268, 581

1982

History and Thought of the Early Church (Collected Studies Series; Variorum: London).

'Priscilliano', in *Dizionario enciclopedico dei religiosi e degli istituti secolari*.

Review of R. MacMullen, *Paganism in the Roman Empire*, in *Times Literary Supplement*, 9 Apr.

Review of A. Kee, *Constantine versus Christ*, in *Times Literary Supplement*, 28 May.

Review of H. W. Goetz, *Die Geschichtstheologie des Orosius*, in *JEH* 33. 159.

Review of H. Cunliffe Jones, *A History of Christian Doctrine*, in *JEH* 33. 87.

SN: *JTS*, NS 33. 283, 345–7, 353, 536, 596, 638–40.

1983

'The Chalcedonian Definition', introduction to A. J. Festugière, *Actes du Concile de Chalcedoine*, sessions III–VI (Patrick Cramer: Geneva).

'New Letters of St. Augustine', *JTS*, NS 34. 425–52.

'Walter Ullmann, 1910–1983', *Cambridge Review*, 18 Nov.

'Canterbury and Rome: Progress and Problems', Cardinal Heenan Memorial Lecture, 1982, *Month* (May), 149–53.

Review of *The Sentences of Sextus*, ed. R. A. Edwards and R. A. Wild, in *JTS*, NS 34. 311.

Review of *Hesychius*, ii, ed. M. Aubineau, in *JTS*, NS 34. 313–14.

Review of Anastasius Sinaita, *Viae Dux*, ed. K. H. Uthemann, in *JTS*, NS 34. 314–15.

Review of John of Damascus, *Opera polemica*, ed. B. Kotter, in *JTS*, NS 34. 316–17.

Review of Irenaeus, *adv. Haereses*, i–ii, ed. A. Rousseau and L. Doutreleau, in *JTS*, NS 34. 630–2.

Review of Origen, *de Principiis*, ed. H. Crouzel and M. Simonetti, in *JTS* NS 34. 632.

Review of the Athenian Corpus of Pachomius, ed. F. Halkin, in *JTS*, NS 34. 633.

Review of M. Wojtowytsch, *Papsttum und Konzile*, in *JTS*, NS 34. 634.

Review of G. E. Caspary, *Politics and Exegesis: Origen and the Two Swords*, in *JEH* 34. 477–8.

Review of J. Fellermayr, *Tradition und Succession*, in *JEH* 34. 480.

SN: *JTS*, NS 34. 396–7, 698–9.

1984

'Oracles of the End in the Conflict of Paganism and Christianity in the Fourth Century', in *Memorial A. J. Festugière* (Patrick Cramer: Geneva).

'Origenes', in *Gestalten der Kirchengeschichte*, i/1 (Kohlhammer: Stuttgart), 134–57.

'Priscillian of Avila', in E. A. Livingstone (ed.), *Studia Patristica*, xv (Texte und Untersuchungen, 128).

'The Great Religions and the Environment', in *Studies in the Archaeology of Jordan*, ii (Department of Antiquities: Amman).

'Lima, ARCIC, and the Church of England', *Theology*, 87 (Jan.), 29–35 (a slightly revised text in *One in Christ* (1984), 31–7).

'Justification by Faith: A Perspective', in *One in Christ*, (1984), 191–225.

'History of the Oxford Movement: 150 Years on', in J. Robert Wright (ed.), *Lift High the Cross* (New York, 1984), 46–80.

'Sir Arthur Armitage', in *Cambridge Review* (Nov.)

'The Oxford Movement and Church Music', in Lionel Dakers (ed.), *The World of Church Music* (Royal School of Church Music: Croydon).

'The Context of Faith and Theology in Anglicanism', in A. A. Vogel (ed.), *Theology in Anglicanism* (London), 11–32.

Review of Hilary of Poitiers, *De Trinitate*, ed. P. Smulders, in *JTS*, NS 35. 548.

Review of Y. Congar, *I Believe in the Holy Spirit*, *JTS* NS 35. 553.

SN: *JTS*, NS 35. 246, 547, 570, 591, 595.

1985

'Augustine on Pagans and Christians: Reflections on Religious and Social Change', in D. Beales and G. Best (eds.), *History, Society and the Churches: Essays in Honour of Owen Chadwick* (Cambridge University Press), 9–27.

Review of R. Macmullen, *Christianizing the Roman Empire*, in the *Times Literary Supplement*, 5 Apr.

'The Ascetic Ideal in the History of the Church', in W. J. Shiels (ed.), *Studies in Church History*, 22, (Presidential Address to the Ecclesiastical History Society, July 1984).

Review of R. Staats, *Makarios-Symeon, Epistola Magna*, ed. R. Staats, in *JTS*, NS 36. 229.

Review of Augustine, *De spiritu et littera*, ed. Marafioti, in *JTS*, NS 36. 389.

SN: *JTS*, NS 36. 280–2, 487, 560–1.

1986

Augustine (Past Masters Series; Oxford University Press). (French trans. *Augustin*, Les Editions du Cerf, 1987; German trans. Vandenhoeck and Ruprecht, 1987.)

'Envoi: On Taking Leave of the Ancient World', in *The Oxford History of the Classical World*.

'Unity and Pluralism', in M. Gourgues and G. D. Mailhiot (eds.), *L'Altérité; Vivre ensemble différents*, Actes du colloque, Ottawa 4–6 Oct. 1984.

'The Petrine Office in the Church', ibid.

'Priscillien', in *Dictionnaire de spiritualité*.

'Stanley Lawrence Greenslade 1905–1977', *Proceedings of the British Academy*, 72.

Review of V. Twomey, *Apostolikos Thronos*, in *JTS*, NS 37. 220.

Review of Augustine, *Contra Adversarium legis et prophetae*, ed. K-D. Daur, in *JTS*, NS 37. 593.

SN: *JTS*, NS 37. 228, 242, 305, 572.

1987

Atlas of the Christian Church (ed. with G. R. Evans) (Macmillan: London).

'Philoponus the Christian Theologian', in R. Sorabji (ed.), *Philoponus and the Rejection of Aristotelian Science* (Duckworth: London).

'Eusebius of Caesarea', *Dictionary of Historians* (Blackwell: Oxford).

'G. D. Mansi', ibid.

Review of S. Lilla, *Codices Vaticani Graeci* in *JTS*, NS 38. 185–6.

Review of Cyril of Alexandria, *Contra Julien*, ed. P. Burguière and P. Évieux, in *JTS*, NS 38. 215–16.

Review of S. O. Horn, *Petrou Kathedra*, in *JTS*, NS 38. 216–17.

SN: *JTS*, NS 38. 294, 297–9.

1988

'Christian Doctrine', in J. H. Burns (ed.), *The Cambridge History of Medieval Political Thought*.

'Royal Supremacy', in B. Bradshaw and E. Duffy (eds.), *John Fisher* (Cambridge University Press).

Selective Index